The Psychoneuroimmunology of Chronic Disease

The Psychoneuroimmunology of Chronic Disease

Exploring the Links Between Inflammation, Stress, and Illness

Edited by
Kathleen Kendall-Tackett

American Psychological Association
Washington, DC

Published by
American Psychological Association
750 First Street, NE
Washington, DC 20002
www.apa.org

To order
APA Order Department
P.O. Box 92984
Washington, DC 20090-2984
Tel: (800) 374-2721; Direct: (202) 336-5510
Fax: (202) 336-5502; TDD/TTY: (202) 336-6123
Online: www.apa.org/books/
E-mail: order@apa.org

In the U.K., Europe, Africa, and the Middle East, copies may be ordered from
American Psychological Association
3 Henrietta Street
Covent Garden, London
WC2E 8LU England

Typeset in Goudy by Stephen McDougal, Mechanicsville, MD

Printer: Maple-Vail Book Manufacturing Group, York, PA
Cover Designer: Watermark Design Office, Alexandria, VA
Technical/Production Editor: Devon Bourexis

The opinions and statements published are the responsibility of the authors, and such opinions and statements do not necessarily represent the policies of the American Psychological Association.

Library of Congress Cataloging-in-Publication Data

The psychoneuroimmunology of chronic disease : exploring the links between inflammation, stress, and illness / edited by Kathleen Kendall-Tackett. — 1st ed.
    p. ; cm.
Includes bibliographical references and index.
ISBN-13: 978-1-4338-0476-2
ISBN-10: 1-4338-0476-X
1. Chronic diseases—Etiology. 2. Psychoneuroendocrinology. 3. Medicine, Psychosomatic. I. Kendall-Tackett, Kathleen A. II. American Psychological Association.
[DNLM: 1. Chronic Disease—psychology. 2. Inflammation—immunology. 3. Nervous System Diseases—immunology. 4. Psychoneuroimmunology—methods. 5. Stress, Psychological—immunology. 6. Stress, Psychological—psychology. WT 500 P9748 2010]
RB156.P79 2010
616'.044—dc22   2009005407

British Library Cataloguing-in-Publication Data
A CIP record is available from the British Library.

Printed in the United States of America
First Edition

CONTENTS

CONTRIBUTORS

Philip C. Calder, PhD, Professor of Nutritional Immunology, Institute of Human Nutrition, School of Medicine, University of Southampton, Southampton, England

Harold Goforth, MD, Assistant Professor of Psychiatry, Duke University Medical Center, Durham, NC

Maureen Groër, RN, PhD, FAAN, Gordon Keller Professor, University of South Florida College of Nursing, Tampa

Angela L. Guillozet-Bongaarts, PhD, Senior Fellow, Department of Pathology, Division of Neuropathology, University of Washington, Seattle

Erin E. Hughes, MS, Doctoral Student, Center for Psychological Studies, Nova Southeastern University, Ft. Lauderdale, FL

Kavita Joshi, MS, Doctoral Student, Center for Psychological Studies, Nova Southeastern University, Ft. Lauderdale, FL

Kathleen Kendall-Tackett, PhD, Clinical Associate Professor of Pediatrics, Texas Tech University School of Medicine, Amarillo

Jeffrey L. Kibler, PhD, Associate Professor, Center for Psychological Studies, Nova Southeastern University, Ft. Lauderdale, FL

Janice Kiecolt-Glaser, PhD, Distinguished University Professor, S. Robert Davis Chair of Medicine, Professor and Director, Division of Health Psychology, Department of Psychiatry, The Ohio State University College of Medicine, Columbus

Mary W. Meagher, PhD, Professor, Department of Psychology, Texas A&M University, College Station

Thomas J. Montine, MD, PhD, Alvord Endowed Chair and Director, Division of Neuropathology; Professor of Pathology, Adjunct Professor of Neurological Surgery, University of Washington, Seattle;

Adjunct Professor of Neurology, Oregon Health & Science University, Portland

Mary Nivison, BA, BS, Doctoral Student, Department of Pathology, Division of Neuropathology, University of Washington, Seattle

Edward C. Suarez, PhD, Associate Professor, Department of Psychiatry and Behavioral Sciences, Duke University Medical Center, Durham, NC

C. Jane R. Welsh, PhD, Associate Professor, Department of Veterinary Integrative Biosciences, College of Veterinary Medicine, Texas A&M University, College Station

Women's Health Research Group, University of South Florida College of Nursing, Tampa

FOREWORD

JANICE KIECOLT-GLASER

This excellent volume presents some of the latest evidence and most exciting discoveries across the broad spectrum of stress, inflammation, and chronic disease. Kathleen Kendall-Tackett has done a superb job in bringing together a stellar set of authors who write about inflammation from very diverse perspectives and who have provided important new ways to think about how psychological distress, in its myriad forms, affects health.

This volume is timely for several reasons. First, it seems like every pre-eminent medical journal has an article in each issue detailing the latest evidence that inflammation plays a role in health. However, although the medical community has clearly embraced inflammation as a key common pathway for so many diseases, what is typically absent is any mention of even the possibility that psychological distress can affect inflammation; indeed, rarely is there any discussion of how psychological states may have contributed to some of the biomedical outcomes. What is more, even though key health behaviors such as sleep and diet have been so clearly tied to inflammation, those behaviors are not discussed as potentially important contributors.

Conversely, in the behavioral medicine literature, a number of elegant studies show that laboratory stressors can reliably provoke changes in inflammation, and very good evidence shows that depressive symptoms, anxiety, hostility, and other relatively persistent variants of negative affect have reliable, longer term consequences for inflammation—but in many cases these changes have been assessed in reasonably healthy populations and have not been related to particular disease outcomes. In yet a third arena, the neuroimmunology literature provides a number of clever and well-designed animal models that have clearly tied various behavioral manipulations to both immune and health outcomes.

This volume addresses all of these facets, and then it goes a step further, providing chapters relevant to treatment and prevention—and the treatments discussed are both biological and psychological. Readers will learn about key physiological pathways and mechanisms as well as research paradigms and pitfalls, and they will have an unparalleled opportunity to glimpse the breadth of an incredibly fascinating and important literature in well-written chapters from experts in the field. This wide-ranging, authoritative, and readable set of chapters offers a valuable window into how and why behavior influences health.

The Psychoneuroimmunology of Chronic Disease

INTRODUCTION

KATHLEEN KENDALL-TACKETT

In the summer of 2006, I was tasked with two apparently separate assignments. The first was to prepare a presentation for a research meeting on the health effects of violence against women, specifically focusing on the impact of violence on the development of heart disease and diabetes. My second task was to prepare for a plenary presentation at the International Lactation Consultant Association on new research in postpartum depression. As a health psychologist, I generally split my time between these two topics. Having written or edited several books on each, I was well aware of what the psychoneuroimmunology (PNI) literature had to say about both. PNI research has been a useful framework for conceptualizing the impact of traumatic events on health and for understanding depression in pregnant and postpartum women (Kendall-Tackett, 2007a, 2007b). What I had not appreciated until that summer, however, was the continuity between these topics. That continuity has significant implications for how disease is understood and treated. The idea for this volume came shortly thereafter.

In the chapters that follow, an elite group of researchers explore the interaction between stress, inflammation, and chronic disease. The findings presented provide evidence of a substantial mind–body connection in health, demonstrating that addressing medical conditions alone while ignoring mental states is incomplete treatment at best. These links have important implications for how we as practitioners advise patients, who may be able to take relatively simple steps to lower their risk of life-threatening disease. We hope to disseminate this information to an audience of researchers, as well as to the wider medical and psychological community, because competent treatment of chronic disease requires a truly interdisciplinary focus.

In recent years, researchers from a variety of fields have discovered that a wide range of illnesses—heart disease, diabetes, multiple sclerosis (MS), Alzheimer's, and autoimmune disorders—have an inflammatory etiology (Kiecolt-Glaser et al., 2007; Pace, Hu, & Miller, 2007; Robles, Glaser, & Kiecolt-Glaser, 2005). But researchers have gone beyond assessing the link between inflammation and disease. As the chapters in this volume attest, psychological or mental states have been found to trigger this same inflammatory process and therefore have an important role in the etiology of a wide range of chronic illnesses. In other words, negative mental states can trigger inflammation, thereby increasing the risk of disease.

The literature is full of instances in which researchers have observed an association between, for instance, depression and heart disease, without necessarily understanding why or how it occurs (Surtees et al., 2008). PNI research allows us to understand the potential mechanisms that underlie the association between negative mental states and poor health. For example, inflammation is often elevated in people with depression. Chronic inflammation appears to damage the endothelium and increase coagulability, thereby increasing the risk of heart attack and stroke among people with depression (Kop & Gottdiener, 2005; Robles et al., 2005).

In perinatal health, the findings are equally intriguing. Take, for example, preterm birth. Recent studies have found, while controlling for other risk factors, that mothers who are depressed or anxious while pregnant have an increased risk of preterm birth (e.g., Dayan et al., 2006; Orr, Reiter, Blazer, & James, 2007). Preterm birth is substantially more common among ethnic minority mothers, particularly among African Americans, who also exhibit high rates of heart disease, metabolic syndrome, and diabetes—all of which are inflammatory illnesses. And, indeed, researchers have found an inflammatory link (Coussons-Read, Okun, Schmitt, & Giese, 2005): The proinflammatory cytokines involved in inflammation (interleukin-6 and tumor necrosis factor-α) also ripen the cervix. Depression increases levels of these proinflammatory cytokines, and thus increased inflammation may cause the baby to be born—even if it is early. These are just a few of the many exciting advances in research that together indicate broad and vital connections between aspects of human functioning that, until quite recently, have been conceptualized as largely unrelated processes.

Many of these findings are addressed in this volume, which is divided into two parts. In Part I, chapter authors address the role of inflammation in disease. In chapter 1, Maureen Groër, Mary W. Meagher, and I provide an overview of the biological process involved in inflammation, with a focus on typical response to threat as well as the long-term effects of stress and chronic inflammation on the immune system. Next, in chapter 2, Mary Nivison, Angela L. Guillozet-Bongaarts, and Thomas J. Montine examine the inflammation process in detail, through a discussion of the process by which polyunsaturated fatty acids undergo free radical damage and thereby contribute to neurodegenerative diseases. In chapter 3, Edward C. Suarez and Harold Goforth examine the central role played by disrupted or reduced sleep in chronic inflammation. Finally, in chapter 4, Philip C. Calder describes the different impacts of omega-6 and omega-3 fatty acids on the inflammation process, and the implications for inflammatory diseases.

In Part II, chapter authors address the role of psychosocial stress in the etiology of inflammatory diseases. These chapters focus on both biological processes and the broader aspects and implications of the link between stress and disease. In chapter 5, I examine the effects of depression, hostility, and posttraumatic stress disorder (PTSD) on inflammation levels, and on chronic diseases accordingly. In chapter 6, Jeffrey L. Kibler, Kavita Joshi, and Erin E. Hughes take a close look at the deleterious effects of PTSD on the immune system, and they examine cognitive–behavioral interventions that may boost immune functioning in people with PTSD. Mary W. Meagher and C. Jane R. Welsh, in chapter 7, discuss recent research that shows that symptoms of chronic diseases such as MS are exacerbated by stress; indeed, chronic stress may be a significant factor in causing MS itself. In chapter 8, Maureen Groër and the Women's Health Research Group at the University of South Florida College of Nursing examine recent research in *allostatic load*, the cumulative effect of alterations in the autonomic nervous system, hypothalamic–pituitary–adrenal axis, and inflammatory response system. The authors use this model to describe social stressors that are specific to women and that place unique strain on the female immune system and increase the risk of disease. Part II ends with chapter 9, in which I examine recent research showing that treatments for depression that lower inflammation also provide benefits for chronic disease. The volume concludes with an epilogue that describes various clinical implications of this material and points toward future directions in PNI research.

Many of the chapters in this book, particularly those in Part I, are strongly research oriented. To aid readers who may be approaching research on psychoneuroimmunology for the first time, the authors end each chapter with a list of key points. A basic overview of inflammation and its role in the stress response is provided in chapter 1.

REFERENCES

Coussons-Read, M. E., Okun, M. L., Schmitt, M. P., & Giese, S. (2005). Prenatal stress alters cytokine levels in a manner that may endanger human pregnancy. *Psychosomatic Medicine, 67,* 625–631.

Dayan, J., Creveuil, C., Marks, M. N., Conroy, S., Herlicoviez, M. A., Dreyfus, M., & Tordjman, S. (2006). Prenatal depression, prenatal anxiety, and spontaneous preterm birth: A prospective cohort study among women with early and regular prenatal care. *Psychosomatic Medicine, 68*, 938–946.

Kendall-Tackett, K. A. (2007a). Cardiovascular disease and metabolic syndrome as sequelae of violence against women: A psychoneuroimmunology approach. *Trauma, Violence, & Abuse, 8*, 117–126.

Kendall-Tackett, K. A. (2007b). A new paradigm for postpartum depression: The central role of inflammation and how breastfeeding and anti-inflammatory treatments decrease risk. *International Breastfeeding Journal, 2*(6). doi:10.1186/1746-4358-2-6

Kiecolt-Glaser, J. K., Belury, M. A., Porter, K., Beversdoft, D., Lemeshow, S., & Glaser, R. (2007). Depressive symptoms, omega-6:omega-3 fatty acids, and inflammation in older adults. *Psychosomatic Medicine, 69*, 217–224.

Kop, W. J., & Gottdiener, J. S. (2005). The role of immune system parameters in the relationship between depression and coronary artery disease. *Psychosomatic Medicine, 67*(Suppl. 1), S37–S41.

Orr, S. T., Reiter, J. P., Blazer, D. G., & James, S. A. (2007). Maternal prenatal pregnancy-related anxiety and spontaneous preterm birth in Baltimore, Maryland. *Psychosomatic Medicine, 69*, 566–570.

Pace, T. W., Hu, F., & Miller, A. H. (2007). Cytokine-effects on glucocorticoid receptor function: Relevance to glucocorticoid resistance and the pathophysiology and treatment of major depression. *Brain, Behavior, and Immunity, 21*, 9–19.

Robles, T. F., Glaser, R., & Kiecolt-Glaser, J. K. (2005). Out of balance: A new look at chronic stress, depression, and immunity. *Current Directions in Psychological Science, 14*, 111–115.

Surtees, P. G., Wainwright, N. W. J., Bockholdt, S. M., Luben, R. N., Warcham, N. J., & Khaw, K.-T. (2008). Major depression, C-reactive protein, and incident ischemic heart disease in health men and women. *Psychosomatic Medicine, 70*, 850–855.

I

THE ROLE OF INFLAMMATION IN DISEASE PROCESS

1

AN OVERVIEW OF STRESS AND IMMUNITY

MAUREEN GROËR, MARY W. MEAGHER,
AND KATHLEEN KENDALL-TACKETT

Stress occurs when environmental demands exceed the individual's adaptive capacity or ability to cope (Cohen, Kessler, & Gordon, 1995). These environmental demands are termed *stressors* and include negative life events such as family conflict, job strain, unemployment, abuse, trauma, and bereavement, as well as physical stressors. To study the process of stress, researchers measure the occurrence of the environmental stressor, behavioral and biological responses to this event, and its long-term consequences.

Stressors appear to have bidirectional effects on the immune system depending on whether they are acute or chronic (Dhabhar & McEwen, 1999; Segerstrom & Miller, 2004). Recent research indicates that acute stressors tend to activate aspects of innate immunity by increasing trafficking of immune cells to the site of challenge and by inducing long-lasting increases in immunological memory (Campisi & Fleshner, 2003; Dhabhar & McEwen, 1997, 1999; Dhabhar & Viswanathan, 2005; Viswanathan, Daugherty, & Dhabhar, 2005). In contrast, chronic stressors are more likely to suppress immune function, resulting in increased susceptibility to infections and cancers (Antoni et al., 2006; Campbell et al., 2001; Dhabhar & McEwen, 1999;

Dobbs, Vasquez, Glaser, & Sheridan, 1993; J. D. Johnson, O'Connor, Watkins, & Maier, 2004; R. R. Johnson et al., 2006; Kelley, Greenfield, Evermann, Parish, & Perryman, 1982; Padgett et al., 1998; Sheridan et al., 1998; Sieve et al., 2004; Spiegel & Giese-Davis, 2003).

HOW DOES STRESS ALTER DISEASE VULNERABILITY?

Considerable evidence suggests that stress can alter vulnerability to infectious, inflammatory, and autoimmune diseases (Ackerman et al., 2002; Backer, 2000; Chida, Sudo, & Kubo, 2005; Dowdell, Gienapp, Stuckman, Wardrop, & Whitacre, 1999; Grant et al., 1989; R. R. Johnson et al., 2006; Matyszak, 1998; McEwen et al., 1997; McGeer & McGeer, 1995, 2004; Meagher et al., 2007; Mei-Tal, Meyerowitz, & Engel, 1970; Mohr et al., 2000; Mohr, Hart, Julian, Cox, & Pelletier, 2004; Rabin, 2002; Sheridan et al., 1998; Sieve et al., 2004; Warren, Greenhill, & Warren, 1982; Warren, Warren, & Cockerill, 1991; Welsh, Meagher, & Sternberg, 2006; Whitton, 2007; R. S. Wilson et al., 2003). Stressors can indirectly alter disease risk by increasing health-compromising behaviors and maladaptive coping strategies, such as increased alcohol consumption, smoking, decreased sleep, and nonadherence to exercise, dietary, and medical regimens. Stressful events also have direct biological effects that alter disease risk. When a stressful event is perceived, the brain activates two primary outflow pathways that alter inflammation and immunity: the sympathetic system and hypothalamic–pituitary–adrenal (HPA) axis.

Sympathetic Adrenomedullary System and Parasympathetic System

The sympathetic adrenomedullary (SAM) system is an essential component of the normal acute alarm response to threat that produces the fight–flight reaction. When stressors are perceived in the limbic system, the brain sends signals through the sympathetic and parasympathetic systems, which generally act to oppose each other. The sympathetic preganglionic neurons send impulses to the adrenal medulla, releasing epinephrine and norepinephrine. Cardiac output is increased through elevated heart rate and stroke volume. Immune cells are redistributed so that they can easily reach a site of injury. Fuel sources are made available. In addition, catecholamines increase the alertness and arousal of the central nervous system (CNS). Although the SAM system predominates in the acute stress response, it can be tonically active in some individuals, that is, highly reactive to minor perturbations.

Opposing the SAM system is the parasympathetic arm of the autonomic nervous system. Vagal nerve activity may regulate allostatic load (Thayer & Sternberg, 2006). Allostasis is the changing of various physiological set points in response to chronic stress, with the effect of producing a "load" that may contribute to pathophysiological process involved in a variety of chronic illnesses. Decreased vagal function is associated with elevated fasting glucose, increased proinflammatory cytokines and acute-phase proteins, and increased cortisol, all of which constitute allostatic load.

Hypothalamic–Pituitary–Adrenal Axis

The HPA axis is activated concomitantly with activation of the SAM system but is more gradual in its effects. Both the SAM system and the HPA axis are activated through the limbic system. HPA axis activation is initiated by release of corticotropin-releasing hormone from the hypothalamus, which stimulates the pituitary to release adrenocorticotropic hormone (ACTH). ACTH then circulates in the blood and acts on adrenal cortical cells, causing the release of glucocorticoids (GCs). Cortisol plays an important adaptive role. For example, cortisol increases food intake and causes glucose to be available as a fuel, and suppresses other functions not immediately essential, such as reproduction (Landys, Ramenofsky, & Wingfield, 2006). GCs increase the efficacy of catecholamines, thus enhancing the effects of the SAM system on cardiovascular function during stress states (McEwen, 2003).

Cortisol is immunosuppressive and anti-inflammatory, and down-regulates the excessive inflammatory and immune processes that might be activated by stressors caused by predation (i.e., injury, bleeding, and infection). By binding to receptors on immune cells, GCs normally decrease gene transcription for proinflammatory cytokines, thereby decreasing inflammation. This mechanism is thought to account in part for the immunosuppressive effects of GCs (Adcock, Ito, & Barnes, 2004).

People with depression may either have abnormally low levels of cortisol or become less sensitive to cortisol. In either case, cortisol fails to restrain the inflammatory response (Dhabhar & McEwen, 2001). Pace, Hu, and Miller (2007) noted that GC resistance has been one of the most reproducible biologic symptoms of depression, and that it occurs in up to 80% of patients with depression. GC resistance may be a result of impaired function of the GC receptors. Chronic exposure to inflammatory cytokines, from either medical illness or chronic stress, likely leads to impaired receptor function.

Without cortisol and other anti-inflammatory molecules, inflammation and tissue destruction could lead to severe and continuous tissue damage. However, excessive secretion of cortisol over a longer term may contribute to allostatic load, and thus to disease. Dysregulation of the HPA axis is a central component of allostatic load, and potentially an early indicator of allostasis. The types of perturbations include hyper- and hypocortisolemia, aberrations in the early morning awakening rise in cortisol, abnormalities in the dexamethasone suppression test, and flattened cortisol rhythms across the day (McEwen, 2003a). Conditions or situations that result in a chronically activated HPA include melancholic depression, anorexia nervosa, obsessive–compulsive disorder, panic anxiety, alcoholism, alcohol and narcotic withdrawal, excessive exercising, poorly controlled diabetes mellitus, hyperthyroidism, and childhood sexual abuse (Tsigos & Chrousos, 2002).

Cortisol is an allostatic hormone that changes on a daily basis depending on time of day, season, and reproductive state. It is now appreciated that the cortisol rise that occurs on awakening is a key determinant of adaptation to routine activities of daily living (Wust, Federenko, Hellhammer, & Kirschbaum, 2000). Even arising from bed in the morning is a sufficient stressor to require both cortisol and the SAM system in order to ensure adequate blood flow to the brain and mobilization of metabolic fuels for the energy needs of the day. It is interesting that the most frequent time for an acute myocardial infarction is in the morning, particularly Monday morning, in association with the morning rise in blood pressure and heart rate (Giles, 2005). The normal circadian rhythm and cortisol response to stressors are healthy phenomena. But prolonged exposure to cortisol is damaging to neural structures. Chronically high and low levels are considered maladaptive (the so-called U-shaped curve; Gunnar & Quevedo, 2007).

Hypocortisolemia is also seen in some chronic stress states. Atypical depression with exhaustion (Gold, Goodman, & Chrousos, 1988), posttraumatic stress disorder (PTSD; Yehuda, 1997), addiction disorders (Schuder, 2005), fibromyalgia (McBeth et al., 2005), and postpartum depression (Groër & Morgan, 2007) are characterized by hypocortisolemia. Several studies have shown that combat veterans with PTSD may have lower morning cortisol (Boscarino, 1996) and lower 24-hour cortisol levels compared with the corresponding values for men without PTSD (Yehuda, 1997). Women exposed to intimate partner violence who develop PTSD actually have higher cortisol levels across the day than do similarly exposed women without PTSD. The inability of organisms to elaborate an adequate cortisol response is an abnormality that contributes to allostatic load.

Inflammatory Cytokines and Acute-Phase Reactants

Inflammation is a rapid and nonspecific response to danger, usually provoked by pathogen-associated molecular patterns, which bind to toll-like receptors on the membranes of immune cells (Beutler, 2004). These cells are also activated by neurotransmitters and neuropeptides (Sternberg, 2006) and "danger signals," such as complement proteins, heat shock proteins, and other products of injured or dying cells (Matzinger, 2002). The neuroimmunological axis is of particular importance in understanding how stress might activate inflammatory pathways. Recent evidence suggests that norepinephrine may play an important role in the induction of stress-induced proinflammatory cytokines within CNS and peripheral circulation (Blandino, Barnum, & Deak, 2006; J. D. Johnson et al., 2005). Virtually every immune organ is innervated by sympathetic fibers; however, the density and distribution of innervation vary between organs. Likewise, immune cells have receptors for one or more of these stress hormones or neurotransmitters, thereby allowing stress response to exert regulatory control over immune function. A stress-induced autonomic–inflammatory reflex may explain how stress is involved in metabolic, vascular, and autoimmune diseases (Bierhaus, Humpert, & Nawroth, 2006).

Inflammatory mediators are capable of tissue damage if not controlled. To prevent such damage, anti-inflammatory processes normally suppress inflammation. These anti-inflammatory molecules include cortisol and cytokines such as interleukin-10 (IL-10) and transforming growth factor-β. The inflammatory response, if inappropriate, excessive, or long-lasting, becomes the underpinning of many human diseases, such as coronary heart disease (CHD).

Inflammatory cytokines are released by many cell types (e.g., macrophages, endothelium, fat cells, muscle cells, liver) in response to danger signals. The action of the proinflammatory cytokines, such as IL-1, IL-6, and tumor necrosis factor-α (TNF-α), is to provoke inflammatory changes locally and act on other systems such as the brain and liver at a distance. One of the most important primary mediators of allostasis is IL-6, an endogenous proinflammatory cytokine produced by adipose tissue, macrophages, adipocytes, T cells, and endothelium. IL-6 stimulates sickness behaviors, fever, fatigue, hematopoiesis, and immune responses; it leads to the acute-phase inflammatory response and controls the hepatic acute-phase response. When exposed to IL-6, hepatocytes augment expression of proteins of the acute-phase response, including fibrinogen and C-reactive protein (CRP). IL-6 has been correlated with measures of CHD and insulin resistance. It is increased in individuals who are obese (Brunn et al., 2003).

CRP is an acute-phase reactant released in response to acute injury, infection, and other inflammatory stimuli, such as inflammatory diseases, necrosis, and trauma (A. Wilson, Ryan, & Boyle, 2006). Largely produced in the liver and synthesized in response to cytokines (predominantly IL-6 and TNF-α), CRP is a marker of low-grade inflammation. High levels of CRP have been associated with obesity, insulin resistance, and an increased risk of developing Type 2 diabetes (Kip et al., 2004; A. Wilson et al., 2006). The usefulness of CRP as a marker of allostatic load in predicting cardiovascular risk has been demonstrated. Cook, Buring, and Ridker (2006) found that adding CRP to a global risk prediction model improved cardiovascular risk classification in participants in the Women's Health Study, particularly for those with a 10-year risk of 5% to 20%. High body mass index showed stronger associations with CRP than did physical activity (Mora, Lee, Buring, & Ridker, 2006).

BIDIRECTIONAL COMMUNICATION BETWEEN
BRAIN AND IMMUNE SYSTEM

Communication between the CNS and immune system is bidirectional in nature. For example, the immune system is able to alter the functioning of the CNS through the release of proinflammatory cytokines (Dantzer & Kelley, 2007; Maier & Watkins, 1998). Cytokines, such as interleukins, are regulatory proteins that are released by cells of the immune system and CNS. Not only do they act as intercellular messengers to alter inflammation and immunity, but cytokines can also influence CNS function and behavior (Maier & Watkins, 1998; Watkins & Maier, 2000). For example, proinflammatory cytokine expression increases in the brain and in the periphery following either immune challenge or exposure to stress. A variety of stressors have also been shown to increase circulating and central levels of proinflammatory cytokines, such as IL-1β and IL-6 (Huang, Takaki, & Arimura, 1997; LeMay, Otterness, Vander, & Kluger, 1990; LeMay, Vander, & Kluger, 1990; Maes, 2001; Shizuya et al., 1997, 1998; Steptoe, Willemson, Owen, Flower, & Mohamed-Ali, 2001; Takaki, Huang, Somogyvari-Vigh, & Arimura, 1994; Zhou, Kusnecov, Shurin, DePaoli, & Rabin, 1993).

Within the CNS, IL-1β and IL-6 can regulate the stress response by binding to receptors that can activate the HPA axis during either an immune or stress response (Bethin, Vogt, & Muglia, 2000; Turnbull & Rivier, 1999). In addition, proinflammatory cytokines have been shown to mediate the sickness syndrome observed following both infection and stress (Bluthe, Michaud, Poli, & Dantzer, 2000; Dantzer & Kelley, 2007; Maier & Watkins, 1998; Watkins & Maier, 2000). Sickness syndrome includes a range of behavioral and physiological changes that have evolved to conserve metabolic resources during periods of challenge, including loss of appetite and consequent weight loss, decreased behavioral activity, loss of interest in pleasurable activities (anhedonia), and enhanced pain sensitivity (hyperalgesia and allodynia).

There is increasing evidence that cross-sensitization can occur between stress-induced and immune-induced proinflammatory cytokines, resulting in the potentiation of CNS cytokine responses (Cunningham, Wilcockson, Campion, Lunnon, & Perry, 2005; Frank, Baratta, Sprunger, Watkins, & Maier, 2007; J. D. Johnson et al., 2002, 2004; Perry, Newman, & Cunningham, 2003; Quan et al., 2001). For example, prior exposure to stress leads to an exacerbation of brain cytokine synthesis after peripheral inflammatory challenge (J. D. Johnson et al., 2002; J. D. Johnson, O'Connor, Watkins, & Maier, 2004; Quan et al., 2001). Other evidence suggests that prior exposure to proinflammatory cytokines can sensitize neuronal, hormonal, cytokine, and behavioral responses to subsequent stress and immune challenges. For example, two prior administrations of IL-6 increased expression of IL-6 in the hypothalamus after a forced swim stress challenge without affecting circulating cytokines, whereas exposure to the forced swim stress alone had no impact (Matsumoto et al., 2006). It appears that prior exposure to IL-6 sensitized the hypothalamic IL-6 response to the subsequent stress challenge. In a similar way, central administration of IL-1β in nonstressed rats results in sensitization of IL-1β responses in the hypothalamus, hippocampus, and cortex to subsequent lipopolysaccharide challenge, without affecting circulating cytokines (J. D. Johnson et al., 2004). Furthermore, prior exposure to IL-1β and TNF-α sensitizes subsequent endocrine, behavioral, and neurochemical responses to the same cytokine or to foot-shock stress (Merali, Lacosta, & Anisman, 1997; Schmidt, Janszen, Wouterlood, & Tilders, 1995).

The phenomenon of cross-sensitization suggests that a shared neural substrate may be primed by either stress or immune activation. Recent evidence suggests that microglia may function as the shared cellular substrate mediating these priming effects of proinflammatory cytokines in the CNS (Cunningham et al., 2005; Frank et al., 2007; Nair & Bonneau, 2006; Perry et al., 2003). Microglia function as the primary immune effector cell in the nervous system and release proinflammatory cytokines. Exposure to stress can activate microglia, resulting in priming or sensitization of microglia to subsequent proinflammatory challenges. Upon subsequent immune challenge, the primed microglia exhibit a potentiated proinflammatory response (Frank et al., 2007). Researchers are just beginning to elucidate the molecular mechanisms that mediate the cross-sensitization of cytokine synthesis (Frank et al., 2007). Whatever the underlying mechanisms may be, cross-sensitization provides a mechanism explaining how stress exacerbates inflammatory disease processes.

SUMMARY

Stressful events, particularly if chronic, can increase the risk of disease. Some of this increased risk is due to psychosocial and behavioral factors, such as smoking and alcohol use. However, there is increasing evidence that stress has a direct biological effect on disease risk, involving the sympathetic nervous system, HPA axis, and inflammatory response system. Communication between the brain and immune system is bidirectional, meaning that stress can cause the brain to trigger the immune response, and the immune response can induce changes in the CNS, resulting in a constellation of behaviors known as sickness syndrome. Chronic stress and immune response become mutually maintaining conditions, increasing the risk of inflammatory, neurodegenerative, and autoimmune diseases.

KEY POINTS

- Stressful events have direct biological effects that increase the risk of disease.

- When the brain perceives danger, it activates the sympathetic nervous system and HPA axis.
- Inflammation increases in response to perceived danger.
- When stress chronically activates these systems, the risk of illnesses such as coronary heart disease, diabetes, neurodegenerative diseases and autoimmunity, is increased.
- Communication between the brain and the immune system is bidirectional.

REFERENCES

Ackerman, K. D., Heyman, R., Rabin, B. S., Anderson, B. P., Houck, P. R., Frank, E., & Baum, A. (2002). Stressful life events precede exacerbations of multiple sclerosis. *Psychosomatic Medicine, 64,* 916–920.

Adcock, I. M., Ito, K., & Barnes, P. J. (2004). Glucocorticoids: Effects on gene transcription. *Proceedings of the American Thoracic Society, 1,* 247–254.

Antoni, M. H., Lutgendorf, S. K., Cole, S. W., Dhabhar, F. S., Sephton, S. E., McDonald, P. G., et al. (2006). The influence of bio-behavioural factors on tumour biology: Pathways and mechanisms. *Nature Reviews: Cancer, 6,* 240–248.

Backer, J. H. (2000). Stressors, social support, coping, and health dysfunction in individuals with Parkinson's disease. *Journal of Gerontological Nursing, 26*(11), 7–16.

Bethin, K. E., Vogt, S. K., & Muglia, L. J. (2000). Interleukin-6 is an essential, corticotropin-releasing hormone-independent stimulator of the adrenal axis during immune system activation. *Proceedings of the National Academy of Sciences USA, 97,* 9317–9322.

Beutler, B. (2004). Innate immunity: An overview. *Molecular Immunology, 40,* 845–859.

Bierhaus, A., Humpert, P., & Nawroth, P. (2006). Linking stress to inflammation. *Anesthesiology Clinics, 24,* 325–340.

Blandino, P., Jr., Barnum, C. J., & Deak, T. (2006). The involvement of norepinephrine and microglia in hypothalamic and splenic IL-1beta responses to stress. *Journal of Neuroimmunology, 173,* 87–95.

Bluthe, R. M., Michaud, B., Poli, V., & Dantzer, R. (2000). Role of IL-6 in cytokine-induced sickness behavior: A study with IL-6 deficient mice. *Physiology & Behavior, 70,* 367–373.

Boscarino, J. (1996). Posttraumatic stress disorder, exposure to combat, and lower plasma cortisol among Vietnam veterans: Findings and clinical implications. *Journal of Consulting and Clinical Psychology, 64,* 191–201.

Brunn, J. M., Lihn, A. S., Verdich, C., Pedersen, S. B., Toubro, S., Astrup, A., et al. (2003). Regulation of adiponectin by adipose tissue-derived cytokines: In vivo and in vitro investigations in humans. *American Journal of Physiology, Endocrinology and Metabolism, 285*, E527–E533.

Campbell, T., Meagher, M. W., Sieve, A., Scott, B., Storts, R., Welsh, T. H., & Welsh, C. J. R. (2001). The effects of restraint stress on the neuropathogenesis of Theiler's virus infection: I. Acute disease. *Brain, Behavior, and Immunity, 15*, 235–254.

Campisi, J., & Fleshner, M. (2003). The role of extracellular HSP72 in acute stress-induced potentiation of innate immunity in physically active rats. *Journal of Applied Physiology, 94*, 43–52.

Chida, Y., Sudo, N., & Kubo, C. (2005). Social isolation stress exacerbates autoimmune disease in MRL/lpr mice. *Journal of Neuroimmunology, 158*, 138–144.

Cohen, S., Kessler, R. C., & Gordon, U. L. (1995). Strategies for measuring stress in studies of psychiatric and physical disorder. In S. Cohen, R. C. Kessler, & U. L. Gordon (Eds.), *Measuring stress: A guide for health and social scientists* (pp. 3–26). New York: Oxford University Press.

Cook, N., Buring, J., & Ridker, P. (2006). The effect of including C-reactive protein in cardiovascular risk prediction models for women. *Annals of Internal Medicine, 145*, 21–29.

Cunningham, C., Wilcockson, D. C., Campion, S., Lunnon, K., & Perry, V. H. (2005). Central and systemic endotoxin challenges exacerbate the local inflammatory response and increase neuronal death during chronic neurodegeneration. *Journal of Neuroscience, 25*, 9275–9284.

Dantzer, R., & Kelley, K. W. (2007). Twenty years of research on cytokine-induced sickness behavior. *Brain, Behavior, and Immunity, 21*, 153–160.

Dhabhar, F. S., & McEwen, B. S. (1997). Acute stress enhances while chronic stress suppresses immune function in vivo: A role for leukocyte trafficking. *Brain, Behavior, and Immunity, 11*, 286–306.

Dhabhar, F. S., & McEwen, B. S. (1999). Enhancing versus suppressive effects of stress hormones on skin immune function. *Proceedings of the National Academy of Sciences USA, 96*, 1059–1064.

Dhabhar, F. S., & McEwen, B. S. (2001). Bidirectional effects of stress and glucocorticoid hormones on immune function: Possible explanations for paradoxical observations. In R. Ader, D. L. Felten, & N. Cohen (Eds.), *Psychoneuroimmunology* (3rd ed., Vol. 1, pp. 301–338). New York: Academic Press.

Dhabhar, F. S., & Viswanathan, K. (2005). Short-term stress experienced at time of immunization induces a long-lasting increase in immunologic memory. *American Journal of Physiology—Regulatory, Integrative and Comparative Physiology, 289*, R738–R744.

Dobbs, C. M., Vasquez, M., Glaser, R., & Sheridan, J. F. (1993). Mechanisms of stress-induced modulation of viral pathogenesis and immunity. *Journal of Neuroimmunology, 48*, 151–160.

Dowdell, K. C., Gienapp, I. E., Stuckman, S., Wardrop, R. M., & Whitacre, C. C. (1999). Neuroendocrine modulation of chronic relapsing experimental autoimmune encephalomyelitis: A critical role for the hypothalamic–pituitary–adrenal axis. *Journal of Neuroimmunology, 100,* 243–251.

Frank, M. G., Baratta, M. V., Sprunger, D. B., Watkins, L. R., & Maier, S. F. (2007). Microglia serve as a neuroimmune substrate for stress-induced potentiation of CNS pro-inflammatory cytokine responses. *Brain, Behavior, and Immunity, 21,* 47–59.

Giles, T. (2005). Relevance of blood pressure variation in the circadian onset of cardiovascular events. *Journal of Hypertension, 23*(Suppl. 1), S35–S39.

Gold, P., Goodman, F., & Chrousos, G. (1988). Clinical and biochemical manifestations of depression: Relation to the neurobiology of stress (1). *The New England Journal of Medicine, 319,* 348–353.

Grant, I., Brown, G. W., Harris, T., McDonald, W. I., Patterson, T., & Trimble, M. R. (1989). Severely threatening events and marked life difficulties preceding onset or exacerbation of multiple sclerosis. *Journal of Neurology, Neurosurgery, & Psychiatry, 52,* 8–13.

Groër, M. W., & Morgan, K. (2007). Immune, health and endocrine characteristics of depressed postpartum mothers. *Psychoneuroendocrinology, 32,* 133–139.

Gunnar, M., & Quevedo, K. (2007). The neurobiology of stress and development. *Annual Review of Psychology, 58,* 145–173.

Huang, Q. H., Takaki, A., & Arimura, A. (1997). Central noradrenergic system modulates plasma interleukin-6 production by peripheral interleukin-1. *American Journal of Physiology—Regulatory, Integrative and Comparative Physiology, 273,* R731–R738.

Johnson, J. D., Campisi, J., Sharkey, C. M., Kennedy, S. L., Nickerson, M., Greenwood, B. N., & Fleshner, M. (2005). Catecholamines mediate stress-induced increases in peripheral and central inflammatory cytokines. *Neuroscience, 135,* 1295–1307.

Johnson, J. D., O'Connor, K. A., Deak, T., Stark, M., Watkins, L. R., & Maier, S. F. (2002). Prior stressor exposure sensitizes LPS-induced cytokine production. *Brain, Behavior, and Immunity, 16,* 461–476.

Johnson, J. D., O'Connor, K. A., Watkins, L. R., & Maier, S. F. (2004). The role of IL-1β in stress-induced sensitization of proinflammatory cytokine and corticosterone responses. *Neuroscience, 127,* 569–577.

Johnson, R. R., Prentice, T., Bridegam P., Young, C. R., Steelman, A. J., Welsh, T. H., et al. (2006). Social stress alters the severity and onset of the chronic phase of Theiler's virus infection. *Journal of Neuroimmunology, 175,* 39–51.

Kelley, K. W., Greenfield, R. E., Evermann, J. F., Parish, S. M., & Perryman, L. E. (1982). Delayed-type hypersensitivity, contact sensitivity, and phytohemagglutinin hemagglutinin skin-test responses of heat- and cold-stressed calves. *American Journal of Veterinary Research, 43,* 775–779.

Kip, K., Marroquin, O., Kelley, D., Johnson, B., Kelsey, S., Shaw, L., et al. (2004). Clinical importance of obesity versus the metabolic syndrome in cardiovascular risk in women: A report from the Women's Ischemia Syndrome Evaluation (WISE) study. *Circulation, 109,* 706–713.

Landys, M., Ramenofsky, M., & Wingfield, J. C. (2006). Actions of glucocorticoids at a seasonal baseline as compared to stress-related levels in the regulation of periodic life processes. *General and Comparative Endocrinology, 148,* 132–149.

LeMay, L. G., Otterness, I. G., Vander, A. J., & Kluger, M. J. (1990). In vivo evidence that the rise in plasma IL 6 following injection of a fever-inducing dose of LPS is mediated by IL 1 beta. *Cytokine, 2,* 199–204.

LeMay, L. G., Vander, A. J., & Kluger, M. J. (1990). The effects of psychological stress on plasma interleukin-6 activity in rats. *Physiology & Behavior, 47,* 957–961.

Maes, M. (2001). Psychological stress and the inflammatory response system. *Clinical Science, 101,* 193–194.

Maier, S. F., & Watkins, L. R. (1998). Cytokines for psychologists: Bidirectional immune-to-brain communication for understanding behavior, mood, and cognition. *Psychological Review, 105,* 83–107.

Matsumoto, T., Komori, T., Yamamoto, M., Shimada, Y., Nakagawa, M., Shiroyama, T., et al. (2006). Prior intraperitoneal injection of rat recombinant IL-6 increases hypothalamic IL-6 contents in subsequent forced swim stressor in rats. *Neuropsychobiology, 54,* 186–194.

Matyszak, M. K. (1998). Inflammation in the CNS: Balance between immunological privilege and immune responses. *Progress in Neurobiology, 56,* 19–35.

Matzinger, P. (2002, April 12). The danger model: A renewed sense of self. *Science, 296,* 301–305.

McBeth, J., Chiu, Y. H., Silman, A., Ray, D., Morriss, R., Dickens, C., et al. (2005). Hypothalamic–pituitary–adrenal stress axis function and the relationship with chronic widespread pain and its antecedents. *Arthritis Research and Therapeutics, 7,* R992–R1000.

McEwen, B. S. (2003). Interacting mediators of allostasis and allostatic load: Towards an understanding of resilience in aging. *Metabolism, 52,* 10–16.

McEwen, B. S., Biron, C. A., Brunson, K. W., Bulloch, K., Chambers, W. H., Dhabhar, F. S., et al. (1997). The role of adrenocorticoids as modulators of immune function in health and disease: Neural, endocrine and immune interactions. *Brain Research Review, 23,* 79–133.

McGeer, P. L., & McGeer, E. G. (1995). The inflammatory response system of brain: Implications for therapy of Alzheimer and other neurodegenerative diseases. *Brain Research Review, 21,* 195–218.

McGeer, P. L., & McGeer, E. G. (2004). Inflammation and the degenerative diseases of aging. *Annals of the New York Academy of Sciences, 1035,* 104–116.

Meagher, M. W., Johnson, R. R., Young, E. E., Vichaya, E. G., Lunt, S., Harden, E., et al. (2007). Interleukin-6 as a mechanism for the adverse effects of social stress on acute Theiler's virus infection. *Brain, Behavior, and Immunity, 21,* 1083–1095.

Mei-Tal, V., Meyerowitz, S., & Engel, G. L. (1970). The role of psychological process in a somatic disorder: Multiple sclerosis: 1. The emotional setting of illness onset and exacerbation. *Psychosomatic Medicine, 32,* 67–86.

Merali, Z., Lacosta, S., & Anisman, H. (1997). Effects of interleukin-1beta and mild stress on alterations of norepinephrine, dopamine and serotonin neurotransmission: A regional microdialysis study. *Brain Research, 761,* 225–235.

Mohr, D. C., Goodkin, D. E., Bacchetti, P., Boudewyn, A. C., Huang, L., Marrietta, P., et al. (2000). Psychological stress and the subsequent appearance of new brain MRI lesions in MS. *Neurology, 55,* 55–61.

Mohr, D. C., Hart, S. L., Julian, L., Cox, D., & Pelletier, D. (2004, March 27). Association between stressful life events and exacerbation in multiple sclerosis: A meta-analysis. *BMJ, 328,* 731–735.

Mora, S., Lee, I., Buring, J., & Ridker, P. (2006). Association of physical activity and body mass index with novel and traditional cardiovascular biomarkers in women. *JAMA, 295,* 1412–1419.

Nair, A., & Bonneau, R. H. (2006). Stress-induced elevation of glucocorticoids increases microglia proliferation through NMDA receptor activation. *Journal of Neuroimmunology, 171,* 72–85.

Pace, T. W., Hu, F., & Miller, A. H. (2007). Cytokine-effects on glucocorticoid receptor function: Relevance to glucocorticoid resistance and the pathophysiology and treatment of major depression. *Brain, Behavior, and Immunity, 21,* 9–19.

Padgett, D. A., Sheridan, J. F., Dorne, J., Berntson, G. G., Candelora, J., & Glaser, R. (1998). Social stress and the reactivation of latent herpes simplex virus Type 1. *Proceedings of the National Academy of Sciences USA, 95,* 7231–7235.

Perry, V. H., Newman, T. A., & Cunningham, C. (2003). The impact of systemic infection on the progression of neurodegenerative disease. *Nature Reviews: Neuroscience, 4,* 103–112.

Quan, N., Avitsur, R., Stark, J. L., He, L., Shah, M., Caliguiri, M., et al. (2001). Social stress increases the susceptibility to endotoxic shock. *Journal of Neuroimmunology, 115,* 36–45.

Rabin, B. S. (2002). Can stress participate in the pathogenesis of autoimmune disease? *Journal of Adolescent Health, 30,* 71–75.

Schmidt, E. D., Janszen, A. W., Wouterlood, F. G., & Tilders, F. J. (1995). Interleukin-1-induced long-lasting changes in hypothalamic corticotropin-releasing hormone (CRH)-neurons and hyperresponsiveness of the hypothalamic–pituitary–adrenal axis. *Journal of Neuroscience, 15,* 7417–7426.

Schuder, S. (2005). Stress-induced hypocortisolemia diagnosed as psychiatric disorders responsive to hydrocortisone replacement. *Annals of the New York Academy of Sciences, 1057,* 466–478.

Segerstrom, S. C., & Miller, G. E. (2004). Psychological stress and the human immune system: A meta-analytic study of 30 years of inquiry. *Psychological Bulletin, 13,* 601–630.

Sheridan, J. F., Dobbs, C., Jung, J., Chu, X., Konstantinos, A., Padgett, D. A., & Glaser, R. (1998). Stress-induced neuroendocrine modulation of viral pathogenesis and immunity. *Annals of the New York Academy of Sciences, 840,* 803–808.

Shizuya, K., Komori, T., Fujiwara, R., Miyahara, S., Ohmori, M., & Nomura, J. (1997). The influence of restraint stress on the expression of mRNAs for IL-6 and the IL-6 receptor in the hypothalamus and midbrain of the rat. *Life Science, 61,* 135–140.

Shizuya, K., Komori, T., Fujiwara, R., Miyahara, S., Ohmori, M., & Nomura, J. (1998). The expressions of mRNAs for interleukin-6 (IL-6) and the IL-6 receptor (IL-6R) in the rat hypothalamus and midbrain during restraint stress. *Life Science, 62,* 2315–2320.

Sieve, A. N., Steelman, A. J., Young, C. R., Storts, R., Welsh, T. H., Welsh, C. J. R., & Meagher, M. W. (2004). Chronic restraint stress during early Theiler's virus infection exacerbates the subsequent demyelinating disease in SJL mice. *Journal of Neuroimmunology, 155,* 103–118.

Spiegel, D., & Giese-Davis, J. (2003). Depression and cancer: Mechanisms and disease progression. *Biological Psychiatry, 54,* 269–282.

Steptoe, A., Willemsen, G., Owen, N., Flower, L., & Mohamed-Ali, V. (2001). Acute mental stress elicits delayed increases in circulating inflammatory cytokine levels. *Clinical Sciences, 101,* 185–192.

Sternberg, E. (2006). Neural regulation of innate immunity: A coordinated nonspecific host response to pathogens. *Nature Reviews: Immunology, 6,* 318–328.

Takaki, A., Huang, Q.-H., Somogyvari-Vigh, A., & Arimura, A. (1994). Immobilization stress may increases plasma interleukin (IL)-6 via central and peripheral catecholamines. *Neuroimmunomodulation, 1,* 335–342.

Thayer, J., & Sternberg, E. (2006). Beyond heart rate variability: Vagal regulation of allostatic systems. *Annals of the New York Academy of Sciences, 1088,* 361–372.

Tsigos, C., & Chrousos, G. P. (2002). Hypothalamic–pituitary–adrenal axis, neuroendocrine factors and stress. *Journal of Psychosomatic Research, 53,* 865–871.

Turnbull, A. V., & Rivier, C. L. (1999). Regulation of the hypothalamic–pituitary–adrenal axis by cytokines: Actions and mechanisms of action. *Physiological Reviews, 79,* 1–71.

Viswanathan, K., Daugherty C., & Dhabhar, F. S. (2005). Stress as an endogenous adjuvant: Augmentation of the immunization phase of cell-mediated immunity. *International Immunology, 17,* 1059–1069.

Warren, S., Greenhill, S., & Warren, K. G. (1982). Emotional stress and the development of multiple sclerosis: Case-control evidence of a relationship. *Journal of Chronic Disease, 35,* 821–831.

Warren, S., Warren, K. G., & Cockerill, R. (1991). Emotional stress and coping in multiple sclerosis (MS) exacerbations. *Journal of Psychosomatic Research, 35,* 37–47.

Watkins, L. R., & Maier, S. F. (2000). The pain of being sick: Implications of immune-to-brain communication for understanding pain. *Annual Review of Psychology, 51,* 29–57.

Welsh, C. J. R., Meagher, M. W., & Sternberg, E. M. (2006). *Neural and neuroendocrine mechanisms in host defense and autoimmunity.* New York: Springer.

Whitton, P. S. (2007). Inflammation as a causative factor in the aetiology of Parkinson's disease. *British Journal of Pharmacology, 150,* 963–976.

Wilson, A., Ryan, M., & Boyle, A. (2006). The novel role of C-reactive protein in cardiovascular disease: Risk marker or pathogen. *International Journal of Cardiology, 106,* 291–297.

Wilson, R. S., Evans, D. A., Bienias, J. L., Mendes de Leon, C. F., Schneider, J. A., & Bennett, D. A. (2003). Proneness to psychological distress is associated with risk of Alzheimer's disease. *Neurology, 61,* 1479–1485.

Wust, S., Federenko, I., Hellhammer, D., & Kirschbaum, C. (2000). Genetic factors, perceived chronic stress, and the free cortisol response to awakening. *Psychoneuroendocrinology, 25,* 707–720.

Yehuda, R. (1997). Sensitization of the hypothalamic–pituitary–adrenal axis in posttraumatic stress disorder. *Annals of the New York Academy of Sciences, 821,* 57–75.

Zhou, D., Kusnecov, A. W., Shurin, M. R., DePaoli, M., & Rabin, B. S. (1993). Exposure to physical and psychological stressors elevates plasma interleukin 6: Relationship to the activation of hypothalamic–pituitary–adrenal axis. *Endocrinology, 133,* 2523–2530.

2

INFLAMMATION, FATTY ACID OXIDATION, AND NEURODEGENERATIVE DISEASE

MARY NIVISON, ANGELA L. GUILLOZET-BONGAARTS, AND THOMAS J. MONTINE

Inflammation is an active defense mechanism against many types of insults to brain. It acts to remove or inactivate pathogens and to inhibit and reverse their detrimental effects. Inflammation in the brain can be triggered by invading microbes such as viruses or bacteria, by injurious chemicals, or by physical insult. It can be initiated from within the organism as well, as happens with diseases affecting the nervous or immune systems. It can be triggered by the accumulation of modified proteins, by the chemical signals from injured neurons, or by an imbalance between proinflammatory and anti-inflammatory processes.

Prolonged or excessive inflammation can be responsible for much of the parenchymal damage in chronic diseases. A prime example is lung damage that accompanies tuberculosis where protracted immune response leads to extensive damage, largely through the actions of the macrophages that produce free radical or oxidative stress. Mounting evidence suggests that similar mechanisms may contribute to neurodegenerative diseases.

FREE RADICAL DAMAGE, IMMUNE ACTIVATION, AND NEURODEGENERATION

Free radical damage, unlike enzyme-catalyzed reactions, is an indiscriminate process that simultaneously modifies multiple targets, including nucleic acids, proteins, and lipids (K. S. Montine, Quinn, & Montine, 2003). This complex process directly damages membranes and generates a number of oxygenated products that can be classified as either chemically reactive or stable products (Esterbauer & Ramos, 1996). The polyunsaturated fatty acids (PUFAs) that make up the cellular membranes, including arachidonic acid (AA), are among the most vulnerable targets for free radical damage, a process termed *lipid peroxidation* (Porter, Caldwell, & Mills, 1995).

Because of the high concentration of PUFAs in brain relative to other organs, lipid peroxidation is one of the major outcomes of free-radical-mediated injury to brain (T. J. Montine, Neely, et al., 2002). A critically important aspect of lipid peroxidation is that it is self-propagating and will proceed until the substrate is consumed or termination occurs. Because it is a self-sustaining process capable of extensive tissue damage, lipid peroxidation is fundamentally different from other forms of free radical injury.

Abundant data strongly implicate free-radical-mediated injury to diseased regions of brain as a shared mechanism of several neurodegenerative diseases. Though free radical damage may be common among neurodegenerative diseases, the sources of the various free radicals are likely specific to different types of neurodegeneration. For example, in vivo and in vitro data indicate that oligomers or higher order aggregates of beta amyloid (Aβ) peptides both directly and indirectly stimulate free radical production in diseased regions of brain of patients with Alzheimer's disease (AD; Butterfield, Drake, Pocernich, & Castegna, 2001). In Parkinson's disease (PD), impaired mitochondrial respiration as a source of increased free radical production has been repeatedly implicated in numerous biochemical, experimental animal, and clinical studies (Orth & Schapira, 2002).

Outcomes of Lipid Peroxidation

There are two broad outcomes to lipid peroxidation: structural damage to membranes and the generation of reactive oxidized products. It is these reactive products that are believed to be the major effectors of tissue damage from lipid peroxidation, including that which leads to neurodegeneration (Feillet-Coudray et al., 1999; T. J. Montine, Markesbery, Morrow, & Roberts, 1998; Pratico et al., 2000). Biochemical studies have demonstrated increased concentrations of reactive products from lipid peroxidation in diseased regions of AD brain. Immunohistochemical studies have localized protein adducts of these molecules to Lewy bodies, neurofibrillary tangles (NFTs), and senile plaques in several neurodegenerative diseases (Ando et al., 1998; Castellani et al., 2002; Lovell, Xie, & Markesbery, 2001; Markesbery & Lovell, 1998; McGrath et al., 2001; K. S. Montine et al., 1998; K. S. Montine, Kim, Olson, Markesbery, & Montine, 1997; K. S. Montine, Olson, et al., 1997; T. J. Montine et al., 1998; Sayre et al., 1997; Smith et al., 1996, 1998; Yoritaka et al., 1996). Some studies have associated either increased magnitude or altered distribution of lipid peroxidation products in AD patients with a specific *APOE* genotype (K. S. Montine, Olson, et al., 1997; Sanan et al., 1994). These reactive products of lipid peroxidation are believed to participate in modifications of the neurofibrillary tangles formed by tau, Aβ peptide aggregates, and α-synuclein aggregates (Duda, Giasson, Mabon, Lee, & Trojanowski, 2002; Giasson et al., 2000).

Numerous studies have demonstrated significantly increased lipid peroxidation-derived aldehydes in diseased regions of brain obtained from deceased patients with AD or PD (Lovell, Ehmann, Butler, & Markesbery, 1995; Lovell, Ehmann, Mattson, & Markesbery, 1997; Lovell et al., 2001; Markesbery & Lovell, 1998; Shelley, 1998). However, activity of some of the major metabolizing enzymes for these reactive products of lipid peroxidation also is altered in diseased regions of brain in AD and PD (Picklo, Olson, Markesbery, & Montine, 2001; K. R. Sidell, Amamath, & Montine, 2001; K. R. Sidell et al., 2003). This finding raises serious issues for interpreting the significance of increased levels of these reactive products in neurodegenerative diseases.

AA is liberated from the phospholipids in cell membranes by the action of phospholipases that are stimulated by a variety of extracellular stimuli, including neurotransmitters, growth factors, and cytokines (Farooqui, Ong, & Horrocks, 2006). Three enzyme systems act on AA to generate (a) prostaglandin H$_2$ via the cyclooxygenase enzymes (COX-1 and COX-2), (b) leukotrienes via the LOX pathways, and (c) epoxyeicosatrienoic acids via the epoxygenase cytochrome P450 pathway (see Figure 2.1). These lipid products are signaling messengers and regulate a wide variety of physiologic functions under basal conditions, including cerebral blood flow and synaptic function. Increases in expression and activity of enzymes in each of these three pathways have been documented in a wide spectrum of neurological diseases, including acute insults such as cerebral ischemia and trauma, as well as chronic neurodegenerative diseases such as AD, PD, and amyotrophic lateral sclerosis (i.e., ALS). Of the three enzymatic pathways, the COX pathway has been most studied, and a significant body of evidence links this pathway and downstream prostanoid products to a broad range of neurological diseases.

The cyclooxygenases COX-1 and COX-2 catalyze the first committed step in prostanoid and thromboxane synthesis (reviewed in Breyer, Bagdassarian, Myers, & Breyer, 2001). The cyclooxygenases convert AA to PGH$_2$, which then serves as a substrate for a family of prostanoid and thromboxane synthases that generate PGE$_2$, PGD$_2$, PGF$_{2\alpha}$, PGI$_2$ (prostacyclin), and TXA$_2$ (thromboxane). These prostaglandins bind to several classes of

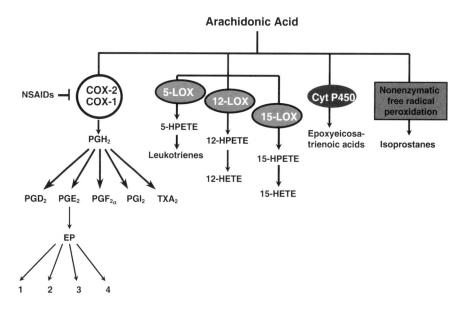

Figure 2.1. Arachidonic acid (AA) is metabolized by three enzyme systems: (a) the cyclooxygenases COX-1 and COX-2 to yield PGH_2, which is converted by specific synthases to the five prostanoids, which are further converted to five prostaglandins; (b) the lipoxygenases 5-LOX, 12-LOX, and 15-LOX to yield leukotrienes and hydroxyeicosatetraenoic (HETE) acids; and (c) the cytochrome P450 epoxygenases to yield epoxyeicosatrienoic acids. AA is also nonenzymatically oxidized by free radicals to form a large family of isoprostanes. HPETE = hydroperoxyeicosatetraenoic acid; NSAIDs = nonsteroidal anti-inflammatory drugs.

G-protein coupled receptors (GPCRs). These GPCRs are designated EP (for E-prostanoid receptor), DP, FP, IP, and TP, respectively. Further complexity arises in there being more than one receptor for each prostaglandin: there are four EP receptors (EP1, EP2, EP3, and EP4) and two DP receptors (DP1 and DP2, also known as CRTH2). In the brain, these prostaglandin receptors have distinct cellular and anatomical distributions, are differentially regulated in response to exogenous stimuli, and have different downstream signaling cascades. Prostaglandin receptor subtypes are distinguished not only by which prostaglandin they bind but also by the specific signal transduction pathway that is activated upon ligand binding. Activation of PG receptors triggers intracellular signals that lead to modifications in production of adenosine 3',5'-cyclic monophosphate (cAMP) and phosphoinositol turnover. Within one family of receptors, subtypes may have opposing effects on cAMP levels, and thus have functionally different downstream effects.

COX-1 and COX-2 are expressed in brain, albeit with significantly different cellular and anatomic distributions. COX-1 is expressed at low levels in all cell types. COX-2 is expressed at moderately robust basal levels in specific neuronal populations, including dentate gyrus, hippocampal pyramidal neurons, efferent layers of cerebral cortex, pyriform cortex, amygdala, and in discrete subpopulations in hypothalamus (Breder, Dewitt, & Kraig, 1995; Yamagata, Andreasson, Kaufmann, Barnes, & Worley, 1993). Within neurons, COX-2 immunoreactivity is localized to postsynaptic sites in dendritic spines, the sites of N-methyl-D-aspartate (NMDA) receptor-mediated neurotransmission (Kaufmann, Worley, Pegg, Bremer, & Isakson, 1996). COX-2 expression is up-regulated in neurons following NMDA receptor-dependent excitatory synaptic activity in paradigms of learning and memory. The fact that COX-2 is specifically localized to postsynaptic structures, and that its expression is increased upon excitatory synaptic activity, points to a role for COX-2 in modulating synaptic transmission under physiologic conditions. Electrophysiologic and in vivo rodent models of learning and memory (Rall, Mach, & Dash, 2003; Shaw, Commins, & O'Mara, 2003; Teather, Packard, & Bazan, 2002) suggest that COX-2 participates in synaptic plasticity, in particular via PGE_2 (Chen & Bazan, 2005; Chen, Magee, & Bazan, 2002; Sang, Zhang, Marcheselli, Bazan, & Chen, 2005). In tests of hippocampal-dependent learning and memory, COX-2 inhibitors given either before or after training inhibited both acquisition and consolidation of spatial memory (Rall et al., 2003; Teather et al., 2002). Mechanisms by which COX-2 and its downstream prostaglandins might function in synaptic remodeling include regulation of downstream growth factors, particularly brain-derived neurotrophic factor (i.e., BDNF; Shaw et al., 2003), and neurovascular coupling in which synaptically active neurons promote local hyperemia (Niwa, Araki, Morham, Ross, & Iadecola, 2000).

Brain Inflammation in Neurodegenerative Disease

Brain inflammation underlies a large number of neurodegenerative diseases as well as normal aging. The prostaglandin products of COX-1 and COX-2 enzymatic activity are important mediators of the inflammatory response. The identification of which prostaglandin receptors promote COX-2 toxicity is currently an active area of research. Because of the number of prostaglandin receptor signaling systems and the complexity of cellular distributions, inducibility, and downstream signaling cascades, this undertaking is quite complex. However, studies using genetic mouse models (Andreasson et al., 2001; Li et al., 2004; Lim et al., 2000; Matsubara et al., 2003; Sung et al., 2004) are beginning to uncover important neurotoxic and proinflammatory functions of selected prostaglandin receptors. Significant headway has been made in examining the function of the PGE_2 EP2 receptor in the lipopolysaccharide (LPS) model of innate immunity and in a transgenic model of familial AD and amyloid deposition.

A first line of defense in the central nervous system against injury or infection is the innate immune response, which activates microglia. Microglia are the macrophages of the brain and respond by producing cytoxic compounds such as reactive oxidative species (ROS) and nitric oxide, as well as by phagocytosing invading pathogens, bacteria or necrotic tissue. Injection of the endotoxin LPS constitutes a primary model of innate immunity, and has been used to study mechanisms of immune activation, including microglial activation and production of ROS, nitric oxide, cytokines, and chemokines, as well as phagocytosis. LPS is a potent and specific stimulus of innate immune response that binds the coreceptors CD14 and TLR4; this is followed by activation of mitogen-activated protein kinases and NFκB, which regulate transcription of proinflammatory genes such as COX-2 and iNOS that function in microglial activation. LPS stimulation also leads to activation of microglial nicotinamide adenine dinucleotide phosphate (i.e., NADPH) oxidase, a major source of superoxide in inflammation. LPS-induced inflammatory changes can increase cognitive decline in aging rodents (Hauss-Wegrzyniak, Lynch, Vraniak, & Wenk, 2002). ROS-induced injury leads to abnormal aging, and impairments in learning are associated with higher levels of oxidative damage (Nicolle et al., 2001).

The Role of EP2

The EP2 receptor functions prominently in the development of oxidative damage in innate immunity triggered by intracerebroventricular (ICV) injection of LPS (Milatovic, Zaja-Milatovic, Montine, Nivison, & Montine, 2005; Milatovic, Zaja-Milatovic, Montine, Shie, & Montine, 2004; T. J. Montine, Milatovic, et al., 2002). In wild type (wt) mice, ICV LPS activates glial innate immunity. We found that this LPS-induced cerebral oxidative damage is abolished in mice lacking EP2 (EP2 -/-; T. J. Montine, Milatovic, et al., 2002). This protective effect is not associated with changes in cerebral eicosanoid production but is partially related to reduced induction of nitric oxide synthase (NOS) activity. We further observed that EP2 -/- mice are completely protected from CD14-dependent synaptodendritic degeneration (Milatovic et al., 2004, 2005). Following ICV LPS injection, hippocampal CA1 pyramidal neurons undergo a delayed, reversible decrease in dendrite length and spine density without neuron death that reaches its nadir at approximately 24 hours and recovers to near basal levels by 72 hours; no change in these endpoints is seen in EP2 -/- mice under the same conditions.

The effect of EP2 deletion on lipid peroxidation parallels what is seen in the simpler LPS model. The CD14-dependent innate immune response to LPS nevertheless is relevant to the immune response to accumulating Aβ peptide because microglial activation and inflammatory mediators are in part CD14-dependent (Fassbender et al., 2004; Milatovic et al., 2004). Thus, the question is raised as to whether the lower oxidative damage in the EP2 -/- background results in a delayed and less severe accumulation of Aβ or, conversely, whether transgenic Aβ production fails to elicit a vigorous oxidative response, which in turn results in a decreased accumulation of Aβ over time. The temporal and causal relationship of inflammatory oxidative stress and

Aβ peptide accumulation is of central relevance to the pathogenesis of AD, where oxidative stress may precede and possibly trigger Aβ deposition (Pratico, Uryu, Leight, Trojanowski, & Lee, 2001).

The hypothesis that the EP2 receptor functions in the innate immune response to Aβ peptides is supported by evidence in nonneuronal systems. Expression of the EP2 receptor is up-regulated in models of innate immunity in peripheral macrophages and antigen presenting cells (Harizi, Grosset, & Gualde, 2003; Hubbard, Lee, Lim, & Erickson, 2001) where the EP2 receptor regulates expression of inflammatory mediators, including tumor necrosis factor-α (Akaogi et al., 2004; Fennekohl et al., 2002; Vassiliou, Jing, & Ganea, 2003), interleukin-6 (Akaogi et al., 2004; Treffkorn, Scheibe, Maruyama, & Dieter, 2004), monocyte chemoattractant protein 1 (Largo et al., 2004), intercellular adhesion molecule (Noguchi et al., 2001), and inducible NOS (Minghetti et al., 1997). Separate studies point to additional roles of EP2 receptor in modulating macrophage migration (Baratelli et al., 2004) and inhibiting phagocytosis of bacterial components by lung alveolar macrophages (Aronoff, Canetti, & Peters-Golden, 2004). A recent intriguing study demonstrated that EP2 -/- microglia exhibit a strong phagocytic response to deposited Aβ not observed in wt microglia (Shie, Breyer, & Montine, 2005). These studies are consistent with others that demonstrate that PGE_2 inhibits phagocytosis by macrophages by a process that is dependent on increased cAMP levels (Aronoff et al., 2004; Borda, Tenenbaum, Sales, Rumi, & Sterin-Borda, 1998; Canning, Hmieleski, Spannhake, & Jakab, 1991; Hutchison & Myers, 1987).

Inflammation in Alzheimer's Disease and Nonsteroidal Anti-Inflammatory Drugs

AD is a common cause of age-dependent dementia, affecting nearly one in three adults over the age of 80. Hallmark pathological features include deposition of Aβ peptide into amyloid plaques in brain parenchyma, NFTs with extensive hippocampal and cortical neuronal loss, and glial activation. A central role of inflammation is postulated in the development and progression of AD (Akiyama et al., 2000). Evidence is accumulating that suggests a substantial role for COX-2 activity and prostaglandin signaling in mediating secondary neuronal injury in chronic degenerative neurological diseases characterized by a predominantly inflammatory pathology. In support of this concept is the fact that in normal aging populations, chronic use of nonsteroidal anti-inflammatory drugs (NSAIDs), which block COX activity, is associated with a significantly lower risk of developing AD (in't Veld, Ruitenberg, Hofman, Stricker, & Breteler, 2001; McGeer, Schulzer, & McGeer, 1996; Stewart, Kawas, Corrada, & Metter, 1997). Conversely, the administration of NSAIDs or COX-2 inhibitors to patients already symptomatic with AD has little benefit (Aisen et al., 2003). These studies indicate that in aging populations, NSAIDs may be effective in the prevention and not the therapy of AD, and that inflammation is an early and potentially reversible preclinical event.

Modeling the effect of NSAIDs in vivo using transgenic mouse models of mutant human alleles of amyloid precursor protein (APP) and presenilin-1 has demonstrated that NSAIDs can reduce amyloid deposition in association with a reversal of behavioral deficits (Hubbard et al., 2001; Jantzen et al., 2002; Lim et al., 2000; Yan et al., 2003). The mechanism by which NSAIDs promote this effect has been attributed to anti-inflammatory effects through inhibition of COX and production of proinflammatory prostaglandins. Recent in vitro studies have demonstrated that high concentrations of some NSAIDs can alter γ-secretase activity and reduce the amount of $A\beta_{42}$, the harmful form of the peptide, in cultured cells (Weggen, Eriksen, Sagi, Pietrzik, Golde, & Koo, 2003; Weggen, Eriksen, Sagi, Pietrzik, Ozols, et al., 2003; Weggen et al., 2001). Whether this mechanism is responsible for the preventive effects of NSAIDs in AD is not clear (Eriksen et al., 2003; Lanz, Fici, & Merchant, 2005). Evidence of significantly decreased levels of microglial activation, an inflammatory response, has been described in patients taking NSAIDs (Mackenzie & Munoz, 1998). In transgenic mouse models of familial AD, NSAIDs reduce $A\beta$ accumulation and markers of microglial activation (Yan et al., 2003).

However, NSAIDs potentiate phagocytosis by macrophages in many studies (Bjornson, Knippenberg, & Bjornson, 1988; Gilmour, Park, Doerfler, & Selgrade, 1993; Gurer et al., 2002; Laegreid et al., 1989). Thus the anti-amyloidogenic properties of NSAIDs in transgenic mutant APP models (Jantzen et al., 2002; Lim et al., 2000; Yan et al., 2003) might be explained by indirect interruption of PGE_2 signaling via the EP2 receptor by COX inhibition, resulting in reduced oxidation and increased phagocytosis and clearance of $A\beta$. These studies suggest a possible dual role for the EP2 receptor in both promoting oxidative damage and inhibiting phagocytosis of $A\beta$. In AD and in models of familial AD, an imbalance develops with aging between the accumulation and clearance of $A\beta$. This imbalance might be occurring because the microglial clearance of $A\beta$ does not keep up with the accumulation of $A\beta$, which is accelerated by the increased oxidative stress elicited by the increasing levels of $A\beta$. An important question in the in vivo development of disease is whether defective phagocytosis leads to further inflammation, oxidative damage, and secondary neurotoxicity, and whether EP2 receptor activation promotes this.

Arachidonic Acid and Isoprostanes

Because of the indiscriminate nature of free radical reactions, multiple products can be formed from AA. These products can modify proteins, nucleic acids, and lipids. In the early 1990s, it was demonstrated that free-radical-mediated damage to AA-generated products that were isometric to prostaglandin products of COX. These newly discovered compounds were termed *isoprostanes* (IsoPs; Morrow et al., 1990). IsoPs are chemically and metabolically stable and therefore suitable as in vivo biomarkers of oxidative damage. These compounds include the families of IsoPs (Morrow et al., 1990), NeuroPs (Reich et al., 2001a), and IsoFs (Fessel, Hulette, Powell, Roberts, & Zhang, 2003).

IsoPs are formed in situ by the peroxidation of AA. Three major structural isomers of IsoPs are formed from a common endoperoxide intermediate (Morrow et al., 1998). We recently demonstrated an oxygen insertion step that diverts intermediates in the IsoP pathway to instead form compounds termed *IsoFs* (Fessel et al., 2003). Like IsoPs, IsoFs are chemically and metabolically stable and so are also well suited to act as in vivo biomarkers. Comparison of IsoP with IsoF formation reflects the local oxygen tension in which free radical damage occurred.

In contrast to AA, which is evenly distributed in all cell types in all regions of brain tissue, docosahexaenoic acid (DHA) is very highly concentrated in neuronal membranes (Salem, Kim, & Yergey, 1986). We have extended the technology for measuring IsoPs to include quantification of oxidation products of DHA, which we have termed *NeuroPs* (Reich et al., 2001b). NeuroPs provide a unique window through which we can quantify oxidative damage, primarily in neuronal membranes in vivo. This approach is fundamentally important when considering neurodegenerative diseases. Under basal conditions, glia outnumber neurons in gray matter 10 to 1, and the ratio is further skewed in neurodegenerative diseases as neuronal death and glial hypertrophy take place. Therefore, experiments that homogenize regions of brain from patients with neurodegenerative disease and then measure indices of oxidative damage are mostly assessing what has occurred in glia. Indeed, we are aware of only one quantitative in vivo marker of oxidative damage that is selective for neurons—NeuroPs.

Because of limitations in quantifying reactive products of lipid peroxidation, we and others have measured IsoPs and related compounds in brain of patients who died with advanced AD. One group has demonstrated elevated IsoP levels in frontal and temporal lobes of patients with AD compared with control participants (Pratico, Lee, Trojanowski, Rokach, & Fitzgerald, 1998). Another group has reported that NeuroPs are elevated in temporal and occipital, but not parietal, lobes of patients with AD compared with control participants, and that NeuroPs are greater than IsoPs in these regions. However, interpretation of data from this study is limited by the long postmortem intervals (average 47 hours in patients with AD; Nourooz-Zadeh, Liu, Yhlen, Anggard, & Halliwell, 1999). This study was expanded by measuring IsoPs and NeuroPs in temporal and parietal cortex, hippocampus, and cerebellum of patients with AD and age-matched control participants, all with short postmortem intervals (Reich et al., 2001a). Total NeuroP, but not total IsoP, levels are greater in patients with AD than in control participants, but only in those brain regions involved by AD. The ratio for specific NeuroPs, but not IsoPs, was 40% to 70% lower in patients with AD compared with control participants. However, this result was found in all brain regions, not only those involved by AD. These data indicate greater free radical damage in DHA-containing compartments in diseased regions of AD brain and suggest diminished reducing capacity in DHA-containing compartments throughout AD brain. This combination raises the possibility of a global vulnerability in neurons of patients with AD that is compounded by factors specific to the brain regions involved in AD.

We recently applied IsoP and IsoF quantification methods to the investigation of PD and related disorders. Despite numerous studies implicating free radical damage to brain in PD, a previous study failed to demonstrate an increase in IsoPs in PD patients (Pratico et al., 1998). However, these investigators evaluated only the cerebral cortex, a region that usually does not demonstrate significant neuronal damage in PD without associated dementia. We recently quantified IsoPs in the substantia nigra (SN), the region of brain most heavily damaged in PD, and in ventricular fluid of patients who had died with PD and were surprised to find no significant increase compared with control individuals (Fessel et al., 2003). One possible explanation is that in the SN of patients with PD, where mitochondrial respiration is impaired, increased cellular oxygen tension favors IsoF over IsoP formation. By contrast, the magnitude of oxidative damage to SN as assessed by these markers is not significantly different in patients with multiple system atrophy–parkinsonian type or AD compared with control participants. Thus, the two neurodegenerative diseases that severely damage the SN—PD and dementia with Lewy bodies (DLB)—are both associated with increased oxidative damage in the SN. Moreover, SN from PD and DLB patients shows a significantly greater proportion of IsoF formation, suggesting locally increased oxygen tension secondary to the mitochondrial dysfunction characteristic of these diseases.

Cerebrospinal fluid (CSF) also has been investigated as a source of central nervous system tissue for the assessment of lipid peroxidation in neurodegenerative diseases. A few studies have determined the concentration of IsoPs and, in one case, NeuroPs, in CSF obtained from the lateral ventricles postmortem and have shown significant elevations in patients with AD compared with age-matched control participants (K. S. Montine et al., 1998; T. J. Montine et al., 1998; T. J. Montine, Markesbery, et al., 1999). In addition, lateral ventricular CSF IsoP concentrations in AD patients are significantly correlated with global indices of neurodegeneration—decreasing brain weight, degree of cerebral cortical atrophy, and increasing Braak stage—but not with *APOE* or the tissue density of neuritic plaques or neurofibrillary tangles (T. J. Montine, Markesbery, et al., 1999). It is noteworthy that all of the postmortem CSF studies in patients with AD used material from individuals with very short (average 2–3 hours) postmortem intervals.

Patients undergoing postmortem examination typically have advanced disease with illness progressing over a decade or more. Therefore, a serious limitation to interpretation of results described earlier is that the increased brain lipid peroxidation might be a late-stage consequence of disease. A late-stage consequence obviously would be a less attractive therapeutic target than would a process contributing to disease progression at an earlier stage. Therefore, we have quantified IsoPs in CSF obtained intra vitam from the lumbar cistern in a number of neurodegenerative diseases earlier in their course, with a focus on AD. Control participants were hospitalized patients who underwent diagnostic evaluation of CSF or elderly volunteers. No control participant had neurodegenerative disease, and no one had evidence of cerebrovascular disease, trauma, or inflammation, unless otherwise specified.

The first study of probable AD patients early in the course of dementia showed that IsoPs are significantly elevated in CSF obtained from the lumbar cistern compared with age-matched hospitalized patients without neurologic disease (T. J. Montine, Beal, Cudkowicz, et al., 1999). The average duration of dementia in these patients with probable AD at the time of CSF examination was less than 2 years; the average duration of AD is between 8 and 12 years. This same result has been observed by us in additional groups of probable AD patients and control participants (T. J. Montine, Beal, Cudkowicz, et al., 1999; T. J. Montine et al., 2001; T. J. Montine, Sidell, et al., 1999). It is notable that a different laboratory examining a third group of probable AD patients and control participants using a similar method obtained similar results and confirmed the difference observed between AD patients and control participants (Pratico et al., 2000). This last study found a correlation between higher CSF IsoP levels and homozygosity for the 4 allele of *APOE*, an association not observed in other CSF and postmortem studies of AD patients (K. S. Montine et al., 1998; T. J. Montine, Markesbery, et al., 1999; T. J. Montine, Montine, et al., 1999; Reich et al., 2001a).

In addition to providing information about neurodegenerative disease pathogenesis and a means to quantitatively assess response to antioxidant therapeutics, CSF IsoP levels also may provide information that is useful in diagnosis of diseases where it is elevated early. We tested the hypothesis that quantification of CSF IsoPs, along with CSF $A\beta_{42}$ and tau levels, improves laboratory diagnostic accuracy for AD in patients with probable AD, dementias other than AD, and age-matched control participants (T. J. Montine et al., 2001). Individuals were classified as AD or non-AD by a commercially available test using CSF $A\beta_{42}$ and tau levels (95% sensitivity, 50% specificity), by CSF IsoP and $A\beta_{42}$ levels (90% sensitivity, 83% specificity), and by combined analysis using CSF IsoP, $A\beta_{42}$, and tau levels (84% sensitivity, 89% specificity). The results indicated that CSF IsoP quantification can enhance the accuracy of the laboratory diagnosis of AD. However, this conclusion is based on a single study, and these findings need to be replicated.

In light of the clear desirability of a peripheral biomarker of oxidative damage, quantification of IsoPs in plasma or urine has been pursued. We performed a large study measuring urine IsoPs and the major urinary metabolite of IsoPs and comparing CSF and urine IsoPs in a subset of nonsmoking individuals (T. J. Montine, Quinn, et al., 2002). This study is by far the largest with 56 AD patients and 34 control participants. There was no difference in urine IsoPs or the IsoP metabolite between AD patients and control participants, nor was there any correlation between urine and CSF IsoPs in 32 AD patients. Taken together, results from all of these studies do not reproducibly support the hypothesis that patients with AD experience increased levels of systemic oxidative stress or that the increased levels of IsoPs observed in CSF are detectable peripherally in patients with AD.

CLINICAL APPLICATIONS

It is now well recognized that the pathologic processes of AD precede clinically diagnosed dementia by as much as 2 or 3 decades. Indeed, as early as 1976, Katzman applied the chronic disease model to AD and proposed the existence of a latent stage during which some structural damage accrues but no functional or behavioral changes, followed by a prodromal stage during which structural damage continues to accrue but now with mild functional and behavioral changes, and culminating in a clinical stage of dementia with substantial irreversible structural damage and extensive functional and behavioral deficits (Katzman, 1976). It is in these early, preclinical stages of AD that the most effective clinical interventions will be able to adequately interrupt disease progression.

Early Biomarkers in Latent Stage Alzheimer's Disease

Several clinicopathologic studies have investigated the latent and prodromal stages of AD, the latter typically presenting as mild cognitive impairment (MCI; Petersen, 2004) or similar forms of cognitive decline without dementia. These have shown that AD-type neurodegenerative changes, namely, neuritic plaques (NPs) and NFTs, are commonly present in postmortem brain from older individuals rigorously demonstrated not to meet criteria for dementia (Arriagada, Marzloff, & Hyma, 1992; Berg, McKeel, Miller, Baty, & Morris, 1993; Crystal et al., 1993; Davis, Schmitt, Wekstein, & Markesbery, 1999; Green, Kaye, & Ball, 2000; Haroutunian et al., 1999; Hulette et al., 1998; J. C. Morris & Price, 2001; Price, Davis, Morris, & White, 1991; Price & Morris, 1999; Riley, Snowdon, & Markesbery, 2002; Schmitt et al., 2000; Xuereb et al., 2000). Across these many studies, about 80% of individuals more than 65 years old who do not have dementia will have NFTs in entorhinal cortex and more than 50% will have NPs in isocortex as identified by standard silver-stain techniques. These data, along with clinical and neuroimaging studies (Adak et al., 2004; Fleisher et al., 2005; Mosconi et al., 2005), form the basis for the widely held view that AD has preclinical stages during which damage accrues but the person does not meet clinical criteria for dementia. Progression to dementia is accompanied by increased density and more extensive distribution of these histopathologic features.

A general consensus from a large number of pathological and experimental studies is that formation of NPs and NFTs lies downstream in a complex molecular cascade that remains to be fully characterized (Hardy & Selkoe, 2002). Important elements in this cascade are the likely interacting processes of formation of nonsoluble protein aggregates, innate immune activation, increased oxidative damage, and synapse loss, among others. Combined with the results of clinicopathologic studies, these imaging and biochemical data support the idea that a very high proportion of older individuals who do not meet clinical criteria for dementia are experiencing not only histopathologic but also other structural and biochemical features of AD-type neurodegeneration. This concept of preclinical AD implies a possible opportunity to intervene before the onset of symptoms to prevent dementia. Indeed, AD latency and prodrome are receiving increasing attention because it is here that effective but safe interventions would have the greatest impact. There is also a growing realization that treatment strategies for these stages may be different from treatment of established dementia (Martin, Meinert, & Breitner, 2002). If true, this has immense implications for future clinical trials of AD because of the large size, long time, and great expense of conducting trials directed at latent or prodromal stages of AD.

One approach to facilitating these trials would be to develop biomarkers for elements in AD pathogenesis that would permit assessment of pharmacologic parameters, such as timing and dose of a new drug needed to suppress oxidative damage, rather than relying on clinical progression from latency to prodrome or from prodrome to dementia as the major end points. Lipid oxidation products must be considered for their use as quantitative biomarkers of free-radical-mediated damage in vivo and their role as targets in therapeutic drug development. Every lipid peroxidation product discussed earlier has been used as a measure of oxidative damage. The goal of a biomarker is to quantitatively reflect changes in free-radical-mediated damage.

Interpretation of biomarkers that are chemically reactive or that are extensively metabolized has inherent limitations. Some of the chemically and metabolically stable oxidation products are useful in vivo biomarkers of lipid peroxidation. These include the IsoPs and IsoFs derived from AA, and the NeuroPs derived from DHA. We have shown increased levels of IsoPs, NeuroPs, and IsoFs in diseased regions of brain from patients who died from advanced AD or PD. Increased CSF levels of IsoPs are present in patients with AD or Huntington's disease (HD) early in the course of their illness, and CSF IsoPs may improve the laboratory diagnostic accuracy for AD. These results indicate that brain lipid peroxidation is a potential therapeutic target early in the course of AD and HD, and that CSF IsoPs may aid in the assessment of antioxidant experimental therapeutics and laboratory diagnosis of AD.

Exquisitely sensitive assays have been developed for IsoPs and, because of the chemical stability and relatively limited metabolism of IsoPs in situ, IsoPs have emerged as a leading quantitative biomarker of lipid peroxidation in vivo (Morrow & Roberts, 1994). IsoPs can be measured in tissue samples where this product of lipid peroxidation remains esterified to phospholipids. Several groups have used measurements of hydrolyzed IsoPs in body fluids in an attempt to quantify the magnitude of oxidative damage in vivo. In AD, there is broad agreement that CSF IsoPs are increased in patients with mild dementia and even in individuals with prodromal dementia (T. J. Montine, Beal, Cudkowicz, et al., 1999; T. J. Montine, Beal, Robertson, et al., 1999; T. J. Montine et al., 2001; T. J. Montine, Sidell, et al., 1999; Pratico, Clark, Liun, Lee, & Trojanowski, 2002; Pratico et al., 2000). Similar to the attempts to identify peripheral biomarkers of other neurodegenerative diseases, attempts to use plasma or urine IsoPs in patients with AD have not yielded reproducible results across centers (Bohnstedt et al., 2003; Feillet-Coudray et al., 1999; T. J. Montine, Beal, Robertson, et al., 1999; T. J. Montine et al., 2000, 2001; Pratico et al., 2000, 2002; Tuppo et al., 2001). This is perhaps not surprising given the small amounts of brain-derived IsoPs relative to peripheral organ-derived IsoPs and the many systemic, dietary, and environmental factors that modulate peripheral IsoPs independent of disease. Although reactive products of lipid peroxidation are likely contributors to neurodegeneration, their use as in vivo biomarkers is severely limited because of their rapid and extensive metabolism and chemical instability (Gutteridge, Westermarck, & Halliwell, 1986; T. J. Montine, Neely, et al., 2002; Moore & Roberts, 1998).

There are many assays of oxidative damage. However, not all provide in vivo quantitative data in the sense that changes in end-organ oxidative damage are proportionally reflected in changes in the peripheral body fluid biomarker (vida infra). Once in vivo quantitative assays are established, the issue of which body fluid to use must be resolved based on the data. In brief, CSF has the advantages of more directly reflecting brain neurochemistry without the confounders associated with dilution into blood, mixing with peripheral pools, or filtration into urine. However, obtaining CSF from a lumbar tap, although considered a limited invasive procedure, is clearly more burdensome to patients, difficult for medical staff, time consuming, and costly than obtaining blood or urine. Restriction to CSF would clearly affect the implementation of biomarkers in large clinical trials. The first question is being addressed by the Biomarkers of Oxidative Stress Study (BOSS), a National Institutes of Health-sponsored multilaboratory study of multiple in vivo biomarkers of oxidative damage (http://www.niehs.nih.gov/research/resources/databases/bosstudy).

The biomarker assays being evaluated are DNA oxidation assays (8-hydroxydeoxyguanosine [8-OHdG], leukocyte DNA-malondialdehyde (MDA) adducts, and DNA-strand breaks), protein oxidation assays (protein carbonyls, various tyrosine products, methionine sulfoxidation), lipid peroxidation assays (lipid hydroperoxides, thiobarbituric acid reactive substances, MDA, IsoPs), and measurements of antioxidants (ascorbic acid, tocopherols, reduced and oxidized glutathione, uric acid, total antioxidant capacity). The initial publications from the BOSS used time- and dose-dependent effects of acute CCl_4 poisoning in rats to determine the most robust plasma or urine biomarkers of the well-established oxidative damage to liver (Kadiiska et al., 2000; Kadiiska, Gladen, Baird, Germolec, et al., 2005). This study concluded that measurements of plasma MDA (GC/MS assay), one class of IsoPs in plasma (GC/NICI-MS assay) or urine (immunoassay), another class of IsoPs in urine (LC/MS/MS assay), and 8-OHdG in urine (immunoassay) yield similar results and are the best biomarkers of oxidative stress in this model. MDA is a product of free-radical-mediated oxidation of fatty acids and is generated by thromboxane synthase. However, a recent report from the BOSS showed that peripheral levels of MDA derive primarily from oxidative injury (Kadiiska, Gladen, Baird, Graham, et al., 2005).

8-OHdG is a commonly assayed product of free-radical-mediated oxidation of DNA. IsoPs are part of a large group of prostaglandin-like isomers generated from free-radical-mediated oxidation of AA (Lawson, Rokach, & FitzGerald, 1999; Morrow et al., 1990, 1992; Pratico, Lawson, & FitzGerald, 1995; Wang et al., 1995), although there is evidence for COX participation in the production of a minor amount of 8-iso-$PGF_{2\alpha}$ (Bachi et al., 1997; Klein, Reutter, Schweer, Seyberth, & Nusing, 1997; Pratico et al., 1995; Schweer, Watzer, Seyberth, & Nusing, 1997). However, multiple studies have now shown that COX isoforms do not significantly contribute to the formation of 8-iso-$PGF_{2\alpha}$ in urine or plasma in humans or animals (Catella et al., 1995; Kadiiska, Gladen, Baird, Graham, et al., 2005; McAdam et al., 2000; Morrow, 2000; Pratico, Smyth, Violi, & FitzGerald, 1996; Reilly, Delanty, Lawson, & FitzGerald, 1996).

The other potential biomarkers tested in the BOSS, although having advantages in experimental settings, showed less or no significant association between serum or urine levels and so did not quantitatively reflect end-organ oxidative damage in peripheral body fluids. Obviously, there are substantial differences between acute CCl_4 poisoning and AD. Nevertheless, if a candidate blood or urine biomarker failed to quantitatively reflect oxidative damage to liver in an acute setting, we cannot reasonably expect it to quantitatively reflect chronic oxidative damage to brain in AD where there is the added complexity of residing behind the blood–brain barrier.

However, several biomarkers of oxidative damage are increased in CSF obtained from patients with mild-to-moderate dementia from AD. Moreover, complementary techniques, such as the different assays for IsoPs, yield quantitatively very similar results in CSF of age-matched control participants or patients with AD (de Leon et al., 2006; T. J. Montine, Beal, Cudkowicz, et al., 1999; T. J. Montine, Beal, Robertson, et al., 1999; T. J. Montine et al., 2001; Pratico et al., 2001, 2002). Of these studies, two have extended these findings to individuals with MCI (de Leon et al., 2006; Pratico et al., 2002). Overall, these studies indicate that multiple BOSS-validated quantitative in vivo biomarkers of oxidative damage are reproducibly increased in CSF in multiple groups of patients with AD, and in two groups of individuals with MCI, compared with age-matched control participants. It should be noted that like most CSF biomarkers for AD, there is considerable overlap in IsoP concentrations between patients and control participants, which impacts the clinical usefulness of CSF IsoPs (vida infra) as well as indicates the need for an ensemble of biomarkers directed at different facets of AD pathogenesis.

In contrast to results from CSF, data from plasma and urine with BOSS-validated oxidative damage biomarkers are not reproducibly changed in AD patients compared with age-matched control participants, either across assays or among different groups of patients with AD. Indeed, MDA, 8-iso-$PGF_{2\alpha}$ as determined by GC/MS in two different laboratories and multiple patient groups, and IsoPs as determined by LC/MS, all failed to demonstrate a difference between patients with AD and control participants in blood or urine (Bohnstedt et al., 2003; Kim, Jung, Paeng, Kim, & Chung, 2004; McGrath et al., 2001; T. J. Montine et al., 2000; T. J. Montine, Quinn, et al., 2002). Finally, we have shown in a rodent model of selective oxidative damage to brain without disruption of the blood–brain barrier that increased cerebral 8-iso-$PGF_{2\alpha}$ is not associated with significant changes in plasma or urine levels (T. J. Montine, Quinn, et al., 2002).

We envision biomarkers of oxidative damage as being useful in enhancing the diagnostic accuracy for AD and for objectively assessing response to therapeutics. To address the first, we tested the hypothesis that CSF 8-iso-$PGF_{2\alpha}$, along with CSF $A\beta_{42}$ and total tau levels, improves laboratory diagnostic accuracy for AD in patients with probable AD, patients with other dementias, and age-matched control participants (T. J. Montine et al., 2001). Laboratory classification of these 37 individuals was performed by combining a commercially available test for CSF $A\beta_{42}$ and tau levels with CSF 8-iso-$PGF_{2\alpha}$ at the average control value from over 50 age-matched control participants aggregated from several studies. Others recently have similarly reported that combining tests increased sensitivity and specificity in test results (de Leon et al., 2006). These studies suggest that combining laboratory tests and perhaps imaging studies may enhance the accuracy of the diagnosis of AD and MCI; however, this conclusion is based on small sample sizes and needs to be replicated.

Resolution of this important issue awaits sharing by laboratories of isotopically labeled standards that are not commercially available, and blinded determinations of the same patient samples similar to the BOSS. In summary, although a peripheral biomarker of oxidative damage in AD is highly desirable, current data point to CSF 8-iso-PGF$_{2\alpha}$ and 8,12-iso-iPF$_{2\alpha}$-VI as the most reliable and reproducible quantitative in vivo biomarkers of oxidative damage in AD. Using the same biomarkers for analyzing oxidative damage in MCI has currently been demonstrated by only one research group and needs to be replicated. Results with peripheral oxidative damage biomarkers in AD have not been reproducible across centers or assays.

Antioxidant Monitoring as a Possible Intervention

A second clinical application of CSF IsoPs is to monitor the antioxidant efficacy of new interventions for AD. Several studies have attempted to assess the efficacy of antioxidants to suppress the risk of subsequently developing AD, presumably by treating latent or prodromal stages, or to treat established dementia from AD. Indeed, in two cohort studies, consumption of diets high in antioxidants, especially α-tocopherol and possibly ascorbate alone, was associated with decreased risk of developing AD-type dementia (Engelhart et al., 2002; M. C. Morris et al., 2002), and another cohort study suggested that supplemental combined ascorbate plus α-tocopherol is associated with lower risk of AD-type dementia (M. C. Morris et al., 1998). Moreover, higher serum levels of antioxidants are associated with better performance on memory tests (Perkins et al., 1999) and cognitive functioning tests in some (Schmidt et al., 1998) but not all (Kalmijn, Feskens, Launer, & Kromhout, 1997) studies. Overall, these data support the proposal that α-tocopherol supplementation, likely in combination with ascorbate, suppresses early processes in preclinical AD and thereby reduces the risk of subsequently developing dementia from AD.

In contrast, clinical trials of α-tocopherol supplementation in patients with MCI or AD-type dementia showed no or limited therapeutic effect (Petersen et al., 2005; Sano et al., 1997). One possible reason for the disparate outcomes suggested in these two studies versus trials is that combined α-tocopherol and ascorbate supplementation may be more potent than single-agent supplementation, so that the trials may not have used the most effective combination of antioxidants.

Our results comparing users of α-tocopherol plus ascorbate with users of α-tocopherol only, although from a small number of patients, are consonant with compelling biochemical data indicating that α-tocopherol acting in concert with ascorbate is a much more potent antioxidant than α-tocopherol alone (T. J. Montine et al., 2003). Indeed, an epidemiologic study concluded that reduced risk of subsequent AD was associated with α-tocopherol plus ascorbate supplementation, but not either agent alone (Zandi et al., 2004). In combination, these results suggest revisiting the conclusions of previous clinical trials.

Other epidemiologic studies have supported the enhanced efficacy of α-tocopherol plus ascorbate at reducing the risk of AD as well (Zandi et al., 2004), and we have demonstrated a likely biochemical basis for this proposal in experimental models of oxidative damage to brain (T. J. Montine et al., 2003). Alternatively, some other more complex mix of dietary antioxidants, perhaps in combination with environmental factors, may be necessary for this apparent protective effect during latency. Finally, it is also quite possible that some therapeutics, such as α-tocopherol supplementation, are effective during AD latency but not prodrome or dementia stages. We think that this area of research can be approached much more rationally if biomarkers of oxidative damage are incorporated into future trials.

Discovering early biomarkers of the various neurodegenerative diseases is an important endeavor. Finding these markers means being able to diagnose the disease earlier, which will allow for better understanding of the disease progression. All of these advances translate into the discovery of better intervention targets for treatment and reversal of the disease. As we learn more about the early course of the different neurodegenerative diseases, we expect to use our expanding knowledge to avert irreversible damage to the brain that accumulates through the progression of the disease and thereby minimize the disease impact on quality of life.

KEY POINTS

- Brain inflammation underlies a large number of neurodegenerative diseases as well as normal aging.
- Lipid peroxidation causes structural damage to membranes and generates products that can cause neurodegeneration.
- COX-1 and COX-2 are important mediators of the inflammatory response.
- The prostaglandin receptor EP2 functions in the development of oxidative damage and microglial activity related to the deposition of Aβ in the brain.
- NSAIDs may be effective in preventing, but not reversing, AD.
- Products of AA peroxidation are chemically and metabolically stable, making them promising biomarkers for assessing neurodegeneration.
- Biomarkers of oxidative damage in the cerebral spinal fluid are useful in latent and prodromal AD and can enhance the diagnostic accuracy of AD.

REFERENCES

Adak, S., Illouz, K., Gorman, W., Tandon, R., Zimmerman, E. A., Guariglia, R., et al. (2004). Predicting the rate of cognitive decline in aging and early Alzheimer disease. *Neurology, 63*, 108–114.

Aisen, P. S., Schafer, K. A., Grundman, M., Pfeiffer, E., Sano, M., Davis, K. L., et al. (2003). Effects of rofecoxib or naproxen vs placebo on Alzheimer disease progression: A randomized controlled trial. *JAMA, 289*, 2819–2826.

Akaogi, J., Yamada, H., Kuroda, Y., Nacionales, D. C., Reeves, W. H., & Satoh, M. (2004). Prostaglandin E2 receptors EP2 and EP4 are up-regulated in peritoneal macrophages and joints of pristane-treated mice and modulate TNF-alpha and IL-6 production. *Journal of Leukocyte Biology, 76*, 227–236.

Akiyama, H., Barger, S., Barnum, S., Bradt, B., Bauer, J., Cole, G. M., et al. (2000). Inflammation and Alzheimer's disease. *Neurobiology of Aging, 21*, 383–421.

Ando, Y., Brannstrom, T., Uchida, K., Nyhlin, N., Nasman, B., Suhr, O., et al. (1998). Histochemical detection of 4-hydroxynonenal protein in Alzheimer amyloid. *Journal of the Neurological Sciences, 156*, 172–176.

Andreasson, K. I., Savonenko, A., Vidensky, S., Goellner, J. J., Zhang, Y., Shaffer, A., et al. (2001). Age-dependent cognitive deficits and neuronal apoptosis in cyclooxygenase-2 transgenic mice. *The Journal of Neuroscience, 21*, 8198–8209.

Aronoff, D. M., Canetti, C., & Peters-Golden, M. (2004). Prostaglandin E2 inhibits alveolar macrophage phagocytosis through an E-prostanoid 2 receptor-mediated increase in intracellular cyclic AMP. *Journal of Immunology, 173*, 559–565.

Arriagada, P. V., Marzloff, K., & Hyma, B. T. (1992). Distribution of Alzheimer-type pathologic changes in nondemented elderly individuals matches the pattern in Alzheimer's disease. *Neurology, 42*, 1681–1688.

Bachi, A., Brambilla, R., Fanelli, R., Bianchi, R., Zuccato, E., & Chiabrando, C. (1997). Reduction of urinary 8-epi-prostaglandin F$_2$ during cyclo-oxygenase inhibition in rats but not in man. *British Journal of Pharmacology, 121*, 1770–1774.

Baratelli, F. E., Heuze-Vourc'h, N., Krysan, K., Dohadwala, M., Riedl, K., Sharma, S., et al. (2004). Prostaglandin E2-dependent enhancement of tissue inhibitors of metalloproteinases-1 production limits dendritic cell migration through extracellular matrix. *Journal of Immunology, 173*, 5458–5466.

Berg, L., McKeel, D. W., Miller, J. P., Baty, J., & Morris, J. C. (1993). Neuropathological indexes of Alzheimer's disease in demented and nondemented persons aged 80 years and older. *Archives of Neurology, 50*, 349–358.

Bjornson, A. B., Knippenberg, R. W., & Bjornson, H. S. (1988). Nonsteroidal anti-inflammatory drugs correct the bactericidal defect of polymorphonuclear leukocytes in a guinea pig model of thermal injury. *Journal of Infectious Diseases, 157*, 959–967.

Bohnstedt, K. C., Karlberg, B., Wahlund, L., Jonhagen, M. E., Basun, H., & Schmidt, S. (2003). Determination of isoprostanes in urine samples from Alzheimer patients using porous graphitic carbon liquid chromatography-tandem mass spectrometry. *Journal of Chromatography B: Analytical Technologies in the Biomedical and Life Sciences, 796,* 11–19.

Borda, E. S., Tenenbaum, A., Sales, M. E., Rumi, L., & Sterin-Borda, L. (1998). Role of arachidonic acid metabolites in the action of a beta adrenergic agonist on human monocyte phagocytosis. *Prostaglandins, Leukotrienes & Essential Fatty Acids, 58,* 85–90.

Breder, C. D., Dewitt, D., & Kraig, R. P. (1995). Characterization of inducible cyclooxygenase in rat brain. *Journal of Comparative Neurology, 355,* 296–315.

Breyer, R. M., Bagdassarian, C. K., Myers, S. A., & Breyer, M. D. (2001). Prostanoid receptors: Subtypes and signaling. *Annual Review of Pharmacology and Toxicology, 41,* 661–690.

Butterfield, D., Drake, J., Pocernich, C., & Castegna, A. (2001). Evidence of oxidative damage in Alzheimer's disease brain: Central role for amyloid beta-peptide. *Trends in Molecular Medicine, 7,* 548–554.

Canning, B. J., Hmieleski, R. R., Spannhake, E. W., & Jakab, G. J. (1991). Ozone reduces murine alveolar and peritoneal macrophage phagocytosis: The role of prostanoids. *American Journal of Physiology—Lung Cellular and Molecular Physiology, 261*(4 Pt 1), L277–L282.

Castellani, R. J., Perry, G., Siedlak, S. L., Nunomura, A., Shimohama, S., Zhang, J., et al. (2002). Hydroxynonenal adducts indicate a role for lipid peroxidation in neocortical and brainstem Lewy bodies in humans. *Neuroscience Letters, 319,* 25–28.

Catella, F., Reilly, M. P., Delanty, N., Lawson, J. A., Moran, N., Meagher, E., et al. (1995). Physiological formation of 8-epi-PGF$_{2\alpha}$ in vivo is not affected by cyclooxygenase inhibition. *Advances in Prostaglandin, Thromboxane, and Leukotriene Research, 23,* 233–236.

Chen, C., & Bazan, N. G. (2005). Endogenous PGE2 regulates membrane excitability and synaptic transmission in hippocampal CA1 pyramidal neurons. *Journal of Neurophysiology, 93,* 929–941.

Chen, C., Magee, J. C., & Bazan, N. G. (2002). Cyclooxygenase-2 regulates prostaglandin E2 signaling in hippocampal long-term synaptic plasticity. *Journal of Neurophysiology, 87,* 2851–2857.

Crystal, H. A., Dickson, D. W., Sliwinski, M. J., Lipton, R. B., Grober, E., Marks-Nelson, H., et al. (1993). Pathological markers associated with normal aging and dementia in the elderly. *Annals of Neurology, 34,* 566–573.

Davis, D. G., Schmitt, F. A., Wekstein, D. R., & Markesbery, W. (1999). Alzheimer neuropathological alterations in aged cognitively normal subjects. *Journal of Neuropathology and Experimental Neurology, 58,* 376–388.

de Leon, M. J., DeSanti, S., Zinkowski, R., Mehta, P. D., Pratico, D., Segal, S., et al. (2006). Longitudinal CSF and MRI biomarkers improve the diagnosis of mild cognitive impairment. *Neurobiology of Aging, 27,* 394–401.

Duda, J. E., Giasson, B. I., Mabon, M. E., Lee, V. M., & Trojanowski, J. Q. (2002). Novel antibodies to synuclein show abundant striatal pathology in Lewy body diseases. *Annals of Neurology, 52,* 205–210.

Engelhart, M. J., Geerlings, M. I., Ruitenberg, A., van Swieten, J. C., Hofman, A., Witteman, J. C., et al. (2002). Dietary intake of antioxidants and risk of Alzheimer disease. *JAMA, 287*, 3223–3229.

Eriksen, J. L., Sagi, S. A., Smith, T. E., Weggen, S., Das, P., McLendon, D. C., et al. (2003). NSAIDs and enantiomers of flurbiprofen target gamma-secretase and lower Abeta 42 in vivo. *Journal of Clinical Investigation, 112*, 440–449.

Esterbauer, H., & Ramos, P. (1996). Chemistry and pathophysiology of oxidation of LDL. *Reviews of Physiology, Biochemistry, and Pharmacology, 127*, 31–64.

Farooqui, A. A., Ong, W. Y., & Horrocks, L. A. (2006). Inhibitors of brain phospholipase A2 activity: Their neuropharmacological effects and therapeutic importance for the treatment of neurologic disorders. *Pharmacological Reviews, 58*, 591–620.

Fassbender, K., Walter, S., Kuhl, S., Landmann, R., Ishii, K., Bertsch, T., et al. (2004). The LPS receptor (CD14) links innate immunity with Alzheimer's disease. *The FASEB Journal, 18*, 203–205.

Feillet-Coudray, C., Tourtauchaux, R., Niculescu, M., Rock, E., Tauveron, I., Alexandre-Gouabau, M. C., et al. (1999). Plasma levels of 8-epiPGF2alpha, an in vivo marker of oxidative stress, are not affected by aging or Alzheimer's disease. *Free Radical Biology & Medicine, 27*, 463–469.

Fennekohl, A., Sugimoto, Y., Segi, E., Maruyama, T., Ichikawa, A., & Puschel, G. P. (2002). Contribution of the two Gs-coupled PGE2-receptors EP2-receptor and EP4-receptor to the inhibition by PGE2 of the LPS-induced TNFalpha-formation in Kupffer cells from EP2-or EP4-receptor-deficient mice: Pivotal role for the EP4-receptor in wild type Kupffer cells. *Journal of Hepatology, 36*, 328–334.

Fessel, J. P., Hulette, C., Powell, S., Roberts, L. J., & Zhang, J. (2003). Isofurans, but not F-2-isoprostanes, are increased in the substantia nigra of patients with Parkinson's disease and with dementia with Lewy body disease. *Journal of Neurochemistry, 85*, 645–650.

Fleisher, A., Grundman, M., Jack, C. R., Jr., Petersen, R. C., Taylor, C., Kim, H. T., et al. (2005). Sex, Apolipoprotein E Epsilon 4 status, and hippocampal volume in mild cognitive impairment. *Archives of Neurology, 62*, 953–957.

Giasson, B. I., Duda, J. E., Murray, I. V., Chen, Q., Souza, J. M., Hurtig, H. I., et al. (2000, November 3). Oxidative damage linked to neurodegeneration by selective alpha-synuclein nitration in synucleinopathy lesions. *Science, 290*, 985–989.

Gilmour, M. I., Park, P., Doerfler, D., & Selgrade, M. K. (1993). Factors that influence the suppression of pulmonary antibacterial defenses in mice exposed to ozone. *Experimental Lung Research, 19*, 299–314.

Green, M. S., Kaye, J. A., & Ball, M. J. (2000). The Oregon Brain Aging Study: Neuropathology accompanying health aging in the oldest old. *Neurology, 54*, 105–113.

Gurer, U. S., Palanduz, A., Gurbuz, B., Yildirmak, Y., Cevikbas, A., & Kayaalp, N. (2002). Effect of antipyretics on polymorphonuclear leukocyte functions in children. *International Immunopharmacology, 2*, 1599–1602.

Gutteridge, J. M. C., Westermarck, T., & Halliwell, B. (1986). Oxygen radical damage in biological systems. In J. E. Johnson, R. Walford, D. Harman, & J. Miquel

(Eds.), *Free radicals, aging, and degenerative diseases* (pp. 99–139). New York: Alan R. Liss.

Hardy, J., & Selkoe, D. J. (2002, July 19). The amyloid hypothesis of Alzheimer's disease: Progress and problems on the road to therapeutics. *Science, 297,* 353–356.

Harizi, H., Grosset, C., & Gualde, N. (2003). Prostaglandin E2 modulates dendritic cell function via EP2 and EP4 receptor subtypes. *Journal of Leukocyte Biology, 73,* 756–763.

Haroutunian, V., Purohit, D. P., Perl, D. P., Marin, D., Khan, K., Lantz, M., et al. (1999). Neurofibrillary tangles in nondemented elderly subjects and mild Alzheimer disease. *Archives of Neurology, 56,* 713–718.

Hauss-Wegrzyniak, B., Lynch, M. A., Vraniak, P. D., & Wenk, G. L. (2002). Chronic brain inflammation results in cell loss in the entorhinal cortex and impaired LTP in perforant path-granule cell synapses. *Experimental Neurology, 176,* 336–341.

Hubbard, N. E., Lee, S., Lim, D., & Erickson, K. L. (2001). Differential mRNA expression of prostaglandin receptor subtypes in macrophage activation. *Prostaglandins, Leukotrienes & Essential Fatty Acids, 65,* 287–294.

Hulette, C. M., Welsh-Bohmer, K. A., Murray, M. G., Saunders, A. M., Mash, D. C., & McIntyre, L. M. (1998). Neuropathological and neuropsychological changes in "normal" aging: Evidence for preclinical Alzheimer disease in cognitively normal individuals. *Journal of Neuropathology and Experimental Neurology, 57,* 1168–1174.

Hutchison, D. L., & Myers, R. L. (1987). Prostaglandin-mediated suppression of macrophage phagocytosis of Listeria monocytogenes. *Cellular Immunology, 110,* 68–76.

in't Veld, B. A., Ruitenberg, A., Hofman, A., Stricker, B. H., & Breteler, M. M. (2001). Antihypertensive drugs and incidence of dementia: The Rotterdam Study. *Neurobiology of Aging, 22,* 407–412.

Jantzen, P. T., Connor, K. E., DiCarlo, G., Wenk, G., Wallace, J., Rojiani, A., et al. (2002). Microglial activation and β-amyloid deposit reduction caused by a nitric oxide-releasing nonsteroidal anti-inflammatory drug in amyloid precursor protein plus presenilin-1 transgenic mice. *Journal of Neuroscience, 22,* 2246–2254.

Kadiiska, M. B., Gladen, B. C., Baird, D. D., Dikalova, A. E., Sohal, R. S., Hatch, G. E., et al. (2000). Biomarkers of Oxidative Stress Study: Are plasma antioxidants markers of CCl_4 poisoning? *Free Radical Biology & Medicine, 2,* 838–845.

Kadiiska, M. B., Gladen, B. C., Baird, D. D., Germolec, D., Graham, L. B., Parker, C. E., et al. (2005). Biomarkers of Oxidative Stress Study: II. Are oxidation products of lipids, proteins, and DNA markers of CCl_4 poisoning? *Free Radical Biology & Medicine, 38,* 698–710.

Kadiiska, M. B., Gladen, B. C., Baird, D. D., Graham, L. B., Parker, C. E., Ames, B. N., et al. (2005). Biomarkers of Oxidative Stress Study: III. Effects of the nonsteroidal anti-inflammatory agents indomethacin and meclofenamic acid on measurements of oxidative products of lipids in CCl_4 poisoning. *Free Radical Biology & Medicine, 38,* 711–718.

Kalmijn, S., Feskens, E. J., Launer, L. J., & Kromhout, D. (1997). Polyunsaturated fatty acids, antioxidants, and cognitive function in very old men. *American Journal of Epidemiology, 145,* 33–41.

Katzman, R. (1976). The prevalence and malignancy of Alzheimer disease: A major killer [Editorial]. *Archives of Neurology, 33,* 217–218.

Kaufmann, W. E., Worley, P. F., Pegg, J., Bremer, M., & Isakson, P. (1996). COX-2, a synaptically induced enzyme, is expressed by excitatory neurons at postsynaptic sites in rat cerebral cortex. *Proceedings of the National Academy of Sciences USA, 93,* 2317–2321.

Kim, K. M., Jung, B. H., Paeng, K. J., Kim, I., & Chung, B. C. (2004). Increased urinary F_2-isoprostanes levels in the patients with Alzheimer's disease. *Brain Research Bulletin, 64,* 47–51.

Klein, T., Reutter, F., Schweer, H., Seyberth, H. W., & Nusing, R. M. (1997). Generation of the isoprostane 8-epi-prostaglandin $F_{2\alpha}$ in vitro and in vivo via the cyclooxygenases. *The Journal of Pharmacology and Experimental Therapeutics, 282,* 1658–1665.

Laegreid, W. W., Liggitt, H. D., Silflow, R. M., Evermann, J. R., Taylor, S. M., & Leid, R. W. (1989). Reversal of virus-induced alveolar macrophage bactericidal dysfunction by cyclooxygenase inhibition in vitro. *Journal of Leukocyte Biology, 45,* 293–300.

Lanz, T. A., Fici, G. J., & Merchant, K. M. (2005). Lack of specific amyloid-{beta}(1-42) suppression by nonsteroidal anti-inflammatory drugs in young, plaque-free Tg2576 mice and in guinea pig neuronal cultures. *The Journal of Pharmacology and Experimental Therapeutics, 312,* 399–406.

Largo, R., Diez-Ortego, I., Sanchez-Pernaute, O., Lopez-Armada, M. J., Alvarez-Soria, M. A., Egido, J., et al. (2004). EP2/EP4 signalling inhibits monocyte chemoattractant protein-1 production induced by interleukin 1beta in synovial fibroblasts. *Annals of the Rheumatic Diseases, 63,* 1197–1204.

Lawson, J. A., Rokach, J., & FitzGerald, G. A. (1999). Isoprostanes: Formation, analysis and use as indices of lipid peroxidation in vivo. *Journal of Biological Chemistry, 274,* 24441–24444.

Li, F., Calingasan, N. Y., Yu, F., Mauck, W. M., Toidze, M., Almeida, C. G., et al. (2004). Increased plaque burden in brains of APP mutant MnSOD heterozygous knockout mice. *Journal of Neurochemistry, 89,* 1308–1312.

Lim, G. P., Yang, F., Chu, T., Chen, P., Beech, W., Teter, B., et al. (2000). Ibuprofen suppresses plaque pathology and inflammation in a mouse model for Alzheimer's disease. *Journal of Neuroscience, 20,* 5709–5714.

Lovell, M., A. Ehmann, W., Butler, S., & Markesbery, W. (1995). Elevated thiobarbituric acid-reactive substances and antioxidant enzyme activity in the brain in Alzheimer's disease. *Neurology, 45,* 1594–1601.

Lovell, M. A., Ehmann, W., Mattson, M., & Markesbery, W. (1997). Elevated 4-hydroxynonenal in ventricular fluid in Alzheimer's disease. *Neurobiology of Aging, 18,* 457–471.

Lovell, M. A., Xie, C., & Markesbery, W. R. (2001). Acrolein is increased in Alzheimer's disease brain and is toxic to primary hippocampal cultures. *Neurobiology of Aging, 22,* 187–194.

Mackenzie, I. R., & Munoz, D. G. (1998). Nonsteroidal anti-inflammatory drug use and Alzheimer-type pathology in aging. *Neurology, 50,* 986–990.

Markesbery, W. R., & Lovell, M. A. (1998). Four-hydroxynonenal, a product of lipid peroxidation, is increased in the brain in Alzheimer's disease. *Neurobiology of Aging, 19,* 33–36.

Martin, B. K., Meinert, C. L., & Breitner, J. C. (2002). Double placebo design in a prevention trial for Alzheimer's disease. *Controlled Clinical Trials, 23,* 93–99.

Matsubara, E., Bryant-Thomas, T., Pacheco Quinto, J., Henry, T. L., Poeggeler, B., Herbert, D., et al. (2003). Melatonin increases survival and inhibits oxidative and amyloid pathology in a transgenic model of Alzheimer's disease. *Journal of Neurochemistry, 85,* 1101–1108.

McAdam, B. F., Mardini, I. A., Habib, A., Burke, A., Lawson, J. A., Kapoor, S., et al. (2000). Effect of regulated expression of human cyclooxygenase isoforms on eicosanoid and isoeicosanoid production in inflammation. *Journal of Clinical Investigation, 105,* 1473–1482.

McGeer, P. L., Schulzer, M., & McGeer, E. G. (1996). Arthritis and anti-inflammatory agents as possible protective factors for Alzheimer's disease: A review of 17 epidemiologic studies. *Neurology, 47,* 425–432.

McGrath, L. T., McGleenon, B. M., Brennan, S., McColl, D., McIlroy, S., & Passmore, A. P. (2001). Increased oxidative stress in Alzheimer's disease as assessed with 4-hydroxynonenal but not malondialdehyde. *QJM, 94,* 485–490.

Milatovic, D., Zaja-Milatovic, S., Montine, K. S., Nivison, M., & Montine, T. J. (2005). CD14-dependent innate immunity-mediated neuronal damage in vivo is suppressed by NSAIDS and ablation of a prostaglandin E$_2$ receptor, EP2. *Current Medicinal Chemistry, 5,* 151–156.

Milatovic, D., Zaja-Milatovic, S., Montine, K. S., Shie, F. S., & Montine, T. J. (2004). Neuronal oxidative damage and dendritic degeneration following activation of CD14-dependent innate immune response in vivo. *Journal of Neuroinflammation, 1*(1), 20.

Minghetti, L., Nicolini, A., Polazzi, E., Creminon, C., Maclouf, J., & Levi, G. (1997). Inducible nitric oxide synthase expression in activated rat microglial cultures is downregulated by exogenous prostaglandin E2 and by cyclooxygenase inhibitors. *Glia, 19,* 152–160.

Montine, K. S., Kim, P. J., Olson, S. J., Markesbery, W. R., & Montine, T. J. (1997). 4-hydroxy-2-nonenal pyrrole adducts in human neurodegenerative disease. *Journal of Neuropathology and Experimental Neurology, 56,* 866–871.

Montine, K. S., Olson, S. J., Amarnath, V., Whetsell, W. O., Graham, D. G., & Montine, T. J. (1997). Immunohistochemical detection of 4-hydroxy-2-nonenal adducts in Alzheimer's disease is associated with inheritance of APOE4. *American Journal of Pathology, 150,* 437–443.

Montine, K. S., Quinn, J., & Montine, T. (2003). Membrane lipid peroxidation. In M. Mattson (Ed.), *Membrane lipid signaling in aging and age-related disease* (pp. 11–26). Amsterdam: Elsevier.

Montine, K. S., Reich, E., Neely, M. D., Sidell, K. R., Olson, S. J., Markesbery, W. R., et al. (1998). Distribution of reducible 4-hydroxynonenal adduct immunoreactivity in Alzheimer disease is associated with APOE genotype. *Journal of Neuropathology and Experimental Neurology, 57,* 415–425.

Montine, T. J., Beal, M. F., Cudkowicz, M. E., O'Donnell, H., Margolin, R. A., McFarland, L., et al. (1999). Increased CSF F-2-isoprostane concentration in probable AD. *Neurology, 52,* 562–565.

Montine, T. J., Beal, M. F., Robertson, D., Cudkowicz, M. E., Biaggioni, I., O'Donnell, H., et al. (1999). Cerebrospinal fluid F2-isoprostanes are elevated in Huntington's disease. *Neurology, 52,* 1104–1105.

Montine, T. J., Kaye, J. A., Montine, K. S., McFarland, L., Morrow, J. D., & Quinn, J. F. (2001). Cerebrospinal fluid A beta(42), tau, and F-2-isoprostane concentrations in patients with Alzheimer disease, other dementias, and in age-matched controls. *Archives of Pathology & Laboratory Medicine, 125,* 510–512.

Montine, T. J., Markesbery, W. R., Morrow, J. D., & Roberts, L. J. (1998). Cerebrospinal fluid F-2-isoprostane levels are increased in Alzheimer's disease. *Annals of Neurology, 44,* 410–413.

Montine, T. J., Markesbery, W. R., Zackert, W., Sanchez, S. C., Roberts, L. J., & Morrow, J. D. (1999). The magnitude of brain lipid peroxidation correlates with the extent of degeneration but not with density of neuritic plaques or neurofibrillary tangles or with APOE genotype in Alzheimer's disease patients. *American Journal of Pathology, 155,* 863–868.

Montine, T. J., Milatovic, D., Gupta, R. C., Valyi-Nagy, T., Morrow, J. D., & Breyer, R. M. (2002). Neuronal oxidative damage from activated innate immunity is EP2 receptor-dependent. *Journal of Neurochemistry, 83,* 463–470.

Montine, T. J., Montine, K. S., Olson, S. J., Graham, D. G., Roberts, L. J., Morrow, J. D., et al. (1999). Increased cerebral cortical lipid peroxidation and abnormal phospholipids in aged homozygous apoE-deficient C57BL/6J mice. *Experimental Neurology, 158,* 234–241.

Montine, T. J., Montine, K. S., Reich, E. E., Terry, E. S., Porter, N. A., & Morrow, J. D. (2003). Antioxidants significantly affect the formation of different classes of isoprostanes and neuroprostanes in rat cerebral synaptosomes. *Biochemical Pharmacology, 65,* 611–617.

Montine, T. J., Neely, M. D., Quinn, J. F., Beal, M. F., Markesbery, W. R., Roberts, L. J., et al. (2002). Lipid peroxidation in aging brain and Alzheimer's disease. *Free Radical Biology & Medicine, 33,* 620–626.

Montine, T. J., Quinn, J. F., Milatovic, D., Silbert, L. C., Dang, T., Sanchez, S., et al. (2002). Peripheral F2-isoprostanes and F4-neuroprostanes are not increased in Alzheimer's disease. *Annals of Neurology, 52,* 175–179.

Montine, T. J., Shinobu, L., Montine, K. S., Roberts, L. J., II, Kowall, N. W., Beal, M. F., et al. (2000). No difference in plasma or urinary F2-isoprostanes among patients with Huntington's disease or Alzheimer's disease and controls. *Annals of Neurology, 48,* 950.

Montine, T. J., Sidell, K. R., Crews, B. C., Markesbery, W. R., Marnett, L. J., Roberts, L. J., et al. (1999). Elevated CSF prostaglandin E-2 levels in patients with probable AD. *Neurology, 53,* 1495–1498.

Moore, K., & Roberts, L. J. (1998). Measurement of lipid peroxidation. *Free Radical Research, 28,* 659–671.

Morris, J. C., & Price, A. L. (2001). Pathologic correlates of nondemented aging, mild cognitive impairment, and early-stage Alzheimer's disease. *Journal of Molecular Neuroscience, 17,* 101–118.

Morris, M. C., Beckett, L. A., Scherr, P. A., Hebert, L. E., Bennett, D. A., Field, D. A., et al. (1998). Vitamin E and vitamin C supplement use and the risk of incident Alzheimer disease. *Alzheimer Disease and Associated Disorders, 12,* 121–126.

Morris, M. C., Evans, D. A., Bienias, J. L., Tangney, C. C., Bennett, D. A., Aggarwal, N., et al. (2002). Dietary intake of antioxidant nutrients and the risk of incident Alzheimer disease in a biracial community study. *JAMA, 287,* 3230–3237.

Morrow, J. D. (2000). The isoprostanes: Their quantification as an index of oxidant stress status in vivo. *Drug Metabolism Reviews, 32,* 377–385.

Morrow, J. D., Awad, J. A., Katoh, T., Takahashi, K., Roberts, L. J., & Burk, R. F. (1992). Formation of novel non-cyclooxygenase derived prostanoids (F_2-isoprostanes) in carbon tetrachloride hepatotoxicity. *Journal of Clinical Investigation, 90,* 2502–2507.

Morrow, J. D., Hill, K. E., Burk, R. F., Nammour, T. M., Badr, K. F., & Roberts, L. J., II. (1990). A series of prostaglandin F2-like compounds are produced in vivo in humans by a non-cyclooxygenase, free radical-catalyzed mechanism. *Proceedings of the National Academy of Sciences USA, 87,* 9383–9387.

Morrow, J. D., & Roberts, L. J., II. (1994). Mass spectrometry of prostanoids: F2-isoprostanes produced by non-cyclooxygenase free radical-catalyzed mechanism. *Methods in Enzymology, 233,* 163–174.

Morrow, J. D., Roberts, L. J., Daniel, V. C., Awad, J. A., Mirochnitchenko, O., Swift, L. L., et al. (1998). Comparison of formation of D2/E2-isoprostanes and F2-isoprostanes in vitro and in vivo—Effects of oxygen tension and glutathione. *Archives of Biochemistry and Biophysics, 353,* 160–171.

Mosconi, L., Tsui, W. H., De Santi, S., Li, J., Rusinek, H., Convit, A., et al. (2005). Reduced hippocampal metabolism in MCI and AD: Automated FDG-PET image analysis. *Neurology, 64,* 1860–1867.

Nicolle, M. M., Gonzalez, J., Sugaya, K., Baskerville, K. A., Bryan, D., Lund, K., et al. (2001). Signatures of hippocampal oxidative stress in aged spatial learning-impaired rodents. *Neuroscience, 107,* 415–431.

Niwa, K., Araki, E., Morham, S. G., Ross, M. E., & Iadecola, C. (2000). Cyclooxygenase-2 contributes to functional hyperemia in whisker-barrel cortex. *Journal of Neuroscience, 20,* 763–770.

Noguchi, K., Iwasaki, K., Shitashige, M., Umeda, M., Izumi, Y., Murota, S., et al. (2001). Downregulation of lipopolysaccharide-induced intercellular adhesion molecule-1 expression via EP2/EP4 receptors by prostaglandin E2 in human fibroblasts. *Inflammation, 25,* 75–81.

Nourooz-Zadeh, J., Liu, E. H., Yhlen, B., Anggard, E. E., & Halliwell, B. (1999). F4-isoprostanes as specific marker of docosahexaenoic acid peroxidation in Alzheimer's disease. *Journal of Neurochemistry, 72,* 734–740.

Orth, M., & Schapira, A. (2002). Mitochondrial involvement in Parkinson's disease. *Neurochemistry International, 40,* 533–541.

Perkins, A. J., Hendrie, H. C., Callahan, C. M., Gao, S., Unverzagt, F. W., Xu, Y., et al. (1999). Association of antioxidants with memory in a multiethnic elderly sample using the Third National Health and Nutrition Examination Survey. *American Journal of Epidemiology, 150,* 37–44.

Petersen, R. C. (2004). Mild cognitive impairment as a diagnostic entity. *Journal of Internal Medicine, 256,* 183–194.

Petersen, R. C., Thomas, R. G., Grundman, M., Bennett, D., Doody, R., Ferris, S., et al. (2005). Vitamin E and donepezil for the treatment of mild cognitive impairment. *The New England Journal of Medicine, 352,* 2379–2388.

Picklo, M. J., Olson, S. J., Markesbery, W. R., & Montine, T. J. (2001). Expression and activities of aldo-keto oxidoreductases in Alzheimer disease. *Journal of Neuropathology and Experimental Neurology, 60,* 686–695.

Porter, N. A., Caldwell, S. E., & Mills, K. A. (1995). Mechanisms of free radical oxidation of unsaturated lipids. *Lipids, 30,* 277–290.

Pratico, D., Clack, C. M., Lee, V. M. Y., Trojanowski, J. Q., Rokach, J., & FitzGerald, G. (2000). Increased 8,12-iso-iPF$_{2\alpha}$-IV in Alzheimer's disease: Correlation of a noninvasive index of lipid peroxidation with disease severity. *Annals of Neurology, 48,* 809–812.

Pratico, D., Clark, C. M., Liun, F., Lee, V. Y.-M., & Trojanowski, J. Q. (2002). Increase of brain oxidative stress in mild cognitive impairment: A possible predictor of Alzheimer disease. *Archives of Neurology, 59,* 972–976.

Pratico, D., Lawson, J. A., & FitzGerald, G. A. (1995). Cyclooxygenase-dependent formation of the isoprostane, 8-epi prostaglandin F$_{2\alpha}$. *Journal of Biological Chemistry, 270,* 9800–9808.

Pratico, D., Lee, V. M. Y., Trojanowski, J. Q., Rokach, J., & Fitzgerald, G. A. (1998). Increased F-2-isoprostanes in Alzheimer's disease: Evidence for enhanced lipid peroxidation in vivo. *The FASEB Journal, 12,* 1777–1783.

Pratico, D., Smyth, E. M., Violi, F., & FitzGerald, G. A. (1996). Local amplification of platelet function by 8-Epi prostaglandin F$_{2\alpha}$ is not mediated by thromboxane receptor isoforms. *Journal of Biological Chemistry, 271,* 14916–14924.

Pratico, D., Uryu, K., Leight, S., Trojanowski, J., & Lee, V. (2001). Increased lipid peroxidation preceded amyloid plaque formation in an animal model of Alzheimer amyloidosis. *Journal of Neuroscience, 21,* 4183–4187.

Price, J. L., Davis, P. B., Morris, J. C., & White, D. L. (1991). The distribution of tangles, plaques and related immunohistochemical markers in healthy aging and Alzheimer's disease. *Neurobiology of Aging, 12,* 295–312.

Price, J. L., & Morris, J. C. (1999). Tangles and plaques in nondemented aging and "preclinical" Alzheimer's disease. *Annals of Neurology, 45,* 358–368.

Rall, J. M., Mach, S. A., & Dash, P. K. (2003). Intrahippocampal infusion of a cyclooxygenase-2 inhibitor attenuates memory acquisition in rats. *Brain Research, 968,* 273–276.

Reich, E. E., Markesbery, W. R., Roberts, L. J., Swift, L. L., Morrow, J. D., & Montine, T. J. (2001a). Brain regional quantification of F-ring and D-/E-ring isoprostanes and neuroprostanes in Alzheimer's disease. *American Journal of Pathology, 158,* 293–297.

Reich, E. E., Markesbery, W. R., Roberts, L. J., Swift, L. L., Morrow, J. D., & Montine, T. J. (2001b). Quantification of F-ring and D-/E-ring isoprostanes and neuroprostanes in Alzheimer's disease. In P. M. Dansette, R. Snyder, M. Delaforge, G. G. Gibson, H. Greim, D. J. Jollow, et al. (Eds.), *Biological Reactive Intermediates VI: Chemical and biological mechanisms in susceptibility to and prevention of environmental diseases* (Vol. 500, pp. 253–256). New York: Kluwer Academic/Plenum Publishers.

Reilly, M., Delanty, N., Lawson, J. A., & FitzGerald, G. A. (1996). Modulation of oxidant stress in vivo in chronic cigarette smokers. *Circulation, 94,* 19–25.

Riley, K. P., Snowdon, D. A., & Markesbery, W. R. (2002). Alzheimer's neurofibrillary pathology and the spectrum of cognitive function: Findings from the nun study. *Annals of Neurology, 51,* 567–577.

Salem, N., Kim, H. Y., & Yergey, J. A. (1986). Docosahexaenoic acid: Membrane function and metabolism. In A. P. Simopoulos, R. R. Kifer, & R. E. Martin (Eds.), *Health effects of polyunsaturated acids in seafoods* (pp. 263–317). New York: Academic Press.

Sanan, D. A., Weisgraber, K. H., Russell, S. J., Mahley, R. W., Huang, D., Saunders, A., et al. (1994). Apolipoprotein E associates with beta amyloid peptide of Alzheimer's disease to form novel monofibrils: Isoform apoE4 associates more efficiently than apoE3. *Journal of Clinical Investigation, 94,* 860–869.

Sang, N., Zhang, J., Marcheselli, V., Bazan, N. G., & Chen, C. (2005). Postsynaptically synthesized prostaglandin E2 (PGE2) modulates hippocampal synaptic transmission via a presynaptic PGE2 EP2 receptor. *Journal of Neuroscience, 25,* 9858–9870.

Sano, M., Ernesto, C., Thomas, R. G., Klauber, M. R., Schafer, K., Grundman, M., et al. (1997). A controlled trial of selegiline, alpha-tocopherol, or both as a treatment for Alzheimer's disease. *The New England Journal of Medicine, 336,* 1216–1222.

Sayre, L. M., Zelasko, D. A., Harris, P. L., Perry, G., Salomon, R. G., & Smith, M. A. (1997). 4-Hydroxynonenal-derived advanced lipid peroxidation end products are increased in Alzheimer's disease. *Journal of Neurochemistry, 68,* 2092–2097.

Schmidt, R., Hayn, M., Reinhart, B., Roob, G., Schmidt, H., Schumacher, M., et al. (1998). Plasma antioxidants and cognitive performance in middle-aged and older adults: Results of the Austrian Stroke Prevention Study. *Journal of the American Geriatrics Society, 46,* 1407–1410.

Schmitt, F. A., Davis, D. G., Wekstein, D. R., Smith, C. D., Ashford, J. W., & Markesbery, W. R. (2000). "Preclinical" AD revisited: Neuropathology of cognitively normal older adults. *Neurology, 55,* 370–376.

Schweer, H., Watzer, B., Seyberth, H. W., & Nusing, R. M. (1997). Improved quantification of 8-epi-prostaglandin F2 alpha and F2-isoprostanes by gas chromatography/triple stage quadrapole mass spectrometry: Partial cyclooxygenase-dependent formation of 8-epi-prostaglandin F2 alpha in humans. *Journal of Mass Spectrometry, 32,* 1362–1370.

Shaw, K. N., Commins, S., & O'Mara, S. M. (2003). Deficits in spatial learning and synaptic plasticity induced by the rapid and competitive broad-spectrum cyclooxygenase inhibitor ibuprofen are reversed by increasing endogenous brain-derived neurotrophic factor. *European Journal of Neuroscience, 17,* 2438–2446.

Shelley, M. L. (1998). 4-hydroxy-2-nonenal may be involved in the pathogenesis of Parkinson's disease. *Free Radical Biology & Medicine, 25,* 169–174.

Shie, F. S., Breyer, R. M., & Montine, T. J. (2005). Microglia lacking E prostanoid receptor Subtype 2 have enhanced A beta phagocytosis yet lack A beta-activated neurotoxicity. *American Journal of Pathology, 166,* 1163–1172.

Sidell, K. R., Amamath, V., & Montine, T. J. (2001). Dopamine thioethers in neurodegeneration. *Current Topics in Medicinal Chemistry, 1,* 519–527.

Sidell, K. R., Montine, K. S., Picklo, M. J., Olsen, S. J., Amarnath, V., & Montine, T. J. (2003). Mercapturate metabolism of 4-hydroxy-2-nonenal in rat and human cerebrum. *Journal of Neuropathology and Experimental Neurology, 62,* 146–153.

Smith, M. A., Perry, G., Richey, P. L., Sayre, L. M., Anderson, V. E., Beal, M. F., et al. (1996). Oxidative damage in Alzheimer's. *Nature, 382,* 120–121.

Smith, M. A., Sayre, L. M., Anderson, V. E., Harris, P. L., Beal, M. F., Kowall, N., et al. (1998). Cytochemical demonstration of oxidative damage in Alzheimer's disease by immunochemical enhancement of the carbonyl reaction with 2,4-dinitrophenylhydrazine. *Journal of Histochemistry and Cytochemistry, 46,* 731–735.

Stewart, W. F., Kawas, C., Corrada, M., & Metter, E. J. (1997). Risk of Alzheimer's disease and duration of NSAID use. *Neurology, 48,* 626–632.

Sung, S., Yao, Y., Uryu, K., Yang, H., Lee, V. M., Trojanowski, J. Q., & Pratico, D. (2004). Early Vitamin E supplementation in young but not aged mice reduces Aβ levels and amyloid deposition in a transgenic model of Alzheimer's disease. *The FASEB Journal, 18,* 323–325.

Teather, L. A., Packard, M. G., & Bazan, N. G. (2002). Post-training cyclooxygenase-2 (COX-2) inhibition impairs memory consolidation. *Learning & Memory, 9,* 41–47.

Treffkorn, L., Scheibe, R., Maruyama, T., & Dieter, P. (2004). PGE2 exerts its effect on the LPS-induced release of TNF-alpha, ET-1, IL-1alpha, IL-6 and IL-10 via the EP2 and EP4 receptor in rat liver macrophages. *Prostaglandins and Other Lipid Mediators, 74,* 113–123.

Tuppo, E. E., Forman, L. J., Spur, B. W., Chan-Ting, R. E., Chopra, A., & Cavalieri, T. A. (2001). Sign of lipid peroxidation as measured in the urine of patients with probable Alzheimer's disease. *Brain Research Bulletin, 54*, 565–568.

Vassiliou, E., Jing, H., & Ganea, D. (2003). Prostaglandin E2 inhibits TNF production in murine bone marrow-derived dendritic cells. *Cellular Immunology, 223*, 120–132.

Wang, Z., Ciabattoni, G., Creminon, C., Lawson, J., Fitzgerald, G. A., Patrono, C., et al. (1995). Immunological characterization of urinary 8-epi-prostaglandin $F_{2\alpha}$ excretion in man. *The Journal of Pharmacology and Experimental Therapeutics, 275*, 94–100.

Weggen, S., Eriksen, J. L., Das, P., Sagi, S. A., Wang, R., Pietzik, C. U., et al. (2001). A subset of NSAIDs lower amyloidogenic Abeta42 independently of cyclooxygenase activity. *Nature, 414*, 212–216.

Weggen, S., Eriksen, J. L., Sagi, S. A., Pietrzik, C. U., Golde, T. E., & Koo, E. H. (2003). Abeta42-lowering nonsteroidal anti-inflammatory drugs preserve intramembrane cleavage of the amyloid precursor protein (APP) and ErbB-4 receptor and signaling through the APP intracellular domain. *Journal of Biological Chemistry, 278*, 30748–30754.

Weggen, S., Eriksen, J. L., Sagi, S. A., Pietrzik, C. U., Ozols, V., Fauq, A., et al. (2003). Evidence that nonsteroidal anti-inflammatory drugs decrease amyloid beta 42 production by direct modulation of gamma-secretase activity. *Journal of Biological Chemistry, 278*, 31831–31837.

Xuereb, J. H., Brayne, C., Dufouil, C., Gertz, H., Wischik, C., Harrington, C., et al. (2000). Neuropathological findings in the very old: Results from the first 101 brains of a population-based longitudinal study of dementing disorders. *Annals of the New York Academy of Sciences, 903*, 490–496.

Yamagata, K., Andreasson, K. I., Kaufmann, W. E., Barnes, C. A., & Worley, P. F. (1993). Expression of a mitogen-inducible cyclooxygenase in brain neurons: Regulation by synaptic activity and glucocorticoids. *Neuron, 11*, 371–386.

Yan, Q., Zhang, J., Liu, H., Babu-Khan, S., Vassar, R., Biere, A. L., et al. (2003). Anti-inflammatory drug therapy alters beta-amyloid processing and deposition in an animal model of Alzheimer's disease. *Journal of Neuroscience, 23*, 7504–7509.

Yoritaka, A., Hattori, N., Uchida, K., Tanaka, M., Stadtman, E., & Mizuno, Y. (1996). Immunohistochemical detection of 4-hydroxynonenal protein adducts in Parkinson's disease. *Proceedings of the National Academy of Sciences USA, 93*, 2696–2701.

Zandi, P. P., Anthony, J. C., Khachaturian, A. S., Stone, S. V., Gustafson, D., Tschanz, J. T., et al. (2004). Reduced risk of Alzheimer disease in users of antioxidant vitamin supplements: The Cache County Study. *Archives of Neurology, 61*, 82–88.

3

SLEEP AND INFLAMMATION: A POTENTIAL LINK TO CHRONIC DISEASES

EDWARD C. SUAREZ AND HAROLD GOFORTH

It is well recognized that changes in sleep patterns, whether difficulties in falling asleep, early rising, shortened sleep periods, or poor restfulness, accompany many stressful life events. What is becoming increasingly evident, however, is that disruptions in sleep have significant impact not only on emotional well-being but also on physical health. Recent epidemiological evidence supports the notion that individual differences in sleep quality and quantity are associated with increased risk of a number of chronic medical conditions (Sleep Disorders Research Task Force, 2003).

Toward understanding how disturbed sleep can contribute to adverse health consequences, this chapter reviews evidence in support of the relation of poor sleep quality to immunological parameters of inflammation implicated in the onset and progression of a number of major chronic medical conditions, including coronary heart disease (CHD), Type 2 diabetes, and hypertension. In so doing, we review data from studies of healthy adults suggesting that various indicators of poor sleep, whether derived from self-report paper-and-pencil questionnaires or polysomnography (PSG), are associated with biomarkers of inflammation, such as C-reactive protein (CRP),

53

interleukin-6 (IL-6), IL-1, and tumor necrosis factor-α (TNF-α), as well as shifts in cellular function. Moreover, we also describe evidence to suggest that levels of inflammatory biomarkers are also associated with sleep dysregulation in people with alcoholism and in people who are depressed, patient populations that show a high prevalence of sleep disturbances.

It is also important to realize that the relation of sleep to immune activity is bidirectional, and it has been suggested that inflammatory cytokines are involved in the regulation of sleep and wakefulness. Studies have shown that inflammatory cytokines have inhibitory as well as somnogenic effects on sleep. The bidirectional nature of this relationship is particularly evident in conditions that use cytokine therapy, in which a high percentage of patients not only develop major depression but also show neurovegetative syndrome that includes sleep disturbances at the onset of cytokine treatment. These results suggest the applicability of the cytokine model in the study of sleep disturbances.

Last, this chapter also reviews the role of gender as a potentially important moderating variable in the relation of sleep to chronic disease and biomarkers of inflammation. It is well recognized that women report more sleep complaints and sleep problems, and these gender differences in subjective reports extend to objective measures of sleep structure derived from PSG (Walsleben et al., 2004). It is surprising that the role of gender has not been well studied because of either limited sample size or exclusion of women from the majority of research studies (Sleep Disorders Research Task Force, 2003). Recent epidemiological studies, however, have suggested that increasing severity of symptoms of sleep disturbance incurs a greater risk of coronary vascular disease (CVD) morbidity and mortality and myocardial infarction (MI). Short sleep duration incurs a greater risk of future hypertension in women than in men, even after adjustments for age and other potential confounding factors (Newman et al., 2000). In light of these gender-specific associations, we review data from our laboratory for mechanisms that may help to explain gender-specific associations between sleep symptoms and chronic diseases characterized by inflammation.

It is important that the reader is made aware that the effect of sleep on the immune system goes beyond that of activation of the inflammatory response system (IRS). Sleep loss and disturbances in sleep have been associated with reduction in lymphocyte responses and natural killer cell activities, the latter an in vitro measure of cellular immune function that serves as a marker for the system's ability to mount a response to viral infection. Although evidence from both animal and humans studies supports the relation of sleep to immune suppression, we do not review those data; instead, we refer the reader to Irwin (2002) and Opp, Born, and Irwin (2007) for reviews of these studies. To begin, we provide a short description of what sleep is and what constitutes poor sleep.

WHAT IS POOR SLEEP?

Sleep is one of the most vital activities that all humans do, and nearly one third of our lifetime is spent sleeping. The importance of sleep is such that prolonged periods of time without sleep can affect our health at a faster rate than can even dietary fasting. Defining what constitutes poor sleep, however, is a complex task because sleep is a multifactorial process that involves a number of systems.

The National Center on Sleep Disorders Research (NCSDR; 2003) has estimated that 50 to 70 million Americans are affected by sleep-related problems that cover a wide spectrum of disorders. In attempting to clarify what constitutes poor sleep, the NCSDR has suggested three broad categories of sleep problems: sleep restrictions, primary sleep disorders, and secondary sleep disorders. Sleep restriction is quantified as a shortened total sleep time (TST) associated with an imposed or self-imposed lifestyle and work schedule. In most studies, short sleepers are individuals who report sleeping fewer than 6 hours/night. Primary sleep disorders as a category encompasses more than 70 types of sleep problems that affect individuals of all ages, including primary insomnia. Secondary sleep disorders are sleep problems associated with chronic diseases that are often characterized by pain, infection, or neurological or psychiatric disorders, including alcohol or substance abuse, which subsequently lead to dysregulations in sleep.

SLEEP MEASURES

The complexity of sleep is also reflected in its assessment. Various approaches have been used to assess sleep in humans; however, self-report scales, actigraphy, and PSG are the most common. Self-report scales offer the advantage of enabling researchers to evaluate a person's own perception of sleep. However, self-perception and physiological sleep are imperfectly linked, so using this tool alone misses important objective sleep components. Subjective self-report scales rely on the individual's (and to some extent the sleep partner's) ability to recall and evaluate different aspects of sleep. Various tools have been developed, and many focus on one or more specific aspects of sleep. For example, the Pittsburgh Sleep Quality Index (PSQI; Buysse, Reynolds, Monk, Berman, & Kupfer, 1989), which is a well-established and frequently used scale, yields an overall index of sleep quality with scores above 5 indicating poor sleep (Carpenter & Andrykowski, 1998).

Other more-focused scales include the Insomnia Severity Index, which measures the degree to which individuals have difficulty falling asleep and staying asleep; the Epworth Sleepiness Scale, which measures the degree of sleepiness during the day; and the International Restless Legs Severity scale, which assess specific symptoms associated with restless leg syndrome. Although PSG and self-report assessment of sleep quality are moderately correlated, it is acknowledged that individuals are not accurate raters of their sleep quality (Buysse et al., 1989).

Actigraphy has been used as a surrogate marker for sleep, but this involves having the patient wear a small wristwatch device to measure movement, and operates on the assumption that a lack of movement correlates into sleep. The obvious disadvantage to this technique is that sedentary periods of rest and relaxation appear the same as sleep periods. So estimation of sleep using these devices is inadequate at best.

PSG currently is considered the gold standard in sleep research because it provides an objective means to evaluate a wide variety of sleep abnormalities, including movement-related sleep disorders and disorders of sleep-related breathing. In addition, PSG allows an objective evaluation of the time spent in various stages of sleep as defined by electroencephalographic and motor activity.

PSG records a number of biophysiological changes that occur during sleep, including brain activity by electroencephalogram (EEG), eye movements by electrooculography, muscle activity or skeletal muscle by electromyography, heart rhythm by electrocardiogram, and breathing function or respiratory effort. As such, PSG provides a wealth of physiological data on sleep reflecting (a) objective sleep disturbances, (b) its distribution over the night, and (c) sleep stage amount and distribution.

During PSG, measurement of brain activities by EEG allows for the identification of the two major phases of sleep referred to as *rapid eye movement* (REM) and *non-REM* (NREM), which can be further divided into slow-wave sleep (SWS) and non-SWS. During REM sleep, EEG tracings reveal several brain regions that are active and, to some degree, more active than during wakefulness. NREM sleep, on the other hand, is characterized by four stages that reflect sleep depth, with Stage 1 representing the transition from wakefulness to sleep. Stage 2 is viewed as light sleep with the presence of sleep spindles (i.e., bursts of sinusoidal waves in the 12- to 14-Hz range), and K-complexes (i.e., transient high-voltage biphasic waves that signal the onset of sleep). Stages 3 and 4 are often referred to as SWS or *deep sleep*, and are characterized by the frequency of high-amplitude, low-frequency waves. Thus, in humans, the transition from wakefulness to sleep begins with NREM sleep, followed by a period of REM sleep, with this cycle repeated four to six times a night. For healthy humans, cycles of REM and NREM periods last between 80 to 110 minutes, with NREM sleep accounting for a majority of the total sleep time.

Thus, defining poor sleep incorporates not only evaluation of the various components of sleep but also different assessment techniques to allow a comprehensive assessment of the sleep disorder. Although these issues are important, they are beyond the scope of this chapter. It is sufficient to say that clinical sleep disorders, individual differences in sleep, and sleep symptoms across the continuum have significant effects on immune function, and these associations have been reported using both subjective and objective measures of sleep.

SLEEP DISORDERS, DISTURBED SLEEP, AND CHRONIC DISEASES

Although negative findings have been reported (e.g., Bjorkelund et al., 2005), a number of clinical studies have suggested that individuals with diagnosed sleep-disordered breathing, and particularly obstructive sleep apnea (OSA; Parati, Lombardi, & Narkiewicz, 2007), are at an increased risk of hypertension (e.g., Young et al., 1997), Type 2 diabetes (e.g., Punjabi & Polotsky, 1998), CHD (e.g., Phillips, 2005), and overall mortality (e.g., Kripke, Garfinkel, Wingard, Klauber, & Marler, 2002). Data from epidemiological studies have also suggested that insomnia is a significant predictor of all-cause mortality, including CVD mortality (e.g., Bryant, Trinder, & Curits, 2004; Foley et al., 1995; Kripke et al., 2002; Mallon, Broman, & Helta, 2002). In statistically evaluating data from 10 epidemiological studies that explicitly asked participants about their sleep complaints, Schwartz et al. (1999) concluded that indices of insomnia, such as trouble falling asleep or staying asleep, were associated with an increased risk of CHD events after adjusting for age and other coronary risk factors. Although fewer studies have examined the relation of sleep disorders to metabolic disorders such as Type 2 diabetes, epidemiological evidence suggests an increased prevalence of sleep-disordered breathing in persons with Type 2 diabetes that is independent of age, gender, and body habitus (e.g., Einhorn et al., 2007; Reichmuth, Austin, Skatrud, & Young, 2005).

It is important to understand that the impact of sleep on chronic disease extends beyond clinical sleep disorders. Emerging evidence suggests that increasing severities of symptoms of poor sleep, including those that do not reach clinical criteria for sleep disorder diagnosis, are also associated with greater risk of CVD (Ayas, White, Al-Delaimy, et al., 2003; Ayas, White, Manson, et al., 2003; Elwood, Hack, Pickering, Hughes, & Gallacher, 2006), Type 2 diabetes (Meisinger et al., 2002; Spiegel, Knutson, Leproult, Tasali, & Van Cauter, 2005; Yaggi, Araujo, & McKinlay, 2006), hypertension (Gangwisch et al., 2006), and the metabolic syndrome (Vgontzas, Bixler, & Chrousos, 2003) as well as overall mortality (Hays, Blazer, & Foley, 1996; Wingard & Berkman, 1983). For example, individuals who report sleeping more than or equal to 9 hours or less than 5 hours demonstrate a greater risk of CHD relative to those who sleep 7 to 8 hours (Ayas, White, Manson, et al., 2003). Similar associations have been reported for hypertension, with those individuals who report sleeping either less than 7 or more than 8 hours as being at an increased risk (Gottlieb et al., 2006). Thus, evidence from prospective and cross-sectional studies has been remarkably consistent in suggesting that short sleep duration and poor sleep quality increase the risk of developing Type 2 diabetes.

Thus, although poor sleep may be an important clinical indicator of current health status, it also appears that poor sleep is associated with increased risk of future poor health. Overall, the weight of the evidence from these prospective studies of initially healthy individuals and clinical samples suggests that disturbed sleep and sleep disorders are associated with an increased risk of CHD, Type 2 diabetes, and hypertension. The relation of sleep to these chronic medical conditions has led researchers to examine potential mechanisms of action whereby sleep disturbances and clinical sleep disorder predict future poor health. One hypothesis that is currently drawing attention posits that the relationship between disturbed sleep and chronic disease is mediated by inflammatory processes (Dickstein & Moldofsky, 1999; Moldofsky & Dickstein, 1999).

Inflammation in Chronic Diseases

It is now understood that specific cellular and molecular responses considered to be inflammatory in nature contribute to the development of the atherosclerotic lesions (Ross, 1999). In response to endothelial dysfunction, the normal homeostatic aspects of the endothelium are altered in such a way as to become more permeable and procoagulant by forming vasoactive molecules, cytokines, and growth factors that stimulate the migration of immune cells, most prominently monocytes and lymphocytes. The process, if unabated, leads to the accumulation of circulating monocytes and lymphocytes at the site of the lesion.

Large cohort studies have shown an association between elevated levels of circulating CRP or fibrinogen and increased risk of cardiac events or death, both in patients who have experienced an episode of unstable coronary artery disease and in apparently healthy individuals. Inflammatory biomarkers have also been implicated in metabolic disorders. Evidence for these associations stems from a number of epidemiological studies showing that inflammatory mediators, such as CRP and IL-6, are associated not only with the prediabetic state and insulin resistance (Haffner, 2003) but also with risk of diabetes (Pradhan, Manson, Rifai, Buring, & Ridker, 2001). Consistent with its role in these chronic conditions, levels of inflammatory biomarkers have been associated with such traditional risk factors as adiposity, smoking, and insulin resistance. However, emerging research is also indicating that sleep dysregulation is associated with inflammatory mediators.

Sleep Dysregulation and Inflammatory Mediators

Given that poor sleep is associated with an increased risk of the most prevalent chronic diseases, researchers have focused on identifying possible mechanisms of action that could underlie this association. Though various mechanisms have been postulated, one possibility is that dysregulated sleep is associated with an activation of the inflammatory response system. A number of studies testing this hypothesis have been conducted in both subjects with diagnosed clinical disorders and healthy individuals. For the most part, most studies have been observational in design, but there is also evidence from a small number of experimental studies using laboratory sleep deprivation.

Sleep Disorders and Inflammation

An important clinical diagnosis that has been shown to increase the risk of the major chronic disease is sleep-related breathing disorders. This group of sleep disorders includes sleep apnea, habitual snoring, Cheyne–Stokes breathing syndrome, and sleep hypoventilation syndrome (American Academy of Sleep Medicine Task Force, 1999). Sleep apnea syndromes are characterized by repeated episodes in which the individual ceases to breathe, thus contributing to partial arousal, sleep dysregulation, and increases in daytime sleepiness. Sleep apneas are typically classified as either central sleep apnea (CSA), obstructive (i.e., OSA), or mixed, with OSA characterized by the presence of an effort to breathe and CSA characterized by the absence of this effort. The most common manifestation of the sleep apnea syndromes is OSA, with estimates of occurrence ranging from 2% to 4% in the general population (Young et al., 1993).

In large epidemiological studies, results have confirmed that OSA is an independent factor for CVD (Foley et al., 1999; Parati et al., 2007), with the relative risk of CVD being 1.42 times greater in individuals with OSA relative to those without (Shahar et al., 2001). The evidence suggesting an increased risk of CVD in individuals with OSA has led researchers to examine its relationship to inflammatory mediators. Although one study did not observe an association of sleep apnea to CRP after adjustment for age, sex, and body mass index (BMI; Taheri et al., 2007), multiple studies have shown that OSA is associated with elevated levels of various inflammatory biomarkers such as CRP, IL-6, TNF-α, and vascular adhesion molecules (Dyugovskaya, Lavie, & Lavie, 2002; Imagawa et al., 2004; Kato et al., 2000; Lavie, 2004; Ohga et al., 1999; Tazaki et al., 2004; Vgontzas et al., 2000; Yokoe et al., 2003).

Elevations in inflammatory cytokines in OSA appear to have some genetic basis, with one recent study suggesting a specific genetic polymorphism associated with increased production of TNF-α being more prevalent among OSA patients (Riha et al., 2005). Inflammatory elevations in OSA appear to respond to treatment, with a number of studies showing that continuous positive airway pressure (CPAP), a recognized treatment for OSA, ameliorates inflammation in most (Drager, Bortolotto, Figueiredo, Krieger, & Lorenzi,

2007; Harsch et al., 2004; Kobayashi et al., 2006; Patruno et al., 2007; Yokoe et al., 2003) but not all studies (Akashiba, Akahoshi, Kawahara, Majima, & Horie, 2005). Others have shown that etanercept, a TNF-α antagonist approved by the federal Food and Drug Administration for the treatment of rheumatoid arthritis, reduced levels of TNF-α and IL-6 but not CRP (Vgontzas et al., 2004).

Emerging, but limited, evidence has recently suggested that primary insomnia, the most commonly occurring primary sleep disorder, is associated with elevations in inflammatory biomarkers. In a study by Vgontzas et al. (2002), participants with primary insomnia, relative to normal control participants, showed a shift in TNF-α and IL-6 levels, with higher levels observed during the daytime hours in those with insomnia. Vgontzas et al. suggested that this shift might explain the greater daytime fatigue often associated with insomnia.

Another recent study examined the relation of proinflammatory cytokine levels in 11 patients with primary insomnia and age- and sex-matched control participants (Burgos et al., 2006). Results showed that nocturnal IL-6 was elevated in insomnia patients, and these elevations were associated with the amount of wake time and SWS. These preliminary, but intriguing, observations suggest that the proinflammatory state associated with a number of chronic diseases may also be present in individuals with primary insomnia.

In addition to studies that have used patient samples with clinical sleep disorders, a number of studies have examined the relation of sleep to inflammatory biomarkers in patient populations of alcohol-dependent adults and people with depression, groups that show high prevalence of sleep problems. Though there is some consensus that moderate intake of alcohol intake may have beneficial effects on CVD via reduction in inflammation (Imhof & Koenig, 2003), emerging evidence suggests that alcohol dependence is associated with an increased risk of coronary disease, especially among populations already at risk, such as patients with affective or psychotic disorders (Denison, Berkowicz, Oden, & Wendestam, 1997; Sundquist & Li, 2006). For example, Irwin et al. (2004) have shown that, independent of potentially confounding factors, levels of IL-6 and TNF-α are elevated in persons with alcohol dependency and that the elevations in IL-6 levels are associated with prolonged sleep latency.

Those results complement the observations by Redwine, Dang, Hall, and Irwin (2003), who showed that IL-6 increased between 3:00 a.m. and 6:30 a.m. for people with alcoholism, whereas control participants showed a decrease in IL-6 during the same time period. Additional analyses by Redwine et al. revealed that, independent of age and chronic alcohol consumption, increases in IL-6 were predicted by increases in REM sleep, suggesting that in persons with chronic alcohol dependency, sleep disturbances are associated with a proinflammatory state.

It is well recognized that sleep dysregulation, and specifically insomnia, is a common complaint of patients with depression. Also, a body of evidence suggests that major depression and severity of depressive symptoms are associated with elevations in inflammatory biomarkers (e.g., Danner, Kasl, Abramson, & Vaccarino, 2003; Panagiotakos et al., 2004; Suarez, 2004). Recent evidence, however, suggests that the relationship between depression and proinflammatory cytokines, specifically IL-6, is fully accounted for by PSG-derived indices of poor sleep. For instance, Motivala, Sarfatti, Olmos, and Irwin (2005) observed that prolonged sleep latency and increases in REM density were associated with elevated levels of IL-6 and soluble intercellular adhesion molecules in patients with depression, and that the elevations in IL-6 were fully accounted for by these two indicators of poor sleep.

As we describe later, sleep disturbances are also common in persons with HIV/AIDS, a disease that is fast becoming a chronic medical condition, with increasing life expectancy reflecting the effectiveness of new retroviral therapies (Altice & Friedland, 1998; James, 1996; Marwick, 1998).

SLEEP DYSREGULATION AND CHRONIC MEDICAL DISORDERS: EVIDENCE FOR INDIVIDUAL DIFFERENCES IN SLEEP QUALITY AND QUANTITY

As indicated in the previous section, the majority of studies in the area of sleep and inflammation have focused on examining clinical sleep disorders and their role in disease and inflammation, with the primary markers being CRP, IL-6, IL-1, and TNF-α. Recent cohort studies, however, have suggested that poor health outcomes are also related to individual differences in sleep quality and quantity. For example, short sleep duration of less than or equal to 5 hours/night was associated with increased risk of hypertension (Gangwisch et al., 2006). These findings were replicated and extended by Gottlieb et al. (2006), who showed that participants of the Sleep Heart Health Study (Quan et al., 1997) who slept less than 7 hours or more than 8 hours were at greater risk of hypertension than were those participants reporting 8 or more hours. The impact of sleep quantity also appears to be related to the risk of Type 2 diabetes.

In the Nurses' Health Study, Ayas, White, Al-Delaimy, et al. (2003) showed that sleep restriction was prospectively associated with increased risk of Type 2 diabetes, with this association potentially mediated by BMI. This association was recently replicated by Gottlieb et al. (2005), who showed that sleep duration of 6 hours or less or 9 hours or more was associated with an increased prevalence of Type 2 diabetes, with the effect being present in persons without insomnia.

Sleep quantity is not the only variable associated with increased risk of poor health. Among a sample of 5,888 older adults, increased daytime sleepiness was associated with CVD morbidity and mortality, MI, and coronary heart failure, even after statistical adjustments for age and other factors (Newman et al., 2000). It is interesting that these observations were stronger in women than in men, suggesting that daytime sleepiness may be an independent risk factor for women (Newman et al., 2000). Similarly, difficulties falling asleep or regular use of hypnotics (an indicator of sleep disturbances) was associated with increased risk of Type 2 diabetes in middle-age men (Nilsson, Roost, Engstrom, Hedblad, & Berglund, 2004). Given these epidemiological observations, we raised the question: Are individual differences in sleep associated with inflammatory biomarkers that are predictive of future risk of CVD and Type 2 diabetes?

Individual Differences in Sleep and Inflammation in Nonclinical Samples

Although clinical studies yielded important and critical data, results may not generalize to general populations. Thus, it is important to examine whether individual differences in sleep quality and quantity are associated with potential mechanisms of action underlying the association between sleep and poor health. The use of nonclinical samples, however, has been limited to a few studies. Nevertheless, the available evidence suggests that variations in sleep and symptoms of sleep disturbances are significantly associated with levels of inflammatory biomarkers. For example, using the PSQI, Friedman et al. (2005) showed that higher levels of IL-6 were associated with poorer sleep efficiency in older healthy women.

In our laboratory, we have observed that increasing levels of CRP and IL-6 are associated with increasing severity of poor sleep, as assessed by the PSQI. CRP and IL-6 were also found to be associated with sleep latency, with individuals reporting sleep latencies of 30 minutes or more showing the highest levels of CRP and IL-6 relative to those participants who took less than 15 minutes or between 15 and 30 minutes to fall asleep. The same association between sleep latency and CRP was observed in a study of older adults. McDade, Hawkley, and Cacioppo (2006) showed that subjective ratings of sleep latency were associated with elevated CRP even after adjustments for potential confounding factors. Thus, it appears that in samples recruited from the community, subjective ratings of overall sleep quality and sleep latency are significantly associated with inflammatory biomarkers, and these associations are not due to potential confounding factors, such as age and BMI.

Studies have also used PSG to examine the relation of objective sleep indices to inflammatory measures in normal participants. The use of PSG allows for studies to examine not only sleep parameters, such as TST, latency to persistent sleep (lps), and length of wake after sleep onset, but also variations in sleep architecture (sleep stages) and EEG waves (e.g., SWS, delta waves), measures that can be assessed only with PSG. One study examined the relation of PSG data to inflammatory biomarkers in healthy, nonapneic, adult participants (Mills et al., 2007). Longer REM latency was associated with higher IL-6 and endothelin-1 (ET-1), and longer lps and shorter Stage 1 sleep were associated with higher ET-1 independent of age and sex (Mills et al., 2007). Results from Mills et al. (2007) replicated previous observations by Hong, Mills, Loredo, Adler, and Dimsdale (2005), who also showed that longer REM latency was significantly associated with elevated IL-6 in a sample of healthy adults. Combined, this preliminary evidence suggests that PSG data, and particularly nocturnal EEG outcomes, are significantly associated with elevations in cardiovascular risk factors in nonclinical samples.

Experimental Studies of Sleep and Inflammation

The studies described in the previous section, while providing positive evidence for an association between inflammatory biomarkers and individual differences in sleep, were observational in nature. There is evidence to suggest, however, that laboratory manipulation of sleep duration can lead to changes in levels of inflammatory markers. In the early 1970s, Moldofsky and his collaborators showed that 40 hours of sleep deprivation in the laboratory led to enhancement in IL-1-like and IL-2-like activities (Moldofsky, Lue, Davidson, & Gorczynski, 1972). Similarly, Vgontzas et al. (1999) showed that total night sleep deprivation was associated with changes in the temporal pattern of circadian IL-6, with daytime elevations in IL-6 being higher following sleep deprivation in young healthy men (Vgontzas et al., 1999). These results were replicated by Redwine, Hauger, Gillin, and Irwin (2000), who showed that partial sleep deprivation in young healthy men led to an increase in IL-6 that was attributed to changes in sleep architecture and a loss of SWS. Extending the observation for IL-6, Meier-Ewert et al. (2004) showed that both *total sleep deprivation* (in this study defined as 88 continuous hours with no sleep) and *partial sleep deprivation* (4.2 hours of sleep/night) were associated with significant increases in CRP from levels observed following a normal night of sleep. In light of the fact that CRP is relatively stable and does not appear to show a circadian rhythm (Danesh et al., 2004), the evidence suggests that in healthy adults the loss of sleep is sufficient to significantly elevate CRP above levels associated with normal sleep.

The effect of laboratory sleep restriction extends beyond increases in circulating levels of inflammatory biomarkers to include changes in cell function and biomarker expression. For example, Redwine, Dang, and Irwin (2004) showed that following partial sleep deprivation, circulating lymphocytes showed increases in the expression of L-selectin and decreases in Mac-1 expression in young healthy men. More recently, Irwin, Wang, Campomayor, Collado-Hidalgo, and Cole (2006) showed that laboratory-induced sleep loss that was operationalized as being awake between 11 p.m. and 3 a.m. led to an increase in the stimulated production of IL-6 and TNF-α by circulating monocytes with sleep loss inducing more than a threefold increased in messenger RNA for IL-6 and a twofold increase in TNF-α messenger RNA.

It is interesting to note that it has been shown that normal sleep also affects cell function. Uthgennant, Schoolmann, Pietrowsky, Fehm, and Born (1995) showed that even after 3 hours of sleep, lipopolysaccharide-stimulated productions of IL-1β and TNF-α by peripheral mononuclear cells were diminished as compared with wake production. In contrast, phytohemagglutinin stimulation increased IL-2 production following 3 hours of sleep. Thus, these data suggest that even short periods of sleep are sufficient to reduce the cellular capacity for cytokine responses to in vitro stimulation, a condition that is consistent with sleep-reducing inflammatory processes.

Combined, the observational and experimental data suggest that in healthy adults without a diagnosis of clinical sleep disorders, factors that reduce sleep quality or quantity promote increases in circulating levels of inflammatory biomarkers known to be associated with increased risk of CVD and Type 2 diabetes. Data also suggest that these effects extend to changes in cellular function that promote and are characteristic of the inflammatory response.

Sleep Disturbances and Cytokine Therapy

Cytokine therapy has been used as a model to examine the impact of cytokines on the development of depression. This model, however, also has applicability for sleep. Studies have shown that the effects of interferon-α (IFN), a cytokine used for the treatment of some cancers, can be characterized by two distinct behavioral syndromes. One reflects neurovegetative symptoms such as sleep disturbances and fatigue. The second syndrome incorporates symptoms such as depressed mood, anxiety, and cognitive dysfunction (Capuron & Miller, 2004).

These distinct behavioral patterns have also been shown to differ in the time that they manifest relative to the initiation of cytokine treatment. Neurovegetative symptoms develop early and are generally present within the first 4 weeks of treatment with IFN-α. They also typically persist throughout the treatment period. Mood and cognitive symptoms, however, develop later between the first and third month of IFN-α exposure (Capuron et al., 2002; Capuron & Miller, 2004). Unlike mood and cognitive symptoms that are responsive to antidepressants, neurovegetative symptoms have been shown to be minimally responsive to antidepressant treatment (Capuron et al., 2002). In light of the effectiveness of IFN-α in the treatment of certain cancers, discontinuation of treatment is not a viable solution. It will be important, therefore, to better understand the actions of IFN-α on neurovegetative symptoms, including sleep disturbances, to develop effective intervention strategies.

Sleep Dysregulation and HIV

As described in the previous section, the relation of sleep to immune function is characterized as bidirectional in nature, with cytokines having effects on sleep quality and quantity. This association can also be noted in medical conditions characterized by inflammation and is perhaps best illustrated in a model of HIV that demonstrates the bidirectional links between inflammation, immunity, and sleep as well as the current areas of controversy regarding these events.

Sleep is altered early in HIV infection, and this alteration appears to occur prior to the onset of AIDS in many individuals. Evidence supports that the virus enters the central nervous system with the assistance of envelope glycoproteins, and these same glycoproteins have also been postulated to play a direct role in disrupting neuronal processes involved in sleep. Other factors identified within this model have included inflammatory cytokines, chemokines, and chemokine receptors, the last of which serve as coreceptors for the HIV envelope glycoproteins. Further, these chemokine receptors appear to also have a role in inducing sleep disturbances in a rat model illustrating the complex host-pathogen interactions in producing and maintaining normal sleep. Hogan, Hutton, Smith, and Opp (2001) found that CCL4/MIP-1β injected centrally into rats prior to dark onset increased non-REM sleep, appeared to fragment sleep, and induced fever—all of which supports an inflammatory role of HIV in inducing sleep disturbance.

The initial chronic asymptomatic stage of HIV infection is associated with an increase in SWS—especially in the latter portions of the sleep cycle, which is unusual in other primary or secondary sleep disorders (White et al., 1995). Researchers have found that these changes are replicable and that they appear to be unrelated to typical psychosocial contributors to insomnia. Instead, Darko, Miller, et al. (1995) noted that evidence is accumulating in linking these sleep disturbances to the increased levels of IL-1β and TNF-α found in the blood of HIV-infected individuals. Both of these cytokines have been noted to be somnogenic in human and animal models, which may reflect increases in fatigue and impaired sleep in this population (Darko, Mitler, & Henriksen, 1995).

HIV envelope glycoprotein 120 (gp120), in particular, appears to induce the synthesis and secretion of both these sleep-promoting cytokines, as well as other cytokines that encourage wakefulness (IL-10, IL-1 receptor antagonist). Opp et al. (1996) used a well-defined rat model to demonstrate that HIV-1 gp120 injected intracerebroventricularly into rats prior to dark onset significantly altered sleep architecture in a dose-dependent model that affected both non-REM and REM sleep architecture. In addition, gp120 appeared to induce both IL-10 as well as IL-1 receptor antagonist in the hypothalamus, which is noted to be a crucial brain structure in sleep regulation.

Despite progress in understanding the physiology of sleep and wakefulness, and their corresponding influences on the immune system, they remain poorly understood as a whole. Considerable evidence exists for interactions between host defense and sleep, and host response mediators, such as IL-1, are likely involved in sleep regulation. Also, data suggest that sleep, and especially non-REM sleep, has an immunosupportive function (Pollmacher, Mullington, Korth, & Hinze-Selch, 1995). Similarly, IL-1β is a well-known HIV-1 replication factor in addition to being an inflammatory cytokine, and inflammation has been noted to worsen the course of HIV-1 infection, which further illustrates the bidirectional nature of sleep and immunity (Wong, Bongiorno, Rettori, McCann, & Licinio, 1997). Other inflammatory cytokines, such as TNF-α, have also been noted to interact synergistically with IL-1 to produce fever, anorexia, lethargy, and sleep. However, in HIV models, TNF-α appears to enhance the effectiveness of killing of HIV-infected cells (Drexler, 1995), which appears to support a positive role of inflammation in the overall disease process, thus illustrating the complex and uncertain nature of these interactions.

Duration of illness appears to play a significant role in the interaction of cytokines and sleep in an HIV disease model, and may be responsible for some of the variations in the presented data. Darko, Miller, et al. (1995) demonstrated a normal, physiological coupling in early HIV seropositive subjects between TNF-α and delta amplitude during sleep, which appears as a cogent link between early HIV infection and the associated increased delta sleep during later stages of the night. However, from a clinical standpoint, sleep patterns often degenerate as HIV infection progresses, and sleep architecture becomes more fragmented and disorganized; similarly, there was a lessened likelihood of TNF-α and delta amplitude coupling in progressive HIV infection in this population (Darko, Miller, et al., 1995). Further data are required to better understand the link between sleep-inflammation processes in early and late disease.

Gender Differences in the Relation of Sleep to Chronic Disease and Inflammation

Although sleep complaints are twice as prevalent in women, with evidence suggesting that the structure of sleep differs between men and women (Goel, Kim, & Lao, 2005), 75% of sleep studies have included only men (NCSDR, 2003). Gender differences in the prevalence of sleep problems and the lack of gender research led the U.S. Department of Health and Human Services along with the National Institutes of Health (NIH), National Heart, Lung and Blood Institute, NCSDR, and the Trans-NIH Sleep Disorder Committee to publish the 2003 National Sleep Disorder Research Plan (NCSDR, 2003). As part of its recommendations, the committee strongly encouraged researchers to include women and examine how sex-related differences in sleep and its regulation influence the mechanisms and risks of developing disease and sleep disorders. In the 3 years since the release of the Research Plan, more studies have included women (e.g., Larkin et al., 2005), but for the most part, these studies continue to be hampered by methodological limitations and small sample size (e.g., Hong, Mills, Loredo, Adler, & Dimsdale, 2005).

The importance of gender has recently been underscored by results from two large epidemiological studies suggesting that the impact of poor sleep on health may differ between men and women. Results from these studies have suggested that symptoms of disturbed sleep incur a greater and significant risk of CVD morbidity and mortality, MI, and hypertension in women than in men, even after adjustments for age and other potential confounding factors (Cappuccio et al., 2007; Newman et al., 2000).

Given these gender-specific associations, we were encouraged to examine the relation of symptoms of poor sleep to circulating levels of inflammatory biomarkers in a sample of 210 nonsmoking, healthy men and women with no history of clinical sleep disorders. Results from multivariate analysis revealed that, independent of potential confounding factors, such as age, BMI, alcohol intake, and ethnicity, higher scores on the PSQI were significantly associated with elevations in CRP and IL-6. But these associations were significant only in women, not in men. To further explore these associations, we examined the relation of PSQI component scores to inflammatory markers. Results indicated that only subjective reporting of more frequent bouts of difficulty falling asleep and greater frequency of sleep disturbances were associated with higher levels of CRP and IL-6 in women but not men.

Although preliminary, these results suggest the plausible biological explanation for the reported gender-specific differences in the relationship between poor sleep and risk of CVD. It will be up to future studies to replicate and expand these preliminary findings to incorporate objective measures of sleep, such as PSG, and determine whether changes in sleep architecture identify specific sleep disturbances that explain our observed differences.

SUMMARY

In this chapter, we reviewed evidence for the relation of sleep disturbances and clinical sleep disorders to the increased risk of the most prevalent major chronic diseases involving the cardiovascular and metabolic systems. Epidemiological evidence points to both clinical diagnosis and individual differences in sleep as important indicators of elevated risk of CVD morbidity and mortality, MI, coronary heart failure, hypertension, and Type 2 diabetes. In attempting to understand the mechanisms underlying these associations, we have examined the relation of sleep to inflammatory biomarkers that have been shown to predict the increased risk of disease, as well as cellular changes implicated in atherogenesis. Given that the association between sleep and proinflammatory cytokines appears to be bidirectional, we suggested that the cytokine therapy model, which has been most often used to describe cytokine-induced depression, may have applicability to cytokine-induced sleep disturbances. To examine further the bidirectional nature of the relationship between sleep and inflammation, we described the effects of HIV/AIDS on sleep disturbances.

Last, we reviewed preliminary data indicating that symptoms of poor sleep are associated with a heightened risk of CVD and hypertension in women but not men. This gender-specific association may be explained by recent observations in our laboratory linking CRP and IL-6 to subjective ratings of poor sleep in women. Taken together, these data, which are derived from various avenues of research, implicate sleep disturbances as a critical factor in inflammation. Furthermore, the association appears bidirectional in nature. If we are to meet the challenges set forth in the Healthy People 2010 agenda to ensure that individuals, communities, and professionals take specific steps to ensure good health and longevity, it will be important to gain a better understanding of the critical contribution sleep has to our health and to find effective ways to improve sleep quality.

KEY POINTS

- Disruptions in sleep have a major impact on mental and physical health.
- Poor sleep quality elevates biomarkers of inflammation, including IL-1, IL-6, and CRP.
- Gender may moderate the relationship between sleep problems and chronic disease and inflammation.
- Markers of poor sleep may account for the relationship between depression and proinflammatory cytokines.
- Sleep deprivation in HIV patients provides a good model for the bidirectional relationship between inflammation and sleep.

REFERENCES

Akashiba, T., Akahoshi, T., Kawahara, S., Majima, T., & Horie, T. (2005). Effects of long-term nasal continuous positive airway pressure on C-reactive protein in patients with obstructive sleep apnea syndrome. *Internal Medicine, 44,* 899–900.

Altice, F. L., & Friedland, G. H. (1998). The era of adherence to HIV therapy. *Annals of Internal Medicine, 129,* 5603–5605.

American Academy of Sleep Medicine Task Force. (1999). Sleep-related breathing disorders in adults: Recommendations for syndrome definition and measurement techniques in clinical research. *Sleep, 22,* 667–689.

Ayas, N. T., White, D. P., Al-Delaimy, W. K., Manson, J. E., Stampfer, M. J., Speizer, F. E., et al. (2003). A prospective study of self-reported sleep duration and incident diabetes in women. *Diabetes Care, 26,* 380–384.

Ayas, N. T., White, D. P., Manson, J. E., Stampfer, M. J., Speizer, F. E., Malhotra, A., & Hu, F. B. (2003). A prospective study of sleep duration and coronary heart disease in women. *Archives of Internal Medicine, 163,* 205–209.

Bjorkelund, C., Bondyr-Carlsson, D., Lapidus, L., Lissner, L., Mansson, J., Skoog, I., & Bengtsson, C. (2005). Sleep disturbances in midlife unrelated to 32-year diabetes incidence: The prospective population study of women in Gothenburg. *Diabetes Care, 28,* 2739–2744.

Bryant, P. A., Trinder, H., & Curtis, N. (2004). Sick and tired: Does sleep have a vital role in the immune system? *Nature Reviews: Immunology, 4,* 457–467.

Burgos, I., Richter, L., Klein, T., Fiebich, B., Feige, B., Lieb, K., et al. (2006). Increased nocturnal interleukin-6 excretion in patients with primary insomnia: A pilot study. *Brain, Behavior, and Immunity, 20,* 246–253.

Buysse, D. J., Reynolds, C. F., III, Monk, T. H., Berman, S. R., & Kupfer, D. J. (1989). The Pittsburgh Sleep Quality Index: A new instrument for psychiatric practice and research. *Psychiatry Research, 28,* 193–213.

Cappuccio, F. P., Stranges, S., Kandala, N.-B., Miller, M. A., Taggart, F. M., Kumari, M., et al. (2007). Gender-specific associations of short sleep duration with prevalent and incident hypertension: The Whitehall II Study. *Hypertension, 50,* 693–700.

Capuron, L., Gummick, J. F., Musselman, D. L., Lawson, D. H., Reemsnyder, A., Nemeroff, C., & Miller, A. H. (2002). Neurobehavioral effects of interferon-alpha in cancer patients: Phenomenological and paroxetine responsiveness of symptom dimensions. *Neuropsychopharmacology, 26,* 643–652.

Capuron, L., & Miller, A. H. (2004). Cytokines and psychopathology: Lessons from interferon-alpha. *Biological Psychiatry, 56,* 819–824.

Carpenter, J. S., & Andrykowski, M. A. (1998). Psychometric evaluation of the Pittsburgh Sleep Quality Index. *Journal of Psychosomatic Research, 45,* 5–13.

Danesh, J., Wheeler, J. G., Hirschfield, G. M., Eda, S., Eiriksdottir, G., Rumley, A., et al. (2004). C-reactive protein and other circulating markers of inflammation in the prediction of coronary heart disease. *The New England Journal of Medicine, 350,* 1387–1397.

Danner, M., Kasl, S. V., Abramson, J. L., & Vaccarino, V. (2003). Association between depression and elevated C-reactive protein. *Psychosomatic Medicine, 65,* 347–356.

Darko, D. F., Miller, J. C., Gallen, C., White, J., Koziol, J., Brown, S. J., et al. (1995). Sleep electroencephalogram delta-frequency amplitude, night plasma levels of tumor necrosis factor alpha, and human immunodeficiency virus infection. *Proceedings of the National Academy of Sciences USA, 92,* 12080–12084.

Darko, D. F., Mitler, M. M., & Henriksen, S. J. (1995). Lentiviral infection, immune response peptides and sleep. *Advances in Neuroimmunology*, *5*, 57–77.

Denison, H., Berkowicz, A., Oden, A., & Wendestam, C. (1997). The significance of coronary death for the excess mortality in alcohol-dependent men. *Alcohol and Alcoholism*, *32*, 517–526.

Dickstein, J. B., & Moldofsky, H. (1999). Sleep, cytokines and immune function. *Sleep Medicine Reviews*, *3*, 219–228.

Drager, L. F., Bortolotto, L. A., Figueiredo, A. C., Krieger, E. M., & Lorenzi, G. F. (2007). Effects of continuous positive airway pressure on early signs of atherosclerosis in obstructive sleep apnea. *American Journal of Respiratory and Critical Care Medicine*, *176*, 706–712.

Drexler, A. M. (1995). Tumor necrosis factor: Its role in HIV/AIDS. *STEP Perspective*, *7*(1), 13–15.

Dyugovskaya, L., Lavie, P., & Lavie, L. (2002). Increased adhesion molecules expression and production of reactive oxygen species in leukocytes of sleep apnea patients. *American Journal of Respiratory and Critical Care Medicine*, *165*, 934–939.

Einhorn, D., Stewart, D. A., Erman, M. K., Gordon, N., Philis-Tsimikas, A., & Casal, E. (2007). Prevalence of sleep apnea in a population of adults with Type 2 diabetes mellitus. *Endocrine Practice*, *13*, 355–362.

Elwood, P., Hack, M., Pickering, J., Hughes, J., & Gallacher, J. (2006). Sleep disturbance, stroke, and heart disease events: Evidence from Caerphilly cohort. *Journal of Epidemiology and Community Health*, *60*, 69–74.

Foley, D. J., Monjan, A. A., Brown, S. L., Simonsick, E. M., Wallace, R. B., & Blazer, D. G. (1995). Sleep complaints among elderly persons: An epidemiologic study of three communities. *Sleep*, *18*, 425–432.

Foley, D. J., Monjan, A. A., Masaki, K. H., Enright, P. L., Quan, S. F., & White, L. R. (1999). Associations of symptoms of sleep apnea with cardiovascular disease, cognitive impairment, and mortality among older Japanese-American men. *Journal of the American Geriatrics Society*, *47*, 524–528.

Friedman, E. M., Hayney, M. S., Love, G. D., Urry, H. L., Rosenkranz, M. A., Davidson, R. J., et al. (2005). Social relationships, sleep quality, and interleukin-6 in aging women. *Proceedings of the National Academy of Sciences USA*, *102*, 18757–18762.

Gangwisch, J. E., Heymsfield, S. B., Boden-Albala, B., Buijs, R. M., Kreier, F., Pickering, T. G., et al. (2006). Short sleep duration as a risk factor for hypertension: Analyses of the first National Health and Nutrition Examination Survey. *Hypertension*, *47*, 833–839.

Goel, N., Kim, H., & Lao, R. P. (2005). Gender differences in polysomnographic sleep in young healthy sleepers. *Chronobiology International*, *22*, 905–915.

Gottlieb, D. J., Punjabi, N. M., Newman, A. B., Resnick, H. E., Redline, S., Baldwin, C. M., & Nieto, F. J. (2005). Association of sleep time with diabetes mellitus and impaired glucose tolerance. *Archives of Internal Medicine*, *165*, 863–867.

Gottlieb, D. J., Redline, S., Nieto, F. J., Baldwin, C. M., Newman, A. B., Resnick, H. E., & Punjabi, N. M. (2006). Association of usual sleep duration with hypertension: The Sleep Heart Health Study. *Sleep, 29,* 1009–1014.

Haffner, S. M. (2003). Insulin resistance, inflammation, and the prediabetic state. *American Journal of Cardiology, 92*(4), 18J–26J.

Harsch, I. A., Koebnick, C., Wallaschofski, H., Schahin, S. P., Hahn, E. G., Ficker, J. H., et al. (2004). Resistin levels in patients with obstructive sleep apnoea syndrome—The link to subclinical inflammation? *Medical Science Monitor, 10,* CR510–CR515.

Hays, J. C., Blazer, D. G., & Foley, D. J. (1996). Risk of napping: Excessive daytime sleepiness and mortality in an older community population. *Journal of the American Geriatrics Society, 44,* 693–698.

Hogan, D., Hutton, L. A., Smith, E. M., & Opp, M. R. (2001). Beta (CC)-chemokines as modulators of sleep: Implications for HIV-induced alterations in arousal state. *Journal of Neuroimmunology, 119,* 317–326.

Hong, S., Mills, P. J., Loredo, J. S., Adler, K. A., & Dimsdale, J. E. (2005). The association between interleukin-6, sleep, and demographic characteristics. *Brain, Behavior, and Immunity, 19,* 165–172.

Imagawa, S., Yamaguchi, Y., Ogawa, K., Obara, N., Suzuki, N., Yamamoto, M., & Nagasawa, T. (2004). Interleukin-6 and tumor necrosis factor-alpha in patients with obstructive sleep apnea-hypopnea syndrome. *Respiration, 71,* 24–29.

Imhof, A., & Koenig, W. (2003). Alcohol inflammation and coronary heart disease. *Addiction Biology, 8,* 271–277.

Irwin, M. R. (2002). Effects of sleep and sleep loss on immunity and cytokines. *Brain, Behavior, and Immunity, 16,* 503–512.

Irwin, M. R., Rinetti, G., Redwine, L., Motivala, S., Dang, J., & Ehlers, C. (2004). Nocturnal proinflammatory cytokine-associated sleep disturbances in abstinent African American alcoholics. *Brain, Behavior, and Immunity, 18,* 349–360.

Irwin, M. R., Wang, M., Campomayor, C. O., Collado-Hidalgo, A., & Cole, S. (2006). Sleep deprivation and activation of morning levels of cellular and genomic markers of inflammation. *Archives of Internal Medicine, 166,* 1756–1762.

James, J. S. (1996). New optimism on controlling HIV infection. *AIDS Treatment News, 249,* 1–3.

Kato, M., Roberts-Thomson, P., Phillips, B. C., Haynes, W. G., Winnicki, M., Accurso, V., & Somers, V. K. (2000). Impairment of endothelium-dependent vasodilation of resistance vessels in patients with obstructive sleep apnea. *Circulation, 102,* 2607–2610.

Kobayashi, K., Nishimura, Y., Shimada, T., Yoshimura, S., Funada, Y., Satouchi, M., & Yokoyama, M. (2006). Effect of continuous positive airway pressure on soluble CD40 ligand in patients with obstructive sleep apnea syndrome. *Chest, 129,* 632–637.

Kripke, D. F., Garfinkel, L., Wingard, D. L., Klauber, M. R., & Marler, M. R. (2002). Mortality associated with sleep duration and insomnia. *Archives of General Psychiatry, 59,* 131–136.

Larkin, E. K., Rosen, C. L., Kirchner, H. L., Storfer-Isser, A., Emancipator, J. L., Johnson, N. L., et al. (2005). Variation of C-reactive protein levels in adolescents: Association with sleep-disordered breathing and sleep duration. *Circulation, 111*, 1978–1984.

Lavie, L. (2004). Sleep apnea syndrome, endothelial dysfunction, and cardiovascular morbidity. *Sleep, 27*, 1053–1054.

Mallon, L., Broman, J. E., & Helta, J. (2002). Sleep complaints predict coronary artery disease mortality in males: A 12-year follow-up study of middle-aged Swedish population. *Journal of Internal Medicine, 251*, 207–216.

Marwick, C. (1998). HIV/AIDS care calls for reallocation of resources. *Journal of the American Medical Association, 279*, 491–493.

McDade, T. W., Hawkley, L. C., & Cacioppo, J. T. (2006). Psychosocial and behavioral predictors of inflammation in middle-aged and older adults: The Chicago Health, Aging, and Social Relations Study. *Psychosomatic Medicine, 68*, 376–381.

Meier-Ewert, H. K., Ridker, P. M., Rifai, N., Regan, M. M., Price, N. J., Dinges, D. F., & Mullington, J. M. (2004). Effect of sleep loss on C-reactive protein, an inflammatory marker of cardiovascular risk. *Journal of the American College of Cardiology, 43*, 678–683.

Meisinger, C., Thorand, B., Schneider, A., Stieber, J., Doring, A., & Lowel, H. (2002). Sex differences in risk factors for incident Type 2 diabetes mellitus: The MONICA Augsburg cohort study. *Archives of Internal Medicine, 162*, 82–89.

Mills, P. J., von Kanel, R., Norman, D., Natarajan, L., Ziegler, M., & Dimsdale, J. E. (2007). Inflammation and sleep in healthy individuals. *Sleep, 30*, 729–735.

Moldofsky, H., & Dickstein, J. B. (1999). Sleep and cytokine-immune functions in medical, psychiatric and primary sleep disorders. *Sleep Medicine Reviews, 3*, 325–337.

Moldofsky, H., Lue, F. A., Davidson, J. R., & Gorczynski, R. (1972). Effects of sleep deprivation on human immune functions. *Federation of the American Society of Experimental Biology Journal, 3*, 1972–1977.

Motivala, S. J., Sarfatti, A., Olmos, L., & Irwin, M. R. (2005). Inflammatory markers and sleep disturbance in major depression. *Psychosomatic Medicine, 67*, 187–194.

National Center on Sleep Disorders Research. (2003). *2003 National Sleep Disorders Research Plan* (03-5209). Bethesda, MD: U.S. Department of Health and Human Services.

Newman, A. B., Spiekerman, C. F., Enright, P., Lefkowitz, D., Manolio, T., Reynolds, C. F., & Robbins, J. (2000). Daytime sleepiness predicts mortality and cardiovascular disease in older adults: The Cardiovascular Health Study Research Group. *Journal of the American Geriatrics Society, 48*, 115–123.

Nilsson, P. M., Roost, M., Engstrom, G., Hedblad, B., & Berglund, G. (2004). Incidence of diabetes in middle-aged men is related to sleep disturbances. *Diabetes Care, 27*, 2464–2469.

Ohga, E., Nagase, T., Tomita, T., Teramoto, S., Matsuse, T., Katayama, H., & Ouchi, Y. (1999). Increased levels of circulating ICAM-1, VCAM-1, and L-selectin in obstructive sleep apnea syndrome. *Journal of Applied Physiology, 87*, 10–14.

Opp, M. R., Born, J., & Irwin, M. R. (2007). Sleep and the immune system. In R. Ader (Ed.), *Psychoneuroimmunology* (Vol. 1, pp. 579–618). New York: Elsevier Academic Press.

Opp, M. R., Rady, P. L., Hughes, T. K. J., Cadet, P., Tyring, S. K., & Smith, E. M. (1996). Human immunodeficiency virus envelope glycoprotein 120 alters sleep and induces cytokine mRNA expression in rats. *American Journal of Physiology—Regulatory, Integrative and Comparative Physiology, 270,* R963–R970.

Panagiotakos, D. B., Pitsavos, C., Chrysohoou, C., Tsetsekou, E., Papageorgiou, C., Christodoulou, G., & Stefanadis, C. (2004). Inflammation, coagulation, and depressive symptomatology in cardiovascular disease-free people: The ATTICA study. *European Heart Journal, 25,* 492–499.

Parati, G., Lombardi, C., & Narkiewicz, K. (2007). Sleep apnea: Epidemiology, pathophysiology, and relation to cardiovascular risk. *American Journal of Physiology—Regulatory, Integrative and Comparative Physiology, 293,* R1671–R1683.

Patruno, V., Aiolfi, S., Costantino, G., Murgia, R., Selmi, C., Malliani, A., & Montano, N. (2007). Fixed and autoadjusting continuous positive airway pressure treatments are not similar in reducing cardiovascular risk factors in patients with obstructive sleep apnea. *Chest, 131,* 1393–1399.

Phillips, B. (2005). Sleep-disordered breathing and cardiovascular disease. *Sleep Medicine Reviews, 9,* 131–140.

Pollmacher, T., Mullington, J., Korth, C., & Hinze-Selch, D. (1995). Influence of host defense activation on sleep in humans. *Advances in Neuroimmunology, 5,* 155–169.

Pradhan, A. D., Manson, J. E., Rifai, N., Buring, J. E., & Ridker, P. M. (2001). C-reactive protein, interleukin 6, and risk of developing Type 2 diabetes mellitus. *Journal of the American Medical Association, 286,* 327–334.

Punjabi, N. M., & Polotsky, V. Y. (1998). Disorders of glucose metabolism in sleep apnea. *Journal of Applied Physiology, 99,* 1998–2007.

Quan, S. F., Howard, B. V., Iber, C., Kiley, J. P., Nieto, F. J., O'Connor, G. T., et al. (1997). The Sleep Heart Health Study: Design, rationale, and methods. *Sleep, 20,* 1077–1085.

Redwine, L., Dang, J., Hall, M., & Irwin, M. (2003). Disordered sleep, nocturnal cytokines, and immunity in alcoholics. *Psychosomatic Medicine, 65,* 75–85.

Redwine, L., Dang, J., & Irwin, M. (2004). Cellular adhesion molecule expression, nocturnal sleep, and partial night sleep deprivation. *Brain, Behavior, and Immunity, 18,* 333–340.

Redwine, L., Hauger, R. L., Gillin, J. C., & Irwin, M. (2000). Effects of sleep and sleep deprivation on interleukin-6, growth hormone, cortisol, and melatonin levels in humans. *The Journal of Clinical Endocrinology & Metabolism, 85,* 3597–3603.

Reichmuth, K. J., Austin, D., Skatrud, J. B., & Young, T. (2005). Association of sleep apnea and Type II diabetes: A population-based study. *American Journal of Respiratory and Critical Care Medicine, 172,* 1590–1595.

Riha, R. L., Brander, P., Vennelle, M., McArdle, N., Kerr, S. M., Anderson, N. H., & Douglas, N. J. (2005). Tumour necrosis factor-alpha (-308) gene polymorphism in obstructive sleep apnoea-hypopnoea syndrome. *European Respiratory Journal, 26,* 673–678.

Ross, R. (1999). Atherosclerosis—An inflammatory disease. *The New England Journal of Medicine, 340,* 115–126.

Schwartz, S., Anderson, W. M., Cole, S. R., Cornoni-Huntley, J., Hays, J. C., & Blazer, D. (1999). Insomnia and heart disease: A review of epidemiologic studies. *Journal of Psychosomatic Research, 47,* 313–333.

Shahar, E., Whitney, C. W., Redline, S., Lee, E. T., Newman, A. B., Javier Nieto, F., et al. (2001). Sleep-disordered breathing and cardiovascular disease: Cross-sectional results of the Sleep Heart Health Study. *American Journal of Respiratory and Critical Care Medicine, 163,* 19–25.

Sleep Disorders Research Task Force. (2003). *2003 National Sleep Disorders Research Plan* (03-5209). Bethesda, MD: U.S. Department of Health and Human Services.

Spiegel, K., Knutson, K., Leproult, R., Tasali, E., & Van Cauter, E. (2005). Sleep loss: A novel risk factor for insulin resistance and Type 2 diabetes. *Journal of Applied Physiology, 99,* 2008–2019.

Suarez, E. C. (2004). C-reactive protein is associated with psychologic risk factors of cardiovascular disease in apparently healthy adults. *Psychosomatic Medicine, 66,* 684–691.

Sundquist, K., & Li, X. (2006). Alcohol abuse partly mediates the association between coronary heart disease and affective or psychotic disorders: A follow-up study in Sweden. *Acta Psychiatrica Scandinavica, 113,* 283–289.

Taheri, S., Austin, D., Lin, L., Nieto, F. J., Young, T., & Mignot, E. (2007). Correlates of serum C-reactive protein (C-REACTIVE PROTEIN)—No association with sleep duration or sleep disordered breathing. *Sleep, 30,* 991–996.

Tazaki, T., Minoguchi, K., Yokoe, T., Samson, K., Minoguchi, H., Tanaka, A., et al. (2004). Increased levels and activity of matrix metallopoteinase-9 in obstructive sleep apnea syndrome. *American Journal of Respiratory and Critical Care Medicine, 170,* 1354–1359.

Uthgennant, D., Schoolmann, D., Pietrowsky, R., Fehm, H., & Born, J. (1995). Effects of sleep on the production of cytokines in humans. *Psychosomatic Medicine, 57,* 97–104.

Vgontzas, A. N., Bixler, E. O., & Chrousos, G. (2003). Metabolic disturbances in obesity verus sleep apnoea: The importance of visceral obesity and insulin resistance. *Journal of Internal Medicine, 254,* 32–44.

Vgontzas, A. N., Papanicolaou, D. A., Bixler, E. O., Hopper, K., Lotsikas, A., Lin, H. M., et al. (2000). Sleep apnea and daytime sleepiness and fatigue: Relation to visceral obesity, insulin resistance, and hypercytokinemia. *The Journal of Clinical Endocrinology & Metabolism, 85,* 1151–1158.

Vgontzas, A. N., Papanicolaou, D. A., Bixler, E. O., Lotsikas, A., Zachman, K., Kales, A., et al. (1999). Circadian interleukin-6 secretion and quantity and depth of sleep. *The Journal of Clinical Endocrinology & Metabolism, 84,* 2603–2607.

Vgontzas, A. N., Zoumakis, E., Lin, H. M., Bixler, E. O., Trakada, G., & Chrousos, G. P. (2004). Marked decrease in sleepiness in patients with sleep apnea by etanercept, a tumor necrosis factor-alpha antagonist. *The Journal of Clinical Endocrinology & Metabolism, 89,* 4409–4413.

Vgontzas, A. N., Zoumakis, M., Papanicolaou, D. A., Bixler, E. O., Prolo, P., Lin, H. M., et al. (2002). Chronic insomnia is associated with a shift of interleukin-6 and tumor necrosis factor secretion from nighttime to daytime. *Metabolism: Clinical and Experimental, 51,* 887–892.

Walsleben, J. A., Kapur, V. K., Newman, A. B., Shahar, E., Bootzin, R. R., Rosenberg, C. E., et al. (2004). Sleep and reported daytime sleepiness in normal subjects: The Sleep Heart Health Study. *Sleep, 27,* 293–298.

White, J. L., Darko, D. F., Brown, S. J., Miller, J. C., Hayduk, R., Kelly, T., & Mitler, M. M. (1995). Early central nervous system response to HIV infection: Sleep distortion and cognitive-motor decrements. *AIDS, 9,* 1043–1050.

Wingard, D. L., & Berkman, L. F. (1983). Mortality risk associated with sleeping patterns among adults. *Sleep, 6,* 102–107.

Wong, M. L., Bongiorno, P. B., Rettori, V., McCann, S. M., & Licinio, J. (1997). Interleukin (IL) 1beta, IL-1 receptor antagonist, IL-10, and IL-13 gene expression in the central nervous system and anterior pituitary during systemic inflammation: Pathophysiological implications. *Proceedings of the National Academy of Sciences USA, 94,* 227–232.

Yaggi, H. K., Araujo, A. B., & McKinlay, J. B. (2006). Sleep duration as a risk factor for the development of Type 2 diabetes. *Diabetes Care, 29,* 657–661.

Yokoe, T., Minoguchi, H., Matsuo, H., Oda, N., Minoguchi, H., Yoshino, G., et al. (2003). Elevated levels of C-reactive protein and interleukin-6 in patients with obstructive sleep apnea syndrome are decreased by nasal continuous positive airway pressure. *Circulation, 107,* 1129–1134.

Young, T., Palta, M., Dempsey, M., Skatrud, J., Weber, S., & Badr, S. (1993). The occurrence of sleep-disordered breathing among middle-aged adults. *The New England Journal of Medicine, 328,* 1230–1235.

Young, T., Peppard, P., Palta, M., Hla, K. M., Finn, L., Morgan, B., & Skatrud, J. (1997). Population-based study of sleep-disordered breathing and hypertension. *Archives of Internal Medicine, 157,* 1746–1752.

4

POLYUNSATURATED FATTY ACIDS, INFLAMMATION, AND INFLAMMATORY DISEASES

PHILIP C. CALDER

There has been a great deal of research in recent years regarding the biological processes by which fatty acids influence inflammation. The findings indicate one connection between the human diet and many common chronic conditions, including arthritis, inflammatory bowel diseases, asthma, multiple sclerosis, and neurodegeneration. Studies indicate that increased intake of certain fatty acids, such as those found in fish oils, may help to reduce inflammation and thereby reduce symptoms associated with these chronic diseases.

In this chapter, the variety of fatty acids in the human diet is described, along with naming conventions and the metabolic relationships between the different types. Next, the effects of omega-3 (n-3) polyunsaturated fatty acids (PUFAs) on several components of the inflammatory process are described. These components include leukocyte chemotaxis (i.e., the process of movement of cells toward a site of inflammatory activity in response to chemicals released at that site). The second component is expression of adhesion molecules that allow leukocytes to interact with the endothelium and so to move from the bloodstream into tissue sites of inflammatory activity.

The final component is production of the classic inflammatory cytokines, such as tumor necrosis factor-α (TNF-α), interleukin-1β (IL-1β), and IL-6, and of the classic inflammatory lipid mediators such as prostaglandin (PG) E$_2$ and the 4-series leukotrienes (LTs). In addition, other fatty acid–derived mediators, such as resolvins and mechanisms of action not involving lipid mediators, are described. Finally, the efficacy of omega-3 PUFAs in selected human inflammatory diseases is discussed.[1]

FATTY ACID STRUCTURE, NOMENCLATURE, SOURCES, INTAKES, AND ROLES

Fatty acids are hydrocarbon chains with a carboxyl group at one end and a methyl group at the other. The carboxyl group is reactive and readily forms ester links with alcohol groups. For example, esterification to glycerol or cholesterol in turn forms acylglycerols (e.g., triacylglycerols, phospholipids) and cholesteryl esters, respectively. The most abundant fatty acids have straight chains of an even number of carbon atoms.

Fatty acid chain lengths vary from 2 to 30 or more, and the chain may contain double bonds. Fatty acids containing double bonds in the acyl chain are referred to as *unsaturated fatty acids*. A fatty acid containing two or more double bonds is called a *polyunsaturated fatty acid*. Saturated fatty acids do not contain double bonds in the acyl chain. The systematic name for a fatty acid is determined simply by the number of carbons and the number of double bonds in the acyl chain (see Table 4.1). However, complications arise in the naming of unsaturated fatty acids because there are multiple possibilities for the position of double bonds within the hydrocarbon chain and because each double bond may be in the *cis* or *trans* configuration. Therefore, when an unsaturated fatty acid is named, it is important that the exact positions of double bonds and their configurations be clearly identified.

The position of double bonds was traditionally identified by naming the carbon number (from carbon 1 [the carboxyl carbon]) on which each double bond occurs. Thus, octadecadienoic acid, an 18-carbon fatty acid with *cis* double bonds between carbons 9 and 10 and carbons 12 and 13, is correctly denoted as *cis* 9, *cis* 12-octadecadienoic acid, or *cis*, *cis*, 9,12-octadecadienoic acid. More recently, an alternative shorthand notation for fatty acids has come into frequent use. This method relies on identifying the number of carbon atoms in the chain, and the number of double bonds and their position. Thus, octadecanoic acid is notated as 18:0, indicating that it has an acyl chain of 18 carbons and does not contain any double bonds. Unsatur-

---

[1]This chapter does not describe the effects of omega-3 fatty acids on dendritic cell or T cell functional activities; recent reviews dealing with this are available (Calder, 2007; Calder, Yaqoob, Thies, Wallace, & Miles, 2002; Yaqoob & Calder, 2007).

TABLE 4.1
Fatty Acid Nomenclature

Systematic name	Trivial name	Shorthand notation
Octanoic	Caprylic	8:0
Decanoic	Capric	10:0
Dodecanoic	Lauric	12:0
Tetradecanoic	Myrsitic	14:0
Hexadecanoic	Palmitic	16:0
Octadecanoic	Stearic	18:0
cis 9-Hexadecenoic	Palmitoleic	16:1n-7
cis 9-Octadecenoic	Oleic	18:1n-9
cis 9, *cis* 12-Octadecadienoic	Linoleic	18:2n-6
All *cis* 9, 12, 15-Octadecatrienoic	α-Linolenic	18:3n-3
All *cis* 6, 9, 12-Octadecatrienoic	γ-Linolenic	18:3n-6
All *cis* 8, 11, 14-Eicosatrienoic	Dihomo-γ-linolenic	20:3n-6
All *cis* 5, 8, 11, 14-Eicosatetraenoic	Arachidonic	20:4n-6
All *cis* 5, 8, 11, 14, 17-Eicosapentaenoic	Eicosapentaenoic	20:5n-3
All *cis* 7, 10, 13, 16, 19-Docosapentaenoic	Docosapentaenoic	22:5n-3
All *cis* 4, 7, 10, 13, 16, 19-Docosahexaenoic	Docosahexaenoic	22:6n-3

ated fatty acids are named simply by identifying the number of double bonds and the position of the first double bond counted from the methyl terminus (with the methyl, or ω, carbon as number 1) of the acyl chain. The way the first double bond is identified is as ω-x, where x is the carbon number on which the double bond occurs. Therefore, *cis*, *cis*, 9,12-octadecadienoic acid is also known as 18:2ω-6. The ω-x nomenclature is sometimes referred to as omega x (e.g., 18:2 omega-6) or n-x (e.g., 18:2n-6). In addition to these nomenclatures, fatty acids are often described by their common names (see Table 4.1). Figure 4.1 shows the structure of several 18-carbon fatty acids indicating the position of the double bonds in the chain and how this is reflected in their naming. Most common unsaturated fatty acids contain *cis* rather than *trans* double bonds. *Trans* double bonds do occur, however, as intermediates in the biosynthesis of fatty acids in ruminant fats (e.g., cow's milk), in plant lipids, and in some seed oils.

There are two principal families of PUFAs: the omega-6 (or n-6) and the omega-3 . The simplest members of each family, linoleic acid (LA; 18:2n-6) and α-linolenic acid (ALA; 18:3n-3), cannot be synthesized by mammals. LA is found in significant quantities in many vegetable oils, including corn, sunflower, and soybean oils, and in products made from such oils, such as margarines (Burdge & Calder, 2004). ALA is found in green plant tissues, in some common vegetable oils, including soybean and rapeseed oils, in some nuts, and in flaxseed (also known as linseed) and flaxseed oil. Between them, LA and ALA contribute over 95%, and perhaps as much as 98%, of dietary

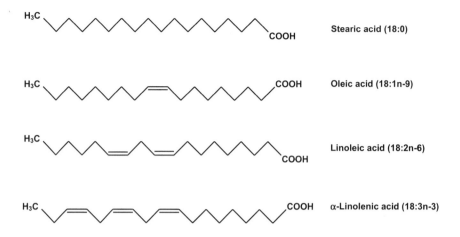

Figure 4.1. The structure and naming of selected 18 carbon fatty acids.

PUFA intake in most Western diets (Burdge & Calder, 2004). The intake of LA in Western countries increased greatly in the second half of the 20th century, following the introduction and marketing of cooking oils and margarines. Typical intakes of both essential fatty acids are in excess of requirements. However, the changed pattern of consumption of LA has resulted in a marked increase in the ratio of omega-6 to omega-3 PUFAs in the diet. This ratio is typically between 5 and 20 in most Western populations (Burdge & Calder, 2004, 2006).

Although LA and ALA cannot be synthesized by humans, they can be metabolized to other fatty acids (see Figure 4.1). This is achieved by the insertion of additional double bonds into the acyl chain (i.e., unsaturation) and by elongation of the acyl chain. Thus, LA can be converted via γ-linolenic acid (GLA; 18:3n-6) and dihomo-γ-linolenic acid (DGLA; 20:3n-6) to arachidonic acid (AA; 20:4n-6; see Figure 4.2). By an analogous set of reactions catalyzed by the same enzymes, ALA can be converted to eicosapentaenoic acid (EPA; 20:5n-3). Both AA and EPA can be further metabolized: EPA gives rise to docosapentaenoic acid (22:5n-3) and docosahexaenoic acid (DHA; 22:6n-3; see Figure 4.2).

Dietary intakes of the longer chain, more unsaturated PUFAs are much, much lower than those of LA and ALA. Some plant oils contain GLA, DGLA, and stearidonic acid (18:4n-3), but typical intakes of these fatty acids from the diet are likely to be less than 10 mg/day. AA is found in meat and offal, and intakes are estimated at 50 to 500 mg/day (Burdge & Calder, 2004). EPA, docosapentaenoic acid, and DHA are found in fish, especially so-called oily fish (e.g., tuna, salmon, mackerel, herring, sardine). One oily fish meal can provide between 1.5 and 3.5 g of these long-chain omega-3 PUFAs (British Nutrition Foundation, 1999).

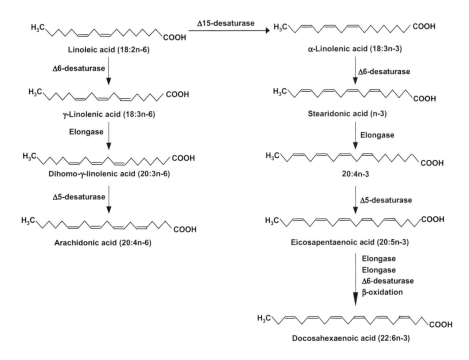

Figure 4.2. The biosynthesis of polyunsaturated fatty acids.

The commercial products known as fish oils also contain these long-chain omega-3 PUFAs, which typically contribute about 30% of the fatty acids present. Thus, consumption of a typical 1-gram fish oil capsule/day can provide about 300 mg of these fatty acids. In the absence of oily fish or fish oil consumption, intake of long-chain omega-3 PUFAs is likely to be less than 100 mg/day (British Nutrition Foundation, 1999; Burdge & Calder, 2004), although foods fortified with these fatty acids are now available in many countries.

PUFAs are important constituents of cells, where they play roles ensuring the correct environment for membrane protein function, maintaining membrane fluidity, and regulating cell signaling, gene expression, and cellular function (Burdge & Calder, 2004). In addition, some PUFAs, particularly AA, act as substrates for synthesis of eicosanoids, which are involved in regulation of many cell and tissue responses (see later discussion).

ARACHIDONIC ACID–DERIVED EICOSANOIDS AND INFLAMMATION

The key link between fatty acids and inflammation is that the eicosanoid family of inflammatory mediators is generated from 20-carbon PUFAs. Be-

TABLE 4.2
Pro- and Anti-Inflammatory Effects of PGE$_2$ and LTB$_4$

PGE$_2$	LTB$_4$
Proinflammatory	Proinflammatory
Induces fever	Increases vascular permeability
Increases vascular permeability	Enhances local blood flow
Increases vasodilatation	Chemotactic agent for leukocytes
Causes pain	Induces release of lysosomal enzymes
Enhances pain caused by other agents	Induces release of reactive oxygen species by granulocytes
Increases production of IL-6	Increases production of TNF, IL-1, and IL-6
Anti-inflammatory	
Inhibits production of TNF and IL-1	
Inhibits 5-LOX (decreases 4-series LT production)	
Induces 15-LOX (increases lipoxin production)	

Note. IL = interleukin; TNF = tumor necrosis factor; LOX = lipoxygenase; LT = leukotriene. From "n-3 Polyunsaturated Fatty Acids, Inflammation, and Inflammatory Diseases," by P. C. Calder, 2006, *American Journal of Clinical Nutrition, 83*(Suppl.), p. 1507S. Copyright 2006 by the American Society for Nutrition. Reprinted with permission.

cause inflammatory cells typically contain a high proportion of the omega-6 PUFA AA and low proportions of other 20-carbon PUFAs, AA is usually the major substrate for eicosanoid synthesis. Eicosanoids, which include PG, thromboxanes (TXs), LT, and other oxidized derivatives, are generated from AA by the metabolic processes summarized in Figure 4.3. Eicosanoids are involved in modulating the intensity and duration of inflammatory responses (see Lewis, Austen, & Soberman, 1990; Tilley, Coffman, & Koller, 2001, for reviews), have cell- and stimulus-specific sources, and frequently have opposing effects (see Table 4.2). Thus, the overall physiological (or pathophysiological) outcome will depend on the cells present, the nature of the stimulus, the timing of eicosanoid generation, the concentrations of different eicosanoids generated, and the sensitivity of target cells and tissues to the eicosanoids generated. Studies have demonstrated that PGE$_2$ induces cyclooxygenase-2 (COX-2) in fibroblast cells and so up-regulates its own production (Bagga, Wang, Farias-Eisner, Glaspy, & Reddy, 2003), induces production of IL-6 by macrophages (Bagga et al., 2003), inhibits 5-lipoxygenase (5-LOX) and so decreases production of 4-series LT (Levy et al, 2001), and induces 15-LOX and so promotes the formation of lipoxins (Levy, Clish, Schmidt, Gronert, & Serhan, 2001; Vachier et al., 2002) that have been found to have anti-inflammatory effects (Gewirtz et al., 2002; Serhan et al., 2003). Thus, PGE$_2$ possesses both pro- and anti-inflammatory actions (see Table 4.2).

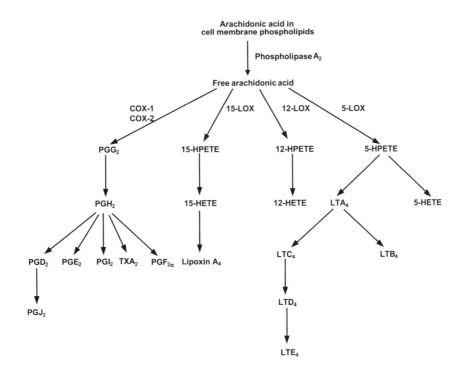

Figure 4.3. Outline of the pathway of eicosanoid synthesis from arachidonic acid. COX = cyclooxygenase; LOX = lipoxygenase; HPETE = hydroperoxyeicosatetraenoic acid; HETE = hydroxyeicosatetraenoic acid; LT = leukotriene; PG = prostaglandin; TX = thromboxane. From "n-3 Polyunsaturated Fatty Acids, Inflammation, and Inflammatory Diseases," by P. C. Calder, 2006 *American Journal of Clinical Nutrition, 83*(Suppl.), p. 1507S. Copyright 2006 by the American Society for Nutrition. Reprinted with permission.

ARACHIDONIC ACID AND INFLAMMATORY MEDIATOR PRODUCTION

Animal feeding studies have shown a strong positive relationship between the amount of AA in inflammatory cells and the ability of those cells to produce eicosanoids such as PGE_2 (Peterson et al., 1998). In turn, the amount of AA in inflammatory cells can be increased by including it in the diet (Peterson et al., 1998; Thies, Nebe-von-Caron, et al., 2001). The amount of AA in inflammatory cells may also be influenced by the dietary intake of its precursor, LA, although the range of LA intake over which this relationship occurs has not been defined for humans. Increasing LA intake by 6.5 g/day in humans habitually consuming 10 to 15 g/day did not alter the AA content of blood mononuclear cells (Yaqoob, Pala, Cortina-Borja, Newsholme, & Calder, 2000). Nevertheless, the role of AA as a precursor for the synthesis of eicosanoids indicates the potential for dietary omega-6 PUFA (LA or AA) to influence inflammatory processes.

Supplementation of the diet of healthy young male participants with 1.5 g AA/day for 7 weeks resulted in a marked increase in production of PGE_2 and LTB_4 by endotoxin-stimulated mononuclear cells, although production of the inflammatory cytokines TNF-α, IL-1β, and IL-6 was not significantly altered (Kelley, Taylor, Nelson, & Mackey, 1998). Thus, increased AA intake may result in changes indicative of selectively increased inflammation or inflammatory responses in humans. Supplementation of the diet of healthy elderly participants with AA (0.7 g/day in addition to a habitual intake of about 0.15 g/day) for 12 weeks did not affect endotoxin-stimulated production of TNF-α, IL-1β, or IL-6 by mononuclear cells and did not alter plasma soluble adhesion molecule concentrations (Thies, Miles, et al., 2001). This lack of effect occurred despite incorporation of AA into target cells (Thies, Nebe-von-Caron, et al., 2001). Taken together, these studies suggest that modestly increased intake of AA results in incorporation of AA into cells involved in inflammatory responses, but incorporation of AA into cells does not affect production of inflammatory cytokines or shedding of adhesion molecules, although production of inflammatory eicosanoids is increased.

LONG-CHAIN OMEGA-3 POLYUNSATURATED FATTY ACIDS AND INFLAMMATORY EICOSANOID PRODUCTION

Increased consumption of long-chain omega-3 PUFAs, such as EPA and DHA, results in increased proportions of those fatty acids in inflammatory cell phospholipids (Caughey, Mantzioris, Gibson, Cleland, & James, 1996; Endres et al., 1989; Gibney & Hunter, 1993; Healy, Wallace, Miles, Calder, & Newsholme, 2000; Lee et al., 1985; Peterson et al., 1998; Sperling et al., 1993; Thies, Nebe-von-Caron, et al., 2001; Wallace, Neely, Miles, & Calder, 2000; Yaqoob et al., 2000). The incorporation of EPA and DHA into human inflammatory cells occurs in a dose–response fashion and is partly at the expense of AA. Because less substrate is available for synthesis of eicosanoids from AA, fish oil supplementation of the human diet has been shown to result in decreased production of PGE_2 (Caughey et al., 1996; Endres et al., 1989; Meydani et al., 1991; Trebble, Wootton, et al., 2003), TXB_2, LTB_4 (Lee et al., 1985; Sperling et al., 1993), 5-hydroxyeicosatetraenoic acid (Lee et al., 1985; Sperling et al., 1993), and LTE_4 (VonSchacky, Kiefl, Jendraschak, & Kaminski, 1993) by inflammatory cells. Although these studies used fish oil, Kelley et al. (1999) demonstrated that 6 g DHA/day resulted in decreased production of PGE_2 (by 60%) and LTB_4 (by 75%) by endotoxin-stimulated mononuclear cells. The reduction in generation of AA-derived mediators that accompanies fish oil consumption has led to the idea that fish oil is anti-inflammatory.

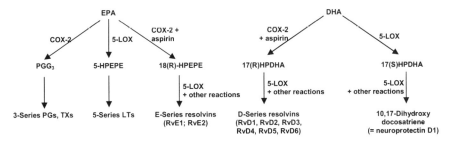

Figure 4.4. Outline of the pathway of synthesis of resolvins and related mediators from eicosapentaenoic acid (EPA) and docosahexaenoic acid (DHA). COX = cyclooxygenase; LOX = lipoxygenase; PG = prostaglandin; HPEPE = hydroperoxy-eicosapentaenoic acid; HPDHA = hydroperoxydocosahexaenoic acid; TX = thromboxane; LT = leukotriene; Rv = resolving.

EPA is also able to act as a substrate for both COX and 5-LOX, giving rise to eicosanoids with a slightly different structure than that of those formed from AA (see Figure 4.4). Thus, fish oil supplementation of the human diet has been shown to result in increased production of LTB$_5$, LTE$_5$, and 5-hydroxyeicosapentaenoic acid by inflammatory cells (Lee et al., 1985; Sperling et al., 1993; Von Schacky et al., 1993), although generation of PGE$_3$ has been more difficult to demonstrate. The functional significance of the production of eicosanoids with different structures is that those formed from EPA are believed to be less potent than those formed from AA. For example, LTB$_5$ is 10- to 100-fold less potent as a neutrophil chemotactic agent than LTB$_4$ (Goldman, Pickett, & Goetzl, 1983; Lee et al., 1984). Recent studies have compared the effects of PGE$_2$ and PGE$_3$ on production of cytokines by cell lines and by human cells. Bagga et al. (2003) reported that PGE$_3$ was a less potent inducer of COX-2 gene expression in fibroblasts and of IL-6 production by macrophages. However, PGE$_2$ and PGE$_3$ had equivalent inhibitory effects on production of TNF-α (Dooper, Wassink, M'Rabet, & Graus, 2002; Miles, Allen, & Calder, 2002) and IL-1β (Miles et al., 2002) by human mononuclear cells stimulated with endotoxin.

In addition to long-chain omega-3 PUFAs modulating the generation of eicosanoids from AA, and to EPA acting as substrate for the generation of alternative eicosanoids, recent studies have identified a novel group of mediators, termed *E-series resolvins*, formed from EPA by COX-2 and 5-LOX (see Figure 4.4) that appear to exert anti-inflammatory actions (Serhan, Clish, Brannon, Colgan, Chiang, & Gronert, 2000; Serhan, Clish, Brannon, Colgan, Gronert, & Chiang, 2000; Serhan et al., 2002). In addition, DHA-derived mediators termed *D-series resolvins*, *docosatrienes*, and *neuroprotectins*, also produced by COX-2, and 5-LOX (see Figure 4.4) have been identified, and these too appear to be anti-inflammatory (Hong, Gronert, Devchand, Moussignac, & Serhan, 2003; Marcheselli et al., 2003; Mukherjee, Marcheselli, Serhan,

& Bazan, 2004). This is an exciting new area of research into omega-3 fatty acids and inflammatory mediators because the discovery of resolvins and related molecules indicates an entirely novel mechanism by which omega-3 PUFAs are anti-inflammatory. Furthermore, the implications for a variety of conditions may be of great importance because the potency of resolvins is high, at least in the experimental systems in which they are examined. This area has been reviewed recently (Serhan, 2005; Serhan, Arita, Hong, & Gotlinger, 2004).

ANTI-INFLAMMATORY EFFECTS OF LONG-CHAIN OMEGA-3 POLYUNSATURATED FATTY ACIDS OTHER THAN ALTERED EICOSANOID PRODUCTION

Although their action in antagonizing AA metabolism is a key anti-inflammatory effect of omega-3 PUFAs, these fatty acids have a number of other anti-inflammatory effects that might be independent of this mechanism. For example, studies have shown that, when consumed in sufficient quantities, dietary fish oil results in decreased leukocyte chemotaxis, decreased production of reactive oxygen species and proinflammatory cytokines, and decreased adhesion molecule expression (see Table 4.3).

Long-Chain Omega-3 Polyunsaturated Fatty Acids and Leukocyte Chemotaxis

Chemotaxis is the process by which leukocytes move toward a site of inflammatory activity in response to the release of chemicals at that site. Such chemicals are termed *chemoattractants* and include the AA-derived eicosanoid LTB_4. A number of dietary supplementation studies that used between 3.1 and 14.4 g EPA+DHA/day have demonstrated a time-dependent decrease in chemotaxis of human neutrophils and monocytes toward various chemoattractants, including LTB_4, bacterial peptides, and human serum (Endres et al., 1989; Lee et al., 1985; Luostarinen, Siegbahn, & Saldeen, 1992; Schmidt et al., 1989, 1992; Sperling et al., 1993). Both the distance of cell migration and the number of cells migrating were decreased. Despite the high dose of long-chain omega-3 PUFAs used in these studies, a dose–response study by Schmidt et al. (1991) suggests that near-maximum inhibition of chemotaxis occurs at an intake of 1.3 g EPA + DHA/day. A lower intake (0.55 g EPA + DHA/day) did not affect monocyte chemotaxis (Schmidt et al., 1996). However, Healy et al. (2000) did not find an effect of several doses of fish oil providing up to 2.25 g EPA + DHA/day on neutrophil chemotaxis. The apparently divergent reports of Schmidt et al. (1996) and Healy et al. (2000) could be explained by the fact that the latter study used a low-EPA/high-DHA fish oil such that the highest dose provided 0.58 g EPA/day, which is less than the amount of EPA provided by the lowest dose of fish oil

TABLE 4.3
Summary of the Anti-Inflammatory Effects of Long-Chain
Omega-3 Fatty Acids

Anti-inflammatory effect	Mechanism(s) likely to be involved
Decreased generation of arachidonic acid-derived eicosanoids (many with inflammatory actions)	Decreased arachidonic acid in cell membrane phospholipids Inhibition of arachidonic acid metabolism Decreased induction of COX-2, 5-LOX, and 5-LOX activating protein
Increased generation of EPA-derived eicosanoids (many with less inflammatory and some with anti-inflammatory actions)	Increased cell membrane phospholipid content of EPA
Increased generation of EPA- and DHA-derived resolvins (some with anti-inflammatory actions)	Increased cell membrane phospholipid content of EPA and DHA
Decreased generation of inflammatory cytokines (TNF-α, IL-1β, IL-6, IL-8)	Decreased activation of NFκB (via decreased phosphorylation of IκB) Activation of PPARγ Altered activity of other transcription factors Differential effects of arachidonic acid- vs. EPA-derived eicosanoids
Decreased expression of adhesion molecules	Decreased activation of NFκB (via decreased phosphorylation of IκB) Altered activity of other transcription factors
Decreased leukocyte chemotaxis	Not clear; perhaps decreased expression of receptors for some chemoattractants
Decreased generation of reactive oxygen species	Not clear; perhaps altered membrane composition affecting signaling processes

Note. COX = cyclooxygenase; LOX = lipoxygenase; EPA = eicosapentaenoic acid; DHA = docosahexaenoic acid; TNF = tumor necrosis factor; NFκB = nuclear factor κB; IκB = inhibitory subunit of NFκB; IL = interleukin; PPAR = peroxisome proliferators activated receptor. From "n-3 Polyunsaturated Fatty Acids, Inflammation, and Inflammatory Diseases," by P. C. Calder, 2006, *American Journal of Clinical Nutrition, 83*(Suppl.), p. 1509S. Copyright 2006 by the American Society for Nutrition. Reprinted with permission.

used by Schmidt et al. If this difference in EPA content is the reason for the different findings of these studies, then the antichemotactic effects of fish oil might be due to EPA rather than DHA.

Long-Chain Omega-3 Polyunsaturated Fatty Acids and Adhesion Molecule Expression

Adhesion molecules are proteins that are expressed on the surface of endothelial cells and leukocytes. These molecules form ligand pairs that promote interaction between the different cell types. It is through these interactions that leukocytes in the bloodstream interact with the blood vessel wall and then leave the bloodstream to move to a site of inflammatory activity. Note that this process will also involve the release of chemoattractants at that site. Cell culture (Collie-Duguid & Wahle, 1996; De Caterina, Cybulsky, Clinton, Gimbrone, & Libby, 1994; De Caterina & Libby, 1996; Hughes, Southon, & Pinder, 1996) and animal feeding studies (Miles, Wallace, & Calder, 2000) have reported decreased expression of some adhesion molecules on the surface of monocytes (Hughes et al., 1996), macrophages (Miles et al., 2000), and endothelial cells (Collie-Duguid & Wahle, 1996; DeCaterina et al., 1994; DeCaterina & Libby, 1996) following exposure to long-chain omega-3 PUFAs. Supplementing the diet of healthy humans with fish oil providing about 1.5 g EPA + DHA/day resulted in a lower level of expression of intercellular adhesion molecule-1 on the surface of blood monocytes stimulated ex vivo with interferon-γ (Hughes, Pinder, Piper, Johnson, & Lund, 1996). Dietary fish oil providing 1.1 g EPA + DHA/day was found to decrease circulating levels of soluble vascular cell adhesion molecule-1 in elderly participants (Miles et al., 2001). But it is not clear whether this result represents decreased surface expression of this protein.

Long-Chain Omega-3 Polyunsaturated Fatty Acids and Reactive Oxygen Species Production

Reactive oxygen species such as superoxide can damage host tissues and so can directly contribute to inflammation. In addition, reactive oxygen species can upregulate other aspects of the inflammatory response (e.g., production of inflammatory cytokines) and so they act to amplify inflammatory processes. Supplementation studies providing 3.1 to 8.4 g EPA+DHA/day have reported 30% to 55% decreases in the production of reactive oxygen species (superoxide or hydrogen peroxide, or both) by stimulated human neutrophils (Luostarinen & Saldeen, 1996; Thompson, Misso, Passarelli, & Phillips, 1991; Varming et al., 1995). Supplementation with 6 g EPA + DHA/day decreased hydrogen peroxide production by human monocytes (Fisher et al., 1990). Studies using lower doses of long-chain omega-3 PUFAs (0.55 to 2.3 g/day) failed to demonstrate effects on reactive oxygen species production by either neutrophils (Healy et al., 2000; Kew et al., 2003; Miles et al., 2004; Thies, Miles, et al., 2001) or monocytes (Schmidt et al., 1996). Halvorsen et al. (1997) reported that 3.8 g of either EPA or DHA/day did not affect production of hydrogen peroxide by human monocytes. This lack of effect might relate either to the different stimulus used in this study (*Escherichia coli*) compared with the other "high-dose" study with monocytes (latex beads; Fisher et al., 1990) or to the fact that 3.8 g long-chain omega-3 PUFA/day is below and 6 g/day is above the threshold that affects hydrogen peroxide production by monocytes.

Long-Chain Omega-3 Polyunsaturated Fatty Acids and Inflammatory Cytokine Production

Cell culture studies demonstrate that EPA and DHA can inhibit the production of IL-1β and TNF-α by monocytes (Babcock et al., 2002) and the production of IL-6 and IL-8 by venous endothelial cells (De Caterina et al., 1994; Khalfoun, Thibault, Watier, Bardos, & Lebranchu, 1997). Fish oil feeding decreased ex vivo production of TNF-α, IL-1β, and IL-6 by rodent macrophages (Billiar et al., 1988; Renier, Skamene, de Sanctis, & Radzioch, 1993; Yaqoob & Calder, 1995). Supplementation of the diet of healthy human volunteers with fish oil providing more than 2 g EPA + DHA/day decreased production of either TNF or IL-1 or IL-6 by mononuclear cells in some studies (Abbate et al., 1996; Caughey et al., 1996; Endres et al., 1989; Gallai et al., 1993; Meydani et al., 1991; Trebble, Arden, et al., 2003). Caughey et al. (1996) reported a significant inverse correlation between the EPA content of mononuclear cells and the ability of those cells to produce TNF-α and IL-1β in response to endotoxin. Kelley et al. (1999) showed that 6 g DHA/day for 12 weeks resulted in decreased production of TNF-α (by 20%) and IL-1β (by 35%) by endotoxin-stimulated mononuclear cells.

Thus, although most studies have used fish oil, it appears that both EPA (Caughey et al., 1996) and DHA (Kelley et al., 1999) are able to decrease inflammatory cytokine production. This assumption was confirmed by a study in which participants with Type 2 diabetes were given 4 g EPA or DHA/day for 6 weeks (Mori et al., 2003). Both EPA and DHA resulted in decreased plasma TNF-α concentrations, although DHA was more potent (35% reduction vs. 20% for EPA). It should be noted that several studies failed to show effects of dietary long-chain omega-3 PUFAs on production of inflammatory cytokines in humans. Some of these studies provided less than 2 g EPA + DHA/day (Cooper, Gibbins, Horan, Little, & Rothwell, 1993; Kew et al., 2003; Schmidt et al., 1996; Thies, Miles, et al., 2001; Wallace, Miles, & Calder, 2003), although others provided higher doses (Blok et al., 1997; Cannon et al., 1995; Kew et al., 2004; Miles et al., 2004; Molvig et al., 1991; Yaqoob et al., 2000). The reason for these discrepancies in the literature is unclear, but technical factors are likely to be contributing factors (Calder, 2001a). The relative contributions of EPA and DHA might also be important in determining the effect of fish oil.

One other factor that has been identified is polymorphisms in genes affecting cytokine production (Grimble et al., 2002). It was found that the effect of dietary fish oil on cytokine production by human mononuclear cells was dependent on the nature of the −308 TNF-α and the +252 TNF-β polymorphisms. This study raises the possibility of being able to identify those who are more likely and those who are less likely to experience specific antiinflammatory effects of fish oil.

Effect of Omega-3 Polyunsaturated Fatty Acids on Inflammatory Gene Expression

Many of the effects of omega-3 PUFAs on inflammatory mediator production appear to be related to altered expression of genes encoding those mediators. For example, de Caterina et al. (1994) demonstrated that the down-regulation of VCAM-1 expression on endothelial cells caused by DHA was exerted at the level of VCAM-1 gene expression and that this effect was independent of effects on eicosanoid production and on antioxidant status. Inclusion of fish oil in the diet completely abolished mRNA for TNF-α, IL-1β, and IL-6 in the kidneys of autoimmune-disease-prone mice (Chandresekar & Fernandes, 1994). Feeding mice a diet rich in fish oil significantly decreased the level of IL-1β mRNA in lipopolysaccharide- or phorbol-ester-stimulated spleen lymphocytes (Robinson et al., 1996); the lower IL-1β mRNA level was due not to accelerated degradation but to impaired synthesis. Fish oil feeding to mice lowered basal and lipopolysaccharide-stimulated TNF-α mRNA levels in peritoneal macrophages (Renier et al., 1993).

The effects of omega-3 PUFAs on inflammatory gene expression suggest that they might act in a way that modifies the activity of transcription factors, most likely NFκB or PPAR-γ, or both. NFκB is activated as a result of a signaling cascade triggered by extracellular inflammatory stimuli and involving phosphorylation of an inhibitory subunit (inhibitory subunit of NFκB [IκB]), which then allows translocation of the remaining NFκB dimer to the nucleus (Perkins, 2007). EPA prevented NFκB activation in response to TNF-α in cultured pancreatic cells, an effect that involved decreased degradation of IκB through decreased phosphorylation (Ross, Moses, & Fearon, 1999). Similarly, EPA or fish oil decreased lipopolysaccharide-induced activation of NFκB in cultured human monocytes (Lo, Chiu, Fu, Lo, & Helton, 1999; Novak, Babcock, Jho, Helton, & Espat, 2003; Zhao, Joshi-Barve, Barve, & Chen, 2004). and this was associated with decreased IκB phosphorylation (Novak et al., 2003; Zhao et al., 2004), perhaps because of decreased activation of mitogen-activated protein kinases (Lo, Chiu, Fu, Chu, & Helton, 2000). These observations suggest direct effects of omega-3 PUFAs on inflammatory gene expression via inhibition of activation of the transcription factor NFκB, although it is not entirely clear which site in the activation cascade they target.

The second transcription factor, PPAR-γ, is believed to act in an anti-inflammatory manner. Although PPAR-γ directly regulates inflammatory gene expression, it also interferes with the activation of NFκB, creating an intriguing interaction between these two transcription factors (Van den Berghe et al., 2003). Omega-3 PUFA might enhance PPAR-γ activity, resulting in anti-inflammatory effects perhaps involving interference in NFκB activation. PPAR-γ is known to bind, and to be activated by, various fatty acids, including omega-3 PUFAs and fatty acid derivatives (Bocos et al., 1995; Forman, Chen, & Evans, 1997; Göttlicher, Widmark, Li, & Gustafsson, 1992; Kliewer et al., 1997). This interaction between fatty acids and PPAR-γ raises the possibility that omega-3 PUFAs might attenuate inflammatory processes through this novel mechanism of action.

CLINICAL APPLICATIONS OF THE ANTI-INFLAMMATORY EFFECTS OF LONG-CHAIN OMEGA-3 POLYUNSATURATED FATTY ACIDS

The roles of omega-6 and omega-3 PUFAs in shaping and regulating inflammatory processes and responses suggest that the balance of these fatty acids might be important in determining the development and severity of inflammatory diseases. The recognition that the long-chain omega-3 PUFAs have anti-inflammatory actions has led to the idea that supplementation of the diet of patients with inflammatory diseases may be of clinical benefit. Supplementation trials have been conducted in a range of such diseases. Those dealing with rheumatoid arthritis, inflammatory bowel diseases (Crohn's disease and ulcerative colitis), and asthma are reviewed here because a larger number of trials have been conducted in these diseases than in the others and because the evidence of benefit is strongest in these diseases.

Rheumatoid Arthritis

Dietary fish oil has been shown to have beneficial effects in animal models of arthritis. For example, compared with vegetable oil, feeding mice fish oil delayed the onset (mean 34 days vs. 25 days) and reduced the incidence (69% vs. 93%) and severity (mean peak severity score 6.7 vs. 9.8) of Type 2 collagen-induced arthritis (Leslie et al., 1985). Both EPA and DHA suppressed Streptococcal cell-wall-induced arthritis in rats, but EPA was more effective (Volker, FitzGerald, & Garg, 2000).

Several studies have reported anti-inflammatory effects of fish oil in patients with rheumatoid arthritis, such as decreased LTB_4 production by neutrophils (Cleland, French, Betts, Murphy, & Elliot, 1988; Kremer et al., 1985, 1987; van der Tempel, Tullekan, Limburg, Muskiet, & van Rijswijk, 1990) and monocytes (Cleland et al., 1988; Tullekan, Limburg, Muskiet, & van Rijswijk, 1990), decreased IL-1 production by monocytes (Kremer et al., 1990), decreased plasma IL-1β concentrations (Esperson et al., 1992), decreased serum C-reactive protein concentrations (Kremer et al., 1985), and normalization of the neutrophil chemotactic response (Sperling et al., 1987).

A number of randomized, placebo-controlled, double-blind studies of fish oil in rheumatoid arthritis have been reported (Adam et al., 2003; Berbert, Kondo, Almendra, Matsuo, & Dichi, 2005; Geusens, Wouters, Nijs, Jiang, & Dequeker, 1994; Kjeldsen-Kragh et al., 1992; Kremer et al., 1995; Lau, Morley, & Belch, 1993; Nielsen et al., 1992; Remans et al., 2004; Skoldstam, Borjesson, Kjallman, Seiving, & Akesson,1992; Sperling et al., 1987; Volker, Fitzgerald, Major, & Garg, 2000). The characteristics and findings of these trials are described in detail elsewhere (Calder, 2006) and are summarized in Table 4.4. The dose of long-chain omega-3 PUFAs used in these trials was between 1.6 and 7.1 g/day and averaged about 3.5 g/day. Almost all of these

TABLE 4.4
Summary of Clinical Trials of Long-Chain Omega-3 Fatty Acids (As Fish
Oil) in Patients With Selected Chronic Inflammatory Diseases

Disease	No. of studies (references)[a]	Doses of EPA+DHA used (g/day)	Duration (weeks)	Improvements seen in
Rheumatoid arthritis	17 (96–102; 104–113)	1.6 to 7.1 (av. 3.5)	12 to 52	Number of swollen and/or tender joints (13 studies) Duration of morning stiffness (7 studies) Time to fatigue (2 studies) Physician's assessment (7 studies) Grip strength (3 studies) Patient's assessment (5 studies) NSAID use (3 studies)
Inflammatory bowel diseases	12 (129,131,136–146)	2.7 to 5.6 (av. 4.5)	12 to 104	Sigmoidoscope score (3 studies) Gut mucosal histology (2 studies) Disease activity (3 studies) Steroid use (3 studies) Relapse (1 study) Remission (2 studies)
Asthma	8 in adults (153,154, 156–161); 2 in children (162,163)	1 to 6 (av. 4.3) in adults	4 to 52	Lung function (2 studies in adults and 1 study in children) Symptom score (1 study in children)

Note. EPA = eicosapentaenoic acid; DHA = docosahexaenoic acid; av. = average; NSAID = nonsteroidal anti-inflammatory drug.
[a]placebo-controlled.

trials showed some benefit of fish oil (see Table 4.4). Such benefits include reduced duration of morning stiffness, reduced number of tender or swollen joints, reduced joint pain, reduced time to fatigue, increased grip strength, and decreased use of nonsteroidal anti-inflammatory drugs (see Table 4.4). Reviews of these trials (Calder, 2001c; Calder & Zurier, 2001; Geusens, 1998; James & Cleland, 1997; Kremer, 2000; Volker & Garg, 1996) have concluded that there is benefit from fish oil. In an editorial commentary discussing the use of fish oil in rheumatoid arthritis, it was concluded that the findings of benefit from fish oil in rheumatoid arthritis are robust, dietary fish oil supplements in rheumatoid arthritis have treatment efficacy, and dietary fish oil supplements should now be regarded as part of the standard therapy for rheumatoid arthritis (Cleland & James, 2000).

Fortin et al. (1995) conducted a meta-analysis that included data from nine trials published between 1985 and 1992 and from one unpublished trial. This analysis concluded that dietary fish oil supplementation for 3 months significantly reduced tender joint count (mean difference –2.9; p = .001) and morning stiffness (mean difference –25.9 minutes; p = .01). Another meta-analysis included data from 10 trials published between 1985 and 2002 (MacLean et al., 2004), although it included 1 study of flaxseed oil, 1 study that did not use a control for fish oil, and 1 study in which transdermal administration of omega-3 PUFAs by ultrasound, rather than the oral route, was used. This meta-analysis concluded that fish oil supplementation has no effect on patient report of pain, swollen joint count, disease activity, or patient's global assessment. However, noting that in a qualitative analysis of seven studies that assessed the effect of omega-3 fatty acids on anti-inflammatory drug or corticosteroid requirement, six demonstrated reduced requirement for these drugs, the authors of the review concluded that omega-3 fatty acids may reduce requirements for corticosteroids. The effects of long-chain omega-3 PUFAs on tender joint count were not assessed in MacLean et al. (2004), which reiterated the findings of the earlier meta-analysis (Fortin et al., 1995) that omega-3 fatty acids reduce tender joint counts.

A new meta-analysis of 17 trials with long-chain omega-3 PUFAs conducted between 1985 and 2005 was published recently (Goldberg & Katz, 2007); this analysis considered six outcomes. It concluded that omega-3 PUFAs for 3 to 4 months reduced patient-reported joint pain intensity (standardized mean difference –0.26; p = .03), duration of morning stiffness (standardized mean difference –0.43; p = .003), number of painful or tender joints (standardized mean difference –0.29; p = .003), and nonsteroidal anti-inflammatory drug consumption (standardized mean difference –0.4; p = .01). Thus, the evidence that long-chain omega-3 PUFAs have clinical benefits in rheumatoid arthritis is fairly robust.

Inflammatory Bowel Diseases

Dietary fish oil has been shown to have beneficial effects in animal models of colitis induced by chemicals (Empey et al., 1991; Nieto, Torres, Rios, & Gil, 2002; Vilaseca et al., 1990; Yuceyar et al., 1999) or by knockout of the IL-10 gene (Chapkin et al., 2007). Long-chain omega-3 PUFAs are incorporated into gut mucosal tissue of patients with inflammatory bowel disease who supplement their diet with fish oil (Hawthorne et al., 1992; Hillier, Jewell, Dorrell, & Smith, 1991; Lorenz et al., 1989), and there are reports that this results in anti-inflammatory effects, such as decreased LTB_4 production by neutrophils (Hawthorne et al., 1992; McCall, O'Leary, Bloomfield, & O'Morain, 1989; Shimizu et al., 2003) and colonic mucosa (Shimizu et al., 2003; Stenson et al., 1992), decreased PGE_2 and TXB_2 production by colonic mucosa (Hillier et al., 1991), and decreased production of PGE_2 by blood mononuclear cells (Trebble et al., 2004).

Small open-label or pilot studies reported clinical benefit of fish oil supplementation in ulcerative colitis (McCall et al., 1989; Salomon, Kornbluth, & Janowitz, 1990). A number of randomized, placebo-controlled, double-blind studies of fish oil in inflammatory bowel disease have been reported (Almallah et al., 1998, 2000; Aslan & Triadafilopoulos, 1992; Belluzzi et al., 1996; Greenfield et al., 1993; Hawthorne et al., 1992; Loeschke et al., 1996; Lorenz et al., 1989; Lorenz-Meyer et al., 1996; Salomon et al., 1990; Trebble et al., 2005; Varghese & Coomansingh, 2000). The characteristics and findings of these trials are provided elsewhere (Calder, 2006) and are summarized in Table 4.4. The dose of long-chain omega-3 PUFAs used in these trials was between 2.7 and 5.6 g/day, and averaged about 4.5 g/day. Some of these trials indicate benefits of fish oil, which include improved clinical score, improved gut mucosal histology, improved sigmoidoscopic score, lower rate of relapse, and decreased use of corticosteroids. One study of special note is that of Belluzzi et al. (1996) in which patients with Crohn's disease in remission were randomized to receive placebo or 2.7 g long-chain omega-3 PUFA/day from an enterically coated fish oil preparation for 1 year. The primary outcome was relapse. However, there was a significant difference in the proportion of patients who relapsed over 12 months: 11/39 (28%) in the fish oil group versus 27/39 (69%) in the placebo group ($p < .001$). Likewise, there was a significant difference in the proportion of patients who remained in remission at 12 months: 59% in the fish oil group versus 26% in the placebo group ($p = .003$).

Reviews of trials of fish oil in inflammatory bowel diseases (Belluzzi, 2000, 2002; Mills, Windsor, & Knight, 2005; Rodgers, 1998; Teitelbaum & Walker, 2001) concluded that there is some benefit from fish oil in inflammatory bowel diseases. A recent meta-analysis identified 13 studies of fish oil supplementation in inflammatory bowel diseases reporting outcomes related to clinical score, sigmoidoscope score, gut mucosal histology score, induced remission, and relapse (MacLean et al., 2004). However, it was concluded that data were sufficient to perform meta-analysis only for relapse and for ulcerative colitis. Relapse was reported in five studies in ulcerative colitis, and three of these were used for meta-analysis. Two of these studies reported a higher rate of relapse with fish oil compared with placebo (Hawthorne et al., 1992; Loeschke et al., 1996), although this finding was not significant in either study, and a third reported no effect (Mantzaris et al., 1996). The pooled risk of relapse with long-chain omega-3 PUFAs relative to placebo was 1.13 (95% confidence interval: 0.91, 1.57). This meta-analysis concluded that omega-3 fatty acids have no effect on relative risk of relapse in ulcerative colitis and there was a statistically nonsignificant reduction in requirement for corticosteroids for omega-3 fatty acids relative to placebo in two studies (MacLean et al., 2004).

Trebble et al. (2005) reported no effect of 2.7 g EPA + DHA/day for 24 weeks on disease activity in patients with Crohn's disease. Thus, despite several favorable studies, the overall view at the moment must be that there is only weak evidence that long-chain omega-3 PUFAs have clinical benefits in inflammatory bowel diseases. However, the apparent ability of long-chain omega-3 PUFAs to retain Crohn's disease patients in remission (Belluzzi et al., 1996) is a striking finding.

Asthma

Several studies have reported anti-inflammatory effects of fish oil in patients with asthma, such as decreased 4-series LT production (Arm et al., 1988; Kirsch et al., 1988; Payan et al., 1986) and leukocyte chemotaxis (Arm et al., 1988; Kirsch et al., 1988). Several uncontrolled or open-label trials of fish oil revealed clinical benefit of fish oil; these are discussed in detail elsewhere (Schachter et al., 2004). A number of randomized, placebo-controlled, double-blind studies of fish oil in asthma have been reported (Arm et al., 1988; Arm, Horton, Spur, Mencia-Huerta, & Lee, 1989; Broughton, Johnson, Pace, Liebman, & Kleppinger, 1997; Dry & Vincent, 1991; Hodge et al., 1998; Kirsch et al., 1988; McDonald, Vecchie, Pierce, & Strauss, 1990; Nagakura, Matsuda, Shichijyo, Sugimoto, & Hata, 2000; Stenius-Aarniala et al., 1989; Thien, Mencia-Huerta, & Lee, 1993; Thien, Woods, De Luca, & Abramson, 2002). The characteristics and findings of these trials are provided elsewhere (Calder, 2006) and are summarized in Table 4.4.

Thien et al. (2002) included eight studies published between 1988 and 2000 in a systematic review. They identified that there was no consistent effect on forced expiratory volume at 1 second, peak flow rate, asthma symptoms, asthma medication use, or bronchia hyperreactivity. They conceded that one study in children showed improved peak flow and reduced asthma medication use. A more recent report covering 26 studies (both randomized, placebo-controlled and others) concluded that no definitive conclusion can yet be drawn regarding the efficacy of omega-3 fatty acid supplementation as a treatment for asthma in children and adults (Schachter et al., 2004). However, the studies of Broughton et al. (1997) and Nagakura et al. (2000) indicated that there may be subgroups of asthmatic subjects who may benefit greatly from long-chain omega-3 PUFAs. It is clear that more needs to be done in this area.

IS THERE A ROLE FOR α-LINOLENIC ACID IN MODULATING INFLAMMATION?

Relatively few studies have examined the effect of the precursor omega-3 PUFA ALA on inflammatory outcomes in humans. Caughey et al. (1996) reported that 13.7 g ALA/day for 4 weeks resulted in a decrease in production of TNF-α and IL-1β by endotoxin-stimulated mononuclear cells by 27% and 30%, respectively. By comparison, fish oil providing 2.7 g EPA + DHA/day decreased production of these cytokines by 70% and 78%, respectively

(Caughey et al., 1996). Thus, on a g/day basis, long-chain omega-3 PUFAs are about 9 times more potent than ALA with respect to this outcome in healthy participants. In contrast to the observations of Caughey et al. (1996), several studies using lower intakes of ALA (2–9.5 g/day) did not find effects on neutrophil chemotaxis (Healy et al., 2000); neutrophil respiratory burst (Healy et al., 2000; Kew et al., 2003; Thies, Miles, et al., 2001); monocyte respiratory burst (Kew et al., 2003; Thies, Miles, et al., 2001); TNF-α, IL-1β, and IL-β production by endotoxin-stimulated mononuclear cells (Kew et al., 2003; Thies, Miles, et al., 2001; Wallace et al., 2003); intercellular adhesion molecule-1 expression on monocytes (Kew et al., 2003); or soluble adhesion molecule concentrations (Thies, Miles, et al., 2001). Taken together, these data suggest that increasing α-linolenic acid intake to more than 10 g/day is required for anti-inflammatory effects to be seen. Even then, the effects will be much more modest than those exerted by long-chain omega-3 PUFAs (Caughey et al., 1996).

CONCLUSIONS

At sufficiently high intakes in humans (at least 2 g/day), long-chain omega-3 PUFAs decrease the production of inflammatory mediators (eicosanoids, cytokines, reactive oxygen species) and the expression of adhesion molecules. They act both directly (e.g., by replacing AA as an eicosanoid substrate and inhibiting AA metabolism) and indirectly (e.g., by altering the expression of inflammatory genes through effects on transcription factor activation; see Calder, 2001b, 2003, 2005). Long-chain omega-3 PUFAs also give rise to anti-inflammatory mediators (resolvins). Thus, omega-3 PUFAs may be potent anti-inflammatory agents. As such, they may be of therapeutic use in a variety of acute and chronic inflammatory settings. However, because information about the relative anti-inflammatory potencies of EPA and DHA is lacking, comparisons between these two fatty acids in various settings should be made. Evidence of the clinical efficacy of long-chain omega-3 PUFAs is strong in some settings (e.g., in rheumatoid arthritis) but weak in others (e.g., in inflammatory bowel diseases and asthma). More, better designed, and larger trials are required in inflammatory diseases to assess the therapeutic potential of long-chain omega-3 PUFAs in these conditions. The precursor omega-3 PUFA α-linolenic acid does not appear to exert anti-inflammatory effects at achievable intakes.

KEY POINTS

- Western diets typically contain an abundance of proinflammatory omega-6 fatty acids and are low in anti-inflammatory omega-3s.

- Fish oil supplements contain EPA and DHA and lower inflammation by decreasing synthesis of proinflammatory cytokines and inflammatory eicosanoids and prostaglandins, thromboxanes, and leukotrienes.
- EPA and DHA also allow the formation of anti-inflammatory resolvins, a novel mechanism by which PUFAs are anti-inflammatory.
- Fish oil supplementation is beneficial in treating some inflammatory diseases, such as rheumatoid arthritis and Crohn's disease. Fish oil is less effective in treating ulcerative colitis and asthma, but some patients might benefit.
- Long-chain omega-3s (EPA and DHA) are 9 times more potent than ALA (the omega-3 found in flaxseed and flax oil) in decreasing proinflammatory cytokines.

REFERENCES

Abbate, R., Gori, A. M., Martini, F., Brunelli, T., Filippini, M., Francalanci, I., et al. (1996). N-3 PUFA supplementation, monocyte PCA expression and interleukin-6 production. *Prostaglandins, Leukotrienes & Essential Fatty Acids, 54,* 439–444.

Adam, O., Beringer, C., Kless, T., Lemmen, C., Adam, A., Wiseman, M., et al. (2003). Anti-inflammatory effects of a low arachidonic acid diet and fish oil in patients with rheumatoid arthritis. *Rheumatology International, 23,* 27–36.

Almallah, Y. Z., Ewen, S. W., El-Tahir, A., Mowat, N. A., Brunt, P. W., Sinclair, T. S., et al. (2000). Distal proctocolitis and n-3 polyunsaturated fatty acids (n-3 PUFA): The mucosal effect in situ. *Journal of Clinical Immunology, 20,* 68–76.

Almallah, Y. Z., Richardson, S., O'Hanrahan, T., Mowat, N. A., Brunt, P. W., Sinclair, T. S., et al. (1998). Distal procto-colitis, natural cytotoxicity, and essential fatty acids. *American Journal of Gastroenterology, 93,* 804–809.

Arm, J. P., Horton, C. E., Mencia-Huerta, J. M., House, F., Eiser, N. M., Clark, T. J., et al. (1988). Effect of dietary supplementation with fish oil lipids on mild asthma. *Thorax, 43,* 84–92.

Arm, J. P., Horton, C. E., Spur, B. W., Mencia-Huerta, J. M., & Lee, T. H. (1989). The effects of dietary supplementation with fish oil lipids on the airways response to inhaled allergen in bronchial asthma. *American Review of Respiratory Disease, 139,* 1395–1400.

Aslan, A., & Triadafilopoulos, G. (1992). Fish oil fatty acid supplementation in active ulcerative colitis: A double-blind, placebo-controlled, crossover study. *American Journal of Gastroenterology, 87,* 432–437.

Babcock, T. A., Novak, T., Ong, E., Jho, D. H., Helton, W. S., & Espat, N. J. (2002). Modulation of lipopolysaccharide-stimulated macrophage tumor necrosis factor-alpha production by omega-3 fatty acid is associated with differential cyclooxygenase-2 protein expression and is independent of interleukin-10. *Journal of Surgical Research, 107,* 135–139.

Bagga, D., Wang, L., Farias-Eisner, R., Glaspy, J. A., & Reddy, S. T. (2003). Differential effects of prostaglandin derived from omega-6 and omega-3 polyunsaturated fatty acids on COX-2 expression and IL-6 secretion. *Proceedings of the National Academy of Sciences USA, 100*, 1751–1756.

Belluzzi, A. (2000). Polyunsaturated fatty acids and inflammatory bowel disease. *American Journal of Clinical Nutrition, 71*(Suppl.), 339S–342S.

Belluzzi, A. (2002). N-3 fatty acids for the treatment of inflammatory bowel diseases. *Proceedings of the Nutrition Society, 61*, 391–395.

Belluzzi, A., Brignola, C., Campieri, M., Pera, A., Boschi, S., & Miglioli, M. (1996). Effect of an enteric-coated fish-oil preparation on relapses in Crohn's disease. *The New England Journal of Medicine, 334*, 1557–1560.

Berbert, A. A., Kondo, C. R., Almendra, C. L., Matsuo, T., & Dichi, I. D. (2005). Supplementation of fish oil and olive oil in patients with rheumatoid arthritis. *Nutrition, 21*, 131–136.

Billiar, T., Bankey, P., Svingen, B., Curran, R. D., West, M. A., Holman, R. T., et al. (1988). Fatty acid uptake and Kupffer cell function: Fish oil alters eicosanoid and monokine production to endotoxin stimulation. *Surgery, 104*, 343–349.

Blok, W. L., Deslypere, J.-P., Demacker, P. N. M., van der Ven-Jonggekrijg, J., Hectors, M. P. C., van der Meer, J. M. W., et al. (1997). Pro- and anti-inflammatory cytokines in healthy volunteers fed various doses of fish oil for 1 year. *European Journal of Clinical Investigation, 27*, 1003–1008.

Bocos, C., Göttlicher, M., Gearing, K., Banner, C., Enmark, E., Teboul, M., et al. (1995). Fatty acid activation of peroxisome proliferator-activated receptor (PPAR). *The Journal of Steroid Biochemistry & Molecular Biology, 53*, 467–473.

British Nutrition Foundation. (1999). *Briefing paper: n-3 fatty acids and health.* London: British Nutrition Foundation.

Broughton, K. S., Johnson, C. S., Pace, B. K., Liebman, M., & Kleppinger, K. M. (1997). Reduced asthma symptoms with n-3 fatty acid ingestion are related to 5-series leukotriene production. *American Journal of Clinical Nutrition, 65*, 1011–1017.

Burdge, G. C., & Calder, P. C. (2004). Fatty acids. In A. Nicolaou & G. Kokotos (Eds.), *Bioactive lipids* (pp. 1–36). Bridgewater, England: The Oily Press.

Burdge, G. C., & Calder, P. C. (2006). Dietary α-linolenic acid and health-related outcomes: A metabolic perspective. *Nutrition Research Reviews, 19*, 26–52.

Calder, P. C. (2001a). N-3 polyunsaturated fatty acids, inflammation and immunity: Pouring oil on troubled waters or another fishy tale? *Nutrition Research, 21*, 309–341.

Calder, P. C. (2001b). Polyunsaturated fatty acids, inflammation and immunity. *Lipids, 36*, 1007–1024.

Calder, P. C. (2001c). The scientific basis for fish oil supplementation in rheumatoid arthritis. In J. K. Ransley, J. K. Donnelly, & N. W. Read (Eds.), *Nutritional supplements in health and disease* (pp. 175–197). London: Springer-Verlag.

Calder, P. C. (2003). N-3 polyunsaturated fatty acids and inflammation: From molecular biology to the clinic. *Lipids, 38*, 342–352.

Calder, P. C. (2005). Polyunsaturated fatty acids and inflammation. *Biochemical Society Transactions, 33*, 423–427.

Calder, P. C. (2006). n-3 polyunsaturated fatty acids, inflammation, and inflammatory diseases. *American Journal of Clinical Nutrition, 83*(Suppl.), 1505S–1519S.

Calder, P. C. (2007). Immunomodulation by omega-3 fatty acids. *Prostaglandins, Leukotrienes & Essential Fatty Acids, 77*, 327–335.

Calder, P. C., Yaqoob, P., Thies, F., Wallace, F. A., & Miles, E. A. (2002). Fatty acids and lymphocyte functions. *British Journal of Nutrition, 87*(Suppl. 1), S31–S48.

Calder, P. C., & Zurier, R. B. (2001). Polyunsaturated fatty acids and rheumatoid arthritis. *Current Opinion in Clinical Nutrition and Metabolic Care, 4*, 115–121.

Cannon, J. G., Fiatarone, M. A., Meydani, M., Gong, J., Scott, L., Blumberg, J. B., et al. (1995). Aging and dietary modulation of elastase and interleukin-2 beta secretion. *American Journal of Physiology—Regulatory, Integrative and Comparative Physiology, 268*, R208–R213.

Caughey, G. E., Mantzioris, E., Gibson, R. A., Cleland, L. G., & James, M. J. (1996). The effect on human tumor necrosis factor-alpha and interleukin 1-beta production of diets enriched in n-3 fatty acids from vegetable oil or fish oil. *American Journal of Clinical Nutrition, 63*, 116–122.

Chandrasekar, B., & Fernandes, G. (1994). Decreased pro-inflammatory cytokines and increased antioxidant enzyme gene expression by omega-3 lipids in murine lupus nephritis. *Biochemical and Biophysical Research Communications, 200*, 893–898.

Chapkin, R. S., Davidson, L. A., Ly, L., Weeks, B. R., Lupton, J. R., & McMurray, D. N. (2007). Immunomodulatory effects of (n-3) fatty acids: Putative link to inflammation and colon cancer. *Journal of Nutrition, 137*, 200S–204S.

Cleland, L. G., French, J. K., Betts, W. H., Murphy, G. A., & Elliot, M. J. (1988). Clinical and biochemical effects of dietary fish oil supplements in rheumatoid arthritis. *Journal of Rheumatology, 15*, 1471–1475.

Cleland, L. G., & James, M. J. (2000). Fish oil and rheumatoid arthritis: Anti-inflammatory and collateral health benefits. *Journal of Rheumatology, 27*, 2305–2307.

Collie-Duguid, E. S., & Wahle, K. W. (1996). Inhibitory effect of fish oil n-3 polyunsaturated fatty acids on the expression of endothelial cell adhesion molecules. *Biochemical and Biophysical Research Communications, 220*, 969–974.

Cooper, A. L., Gibbins, L., Horan, M. A., Little, R. A., & Rothwell, N. J. (1993). Effect of dietary fish oil supplementation on fever and cytokine production in human volunteers. *Clinical Nutrition, 12*, 321–328.

De Caterina, R., Cybulsky, M. I., Clinton, S. K., Gimbrone, M. A., & Libby, P. (1994). The omega-3 fatty acid docosahexaenoate reduces cytokine-induced expression of proatherogenic and proinflammatory proteins in human endothelial cells. *Arteriosclerosis and Thrombosis, 14*, 1829–1836.

De Caterina, R., & Libby, P. (1996). Control of endothelial leukocyte adhesion molecules by fatty acids. *Lipids, 31*(Suppl.), S57–S63.

Dooper, M. W., Wassink, L., M'Rabet, L., & Graus, Y. M. (2002). The modulatory effects of prostaglandin-E on cytokine production by human peripheral blood mononuclear cells are independent of the prostaglandin subtype. *Immunology*, *107*, 152–159.

Dry, J., & Vincent, D. (1991). Effect of a fish oil diet on asthma: Results of a 1-year double-blind study. *International Archives of Allergy and Applied Immunology*, *95*, 156–157.

Empey, L. R., Jewell, L. D., Garg, M. L., Thomson, A. B., Clandinin, M. T., & Fedorak, R. N. (1991). Fish oil-enriched diet is mucosal protective against acetic acid-induced colitis in rats. *Canadian Journal of Physiology and Pharmacology*, *69*, 480–487.

Endres, S., Ghorbani, R., Kelley, V. E., Georgilis, K., Lonnemann, G., van der Meer, J. M. W., et al. (1989). The effect of dietary supplementation with n-3 polyunsaturated fatty acids on the synthesis of interleukin-1 and tumor necrosis factor by mononuclear cells. *The New England Journal of Medicine*, *320*, 265–271.

Esperson, G. T., Grunnet, N., Lervang, H. H., Nielsen, G. L., Thomsen, B. S., Faarvang, K. L., et al. (1992). Decreased interleukin-1 beta levels in plasma from rheumatoid arthritis patients after dietary supplementation with n-3 polyunsaturated fatty acids. *Clinical Rheumatology*, *11*, 393–395.

Fisher, M., Levine, P. H., Weiner, B. H., Johnson, M. H., Doyle, E. M., Ellis, P. A., et al. (1990). Dietary n-3 fatty acid supplementation reduces superoxide production and chemiluminescence in monocyte enriched preparation of leukocytes. *American Journal of Clinical Nutrition*, *51*, 804–808.

Forman, B. M., Chen, J., & Evans, R. M. (1997). Hypolipidemic drugs, polyunsaturated fatty acids, and eicosanoids are ligands for peroxisome proliferator-activated receptors alpha and delta. *Proceedings of the National Academy of Sciences USA*, *94*, 4312–4317.

Fortin, P. R., Lew, R. A., Liang, M. H., Wright, E. A., Beckett, L. A., Chalmers, T. C., et al. (1995). Validation of a meta-analysis: The effects of fish oil in rheumatoid arthritis. *Journal of Clinical Epidemiology*, *48*, 1379–1390.

Gallai, V., Sarchielli, P., Trequattrini, A., Franceschini, M., Floridi, A., Firenze, C., et al. (1993). Cytokine secretion and eicosanoid production in the peripheral blood mononuclear cells of MS patients undergoing dietary supplementation with n-3 polyunsaturated fatty acids. *Journal of Neuroimmunology*, *56*, 143–153.

Geusens, P. P. (1998). N-3 fatty acids in the treatment of rheumatoid arthritis. In J. M. Kremer (Ed.), *Medicinal fatty acids in inflammation* (pp. 111–123). Basel, Switzerland: Birkhauser Verlag.

Geusens, P. P., Wouters, C., Nijs, J., Jiang, Y., & Dequeker, J. (1994). Long-term effect of omega-3 fatty acid supplementation in active rheumatoid arthritis. *Arthritis & Rheumatism*, *37*, 824–829.

Gewirtz, A. T., Collier-Hyams, L. S., Young, A. N., Kucharzik, T., Guilford, W. J., Parkinson, J. F., et al. (2002). Lipoxin A4 analogs attenuate induction of intestinal epithelial proinflammatory gene expression and reduce the severity of dextran sodium sulfate-induced colitis. *Journal of Immunology*, *168*, 5260–5267.

Gibney, M. J., & Hunter, B. (1993). The effects of short- and long-term supplementation with fish oil on the incorporation of n-3 polyunsaturated fatty acids into cells of the immune system in healthy volunteers. *European Journal of Clinical Nutrition, 47,* 255–259.

Goldberg, R. J., & Katz, J. (2007). A meta-analysis of the analgesic effects of omega-3 polyunsaturated fatty acid supplementation for inflammatory joint pain. *Pain, 129,* 210–223.

Goldman, D. W., Pickett, W. C., & Goetzl, E. J. (1983). Human neutrophil chemotactic and degranulating activities of leukotriene B5 (LTB5) derived from eicosapentaenoic acid. *Biochemical and Biophysical Research Communications, 117,* 282–288.

Göttlicher, M., Widmark, E., Li, Q., & Gustafsson, J. A. (1992). Fatty acids activate a chimera of the clofibric acid-activated receptor and the glucocorticoid receptor. *Proceedings of the National Academy of Sciences USA, 89,* 4653–4657.

Greenfield, S. M., Green, A. T., Teare, J. P., Jenkins, A. P., Punchard, N. A., Ainley, C. C., et al. (1993). A randomized controlled study of evening primrose oil and fish oil in ulcerative colitis. *Alimentary Pharmacology & Therapy, 7,* 159–166.

Grimble, R. F., Howell, W. M., O'Reilly, G., Turner, S. J., Markovic, O., Hirrell, S., et al. (2002). The ability of fish oil to suppress tumor necrosis factor-alpha production by peripheral blood mononuclear cells in healthy men is associated with polymorphisms in genes that influence tumor necrosis factor-alpha production. *American Journal of Clinical Nutrition, 76,* 454–459.

Halvorsen, D. A., Hansen, J.-B., Grimsgaard, S., Bonna, K. H., Kierulf, P., & Nordoy, A. (1997). The effect of highly purified eicosapentaenoic and docosahexaenoic acids on monocyte phagocytosis in man. *Lipids, 32,* 935–942.

Hawthorne, A. B., Daneshmend, T. K., Hawkey, C. J., Belluzzi, A., Everitt, S. J., Holmes, G. K., et al. (1992). Treatment of ulcerative colitis with fish oil supplementation: A prospective 12 month randomised controlled trial. *Gut, 33,* 922–928.

Healy, D. A., Wallace, F. A., Miles, E. A., Calder, P. C., & Newsholme, P. (2000). The effect of low to moderate amounts of dietary fish oil on neutrophil lipid composition and function. *Lipids, 35,* 763–768.

Hillier, K., Jewell, R., Dorrell, L., & Smith, C. L. (1991). Incorporation of fatty acids from fish oil and olive oil into colonic mucosal lipids and effects upon eicosanoid synthesis in inflammatory bowel disease. *Gut, 32,* 1151–1155.

Hodge, L., Salome, C. M., Hughes, J. M., Liu-Brennan, D., Rimmer, J., Allman, M., et al. (1998). Effect of dietary intake of omega-3 and omega-6 fatty acids on severity of asthma in children. *European Respiratory Journal, 11,* 361–365.

Hong, S., Gronert, K., Devchand, P., Moussignac, R.-L., & Serhan, C. N. (2003). Novel docosatrienes and 17S-resolvins generated from docosahexaenoic acid in murine brain, human blood and glial cells: Autocoids in anti-inflammation. *Journal of Biological Chemistry, 278,* 14677–14687.

Hughes, D. A., Pinder, A. C., Piper, Z., Johnson, I. T., & Lund, E. K. (1996). Fish oil supplementation inhibits the expression of major histocompatibility complex Class II molecules and adhesion molecules on human monocytes. *American Journal of Clinical Nutrition, 63,* 267–272.

Hughes, D. A., Southon, S., & Pinder, A. C. (1996). (n-3) Polyunsaturated fatty acids modulate the expression of functionally associated molecules on human monocytes in vitro. *Journal of Nutrition, 126,* 603–610.

James, M. J., & Cleland, L. G. (1997). Dietary n-3 fatty acids and therapy for rheumatoid arthritis. *Seminars in Arthritis and Rheumatism, 27,* 85–97.

Kelley, D. S., Taylor, P. C., Nelson, G. J., & Mackey, B. E. (1998). Arachidonic acid supplementation enhances synthesis of eicosanoids without suppressing immune functions in young healthy men. *Lipids, 33,* 125–130.

Kelley, D. S., Taylor, P. C., Nelson, G. J., Schmidt, P. C., Ferretti, A., Erickson, K. L., et al. (1999). Docosahexaenoic acid ingestion inhibits natural killer cell activity and production of inflammatory mediators in young healthy men. *Lipids, 34,* 317–324.

Kew, S., Banerjee, T., Minihane, A. M., Finnegan, Y. E., Muggli, R., Albers, R., et al. (2003). Lack of effect of foods enriched with plant- or marine-derived n-3 fatty acids on human immune function. *American Journal of Clinical Nutrition, 77,* 1287–1295.

Kew, S., Mesa, M. D., Tricon, S., Buckley, R., Minihane, A. M., & Yaqoob, P. (2004). Effects of oils rich in eicosapentaenoic and docosahexaenoic acids on immune cell composition and function in healthy humans. *American Journal of Clinical Nutrition, 79,* 674–681.

Khalfoun, B., Thibault, F., Watier, H., Bardos, P., & Lebranchu, Y. (1997). Docosahexaenoic and eicosapentaenoic acids inhibit in vitro human endothelial cell production of interleukin-6. *Advances in Experimental Medicine and Biology, 400,* 589–597.

Kirsch, C. M., Payan, D. G., Wong, M. Y., Dohlman, J. G., Blake, V. A., Petri, M. A., et al. (1988). Effect of eicosapentaenoic acid in asthma. *Clinical Allergy, 18,* 177–187.

Kjeldsen-Kragh, J., Lund, J. A., Riise, T., Finnanger, B., Haaland, K., Finstad, R., et al. (1992). Dietary omega-3 fatty acid supplementation and naproxen treatment in patients with rheumatoid arthritis. *Journal of Rheumatology, 19,* 1531–1536.

Kliewer, S. A., Sundseth, S. S., Jones, S. A., Brown, P. J., Wisely, G. B., Koble, C. S., et al. (1997). Fatty acids and eicosanoids regulate gene expression through direct interactions with peroxisome proliferator-activated receptors alpha and gamma. *Proceedings of the National Academy of Sciences USA, 94,* 4318–4323.

Kremer, J. M. (2000). N-3 fatty acid supplements in rheumatoid arthritis. *American Journal of Clinical Nutrition, 71*(Suppl.), 349S–351S.

Kremer, J. M., Bigauoette, J., Michalek, A. V., Timchalk, M. A., Lininger, L., Rynes, R. I., et al. (1985, January 26). Effects of manipulation of dietary fatty acids on manifestations of rheumatoid arthritis. *The Lancet, 1,* 184–187.

Kremer, J. M., Jubiz, W., Michalek, A., Rynes, R. I., Bartholomew, L. E., Bigouette, J., et al. (1987). Fish-oil supplementation in active rheumatoid arthritis. *Annals of Internal Medicine, 106,* 497–503.

Kremer, J. M., Lawrence, D. A., Jubiz, W., DiGiacomo, R., Rynes, R., Bartholomew, L. E., et al. (1990). Dietary fish oil and olive oil supplementation in patients with rheumatoid arthritis. *Arthritis & Rheumatism, 33,* 810–820.

Kremer, J. M., Lawrence, D. A., Petrillo, G. F., Litts, L. L., Mullaly, P. M., Rynes, R. I., et al. (1995). Effects of high-dose fish oil on rheumatoid arthritis after stopping nonsteroidal antiinflammatory drugs: Clinical and immune correlates. *Arthritis & Rheumatism, 38,* 1107–1114.

Lau, C., Morley, K. D., & Belch, J. J. F. (1993). Effects of fish oil supplementation on non-steroidal anti-inflammatory drug requirement in patients with mild rheumatoid arthritis. *British Journal of Rheumatology, 32,* 982–989.

Lee, T. H., Hoover, R. L., Williams, J. D., Sperling, R. I., Ravalese, J., Spur, B. W., et al. (1985). Effects of dietary enrichment with eicosapentaenoic acid and docosahexaenoic acid on in vitro neutrophil and monocyte leukotriene generation and neutrophil function. *The New England Journal of Medicine, 312,* 1217–1224.

Lee, T. H., Mencia-Huerta, J. M., Shih, C., Corey, E. J., Lewis, R. A., & Austen, K. F. (1984). Characterization and biologic properties of 5,12-dihydroxy derivatives of eicosapentaenoic acid, including leukotriene-B5 and the double lipoxygenase product. *Journal of Biological Chemistry, 259,* 2383–2389.

Leslie, C. A., Gonnerman, W. A., Ullman, M. D., Hayes, K. C., Franzblau, C., & Cathcart, E. S. (1985). Dietary fish oil modulates macrophage fatty acids and decreases arthritis susceptibility in mice. *Journal of Experimental Medicine, 162,* 1336–1349.

Levy, B. D., Clish, C. B., Schmidt, B., Gronert, K., & Serhan, C. N. (2001). Lipid mediator class switching during acute inflammation: Signals in resolution. *Nature: Immunology, 2,* 612–619.

Lewis, R. A., Austen, K. F., & Soberman, R. J. (1990). Leukotrienes and other products of the 5-lipoxygenase pathway: Biochemistry and relation to pathobiology in human diseases. *The New England Journal of Medicine, 323,* 645–655.

Lo, C. J., Chiu, K. C., Fu, M. J., Chu, A., & Helton, S. (2000). Fish oil modulates macrophage P44/42 mitogen-activated protein kinase activity induced by lipopolysaccharide. *Journal of Parenteral and Enteric Nutrition, 24,* 159–163.

Lo, C. J., Chiu, K. C., Fu, M., Lo, R., & Helton, S. (1999). Fish oil decreases macrophage tumor necrosis factor gene transcription by altering the NF kappa B activity. *Journal of Surgical Research, 82,* 216–222.

Loeschke, K., Ueberschaer, B., Pietsch, A., Gruber, E., Ewe, K., Wiebecke, B., et al. (1996). N-3 fatty acids only delay early relapse of ulcerative colitis in remission. *Digestive Diseases and Sciences, 41,* 2087–2094.

Lorenz, R., Weber, P. C., Szimnau, P., Heldwein, W., Strasser, T., & Loeschke, K. (1989). Supplementation with n-3 fatty acids from fish oil in chronic inflammatory bowel disease—A randomized, placebo-controlled, double-blind crossover trial. *Journal of Internal Medicine Supplement, 731,* 225–232.

Lorenz-Meyer, H., Bauer, P., Nicolay, C., Schulz, B., Purrmann, J., Fleig, W. E., et al. (1996). Omega-3 fatty acids and low carbohydrate diet for maintenance of remission in Crohn's disease: A randomized controlled multicenter trial. *Scandinavian Journal of Gastroenterology*, 31, 778–785.

Luostarinen, R., & Saldeen, T. (1996). Dietary fish oil decreases superoxide generation by human neutrophils: Relation to cyclooxygenase pathway and lysosomal enzyme release. *Prostaglandins, Leukotrienes & Essential Fatty Acids*, 55, 167–172.

Luostarinen, R., Siegbahn, A., & Saldeen, T. (1992). Effect of dietary fish oil supplemented with different doses of Vitamin E on neutrophil chemotaxis in healthy volunteers. *Nutrition Research*, 12, 1419–1430.

MacLean, C. H., Mojica, W. A., Morton, S. C., Pencharz, J., Hasenfeld Garland, R., Tu, W., et al. (2004). *Effects of omega-3 fatty acids on inflammatory bowel disease, rheumatoid arthritis, renal disease, systemic lupus erythematosus, and osteoporosis.* Rockville, MD: Agency for Healthcare Research and Quality.

Mantzaris, G., Archavlis, E., Zografos, C., Petraki, K., Spiliades, C., & Triantafyllou, G. (1996). A prospective, randomized, placebo-controlled study of fish oil in ulcerative colitis. *Hellenic Journal of Gastroenterology*, 9, 138–141.

Marcheselli, V. L., Hong, S., Lukiw, W. J., Hua Tian, X., Gronert, K., Musto, A., et al. (2003). Novel docosanoids inhibit brain ischemia reperfusion-mediated leukocyte infiltration and pro-inflammatory gene expression. *Journal of Biological Chemistry*, 278, 43807–43817.

McCall, T. B., O'Leary, D., Bloomfield, J., & O'Morain, C. A. (1989). Therapeutic potential of fish oil in the treatment of ulcerative colitis. *Alimentary Pharmacology & Therapy*, 3, 415–424.

McDonald, C. F., Vecchie, L., Pierce, R. J., & Strauss, B. J. B. (1990). Effect of fish oil derived omega-3 fatty acid supplements on asthma control. *Australia and New Zealand Journal of Medicine*, 20, 526.

Meydani, S. N., Endres, S., Woods, M. M., Goldin, B. R., Soo, C., Morrill-Labrode, A., et al. (1991). Oral (n-3) fatty acid supplementation suppresses cytokine production and lymphocyte proliferation: Comparison between young and older women. *Journal of Nutrition*, 121, 547–555.

Miles, E. A., Allen, E., & Calder, P. C. (2002). In vitro effects of eicosanoids derived from different 20-carbon fatty acids on production of monocyte-derived cytokines in human whole blood cultures. *Cytokine*, 20, 215–223.

Miles, E. A., Banerjee, T., Dooper, M. W. B. W., M'Rabet, L., Graus, Y. M. F., & Calder, P. C. (2004). The influence of different combinations of α-linolenic acid, stearidonic acid and EPA on immune function in healthy young male subjects. *British Journal of Nutrition*, 91, 893–903.

Miles, E. A., Thies, F., Wallace, F. A., Powell, J. R., Hirst, T. L., Newsholme, E. A., et al. (2001). Influence of age and dietary fish oil on plasma soluble adhesion molecule concentrations. *Clinical Science*, 100, 91–100.

Miles, E. A., Wallace, F. A., & Calder, P. C. (2000). Dietary fish oil reduces intercellular adhesion molecule 1 and scavenger receptor expression on murine macrophages. *Atherosclerosis*, 152, 43–50.

Mills, S. C., Windsor, A. C., & Knight, S. C. (2005). The potential interactions between polyunsaturated fatty acids and colonic inflammatory processes. *Clinical Experimental Immunology, 142*, 216–228.

Molvig, J., Pociot, F., Worsaae, H., Wogensen, L. D., Baek, L., Christensen, P., et al. (1991). Dietary supplementation with omega 3 polyunsaturated fatty acids decreases mononuclear cell proliferation and interleukin 1 beta content but not monokine secretion in healthy and insulin dependent diabetic individuals. *Scandinavian Journal of Immunology, 34*, 399–410.

Mori, T. A., Woodman, R. J., Burke, V., Puddey, I. B., Croft, K. D., & Beilin, L. J. (2003). Effect of eicosapentaenoic acid and docosahexaenoic acid on oxidative stress and inflammatory markers in treated-hypertensive type 2 diabetic subjects. *Free Radical Biology & Medicine, 35*, 772–781.

Mukherjee, P. K., Marcheselli, V. L., Serhan, C. N., & Bazan, N. G. (2004). Neuroprotectin D1: A docosahexaenoic acid-derived docosatriene protects human retinal pigment epithelial cells from oxidative stress. *Proceedings of the National Academy of Sciences USA, 101*, 8491–8496.

Nagakura, T., Matsuda, S., Shichijyo, K., Sugimoto, H., & Hata, K. (2000). Dietary supplementation with fish oil rich in omega-3 polyunsaturated fatty acids in children with bronchial asthma. *European Respiratory Journal, 16*, 861–865.

Nielsen, G. L., Faarvang, K. L., Thomsen, B. S., Teglbjaerg, K. L., Jensen, L. T., Hansen, T. M., et al. (1992). The effects of dietary supplementation with n-3 polyunsaturated fatty acids in patients with rheumatoid arthritis: A randomized, double blind trial. *European Journal of Clinical Investigation, 22*, 687–691.

Nieto, N., Torres, M. I., Rios, A., & Gil, A. (2002). Dietary polyunsaturated fatty acids improve histological and biochemical alterations in rats with experimental ulcerative colitis. *Journal of Nutrition, 132*, 11–19.

Novak, T. E., Babcock, T. A., Jho, D. H., Helton, W. S., & Espat, N. J. (2003). NF-kappa B inhibition by omega-3 fatty acids modulates LPS-stimulated macrophage TNF-alpha transcription. *American Journal of Physiology—Lung Cellular and Molecular Physiology, 284*, L84–L89.

Payan, D. G., Wong, M. Y., Chernov-Rogan, T., Valone, F. H., Pickett, W. C., Blake, V. A., et al. (1986). Alterations in human leukocyte function induced by ingestion of eicosapentaenoic acid. *Journal of Clinical Immunology, 6*, 402–410.

Perkins, N. D. (2007). Integrating cell-signalling pathways with NF-kappaB and IKK function. *Nature Reviews: Molecular Cell Biology, 8*, 49–62.

Peterson, L. D., Jeffery, N. M., Thies, F., Sanderson, P., Newsholme, E. A., & Calder, P. C. (1998). Eicosapentaenoic and docosahexaenoic acids alter rat spleen leukocyte fatty acid composition and prostaglandin E2 production but have different effects on lymphocyte functions and cell-mediated immunity. *Lipids, 33*, 171–180.

Remans, P. H., Sont, J. K., Wagenaar, L. W., Wouters-Wesseling, W., Zuijderduin, W. M., Jongma, A., et al. (2004). Nutrient supplementation with polyunsaturated fatty acids and micronutrients in rheumatoid arthritis: Clinical and biochemical effects. *European Journal of Clinical Nutrition, 58*, 839–845.

Renier, G., Skamene, E., de Sanctis, J., & Radzioch, D. (1993). Dietary n-3 polyunsaturated fatty acids prevent the development of atherosclerotic lesions in mice: Modulation of macrophage secretory activities. *Arteriosclerosis and Thrombosis, 13*, 1515–1524.

Robinson, D. R., Urakaze, M., Huang, R., Taki, H., Sugiyama, E., Knoell, C. T., et al. (1996). Dietary marine lipids suppress continuous expression of interleukin-1-beta gene expression. *Lipids, 31*(Suppl.), S23–S31.

Rodgers, J. B. (1998). N-3 fatty acids in the treatment of ulcerative colitis. In J. M. Kremer (Ed.), *Medicinal fatty acids in inflammation* (pp. 103–109). Basel, Switzerland: Birkhauser Verlag.

Ross, J. A., Moses, A. G. W., & Fearon, K. C. H. (1999). The anti-catabolic effects of n-3 fatty acids. *Current Opinion in Clinical Nutrition and Metabolic Care, 2*, 219–226.

Salomon, P., Kornbluth, A. A., & Janowitz, H. D. (1990). Treatment of ulcerative colitis with fish oil n-3-omega-fatty acid: An open trial. *Journal of Clinical Gastroenterology, 12*, 157–161.

Schachter, H., Reisman, J., Tran, K., Dales, B., Kourad, K., Barnes, D., et al. (2004). *Health effects of omega-3 fatty acids on asthma* (AHRQ Publication No. 04-E013-2). Rockville, MD: Agency for Healthcare Research and Quality.

Schmidt, E. B., Pedersen, J. O., Ekelund, S., Grunnet, N., Jersild, C., & Dyerberg, J. (1989). Cod liver oil inhibits neutrophil and monocyte chemotaxis in healthy males. *Atherosclerosis, 77*, 53–57.

Schmidt, E. B., Pedersen, J. O., Varming, K., Ernst, E., Jersild, C., Grunnet, N., & Dyerberg, J. (1991). N-3 fatty acids and leukocyte chemotaxis: Effects in hyperlipidemia and dose–response studies in healthy men. *Arteriosclerosis and Thrombosis, 11*, 429–435.

Schmidt, E. B., Varming, K., Møller, J. M., Bülow Pedersen, I., Madsen, P., & Dyerberg, J. (1996). No effect of a very low dose of n-3 fatty acids on monocyte function in healthy humans. *Scandinavian Journal of Clinical and Laboratory Investigation, 56*, 87–92.

Schmidt, E. B., Varming, K., Perdersen, J. O., Lervang, H. H., Grunnet, N., Jersild, C., et al. (1992). Long term supplementation with n-3 fatty acids: II. Effect on neutrophil and monocyte chemotaxis. *Scandinavian Journal of Clinical & Laboratory Investigation, 52*, 229–236.

Serhan, C. N. (2005). Novel eicosanoid and docosanoid mediators: Resolvins, docosatrienes, and neuroprotectins. *Current Opinion in Clinical Nutrition and Metabolic Care, 8*, 115–121.

Serhan, C. N., Arita, M., Hong, S., & Gotlinger, K. (2004). Resolvins, docosatrienes, and neuroprotectins, novel omega-3-derived mediators, and their endogenous aspirin-triggered epimers. *Lipids, 39*, 1125–1132.

Serhan, C. N., Clish, C. B., Brannon, J., Colgan, S. P., Chiang, N., & Gronert, K. (2000). Novel functional sets of lipid-derived mediators with anti-inflammatory actions generated from omega-3 fatty acids via cyclooxygenase 2-nonsteroidal antiinflammatory drugs and transcellular processing. *Journal of Experimental Medicine, 192,* 1197–1204.

Serhan, C. N., Clish, C. B., Brannon, J., Colgan, S. P., Gronert, K., & Chiang, N. (2000). Anti-inflammatory lipid signals generated from dietary n-3 fatty acids via cyclooxygenase-2 and transcellular processing: A novel mechanism for NSAID and n-3 PUFA therapeutic actions. *Journal of Physiology and Pharmacology, 4,* 643–654.

Serhan, C. N., Hong, S., Gronert, K., Colgan, S. P., Devchand, P. R., Mirick, G., et al. (2002). Resolvins: A family of bioactive products of omega-3 fatty acid transformation circuits initiated by aspirin treatment that counter pro-inflammation signals. *Journal of Experimental Medicine, 196,* 1025–1037.

Serhan, C. N., Jain, A., Marleau, S., Clish, C., Kantarci, A., Behbehani, B., et al. (2003). Reduced inflammation and tissue damage in transgenic rabbits overexpressing 15-lipoxygenase and endogenous anti-inflammatory lipid mediators. *Journal of Immunology, 171,* 6856–6865.

Shimizu, T., Fujii, T., Suzuki, R., Igarashi, J., Ohtsuka, Y., Nagata, S., et al. (2003). Effects of highly purified eicosapentaenoic acid on erythrocyte fatty acid composition and leukocyte and colonic mucosa leukotriene B4 production in children with ulcerative colitis. *Journal of Pediatric Gastroenterology and Nutrition, 37,* 581–585.

Skoldstam, L., Borjesson, O., Kjallman, A., Seiving, B., & Akesson, B. (1992). Effect of six months of fish oil supplementation in stable rheumatoid arthritis: A double blind, controlled study. *Scandinavian Journal of Rheumatology, 21,* 178–185.

Sperling, R. I., Benincaso, A. I., Knoell, C. T., Larkin, J. K., Austen, K. F., & Robinson, D. R. (1993). Dietary ω-3 polyunsaturated fatty acids inhibit phosphoinositide formation and chemotaxis in neutrophils. *Journal of Clinical Investigation, 91,* 651–660.

Sperling, R. I., Weinblatt, M., Robin, J. L., Ravalese, J., Hoover, R. L., House, F., et al. (1987). Effects of dietary supplementation with marine fish oil on leukocyte lipid mediator generation and function in rheumatoid arthritis. *Arthritis & Rheumatism, 30,* 988–997.

Stenius-Aarniala, B., Aro, A., Hakulinen, A., Ahola, I., Seppala, E., & Vapaatalo, H. (1989). Evening primrose oil and fish oil are ineffective as supplementary treatment of bronchial asthma. *Annals of Allergy, 62,* 534–537.

Stenson, W. F., Cort, D., Rodgers, J., Burakoff, R., DeSchryver-Kecskemeti, K., Gramlich, T. L., et al. (1992). Dietary supplementation with fish oil in ulcerative colitis. *Annals of Internal Medicine, 116,* 609–614.

Teitelbaum, J. E., & Walker, W. A. (2001). Review: The role of omega 3 fatty acids in intestinal inflammation. *Journal of Nutritional Biochemistry, 12,* 21–32.

Thien, F. C. K., Mencia-Huerta, J. M., & Lee, T. H. (1993). Dietary fish oil effects on seasonal hay fever and asthma in pollen-sensitive subjects. *American Review of Respiratory Disease, 147,* 1138–1143.

Thien, F. C. K., Woods, R., De Luca, S., & Abramson, M. J. (2002). Dietary marine fatty acids (fish oil) for asthma in adults and children. *Cochrane Database of Systematic Reviews, 2,* CD001283.

Thies, F., Miles, E. A., Nebe-von-Caron, G., Powell, J. R., Hurst, T. L., Newsholme, E. A., et al. (2001). Influence of dietary supplementation with long chain n-3 or n-6 polyunsaturated fatty acids on blood inflammatory cell populations and functions and on plasma soluble adhesion molecules in healthy adults. *Lipids, 36,* 1183–1193.

Thies, F., Nebe-von-Caron, G., Powell, J. R., Yaqoob, P., Newsholme, E. A., & Calder, P. C. (2001). Dietary supplementation with gamma-linolenic acid or fish oil decreases T lymphocyte proliferation in healthy older humans. *Journal of Nutrition, 131,* 1918–1927.

Thompson, P. J., Misso, N. L. A., Passarelli, M., & Phillips, M. J. (1991). The effect of eicosapentaenoic acid consumption on human neutrophil chemiluminescence. *Lipids, 26,* 1223–1226.

Tilley, S. L., Coffman, T. M., & Koller, B. H. (2001). Mixed messages: Modulation of inflammation and immune responses by prostaglandins and thromboxanes. *Journal of Clinical Investigation, 108,* 15–23.

Trebble, T. M., Arden, N. K., Stroud, M. A., Wootton, S. A., Burdge, G. C., Miles, E. A., et al. (2003). Inhibition of tumour necrosis factor-alpha and interleukin-6 production by mononuclear cells following dietary fish-oil supplementation in healthy men and response to antioxidant co-supplementation. *British Journal of Nutrition, 90,* 405–412.

Trebble, T. M., Arden, N. K., Wootton, S. A., Calder, P. C., Mullee, M., Fine, D. R., et al. (2004). Fish oil and antioxidants alter the composition and function of circulating mononuclear cells in Crohn's disease. *American Journal of Clinical Nutrition, 80,* 1137–1144.

Trebble, T. M., Stroud, M. A., Wootton, S. A., Calder, P. C., Fine, D. R., Mullee, M. A., et al. (2005). High dose fish oil and antioxidants in Crohn's disease and the response of bone turnover: A randomised controlled trial. *British Journal of Nutrition, 94,* 253–261.

Trebble, T. M., Wootton, S. A., Miles, E. A., Mullee, M., Arden, N. K., Ballinger, A. B., et al. (2003). Prostaglandin E2 production and T-cell function after fish-oil supplementation: Response to antioxidant co-supplementation. *American Journal of Clinical Nutrition, 78,* 376–382.

Tullekan, J. E., Limburg, P. C., Muskiet, F. A. J., & van Rijswijk, M. H. (1990). Vitamin E status during dietary fish oil supplementation in rheumatoid arthritis. *Arthritis & Rheumatism, 33,* 1416–1419.

Vachier, I., Chanez, P., Bonnans, C., Godard, P., Bousquet, J., & Chavis, C. (2002). Endogenous anti-inflammatory mediators from arachidonate in human neutrophils. *Biochemical and Biophysical Research Communications, 290,* 219–224.

Van den Berghe, W., Vermeulen, L., Delerive, P., De Bosscher, K., Staels, B., & Haegeman, G. (2003). A paradigm for gene regulation: Inflammation, NF-kappaB and PPAR. *Advances in Experimental Medicine and Biology, 544,* 181–196.

van der Tempel, H., Tullekan, J. E., Limburg, P. C., Muskiet, F. A. J., & van Rijswijk, M. H. (1990). Effects of fish oil supplementation in rheumatoid arthritis. *Annals of the Rheumatic Diseases, 49,* 76–80.

Varghese, T., & Coomansingh, D. (2000). Clinical response of ulcerative colitis with dietary omega-3 fatty acids: A double-blind randomized study. *British Journal of Surgery, 87*(Suppl. 1), 73.

Varming, K., Schmidt, E. B., Svaneborg, N., Moller, J. M., Lervang, H. H., Grunnet, N., et al. (1995). The effect of n 3 fatty acids on neutrophil chemiluminescence. *Scandinavian Journal of Clinical & Laboratory Investigation, 55,* 47–52.

Vilaseca, J., Salas, A., Guarner, F., Rodriguez, R., Martinez, M., & Malagelada, J.-R. (1990). Dietary fish oil reduces progression of chronic inflammatory lesions in a rat model of granulomatous colitis. *Gut, 31,* 539–544.

Volker, D. H., Fitzgerald, P. E. B., & Garg, M. L. (2000). The eicosapentaenoic to docosahexaenoic acid ratio of diets affects the pathogenesis of arthritis in Lew/ SSN rats. *Journal of Nutrition, 130,* 559–565.

Volker, D. H., Fitzgerald, P. E. B., Major, G., & Garg, M. (2000). Efficacy of fish oil concentrate in the treatment of rheumatoid arthritis. *Journal of Rheumatology, 27,* 2343–2346.

Volker, D. H., & Garg, M. (1996). Dietary n-3 fatty acid supplementation in rheumatoid arthritis—Mechanisms, clinical outcomes, controversies, and future directions. *Journal of Clinical Biochemistry and Nutrition, 20,* 83–87.

Von Schacky, C., Kiefl, R., Jendraschak, E., & Kaminski, W. E. (1993). N-3 fatty acids and cysteinyl-leukotriene formation in humans in vitro, ex vivo and in vivo. *Journal of Laboratory and Clinical Medicine, 121,* 302–309.

Wallace, F. A., Miles, E. A., & Calder, P. C. (2003). Comparison of the effects of linseed oil and different doses of fish oil on mononuclear cell function in healthy human subjects. *British Journal of Nutrition, 89,* 679–689.

Wallace, F. A., Neely, S. J., Miles, E. A., & Calder, P. C. (2000). Dietary fats affect macrophage-mediated cytotoxicity towards tumour cells. *Immunology & Cell Biology, 78,* 40–48.

Yaqoob, P., & Calder, P. C. (1995). Effects of dietary lipid manipulation upon inflammatory mediator production by murine macrophages. *Cell Immunology, 163,* 120–128.

Yaqoob, P., & Calder, P. C. (2007). Fatty acids and immune function: New insights into mechanisms. *British Journal of Nutrition, 98*(Suppl. 1), S41–S45.

Yaqoob, P., Pala, H. S., Cortina-Borja, M., Newsholme, E. A., & Calder, P. C. (2000). Encapsulated fish oil enriched in alpha-tocopherol alters plasma phospholipid and mononuclear cell fatty acid compositions but not mononuclear cell functions. *European Journal of Clinical Investigation, 30,* 260–274.

Yuceyar, H., Ozutemiz, O., Huseyinov, A., Saruc, M., Alkanat, M., Bor, S., et al. (1999). Is administration of n-3 fatty acids by mucosal enema protective against trinitrobenzene-induced colitis in rats? *Prostaglandins, Leukotrienes & Essential Fatty Acids, 61,* 339–345.

Zhao, Y., Joshi-Barve, S., Barve, S., & Chen, L. H. (2004). Eicosapentaenoic acid prevents LPS-induced TNF-alpha expression by preventing NF-kappaB activation. *Journal of the American College of Nutrition, 23,* 71–78.

II

THE LINK BETWEEN STRESS, INFLAMMATION, AND DISEASE

5

DEPRESSION, HOSTILITY, POSTTRAUMATIC STRESS DISORDER, AND INFLAMMATION: THE CORROSIVE HEALTH EFFECTS OF NEGATIVE MENTAL STATES

KATHLEEN KENDALL-TACKETT

Negative emotions, such as depression, anxiety, pessimism, hopelessness, anger, and shame, have a well-documented deleterious effect on health (Frasure-Smith & Lesperance, 2005; Kendall-Tackett, 2007; Kubzansky, Davidson, & Rozanski, 2005; Surtees et al., 2008). They also increase inflammation. This chapter describes research on three common negative mental states—depression, hostility, and posttraumatic stress disorder (PTSD)—their impact on inflammation and how mental-state-related inflammation impacts health. Finally, clinical applications based on these findings are presented.

DEPRESSION

Depression and Inflammation

More than a decade ago, researchers first noted that high levels of proinflammatory cytokines increased the risk of depression (Maes & Smith,

1998). Furthermore, these researchers also found that psychological stress leads to an increase in inflammation. The proinflammatory cytokines identified most often in depression research are interleukin-1β (IL-1β), IL-6, and tumor necrosis factor-α (TNF-α). Researchers sometimes include other measures of inflammation in their studies. These include interferon-γ (IFN-γ), intercellular adhesion molecule, or C-reactive protein (CRP; Pace, Hu, & Miller, 2007). Fibrinogen, a soluble protein that aids in clotting, is another marker of inflammation. Because it increases the speed of platelet aggregation and thrombus formation, a high level of fibrinogen is a risk factor for cardiovascular disease (CVD) and predicts cardiac events. Maes (2001) described the stress–depression–inflammation connection as follows:

> The discovery that psychological stress can induce the production of proinflammatory cytokines has important implications for human psychopathology and, in particular, for the aetiology of major depression. Psychological stressors, such as negative life events, are emphasized in the aetiology of depression. Thus psychosocial and environmental stressors play a role as direct precipitants of major depression or they function as vulnerability factors which predispose humans to develop major depression. Major depression is accompanied by activation of the inflammatory response system (IRS) with, among other things, an increased production of proinflammatory cytokines, such as IL-1β, IL-6, TNF-α and IFN-γ, signs of monocytic- and T-cell activation and an acute-phase response. (p. 193)

How Depression Influences Health

Depression is one of the most common of all mood disorders, and it is the mental state with the most clearly documented impact on health (Frasure-Smith & Lesperance, 2005). Depression increases the risk of a number of health problems, including coronary heart disease, myocardial infarction, chronic pain syndromes, premature aging, impaired immune function, impaired wound healing, and Alzheimer's disease (Kiecolt-Glaser et al., 2005; Pace et al., 2007; Surtees et al., 2008; Wilson, Finch, & Cohen, 2002). In a large study of U.S. veterans (N = 35,715), patients with depression were at increased risk of dying over a 5-year period (Kinder et al., 2008). This was not true for those with PTSD and no depression, nor for those who had neither depression nor PTSD.

Most of the research on depression and health has examined the link between depression and CVD. Depression is a robust risk factor for CVD, cardiovascular events, and cardiac-related mortality (Frasure-Smith & Lesperance, 2005; Rutledge et al., 2006). Patients with depression have more frequent and earlier hospital readmissions and are more likely to have a number of behavioral risk factors, including smoking, obesity, and a sedentary lifestyle (Rieckmann et al., 2006). The risk was not only for those with major depression but also for those with milder forms. But behavior alone cannot account for the increased risk. Depression changes the inflammatory response system and more directly influences cardiac risk.

Depression, Inflammation, and Heart Disease

Inflammation is a crucial factor in atherogenesis and the progression of coronary artery disease (Zouridakis, Avanzas, Arroyo-Espliguero, Fredericks, & Kaski, 2004). Inflammatory factors are not simply markers. They have a pathogenic role to play, and these inflammatory markers, including CRP and proinflammatory cytokines, are often elevated in people with depression.

Several studies have found elevated CRP in patients with depression and heart disease. In a study of men and women at risk of heart disease ($N = 68$), Taylor et al. (2006) found that patients with depression had elevated CRP compared with the control participants. The patients with depression also had abnormally low cortisol levels in response to stress, and a lower respiratory sinus arrhythmia. The mean age of the patients was 62 years.

Surtees et al. (2008) compared a large sample of patients with ischemic heart disease with a sample of matched control participants. They found that major depression in the previous year increased CRP levels. Those with higher CRP had an odds ratio of 2.02 for incident ischemic heart disease, even when adjusting for other risk factors, including cigarette smoking, diabetes, systolic blood pressure, body mass index (BMI), and cholesterol.

Eighteen elderly patients with chronic heart failure and major depression were compared with 16 patients with heart failure and no depression, and 13 healthy control participants (Andrei et al., 2007). Patients with chronic heart failure and major depression had significantly higher CRP levels than did the healthy control participants. The CRP levels of the heart patients without depression were elevated compared with the healthy control participants, but not significantly so. There were no differences in TNF-α or IL-6 between the groups.

Coagulability may also be a factor in depression's impact on heart disease. A study of patients 65 and older found that depression was related to both CRP and coagulation factors (Kop et al., 2002). This study included 4,268 patients who were free of CVD (mean age = 72.4 years). Men and women with depression had elevated CRP, elevated white blood cell count, and increased markers of coagulability.

Similarly, coagulation was also related to depression and cardiovascular risk in a study of 3,292 perimenopausal women (Matthews et al., 2007). This study included five markers of hemostasis and inflammation. Over the 5-year period, once the model was adjusted for health history, medication use, ethnicity, and menopausal status, depressive symptoms were related to fibrinogen and PAI-1. CRP was not elevated in women with depressive symptoms. The authors concluded that depressive symptoms may be associated with increased cardiovascular risk through hypercoagulability.

Depression has also been related to cardiac-related mortality risk. It predicted cardiac symptoms in a sample of 750 middle-age women with suspected myocardial ischemia (Rutledge et al., 2006). Both treatment for depression and current depression severity were related to cardiac symptoms and outcomes over the course of the 2.3-year follow-up. The more severe the depression, the higher the mortality risk; each point increase on the Beck Depression Inventory was associated with a 3% increase in mortality risk even after adjusting for age, disease severity, and other coronary artery disease risk factors.

Eighteen patients with congestive heart failure and depressive symptoms were enrolled in the study, and levels of IFN-γ, IL-6, and IL-10 CD4+ T cells were assessed (Redwine et al., 2007). The researchers found that higher depressive symptoms led to a prospective increase in cardiac rehospitalization or death over a 2-year period. Lower IFN-γ and anti-inflammatory IL-10 were prospectively related to increased depressive symptoms, cardiac rehospitalization, or death. Contrary to expectation, they did not find that IL-6 was elevated in patients with depression.

Treating depression without addressing inflammation may not be sufficient to reverse cardiac risk. In a sample of 129 patients with heart failure, soluble TNF-α levels were significantly higher in patients with depression than in patients without depression and also for a subgroup of patients who were no longer depressed but were on antidepressant medications (Moorman et al., 2007). These findings suggest that medications were treating depression but not adequately reversing inflammation. There were no significant differences between the depressed and nondepressed groups in IL-1β or IL-6.

Summary

Depression is associated with increased levels of proinflammatory cytokines, C-reactive protein, and other markers of inflammation, such as coaguability. Not surprisingly, depression is related to heart disease and predicts new cardiac events. Unfortunately, depression is not alone in increasing risk of disease. Hostility is a related mental state that also increases risk of both cardiac and metabolic diseases. These studies are described in the next section.

HOSTILITY AND OTHER NEGATIVE SOCIAL APPRAISALS

For men and women with a hostile world view, life is not benign. Hostile people do not trust others, are suspicious and cynical about human nature, and have a tendency to interpret the actions of others as negative (Kubzansky et al., 2005; Smith, 1992). Trait hostility increases physiological arousal because of the way hostile people interpret the world; they are more likely to perceive even neutral events as negative, responding strongly because they perceive interpersonal threat (Kiecolt-Glaser & Newton, 2001).

Health Effects of Hostility

Hostility has garnered a great deal of attention because, like depression, it increases the risk of CVD (Smith et al., 2007). Smith and Ruiz's (2002) review noted that people who are high in trait hostility are more prone to ischemia and constriction of the coronary arteries during mental stress. Trait hostility predicted new coronary events in previously healthy people. And for patients who already had coronary heart disease, hostility sped up progression of the disease.

Hostility also has metabolic effects. In a sample of 1,081 older men, hostility was related to several indices of metabolic syndrome (Niaura et al., 2000). Hostility was positively associated with higher waist-to-hip ratio, BMI, total caloric intake, fasting insulin level, and serum triglycerides. It was inversely related to education and high-density lipoprotein (HDL) cholesterol. The authors concluded that their results were consistent with previous studies indicating that hostility was associated with a pattern of obesity, central adiposity, and elevated insulin levels.

Hostility also increases the risk of metabolic syndrome in teens. In a 3-year follow-up of 134 White and African American adolescents, hostility at Time 1 predicted risk factors for metabolic syndrome at Time 2 (Raikkonen, Matthews, & Salomon, 2003). These risk factors were at the 75th percentile for age, gender, and race and included BMI, insulin resistance, a high ratio of triglycerides to HDL cholesterol, and mean arterial blood pressure. Unfortunately, lipid profiles, blood pressure, and insulin resistance are not the only things that hostility affects. As with depression, hostility also increases inflammation.

Hostility and Inflammation

A study of 6,814 healthy men and women found that participants with higher levels of cynical distrust, chronic stress, or depression had higher levels of inflammation (Ranjit et al., 2007). Inflammation included elevated CRP, IL-6, and fibrinogen. Chronic stress was associated with higher IL-6 and CRP, and depression was associated with higher IL-6. All are risk factors for heart disease.

Hostility was associated with higher levels of circulating proinflammatory cytokines IL-1α, IL-1β, and IL-8 in 44 healthy, nonsmoking, premenopausal women. The combination of depression and hostility was particularly harmful and increased levels of IL-1β, IL-8, and TNF-α (Suarez, Lewis, Krishnan, & Young, 2004). There was a dose–response effect: The more severe the depression and hostility, the greater the production of cytokines. A study with men had similar results (Suarez, 2003). The author noted that increased levels of IL-6 predicted both future risk of cardiac events and all-cause mortality. He hypothesized that IL-6 may mediate the relationship between hostility and these health problems.

Suarez (2006) also studied 135 healthy patients (75 men, 60 women) with no symptoms of diabetes. He found that women who had higher levels of depression and hostility, and who had a propensity to express anger, also had higher levels of fasting insulin, glucose, and insulin resistance. These findings were not true for men, and they were independent of other risk factors for metabolic syndrome, including BMI, age, fasting triglycerides, exercise regularity, or ethnicity. The author indicated that these findings were significant because prestudy glucose levels were in the nondiabetic range. The author noted that inflammation, particularly elevated IL-6 and CRP, may mediate the relationship between depression and hostility and between risk of Type 2 diabetes and CVD, possibly because IL-6 and CRP increase insulin resistance.

Hostility and Social Relationships

Hostility also has indirect effects on health by affecting quality of relationships. Hostile persons can undermine relationships through their mistrustful thoughts and antagonistic actions, and they are more likely to have negative social relations with others (Smith & Ruiz, 2002). Hostile people are more likely to be socially isolated, to be insecure about current relationships, and to perceive that others are making negative judgments about them. Because of this, trait hostility has a serious impact on marriage and other important relationships, and quality of social relationships, especially marriage, can have a significant impact on health.

Health Effects of Marriage and Marital Strife

Of all social relationships, marriage has the strongest effect on health. Marriage seems particularly protective of men's health. In a review of the literature on marriage and health, Kiecolt-Glaser and Newton (2001) found that being married reduced premature mortality by 500% for men. For women, marriage reduced premature mortality by only 50%. This sex difference may be due to women having larger social networks outside of marriage than do men.

In data from the Framingham Offspring Study, married men were half as likely to die during the follow-up period as were unmarried men (Eaker, Sullivan, Kelly-Hayes, D'Agostino, & Benjamin, 2007). The Framingham Offspring Study is the second generation of data collection from the Framingham Heart Study, a major study of CVD, now following the second and third generations of study participants. The results were more complex for women. Marital status alone was not enough to prolong life; however, aspects of how women handled marital conflict were. Women who "self-silenced" in conflicts were 4 times more likely to die compared with those who did not. The findings were true even after adjusting for systolic blood pressure, age, BMI, cigarette smoking, diabetes, and cholesterol.

Though the effects of marriage on health are generally good, ongoing marital strife is not. In fact, it increases the risk of heart disease, particularly for women. A 13-year longitudinal study of married women found that women with poor-quality marriages had higher rates of several markers for CVD: low HDL cholesterol, high triglycerides, and higher BMI, blood pressure, depression, and anger (Gallo, Troxel, Matthews, & Kuller, 2003). In a study from Sweden, Orth-Gomer et al. (2000) followed 292 women for 5 years after a myocardial infarction. They found that women with high levels of marital strife were nearly 3 times more likely to have another heart attack or other coronary event than were women who were married but not distressed. This relationship held even after adjusting for age, estrogen levels, education, and smoking.

In a study of 300 married couples (average age = 54.4) with no coronary artery disease, participants completed four measures of hostility (Smith et al., 2007). The measures were self-reports and spouse ratings of angry hostility (a tendency to experience anger) and antagonism, which included argumentative, mistrusting, and cold interpersonal behavior. The researchers found that self-reports of hostility and antagonism were not related to coronary artery calcification, a marker for potential atherosclerosis. But spouse ratings of the person were. These findings were true for the older, but not middle-age, participants, independent of socioeconomic status (SES), marital satisfaction, age, and gender. These findings were also independent of exercise, smoking, and alcohol use. The authors concluded that hostility was related to asymptomatic coronary artery disease but that self-reports likely underestimated this variable.

Social Integration

Much of what is known about the health effects of social relationships comes from studying its absence, in the form of social isolation and low social integration. Hostile people are more likely to have low social integration and be more socially isolated—another way that hostility can influence health. In older men, low social integration was associated with increased fibrinogen, even after adjusting for smoking, alcohol consumption, physical activity, BMI, age, race, and education (Loucks, Berkman, Cruenewald, & Seeman, 2005). There was no relation between social integration and fibrinogen for women. This study included 800 high-functioning men and women (ages 70–79) who were part of the MacArthur Successful Aging Study. The researchers calculated social integration using marital status, number of contacts with family and friends, frequency of religious service attendance, and participation in volunteer organizations.

In a sample of 783 middle-age and older adults, social isolation increased levels of coronary artery calcification. The researchers found that 49% of subjects had calcification. The risk was higher in participants with diabetes mellitus, and men had higher levels of calcification than did women. Social isolation (measured as being single or widowed) was related to calcification, even after adjusting for age, sex, systolic blood pressure, blood glucose, and low-density lipoprotein cholesterol. In contrast, health behaviors, socioeconomic status, and depression were not related to calcification (Kop et al., 2005). The authors proposed several possible mechanisms for this effect. Social isolation increases rates of serum norepinephrine and cortisol as well as elevated heart rate. Therefore, isolation could induce sustained sympathetic hyperresponsiveness, which may promote vascular injury. Social isolation may also increase the risk of high-risk health behaviors, such as smoking and maintaining a high-fat diet.

Secure Relationships and Sleep Quality

Another way that problem relationships may increase cardiovascular risk is by affecting sleep. Two recent studies examined the relationship between security of attachments between adult partners and sleep quality. Sleep is a physiologically vulnerable state. To sleep soundly, people must feel sufficiently secure so they can down-regulate vigilance and alertness. To feel this secure, they must be secure in key social relationships (Troxel, Cyranowski, Hall, Frank, & Buysee, 2007).

In the first study, 78 married adults completed questionnaires about their sleep quality, quality of current partnership (secure vs. insecure attachment), and depression (Carmichael & Reis, 2005). Married participants who were anxious about their current relationships reported poorer sleep quality, even after controlling for depression. Women with insecure attachments were concerned that their partners were emotionally unavailable and not trustworthy. The researchers indicated that one limitation of their study was that they used a self-report measure of sleep, rather than assessing sleep directly.

Troxel et al. (2007) addressed that limitation by using polysomnographic studies to assess sleep directly. In a study of 107 women with recurrent major depression, marital status and security of that relationship predicted quality and efficiency of sleep. If women had anxious attachments, particularly if they were separated or widowed, they had a significantly smaller percentage of Stage 3–4 sleep than did women who were currently partnered and who had secure attachments. The authors noted the importance of Stage 3–4 sleep in protecting individuals from cardiovascular and metabolic diseases.

McEwen (2003) reported that even short periods of sleep deprivation can elevate cortisol and glucose levels and can increase both insulin and insulin resistance. Sleep deprivation also provokes an inflammatory response because the body thinks it is under attack. Long-term sleep deprivation can seriously impair health, which could be a health risk factor for men and women who are not in stable, secure relationships (Stein, Belik, Jacobi, & Sareen, 2008). Suarez and Goforth (see chap. 3, this volume) also described how sleep problems increase inflammation and the importance of sleep in preventing cardiovascular and metabolic diseases.

Social Stratification and Cardiac Risk Factors

Where people fall on the social hierarchy also has an impact on their cardiovascular health. If men or women perceive that they have low social status—because of education, ethnicity, vocation, or income level—their risk of CVD increases. Perceived social status involves negative appraisals of what others think of them and triggers the inflammatory response.

Low social status was associated with two measures of vascular inflammation related to blood pressure in a sample of 121 White and African American men and women (Hong, Neleson, Krohn, Mills, & Dimsdale, 2006). In this sample, researchers measured soluble intercellular adhesion molecule (sICAM) and endothelin-1 (ET-1). Men and women in the lowest social class had the highest levels of sICAM and ET-1. Social status was calculated based on measures of occupation and education. These findings were independent of hypertension status and ethnicity but were related to gender and health behaviors.

Low status was also reflected in the measure of CRP in a 3-year longitudinal study of 188 middle-age and older adults, ages 52 to 70 (McDade, Hawkley, & Cacioppo, 2006). In this sample, African Americans, women, and those with lower education had the highest levels of CRP. However, ethnic group differences disappeared once health behaviors were factored in. Waist circumference, latency to sleep, smoking, and perceived stress were independently associated with increased CRP. Men and women who took longer to get to sleep had higher levels of CRP. The authors concluded that psychosocial stress and health behaviors are both important determinants of systemic inflammation and increased cardiac risk.

Low parental education level, another marker of social status, predicted metabolic and cardiovascular risk factors in 758 Black and White high school students. Students with low social status had higher insulin levels, higher glucose, greater insulin resistance, higher low-density lipoprotein and lower HDL cholesterol, higher waist circumference, and higher BMI than did students with high status (Goodman, McEwen, Huang, Dolan, & Adler, 2005). The authors hypothesized that cortisol and insulin are the primary hormonal factors regulating carbohydrate metabolism, inflammation, cholesterol metabolism, and adiposity, and that the chronic stress of low social status dysregulates these processes. They concluded that low parental education was associated with multiple metabolic risks, suggesting an intergenerational transfer of risks for CVD.

Low SES was also related to increased sympathetic nervous system activity in a study of 672 participants, ages 18 to 30 (Janicki-Deverts et al.,

2007). In this study, 12-hour overnight urine samples were analyzed for norepinephrine and epinephrine. Participants also completed questionnaires that assessed demographic variables, health behavior, and psychosocial variables (e.g., perceived discrimination, negative support, depression). The researchers measured SES by income, education, and occupation. Regardless of which measure of SES they used, those with higher SES had lower norepinephrine and epinephrine. This effect was independent of race, age, and gender, and was similar for Blacks and Whites. Two factors that mediated the effects were depressive symptoms and smoking.

Chronic exposure to discrimination was significantly associated with coronary artery calcification, even after controlling for demographics, standard cardiac risk factors, and BMI in a sample of middle-age African American women (Lewis et al., 2006). The women were assessed over a 5-year period. Recent discrimination was only marginally associated with coronary artery calcification, and multiple forms of discrimination were more powerfully associated than was racial discrimination alone.

Summary

Human social relationships either increase or decrease our vulnerability to stress. If humans make consistently negative or hostile appraisals of the motives of others, they increase their risk of disease directly and indirectly by impacting the quality of their social relationships. This vulnerability manifests through several physiological mechanisms, including inflammation. These findings indicate that humans are social animals and that social support, social integration, and perceived social status have measurable effects on health. Indeed, loved ones, and others in our social orbit, help regulate our internal states. Hostility and disruptions to social networks have a negative impact on health and can result in diseases such as heart disease, metabolic syndrome, and diabetes.

POSTTRAUMATIC STRESS DISORDER

Trauma survivors are significantly more likely to have a number of serious illnesses and to die prematurely than are their nontraumatized counterparts (Felitti et al., 2001; Kendall-Tackett, 2003). For example, the National Comorbidity Study found that women who were maltreated as children had a ninefold increase in CVD compared with nonmaltreated women (Batten, Aslan, Maciejewski, & Mazure, 2004). Data from the Canadian Community Health Survey ($N = 36,984$) indicated that participants with PTSD had significantly higher rates of several illnesses, including CVD, respiratory diseases, chronic pain syndromes, gastrointestinal illnesses, and cancer (Sareen, Cox, Stein, Afifi, Fleet, & Asmundson, 2007). PTSD was also strongly associated with chronic fatigue syndrome and multiple-chemical sensitivity, but there was no significant difference in rates of diabetes.

PTSD following a manmade disaster showed similar health effects (N = 896; Dirkzwager, van der Velden, Grievink, & Yzermans, 2007). In this study, PTSD was associated with new vascular events as well as physician-reported vascular, musculoskeletal, and dermatological problems. These problems appeared even after controlling for previous health problem, smoking, and demographic characteristics.

It is not surprising that people with PTSD use more health care services. In a study of women seeking health care at Veterans Administration facilities (Dobie et al., 2006), the women with PTSD had more outpatient visits to the emergency department, primary care, or medical or surgery subspecialties; ancillary services; and diagnostic tests. They also had higher rates of hospitalizations and surgical procedures. Women with PTSD were significantly more likely to have a service-related disability, have chronic pain, and to be obese. They were also more likely to smoke and abuse alcohol. Comorbid depression rates were also high: Seventy-five percent of the women with PTSD also screened positive for depression.

Inflammation in Trauma Survivors

Although the area of study is a relatively new one, several researchers have found that traumatic events increase levels of proinflammatory cytokines in trauma survivors. The increase in inflammation may mediate the relationship between trauma and health problems.

Childhood maltreatment was shown to affect clinically relevant levels of CRP when measured 20 years later in abuse survivors (Danese, Pariante, Caspi, Taylor, & Poulton, 2007). The participants (N = 1,037) were part of the Dunedin Multidisciplinary Health and Development Study, a study of health behavior in a complete birth cohort in New Zealand. Participants were assessed every 2 to 3 years throughout childhood, and every 5 to 6 years through age 32. The effect of child maltreatment on inflammation was independent of co-occurring life stresses in adulthood, early-life risks, or adult health or health behavior. Severity of abuse was related, in a dose-responsive way, to severity of inflammation.

In a study of intimate partner violence (IPV), 62 women who had had abusive partners had significantly higher IFN-γ levels than did nonabused women (Woods et al., 2005). Of women in the IPV group, 52% reported depression and 39% had high levels of PTSD symptoms. These findings demonstrated the lingering health effects of IPV in women who experienced violence 8 to 11 years previously yet were still manifesting significantly physical symptomatology.

Inflammation was also elevated in a study of rape (Groër, Thomas, Evans, Helton, & Weldon, 2006). In this study, 15 women who had been raped were compared with 16 women who had not been sexually assaulted on immune markers 24 to 72 hours after their assault. Women who had been sexually assaulted had higher adrenocorticotropic hormone, CRP, IL-6, IL-10, and IFN-γ than did women in the control group. In addition, the assaulted women had lower B lymphocyte counts and decreased lymphocyte proliferation. The researchers interpreted their findings as indicating that sexual assault activated innate immunity and suppressed some aspects of adaptive immunity. If these long-term alterations persist, they could lead to health problems in rape survivors.

In a sample of 14 otherwise healthy patients with PTSD and a matched group on age and gender of 14 patients without PTSD, von Kanel et al. (2006) investigated PTSD and blood coagulation by measuring clotting factors, fibrinogen, and D-dimer in the plasma. They found that the more severe the PTSD, the higher the levels of fibrinogen and the clotting factor FVIII:C. They concluded that PTSD may elicit hypercoagulability, even at subthreshold levels, which may increase risk of CVD in trauma survivors.

Sleep Disorders in Posttraumatic Stress Disorder

Sleep disorders are also common in PTSD, with disturbed sleep and nightmares being key symptoms (Morin & Ware, 1996). As Suarez and Goforth (see chap. 3, this volume) described, sleep problems could be another way that PTSD affects health. A number of studies have documented disturbed sleep patterns in men and women who have experienced a wide range of violence. For example, in a European community sample, 68% of sexual abuse survivors reported having sleep difficulties, with 45% having repetitive nightmares (Teegen, 1999). In a French sample, 33% of teens who had been raped indicated that they "slept badly" compared with 16% of the nonassaulted control group. Of the assaulted teens, 28% had nightmares (compared with 11%), and 56% woke during the night (compared with 21%; Choquet, Darves-Bornoz, Ledoux, Manfredi, & Hassler, 1997).

Hulme (2000) found that sleep problems among female sexual abuse survivors were common in a primary-care sample. Fifty-two percent of sexual abuse survivors reported that they could not sleep at night (compared with 24% of the nonabused group), and 36% reported nightmares (compared with 13%). Intrusive symptoms were also common, with 53% of sexual abuse survivors reporting sudden thoughts or images of past events (compared with 18% of the nonabused group).

In a sample of battered women living in shelters ($N = 50$), 70% reported poor sleep quality, 28% went to bed very fatigued, and 40% woke up feeling very fatigued (Humphreys, Lee, Neylan, & Marmar, 1999). Moreover, 82% described one or more of the following characteristics of disturbed sleep: many wakings over the course of the night, restless sleep, and early-morning waking. Six described vivid nightmares that included recent incidents of abuse.

In a study of sleep disorders in sexual assault survivors, 80% had either sleep-breathing or sleep-movement disorders. Both of these disorders were linked to higher levels of depression and suicidality, and women who had both types of sleep disorders had the most severe symptoms. The authors speculated that fragmented sleep potentiated the symptoms for women after a sexual assault, stretching their fragile coping abilities to the breaking point (Krakow, Artar, et al., 2000).

Sleep problems may also keep symptoms of PTSD active. In a study of 23 patients who suffered from chronic nightmares and obstructive sleep apnea, patients who had completed a treatment program for their sleep problems ($N = 14$) were compared with patients who had dropped out of the program ($N = 9$). Twenty-one months later, those who completed the program had substantially improved sleep compared with those who had not. When the patients with PTSD were compared with the PTSD/no-treatment patients, those in the treatment group had a 75% improvement in their PTSD symptoms. In contrast, the six patients in the PTSD/no-treatment group reported a 43% worsening of symptoms. The authors concluded that treating sleep difficulties appeared to also improve PTSD symptoms, and they recommended a full evaluation of sleep in patients with PTSD (Krakow, Lowry, et al., 2000).

Summary

PTSD and trauma exposure impact health in ways similar to that of depression by raising inflammation and impacting sleep quality. The link between PTSD and health has other components, as described in chapters 6 and 7 of this volume. The studies presented in this chapter suggest two possible interventions for trauma survivors. The first is assessing them for, and then treating, sleep disorders. The second is to target inflammation specifically, which will require a multimodal approach. Treatment will be visited again in chapter 8.

SUMMARY

Depression, hostility, and PTSD are all negative mental states that increase the risk of physical illness—and they often co-occur. Of more concern is the recognition that when these states do co-occur, they actually compound the negative health effects and increase inflammatory markers. These findings suggest that treating depression and PTSD will likely improve physical health by lowering inflammation and improving sleep quality. Cognitive interventions that address hostility and related negative beliefs will also likely have a positive physical effect. And practitioners may also want to specifically address inflammation via exercise, omega-3 fatty acids, and conventional antidepressants. These approaches are described more fully in chapter 9 of this volume.

KEY POINTS

- Negative emotional states impair health via a number of mechanisms, including high-risk behavior and low social support.
- Negative emotions also chronically activate the inflammatory response system, which increases the risk of disease.
- Depression has a well-established link to heart disease, cardiac events, and cardiac-related mortality. This is likely due to increased CRP and coagulability in people with depression.
- Hostility contributes to heart disease and is related to symptoms of metabolic syndrome, including insulin resistance.
- Hostility also affects health by impairing social relationships, contributing to strife within relationships, and increasing social isolation.
- New studies show that PTSD also contributes to health problems by increasing inflammation and causing sleep problems—even years after the traumatic event.

REFERENCES

Andrei, A. M., Fraguas, R., Jr., Telles, R. M., Alves, T. C., Strunz, C. M., Nussbacher, A., et al. (2007). Major depressive disorder and inflammatory markers in elderly patients with heart failure. *Psychosomatics*, 48, 319–324.

Batten, S. V., Aslan, M., Maciejewski, P. K., & Mazure, C. M. (2004). Childhood maltreatment as a risk factor for adult cardiovascular disease and depression. *Journal of Clinical Psychiatry*, 65, 249–254.

Carmichael, C. L., & Reis, H. T. (2005). Attachment, sleep quality, and depressed affect. *Health Psychology*, 24, 526–531.

Choquet, M., Darves-Bornoz, J.-M., Ledoux, S., Manfredi, R., & Hassler, C. (1997). Self-reported health and behavioral problems among adolescent victims of rape in France: Results of a cross-sectional survey. *Child Abuse & Neglect*, 21, 823–832.

Danese, A., Pariante, C. M., Caspi, A., Taylor, A., & Poulton, R. (2007). Childhood maltreatment predicts adult inflammation in a life-course study. *Proceedings of the National Academy of Sciences USA*, 104, 1319–1324.

Dirkzwager, A. J., van der Velden, P. G., Grievink, L., & Yzermans, C. J. (2007). Disaster-related posttraumatic stress disorder and physical health. *Psychosomatic Medicine, 69,* 435–440.

Dobie, D. J., Maynard, C., Kivlahan, D. R., Johnson, K. M., Simpson, T., David, A. C., et al. (2006). Posttraumatic stress disorder screening status is associated with increased VA medical and surgical utilization in women. *Journal of General Internal Medicine, 21*(Suppl. 3), S58–S64.

Eaker, E. D., Sullivan, L. M., Kelly-Hayes, M., D'Agostino, R. B., & Benjamin, E. J. (2007). Marital status, marital strain, and risk of coronary heart disease or total mortality: The Framingham Offspring Study. *Psychosomatic Medicine, 69,* 509–513.

Felitti, V. J., Anda, R. F., Nordenberg, D., Williamson, D. F., Spitz, A. M., Edwards, V., et al. (2001). Relationship of childhood abuse and household dysfunction to many of the leading causes of death in adults. In K. Franey, R. Geffner, & R. Falconer (Eds.), *The cost of child maltreatment: Who pays? We all do* (pp. 53–69). San Diego, CA: Family Violence and Sexual Assault Institute.

Frasure-Smith, N., & Lesperance, F. (2005). Reflections on depression as a cardiac risk factor. *Psychosomatic Medicine, 67*(Suppl. 1), S19–S25.

Gallo, L. C., Troxel, W. M., Matthews, K. A., & Kuller, L. H. (2003). Marital status and quality in middle-aged women: Associations with levels and trajectories of cardiovascular risk factors. *Health Psychology, 22,* 453–463.

Goodman, E., McEwen, B. S., Huang, B., Dolan, L. M., & Adler, N. E. (2005). Social inequalities in biomarkers of cardiovascular risk in adolescence. *Psychosomatic Medicine, 67,* 9–15.

Groër, M. W., Thomas, S. P., Evans, G. W., Helton, S., & Weldon, A. (2006). Inflammatory effects and immune system correlates of rape. *Violence and Victims, 21,* 796–808.

Hong, S., Nelesen, R. A., Krohn, P. L., Mills, P. J., & Dimsdale, J. E. (2006). The association of social status and blood pressure with markers of vascular inflammation. *Psychosomatic Medicine, 68,* 517–523.

Hulme, P. A. (2000). Symptomatology and health care utilization of women primary care patients who experienced childhood sexual abuse. *Child Abuse & Neglect, 24,* 1471–1484.

Humphreys, J. C., Lee, K. A., Neylan, T. C., & Marmar, C. R. (1999). Sleep patterns of sheltered battered women. *Journal of Nursing Scholarship, 31,* 139–143.

Janicki-Deverts, D., Cohen, S., Adler, N. E., Schwartz, J. E., Matthews, K. A., & Seeman, T. E. (2007). Socioeconomic status is related to urinary catecholamines in the Coronary Artery Risk Development in Young Adults (CARDIA) Study. *Psychosomatic Medicine, 69,* 514–520.

Kendall-Tackett, K. A. (2003). *Treating the lifetime health effects of childhood victimization.* Kingston, NJ: Civic Research Institute.

Kendall-Tackett, K. A. (2007). Cardiovascular disease and metabolic syndrome as sequelae of violence against women: A psychoneuroimmunology approach. *Trauma, Violence, & Abuse, 8,* 117–126.

Kiecolt-Glaser, J. K., Loving, T. J., Stowell, J. R., Malarkey, W. B., Lemeshow, S., Dickinson, S. L., & Glaser, R. (2005). Hostile marital interactions, proinflammatory cytokine production, and wound healing. *Archives of General Psychiatry*, *62*, 1377–1384.

Kiecolt-Glaser, J. K., & Newton, T. L. (2001). Marriage and health: His and hers. *Psychological Bulletin*, *127*, 472–503.

Kinder, L. S., Bradley, K. A., Katon, W. J., Ludman, E., McDonnel, M. B., & Bryson, C. L. (2008). Depressions, posttraumatic stress disorder, and mortality. *Psychosomatic Medicine*, *70*, 20–26.

Kop, W. J., Berman, D. S., Gransar, H., Wong, N. D., Miranda-Peats, R., White, M. D., et al. (2005). Social networks and coronary artery calcification in asymptomatic individuals. *Psychosomatic Medicine*, *67*, 343–352.

Kop, W. J., Gottdiener, J. S., Tangen, C. M., Fried, L. P., McBurnie, M. A., Walston, J., et al. (2002). Inflammation and coagulation factors in persons > 65 years of age with symptoms of depression but without evidence of myocardial ischemia. *American Journal of Cardiology*, *89*, 419–424.

Krakow, B., Artar, A., Warner, T. D., Melendez, D., Johnston, L., Hollifield, M., et al. (2000). Sleep disorder, depression, and suicidality in female sexual assault survivors. *Crisis*, *21*, 163–170.

Krakow, B., Lowry, C., Germain, A., Gaddy, L., Hollifield, M., Koss, M., et al. (2000). A retrospective study on improvements in nightmares and post-traumatic stress disorder following treatment for co-morbid sleep-disordered breathing. *Journal of Psychosomatic Research*, *49*, 291–298.

Kubzansky, L. D., Davidson, K. W., & Rozanski, A. (2005). The clinical impact of negative psychological states: Expanding the spectrum of risk for coronary artery disease. *Psychosomatic Medicine*, *67*(Suppl. 1), S10–S14.

Lewis, T. T., Everson-Rose, S. A., Powell, L. H., Matthews, K. A., Brown, C., Karavolos, K., et al. (2006). Chronic exposure to everyday discrimination and coronary artery calcification in African American women: The SWAN Heart Study. *Psychosomatic Medicine*, *68*, 362–368.

Loucks, E. B., Berkman, L. F., Cruenewald, T. L., & Seeman, T. E. (2005). Social integration is associated with fibrinogen concentration in elderly men. *Psychosomatic Medicine*, *67*, 353–358.

Maes, M. (2001). Psychological stress and the inflammatory response system. *Clinical Science*, *101*, 193–194.

Maes, M., & Smith, R. S. (1998). Fatty acids, cytokines, and major depression. *Biological Psychiatry*, *43*, 313–314.

Matthews, K. A., Schott, L. L., Bromberger, J., Cyranowski, J., Everson-Rose, S. A., & Sowers, M. F. (2007). Associations between depressive symptoms and inflammatory/hemostatic markers in women during the menopausal transition. *Psychosomatic Medicine*, *69*, 124–130.

McDade, T. W., Hawkley, L. C., & Cacioppo, J. T. (2006). Psychosocial and behavioral predictors of inflammation in middle-aged and older adults: The Chicago

Health, Aging, and Social Relations Study. *Psychosomatic Medicine, 68,* 376–381.

McEwen, B. S. (2003). Mood disorders and allostatic load. *Biological Psychiatry, 54,* 200–207.

Moorman, A. J., Mozaffarian, D., Wilkinson, C. W., Lawler, R. L., McDonald, G. B., Crane, B. A., et al. (2007). In patients with heart failure elevated soluble TNF-receptor 1 is associated with higher risk of depression. *Journal of Cardiac Failure, 13,* 738–743.

Morin, C. M., & Ware, J. C. (1996). Sleep and psychopathology. *Applied & Preventive Psychology, 5,* 211–224.

Niaura, R., Banks, S. M., Ward, K. D., Stoney, C. M., Spiro, A., III, Aldwin, C. M., et al. (2000). Hostility and the metabolic syndrome in older males: The normative aging study. *Psychosomatic Medicine, 62,* 7–16.

Orth-Gomer, K., Wamala, S. P., Horsten, M., Schenk-Gustafsson, K., Schneiderman, N., & Mittleman, M. A. (2000). Marital stress worsens prognosis in women with coronary heart disease: The Stockholm Female Coronary Risk Study. *JAMA, 284,* 3008–3014.

Pace, T. W., Hu, F., & Miller, A. H. (2007). Cytokine-effects on glucocorticoid receptor function: Relevance to glucocorticoid resistance and the pathophysiology and treatment of major depression. *Brain, Behavior, and Immunity, 21,* 9–19.

Raikkonen, K., Matthews, K. A., & Salomon, K. (2003). Hostility predicts metabolic syndrome risk factors in children and adolescents. *Health Psychology, 22,* 279–286.

Ranjit, N., Diez-Roux, A. V., Shea, S., Cushman, M., Seeman, T., Jackson, S. A., & Ni, H. (2007). Psychosocial factors and inflammation in the Multi-Ethnic Study of Atherosclerosis. *Archives of Internal Medicine, 167,* 174–181.

Redwine, L. S., Mills, P. J., Hong, S., Rutledge, T., Reis, V., Maisel, A., et al. (2007). Cardiac-related hospitalization and/or death associated with immune dysregulation and symptoms of depression in heart failure patients. *Psychosomatic Medicine, 69,* 23–29.

Rieckmann, N., Gerin, W., Kronish, I. M., Burg, M. M., Chaplin, W. F., Kong, G., et al. (2006). Course of depressive symptoms and medication adherence after acute coronary syndromes: An electronic medication monitoring study. *Journal of the American College of Cardiology, 48,* 2218–2222.

Rutledge, T., Reis, S. E., Olson, M., Owens, J., Kelsey, S. F., Pepine, C. J., et al. (2006). Depression is associated with cardiac symptoms, mortality risk, and hospitalization among women with suspected coronary disease: The NHLBI-sponsored WISE study. *Psychosomatic Medicine, 68,* 217–223.

Sareen, J., Cox, B. J., Stein, M. B., Afifi, T. O., Fleet, C., & Asmundson, G. J. (2007). Physical and mental comorbidity, disability, and suicidal behavior associated with posttraumatic stress disorder in a large community sample. *Psychosomatic Medicine, 69,* 242–248.

Smith, T. W. (1992). Hostility and health: Current status of a psychosomatic hypothesis. *Health Psychology*, *11*, 139–150.

Smith, T. W., & Ruiz, J. M. (2002). Psychosocial influences on the development and course of coronary heart disease: Current status and implications for research and practice. *Journal of Consulting and Clinical Psychology*, *70*, 548–568.

Smith, T. W., Uchino, B. N., Berg, C. A., Florsheim, P., Pearce, G., Hawkins, M., et al. (2007). Hostile personality traits and coronary artery calcification in middle-aged and older married couples: Different effects for self-reports versus spouse ratings. *Psychosomatic Medicine*, *69*, 441–448.

Stein, M. B., Belik, S.-L., Jacobi, F., & Sareen, J. (2008). Impairment associated with sleep problems in the community: Relationships to physical and mental health comorbidity. *Psychosomatic Medicine*, *70*, 913–919.

Suarez, E. C. (2003). Joint effect of hostility and severity of depressive symptoms on plasma interleukin-6 concentration. *Psychosomatic Medicine*, *65*, 523–527.

Suarez, E. C. (2006). Sex differences in the relation of depressive symptoms, hostility, and anger expression to indices of glucose metabolism in nondiabetic adults. *Health Psychology*, *25*, 484–492.

Suarez, E. C., Lewis, J. G., Krishnan, R. R., & Young, K. H. (2004). Enhanced expression of cytokines and chemokines by blood monocytes to in vitro lipopolysaccharide stimulation are associated with hostility and severity of depressive symptoms in healthy women. *Psychoneuroendocrinology*, *29*, 1119–1128.

Surtees, P. G., Wainwright, N. W. J., Bockholdt, S. M., Luben, R. N., Warcham, N. J., & Khaw, K.-T. (2008). Major depression, C-reactive protein, and incident ischemic heart disease in health men and women. *Psychosomatic Medicine*, *70*, 850–855.

Taylor, C. B., Conrad, A., Wilhelm, F. H., Neri, E., DeLorenzo, A., Kramer, M. A., et al. (2006). Psychophysiological and cortisol responses to psychological stress in depressed and nondepressed older men and women with elevated cardiovascular disease risk. *Psychosomatic Medicine*, *68*, 538–546.

Teegen, F. (1999). Childhood sexual abuse and long-term sequelae. In A. Maercker, M. Schutzwohl, & Z. Solomon (Eds.), *Posttraumatic stress disorder: A lifespan developmental perspective* (pp. 97–112). Seattle, WA: Hogrefe & Huber.

Troxel, W. M., Cyranowski, J. M., Hall, M., Frank, E., & Buysee, D. J. (2007). Attachment anxiety, relationship context, and sleep in women with recurrent major depression. *Psychosomatic Medicine*, *69*, 692–699.

von Kanel, R., Hepp, U., Buddeberg, C., Keel, M., Mica, L., Aschbacher, K., et al. (2006). Altered blood coagulation in patients with posttraumatic stress disorder. *Psychosomatic Medicine*, *68*, 598–604.

Wilson, C. J., Finch, C. E., & Cohen, H. J. (2002). Cytokines and cognition—The case for a head-to-toe inflammatory paradigm. *Journal of the American Geriatrics Society*, *50*, 2041–2056.

Woods, A. B., Page, G. G., O'Campo, P., Pugh, L. C., Ford, D., & Campbell, J. C. (2005). The mediation effect of posttraumatic stress disorder symptoms on the relationship of intimate partner violence and IFN-gamma levels. *American Journal of Community Psychology, 36,* 159–175.

Zouridakis, E., Avanzas, P., Arroyo-Espliguero, R., Fredericks, S., & Kaski, J. C. (2004). Markers of inflammation and rapid coronary artery disease progression in patients with stable angina pectoris. *Circulation, 110,* 1747–1753.

6

COGNITIVE AND BEHAVIORAL REACTIONS TO STRESS AMONG ADULTS WITH PTSD: IMPLICATIONS FOR IMMUNITY AND HEALTH

JEFFREY L. KIBLER, KAVITA JOSHI, AND ERIN E. HUGHES

Adults who meet criteria for a posttraumatic stress disorder (PTSD) diagnosis have poorer health on average, and their health problems occur earlier in life, compared with adults in the general population (Beckham et al., 1998; Butterfield, Forneris, Feldman, & Beckham, 2000; Schnurr & Janikowski, 1999). Furthermore, one study showed that the relationship of PTSD to physical health was independent of age, depression, or other comorbid anxiety disorders (Zayfert, Dums, Ferguson, & Hegel, 2002). For some individuals, the health consequences of trauma may begin with traumatic childhood experiences. Two separate large-scale epidemiological studies in the United States and United Kingdom demonstrated linear relationships between the number of adverse childhood experiences (e.g., abuse, other potentially traumatic event) and cardiovascular risk factors evidenced as adults (Felitti et al., 1998; Surtees et al., 2003). Data from the U.S. National Comorbidity Study indicated childhood sexual abuse was associated with increased risk of cardiovascular disease (CVD; R. D. Goodwin & Stein, 2004).

A growing literature also indicates a relationship between PTSD diagnosis and CVD (Boscarino & Chang, 1999a; Hovens et al., 1998; McFarlane, Achison, Rafalowicz, & Papay, 1994; Schnurr, Spiro, & Paris, 2000). In a study of Vietnam veterans, participants with PTSD were more likely to display an abnormal electrocardiogram (28% vs. 15%) and were more likely to evidence atrioventricular conduction defects and history of myocardial infarction than were veterans without PTSD (Boscarino & Chang, 1999a). Heart disease was nearly 2.5 times as common in World War II resistance veterans with PTSD than in a nonveteran, same-age control group (Hovens et al., 1998). Other studies have also identified significantly higher rates of CVD in World War II and Korean veterans with PTSD (Schnurr et al., 2000), as well as in firefighters with PTSD (McFarlane et al., 1994), compared with control participants. Together, these retrospective studies provide convincing evidence for the association between PTSD and CVD.

There are several potential mechanisms by which PTSD might confer health risks. One hypothesis is that health-related behaviors, which are often related to coping with stress, are affected by posttraumatic stress and directly affect health status. A second hypothesis is that posttraumatic stress has direct deleterious effects on the central nervous system (e.g., altering brain structure or function, changing the way stimuli are perceived neurologically). A third hypothesis is that immune dysregulation serves as a mediator between stress reactions and health problems among individuals who have experienced traumatic stress. We contend that stress-related health risks, coupled with stress-related immune responses, play a significant role in the high rates of chronic illness in PTSD.

In the present chapter, we first discuss the behavioral and cognitive reactions to stress in PTSD (including health risk behaviors and physiological reactivity), and the ways these reactions may be related to illness. Then we discuss research that addresses the general relationships of psychological, behavioral, and psychophysiological variables to immune function, and the relevance of these relationships to the data on immune alterations in PTSD.

BEHAVIORAL REACTIONS AND COPING RESPONSES IN POSTTRAUMATIC STRESS DISORDER

The ways in which people with PTSD cope behaviorally with posttraumatic stress and other stressors in their lives are sometimes unhealthy from a physical standpoint, posing a risk of chronic illnesses, such as CVD and HIV. There is some evidence of increased prevalence of unhealthy lipid levels, cigarette smoking, obesity, and high blood pressure (BP), as well as alcohol abuse and high-risk sexual behavior, among individuals with PTSD.

Most studies that have examined cardiovascular risk factors in PTSD have not examined more than one or two risk variables, such as smoking or cholesterol. However, in a small pilot study we conducted (Kibler et al., 2007), five CVD risk variables were assessed (i.e., BP, weight, physical inactivity, lipid levels, and smoking). The pilot study was an examination of CVD risk among individuals with current posttraumatic stress and nonclinical control participants with no, or minimal, PTSD symptoms (and no other mental health conditions). Included were participants who were between the ages of 18 and 49, and who had no history of chronic illness. A group of 11 individuals with PTSD or significant PTSD symptoms that did not meet full diagnostic criteria (symptoms were assessed using a structured diagnostic interview) were compared with a nonclinical control group of 9 participants. The control group was comparable to the PTSD group with regard to age ($M \pm SD$ age = 24 ± 8 years in the control group and $M \pm SD$ age = 25 ± 10 years for PTSD group). Participants were women, except for one African American man in each group.

The PTSD group was composed of 8 African American and three Caucasian participants, and the control group consisted of seven African American participants and two Caucasian participants. The PTSD group evidenced more than twice as many risk factors ($M \pm SD$ = 1.4 ± 1.2) as the control group ($M \pm SD$ = 0.6 ± 0.5; one-tailed t = 1.85, $p < .05$). Sample size was not sufficient to test for statistically significant group differences for each risk factor, but effect size calculations (Cohen's d) indicated a large effect for greater mean weight in the PTSD group (d = .78; respective Ms = 190 lb vs. 154 lb), a medium effect for greater diastolic BP in the PTSD group (d = .49; respective Ms = 75.7 mmHg vs. 72.5 mmHg), and a small effect for greater systolic BP in the PTSD group (d = .15; respective Ms = 112.2 mmHg vs. 110.0 mmHg).

Overweight and Obesity

Other studies have indicated comparable mean body weight between PTSD and non-PTSD groups, but greater variability in weight and a higher rate of obesity in PTSD among combat veterans (Shalev, Bleich, & Ursano, 1990) and relatively young women (Lemieux, 1998; Lemieux & Coe, 1995). These findings of greater rates of obesity, as well as the finding of unhealthy lipids in PTSD (Filakovic et al., 1997; Kagan, Leskin, Haas, Wilkins, & Foy, 1999), suggest that overeating, overconsumption of high-fat foods, or lack of exercise may contribute to health problems.

For women who have been victims of sexual assault or abuse, one hypothesis is that the desire to be overweight serves as a protective mechanism— sexual trauma victims may consider themselves less attractive to other perpetrators because they are overweight (e.g., Weiner & Stephens, 1996). A related phenomenon is the effect of negative self-image on body weight. Women who have been abused commonly have a disrupted sense of self-worth and their own beauty, losing confidence in their ability to be valued and seen as beautiful to others; these beliefs can be manifested in diminished self-care, including overeating and physical inactivity (Robinson, 2000).

Physical Inactivity

Physical inactivity is associated with obesity, elevated BP, and a poor lipid profile. Conversely, regular physical activity has desirable effects on several important outcomes relevant to cardiovascular risk, such as BP and central body fat (Sallis & Owen, 1999). There is not sufficient evidence to determine whether there is a difference in physical activity in PTSD. However, one study showed that high anxiety sensitivity, a common symptom in PTSD, is associated with low exercise motivation among male veterans in treatment for posttraumatic stress (Lyons, McClendon, & Dubbert, 1994). This finding suggests that heightened concern regarding increases in physical arousal in PTSD may discourage healthy activity levels. This hypothesis is plausible because behavioral avoidance of physiological arousal and startling stimuli are hallmark components of PTSD (Meadows & Foa, 1998; Tull & Roemer, 2003). Another study provided evidence that veterans with PTSD are less physically fit than control participants on the basis of poorer performance on an ergometric workload test and greater levels of self-reported "effort symptoms," such as shortness of breath and weakness (Shalev et al., 1990).

Smoking

Smoking and other forms of substance use are more common among individuals with a history of PTSD when compared with non-PTSD control participants, and are thought to be used as a coping strategy for trauma memories and negative affect (Beckham et al., 1997; Brown, Read, & Kahler, 2003; Shalev et al., 1990; Wyatt, Vargas-Carmona, Burns-Loeb, & Williams, 2005). Smokers with PTSD tend to be heavier smokers than are control smokers without PTSD (Beckham et al., 1997; Shalev et al., 1990). Within a PTSD sample, smokers tend to have higher levels of PTSD symptoms (Beckham et al., 1995), suggesting that greater severity of PTSD may contribute to smoking status. Smoking in combination with hypertension and unhealthy lipids increases cardiovascular risk by a factor greater than the sum of their independent risks (Ockene & Houston-Miller, 1997).

Elevated Blood Pressure

Some individuals with PTSD may be at risk of CVD by virtue of elevated casual BP. Elevated BP is evident in combat veterans with PTSD in both laboratory and 24-hour ambulatory environments (Blanchard, 1990;

Buckley & Kaloupek, 2001; McFall, Murburg, Ko, & Veith, 1990; Muraoka, Carlson, & Chemtob, 1998). These findings reflect a condition of sympathetic nervous system overdrive in PTSD, which may put the system at risk of cardiovascular injury. In addition to the biological influences, elevated BP is affected by behavioral and psychological factors as well (e.g., Carels, Sherwood, & Blumenthal, 1998; Harrell, 1980). High levels of distress tend to be associated with higher 24-hour BP levels (Kamarck et al., 2005), whereas interventions to improve stress-coping strategies can assist with BP management (e.g., Clifford, Tan, & Gorsuch, 1991; Steptoe, 1988).

Stress Reactivity

In addition to resting or casual measures of physiological parameters, such as BP or heart rate, autonomic nervous system (ANS) reactivity to stress has also received considerable attention in the PTSD literature. Studies of cardiovascular responses to stress in PTSD have led to the conclusion that there is ANS hyperreactivity in PTSD (e.g., Kosten, Mason, Giller, Ostroff, & Harkness, 1987; Southwick, Yehuda, & Morgan, 1995). Exaggerated cardiovascular reactivity to psychological stress is a proposed mechanism by which negative emotions can confer risk of CVD via chronic overstimulation of the ANS; this *reactivity hypothesis* posits that exaggerated reactivity to mental challenge in the laboratory is representative of increased ANS arousal in response to prolonged psychological stress in the natural environment (Blascovich & Katkin, 1993; Krantz & Manuck, 1984; Obrist, 1981). Heightened cardiovascular reactivity may reflect the negative emotions and altered autonomic control in PTSD during day-to-day environmental stressors (Cohen et al., 1998; Kosten et al., 1987; McFall et al., 1990; Schnurr & Janikowski, 1999; Southwick et al., 1995). Furthermore, a positive relationship has been observed between cardiovascular reactivity and unhealthy lipid levels (Kagan et al., 1999).

An issue pertinent to the discussion of stress reactivity and PTSD is whether exaggerated ANS responses are specific to trauma-relevant stressors. A large body of research has shown greater cardiovascular reactivity (e.g., heart rate, skin conductance, BP) to trauma-related cues in PTSD (e.g., Orr, Pitman, Lasko, & Herz, 1993; Wolfe et al., 2000). These findings have been interpreted as conditioned learning of ANS hyperarousal. However, studies of cardiovascular reactivity in PTSD that have used generic, non-trauma-related stress paradigms (e.g., anger recall, mental arithmetic) had mixed results. Some studies have shown that men and women with PTSD exhibit greater reactivity during psychological stress in laboratory settings (Beckham et al., 2002; Goldfinger, Amdur, & Liberzon, 1998; Metzger et al., 1999) and that male veterans with PTSD also have greater ambulatory BP reactivity to distress outside the lab (Beckham et al., 2003; Buckley, Holohan, Greif, Bedard, & Suvak, 2004).

Other studies have indicated no differences in reactivity (e.g., McFall et al., 1990; Orr, Meyerhoff, Edwards, & Pitman, 1998; Pitman, Orr, Forgue, de Jong, & Caiborn, 1987; Shalev, Orr, & Pitman, 1993). Among studies yielding no reactivity differences to generic stressors, methodological features have limited interpretation. For example, one study used the period following task instruction and immediately preceding the stress tasks, rather than a preinstruction rest period, as the prestressor baseline (Orr et al., 1998); this method is confounded by anticipatory reactivity. Studies have also reported the use of stress reactivity paradigms (Pitman et al., 1987; Shalev et al., 1993) that produced heart rate responses that were very small (less than 3 bpm) and therefore may not be clinically meaningful experimental manipulations. Taken together, these studies suggest limited preliminary evidence that psychophysiological responses in PTSD are altered in situations that are not trauma-related.

In addition to the assessment of cardiovascular reactivity, measurement of cardiovascular recovery from stress may prove to be an important index of exaggerated physiological arousal and disease risk (Brosschot & Thayer, 1998; Gregg, James, Matyas, & Thorsteinsson, 1999). Little research to date has examined cardiovascular recovery from stress in PTSD. In one study, higher PTSD symptom levels were associated with longer heart rate recovery following startle tones (Kibler & Lyons, 2004). In another study, systolic and diastolic BP recovery periods were longer following an anger recall task in veterans with PTSD than in veterans without PTSD (Beckham et al., 2002). These findings provide preliminary evidence for prolonged cardiovascular responses to stress in PTSD. The recovery period following a stressor may have even more relevance than reactivity measures in identifying maladaptive cardiovascular adaptations (Brosschot & Thayer, 1998; Gregg et al., 1999) because slow recovery is thought to reflect extended maintenance of physiological stress reactions.

Sexual Risk Behaviors

A history of posttraumatic stress may also be associated with sexual risk behaviors. It has been suggested that increased sexual behavior and promiscuity serve as possible mechanisms for coping with shame and guilt among abuse victims (Arata, 2000). Evidence suggests women who are HIV positive report greater prevalence of sexual trauma and PTSD (Kimerling et al., 1999; Wyatt et al., 2002). In addition, sexual abuse history, physical abuse history, and number of PTSD symptoms have all been associated with greater engagement in high-risk sexual behaviors (Bensley, Eenwyk, & Simmons, 2000; Brener, McMahon, Warren, & Douglas, 1999; Zierler et al., 1991). Exposure to interpersonal violence during adolescence is also a predictor of risky sexual behaviors among college women (Green et al., 2005). The mechanism by which posttraumatic stress may be related to sexual risk behavior has not been clearly established. Little emphasis has been placed on specific psychological or emotional factors that might mediate relationships between posttraumatic stress and sexual risk behaviors. However, it is possible that the high rates of substance abuse in traumatized populations, or other psychological variables, will help explain the relationship between trauma and sexual risk.

COGNITIONS AND EMOTIONAL REACTIONS IN POSTTRAUMATIC STRESS DISORDER

The cognitive aspects of PTSD (e.g., negative cognitions) and their relationships to emotional functioning provide a theoretical framework for understanding patterns of cardiovascular reactivity and unhealthy behaviors in PTSD (Aldwin & Yancura, 2004; Rogers, Norman, Thorp, Lang, & Lebeck, 2005; Schnurr & Green, 2004). Inherent in this model is the assumption that unhealthy behaviors often occur in the context of poor coping with PTSD-related distress (Aldwin & Yancura, 2004). The emotional dysregulation and avoidance symptoms of PTSD make it especially difficult to adopt and maintain healthy behaviors.

Theoretical models have recently been developed that adequately incorporate the cognitive component of PTSD (i.e., the role that faulty thinking or assumptions and other disrupted cognitions may play in emotional and behavioral reactions) and its potential role in treatment (Chemtob, Roitblat, Hamada, Carlson, & Twentyman, 1988; Ehlers & Clark, 2000; Resick & Schnicke, 1992). These theoretical models suggest that cognitive appraisals may become habitually disrupted in PTSD if not targeted by treatment. The cognitive structures or schemas that develop as a result of a traumatic event (e.g., thoughts concerning safety and justice, negative self-evaluations, self-blame) pervasively affect the way victims with PTSD view and approach their environment (Foa & Rauch, 2004). Chemtob's cognitive action theory proposes that the threat schema is always at least weakly potentiated (Chemtob, Roitblat, Hamada, Carlson, & Twentyman, 1988), leading to a pervasive expectation that a threat will occur. Indeed, heightened perception of threat is consistently observed in PTSD (e.g., Amir, McNally, & Wiegartz, 1996; McNally, Amir, & Lipke, 1996; Trandel & McNally, 1987; A. E. Wilson, Calhoun, & Bernat, 1999).

It is commonly accepted that the perception or cognitive appraisal of a stressor plays a significant role in the emotional response and long-term coping with stressful situations (Folkman, Lazarus, Dunkel-Schetter, DeLongis, & Gruen, 1986; Lazarus & Folkman, 1984). Cognitive appraisals of high threat coupled with low perceived coping ability can lead to discomfort or anxiety and diminished performance (Lazarus & Folkman, 1984). Challenge appraisals (i.e., high perceived coping ability relative to perceived threat), however, tend to be associated with positive emotions and drive to achieve or excel (Folkman et al., 1986; Lazarus & Folkman, 1984; Tomaka, Blascovich, Kelsey, & Leitten, 1993). Thus, the styles of coping that follow from threat and challenge appraisals are qualitatively different. The findings that these appraisals are associated with specific patterns of ANS reactivity (Tomaka, Blascovich, Kibler, & Ernst, 1997; Tomaka et al., 1993) are conceptually meaningful for understanding behavioral and physiological responses to stress in PTSD. These studies have indicated that exaggerated vascular or BP responses are associated with greater perceived threat, whereas moderate cardiac responses (viewed as healthy and performance-enhancing) are associated with greater perceived challenge (Tomaka et al., 1993, 1997).

A conceptual implication of these findings is that challenge orientation and a propensity toward moderate cardiac responses to stress enhance adaptive behavioral coping because the physiological functioning associated with challenge (adequate oxygen delivery to brain and musculature) would promote problem solving and performance. There is support for the hypothesis that cognitive appraisal is related to coping (e.g., Folkman et al., 1986; Lowe et al., 2003). However, this model has not been widely applied to health behaviors or unhealthy practices (as potential stress-coping responses). Although the implications of cognitive appraisals for ANS responses and health behaviors in PTSD have not been determined, Lazarus and Folkman's (1984) cognitive appraisal theory of stress and coping suggests that the disrupted cognitions experienced in PTSD would interfere with the active pursuit of healthy lifestyle behaviors (e.g., exercise, problem-focused coping without the overuse of substances or unhealthy foods).

In sum, dysregulated behavioral and cognitive functioning in PTSD may be related to health outcomes. In the next section, we address how stress reactions are generally related to immune and endocrine function before turning to the potential role of immune function for health outcomes in PTSD.

STRESS REACTIONS, IMMUNITY, AND HEALTH

An extensive literature within psychoneuroimmunology relates psychological and emotional variables to immune status and immune function. Therefore, we only briefly summarize findings that may be of relevance to the discussion of PTSD and health.

Exposure to stress can increase susceptibility to physical illnesses such as coronary heart disease, upper respiratory infections, and cancer (Kiecolt-Glaser, Dura, Speicher, Trask, & Glaser, 1991; Stone, Mezzacappa, Donatone, & Gonder, 1999). Stress plays an important role in how the immune system functions. When stress activates the sympathetic nervous system (SNS), catecholamines, such as norepinephrine and epinephrine, are released into the bloodstream. The release of catecholamines creates flight responses, such as increases in BP, mental agility, heart rate, breathing rate, and sweating. Activation of the SNS in the presence of a stressor results in suppression of the immune system, thereby increasing the body's susceptibility to disease when stressors are ongoing. Animal models have shown an increase in tumor cell growth when natural killer (NK) cells were inhibited by stress (Ben-Eliyahu, Shakhar, Page, Stefanski, & Shakhar, 2000). The NK cells are responsible for killing tissue cells that are infected by viruses. When NK cells are inhibited, they are unable to fight the viruses.

Physiological Reactivity to Psychological Stress and Immunity

Not only is stress associated with activation of the SNS, but it can also play a role in the central nervous system along the hypothalamic–pituitary–adrenal (HPA) axis. When catecholamines are being released, the hypothalamus simultaneously secretes corticotropin-releasing factor. The release of corticotropin-releasing factor produces adrenocorticotropic hormone from the anterior lobe of the pituitary gland. This hormone in turn stimulates the adrenal cortices to release *cortisol*, a stress hormone that helps the immune system to operate efficiently. The release of catecholamines and cortisol allows the body to break down sugar as a source of available energy. This process results in enough energy to produce the flight response typically seen in stress reactions (Schneiderman, Ironson, & Siegal, 2005).

Acute Stress

Many types of stressors create physiological and immunological changes in the body. Laboratory settings have often been used for the study of acute-stress-related immunity. In a study assessing the stress of examinations in medical students, NK cell activity declined during the examination period (Kiecolt-Glaser et al., 1984). Further studies identified additional changes in the immune system, such as reduced responsiveness of T lymphocytes to mitogen stimulation in medical students during examination times, which resulted in decreased immunity defenses (Glaser, Kiecolt-Glaser, Speicher, & Holliday, 1985).

Acute stress has also been examined in people before and after receiving a vaccination. Edwards et al. (2006) found that acute physical and mental stress, prior to influenza vaccination, increased antibody responsiveness in women. This finding suggests that immunoenhancement may occur in the presence of an acute stressor. Another study found that individuals with higher Hepatitis B antibody levels had higher cortisol levels during an acute-stress task and recovery period than did individuals with lower levels of the vaccination antibody (Burns, Ring, Drayson, & Carroll, 2002). This finding suggests that amount of antibodies present in the body influences cortisol outputs during an acute stressor.

The effects of acute stressors may also be increased by the presence of a chronic stressor (G. E. Miller & Chen, 2006). Women with an episodic stressor superimposed on a chronic interpersonal stressor had increased cortisol output throughout the day and reductions in the expression of GR mRNA and C-reactive protein (Marin, Martin, Blackwell, Stetler, & Miller, 2007). The increased cortisol levels and reduction of glucocorticoid receptors in leukocytes may potentially increase the risk of cardiac or metabolic problems, whereas reductions in C-reactive protein may potentially offset this risk of cardiac problems. Future studies may further clarify the long-term immunological effects of simultaneously experiencing chronic and episodic stressors.

Chronic Stress

The physiological reaction to stress may be harmful if the stressor persists for an extended period (Selye, 1956). Research suggests that chronic overactivation of the SNS may suppress immune function by interfering with the production of cytokines, which are responsible for up-regulating or down-regulating the activity of many types of immune cells. For instance, parents of children with cancer are less able to suppress the production of interleukin-6 (IL-6), a proinflammatory cytokine that stimulates immune responses to trauma. Similarly, caregivers of individuals with Alzheimer's dementia (AD) have demonstrated compromised immune function, even years after the person with AD had died (Wu et al., 1999).

Marital discord may also be considered a chronic stressor (J. S. Goodwin, Hunt, Key, & Samet, 1987; Kiecolt-Glaser & Newton, 2001). Poor marital relationships have been associated with cardiovascular and endocrine system dysregulation (Kiecolt-Glaser et al., 1997; Malarkey, Kiecolt-Glaser, Pearl, & Glaser, 1994). However, women with rheumatoid arthritis and a good spousal relationship were less likely to experience disease-related problems (Zautra et al., 1998). Thus, negative marital experiences appear to lead to poorer health effects because of the chronically stressful nature of marital discord, whereas positive marital relations have been associated with health-buffering effects.

Stress Reactivity, Immune Function, and Autoimmune Diseases

Research has also shown that stress can worsen the conditions of autoimmune diseases (Harbuz, Chover-Gonzalez, & Jessop, 2003). For example, stressful life events have been associated with the occurrence of rheumatoid arthritis (G. H. Baker & Brewerton, 1981). Stress can alter the course of multiple sclerosis, resulting in deleterious cellular changes (Ackerman, Martino, Heyman, Moyna, & Rabin, 1998; see also chap. 7, this volume).

HIV has been of great interest to researchers, with much research focusing on tracking immunological changes as a result of stressors. For example, Hurwitz et al. (2005) examined differences in stress-induced cellular immune parameters between HIV-seronegative, HIV-positive asymptomatic, and HIV-positive symptomatic individuals. Participants in this study performed a laboratory speech stressor. The HIV-positive groups experienced an increase in T cell and CD8 reactivity, whereas the HIV-negative group did not. Findings from this study suggest that individuals infected with HIV experienced greater T cell and CD8 mobilization to stress-induced physiological changes because the immune systems of these individuals have heightened awareness of immunological changes.

In sum, the stress reactions observed in individuals with autoimmune diseases may be caused by the constant activation of an acute stress response. People with autoimmune disease, in comparison with healthy individuals, exhibit overactive proinflammatory cytokine production (Schneiderman et al., 2005). Therefore, the stressor may be overexerting the immune system.

Behavioral and Psychological Reactions and Immunity

Behavioral factors, such as physical activity and social support, may contribute to differences in stress adaptation and immune function (Forcier et al., 2006; Kemp & Hatmaker, 1989; R. A. Miller, 1996). One study found that individuals who exercised in moderate amounts had a lower chance of developing an upper respiratory infection than did people who engaged in extreme exercise (Nieman, 1994). This finding is consistent with research indicating that moderate amounts of exercise are beneficial in preventing illnesses such as cancer, stroke, and respiratory infections.

Social support is another behavioral factor that may relate to immune function. In animal studies, when monkeys were separated, the isolated monkeys exhibited signs of depression and reduced lymphocyte function (Boccia et al., 1997). Indeed, the impacts of social isolation are often negative, whereas social support has been associated with positive effects. In human studies, individuals who were married had fewer incidences of diseases and released more antibodies in reaction to an immunization (Kiecolt-Glaser, Glaser, Cacioppo, & Malarkey, 1998). Ditzen et al. (2007) showed that positive interactions between couples buffered reactions to stress: Women who received positive physical contact from their partner prior to laboratory stress evidenced cortisol-free salivary assays. Social support may assist in preventing illnesses, whereas social isolation has the potential for negative health outcomes. An important implication for behavioral correlates of immune function is that some may be altered to promote healthy lifestyles.

Research suggests that the impact of negative emotions and negative thoughts may impair normal functioning of the immune system. Negative emotions have been found to stimulate overproduction of proinflammatory cytokines (Catania et al., 1997). The same response occurs when the body is exposed to chronic infections, whereupon the overproduction of cytokines may lead to inhibition of immune responses. In a recent study by Jain, Mills, von Kanel, Hong, and Dimsdale (2007), healthy people who perceived minor life events in a negative way had an increase in inflammatory responses. A study assessing the impact of major life regrets found that older individuals who had more intense regret over a major life event demonstrated irregular cortisol secretions and higher amounts of physical health problems (Wrosch, Bauer, Miller, & Lupien, 2007).

What Happens When Stress Is Reduced?

Several approaches, such as cognitive–behavioral stress management (CBSM) and relaxation techniques, have been used to help people manage stress. Antoni et al. (1999) conducted a study to determine whether CBSM reduces distress associated with HIV serostatus notification in healthy gay men. Results showed that individuals assigned to a CBSM group had lower depression levels and better immune function. Another study found that relaxation increased NK cell activity and decreased herpes simplex virus antibody titers among 45 older adults (Kiecolt-Glaser et al., 1985). This finding indicated improvements in immune functioning 1 month after the relaxation intervention. Stress management and relaxation interventions may hold promise for reducing some of the adverse immunological effects of stress.

IMMUNITY AND ENDOCRINE FUNCTION IN POSTTRAUMATIC STRESS DISORDER: RELATIONSHIPS TO STRESS AND HEALTH

Multiple systems in the body, including the neural, cardiovascular, metabolic, and immune systems (Kronfol & Remick, 2000), appear to be influenced by posttraumatic stress reactions. Physiologic changes or abnormalities in the major stress response systems—the HPA axis and the SNS—have been observed in PTSD (D. G. Baker et al., 2001; Yehuda, 1998). Stress normally affects the immune system by causing the HPA axis to temporarily suppress immune function through secretion of glucocorticoids, such as cortisol. With low levels of cortisol, the immune system is left in a state of increased activation. Some evidence suggests secretion of cortisol is low in PTSD. Cortisol has been shown to be decreased in both plasma and urinary samples in participants with PTSD (see Yehuda, 1998). Veterans with PTSD have been shown to have lower circulating levels of cortisol and higher circulating catecholamine levels (Boscarino & Chang, 1999b).

Immune Function in Posttraumatic Stress Disorder

The available evidence suggests possible cytokine dysregulation in PTSD (e.g., Maes, Lin, Delmeire, Van Gastel, & Kennis, 1999; Spivak et al., 1997). Cytokines are protein substances released by cells that serve as intercellular signals to regulate the balance of cell-mediated and humoral immune response to injury and infection (Kiecolt-Glaser, McGuire, Robles, & Glaser, 2002). This important natural defense mechanism is part of the normal immune response (Everson, Kotler, & Blackburn, 1999). Proinflammatory cytokines promote inflammation, meaning they attract other immune cells to the site of injury or infection and cause them to become activated to respond. Proinflammatory cytokines are involved in the modulation of anxiety and stress reactions, and are released in greater volume when a person is under stress. It follows that PTSD, which can be conceptualized as a state of chronic stress or hyperarousal, might be associated with elevated levels of proinflammatory cytokines. This increase in the inflammatory response is a potential pathway to multiple disease processes and has been well-documented in PTSD (Burges-Watson, Muller, Jones, & Bradley, 1993; Ironson et al., 1997; Solomon, Segerstrom, & Grohr, 1997; Spivak et al., 1997).

Levels of the proinflammatory cytokine IL-6 have been found to be increased in the serum of accident victims with PTSD, as well as in the cerebrospinal fluid of veterans with combat-related PTSD (Maes et al., 1999). IL-1β, another proinflammatory cytokine that is critical in mediating immune and inflammatory responses (Dinarello, 1994; Duram & Oppenheim, 1989), has been found to be increased in combat veterans with PTSD (Spivak et al., 1997). Elevated levels of IL-1β may impact a person's behavior, causing psychomotor retardation, sleep disorders, reduced exploratory and sexual behavior, fear reactions, anorexia, weight loss, and decreased energy (Kent, Bluthe, Kelley, & Dantzer, 1992; Yirmiya, Avitsur, Donchin, & Cohen, 1995). The release of IL-1β also stimulates central catecholaminergic activity, SNS activity (Dunn, 1988; Rivier, Vale, & Brown, 1989), and HPA axis activity (Fukata, Usui, Naitoh, Nakai, & Imura, 1989), and regulates the serotonin transporter gene (Ramamoorthy, Ramamoorthy, & Prasad, 1995).

A study of peripheral blood lymphocytes and PTSD resulting from childhood sexual abuse revealed that patients with PTSD had significantly higher levels of lymphocyte activation, suggesting hyperelevated immune function (S. N. Wilson, van der Kolk, Burbridge, Fisler, & Kradin, 1999). In another study, patients with PTSD had significantly higher NK cell activity, and higher numbers of CD4 and CD8 cells, compared with control participants (Laudenslager et al., 1998).

In addition to showing that participants with PTSD had significantly higher levels of leukocytes, lymphocytes, and CD4 and CD8 T cell lymphocytes, Boscarino and Chang (1999b) found that participants with PTSD have delayed reactive skin hypersensitivity. This finding suggests the presence of hypersensitized T cell lymphocytes, which are related to autoimmune diseases such as diabetes and multiple sclerosis (D. G. Baker, Mendenhall, Simbarti, Magan, & Steinberg, 1997; Carrithers, 1997). More research in this area is needed because mononuclear leukocytes are implicated in many disease processes, including atherosclerosis and rheumatoid arthritis

(Boscarino, 1997). It is hypothesized that the elevated leukocyte levels in PTSD are associated with low levels of cortisol secretion. In addition, chronic HPA axis activation, also seen in people with PTSD, changes adrenal androgen hormones, which may lead to the increase of Type 2 T cells (Boscarino & Chang, 1999b).

In a study of survivors of hurricane Andrew, participants with greater losses to their home or property, or PTSD symptoms, exhibited significantly lower levels of NK cell cytotoxic (NKCC) activity as well as lower levels of CD4+ and CD8+ lymphocytes (Ironson et al., 1997). White blood cell (WBC) counts were also positively correlated with the degree of loss experienced and later symptoms of PTSD. This finding supports previous research that showed increases in WBC after stress (Herbert & Cohen, 1993). In addition, in the hurricane survivors, the changes in WBC and NKCC were related to increased self-reported somatic symptoms. The increased number of NK cells in this study may be a compensatory mechanism to try to offset the decreased activity of the cells. The level of NKCC may play an important role in some diseases, including cancer, chronic viral infections, autoimmune diseases (Whiteside, Bryant, & Day, 1990), and chronic fatigue syndrome (Klimas, Salvato, Morgan, & Fletcher, 1990).

Glover, Steele, Stuber, and Fahey (2005) found that participants with posttraumatic stress symptoms had significantly higher levels of CD4+ cells, lower levels of CD8+ cells, and blunted NK cell activity compared with nonsymptomatic participants. These findings support Boscarino and Chang's (1999b) findings of increased levels of CD4+ cells in male combat veterans with chronic PTSD. The low levels of CD8+ are consistent with the Ironson et al. (1997) study. However, these findings conflict with other findings (Boscarino & Chang, 1999b; Laudenslager et al., 1998; S. N. Wilson et al., 1999).

Acute symptomatic PTSD has been shown to be associated with an increase in physiological reactivity to stress, which could increase cell-mediated immune function as there is robust evidence that acute stress can increase cell-mediated immunity (see Dhabhar & McEwen, 1999). Cell-mediated immunity is a system that protects against viruses, fungi, and other foreign pathogens and also affects cognition (Walker et al., 1997). A study investigating delayed-type hypersensitivity, a measure of cell-mediated immunity, found significantly increased levels of cell-mediated immunity in women with PTSD related to a childhood history of physical or sexual abuse (Altemus, Cloitre, & Dhabhar, 2003). This finding is consistent with previous work by Burges-Watson et al. (1993) indicating increased delayed-type sensitivity in Australian male combat veterans with PTSD, as well as findings of higher plasma levels of proinflammatory cytokines (Maes et al., 1999; Spivak et al., 1997) and increased activation of T lymphocytes (S. N. Wilson et al., 1999) in people with PTSD. There is, however, some conflicting evidence, as decreased cell-mediated immunity has been found in PTSD in Gulf War veterans (Schnurr et al., 2000).

Clinical Implications

The primary implication of the literature relating PTSD to behavioral health risks is that comprehensive clinical care for PTSD may need to include health-related prevention and treatment as an adjunct to empirically validated psychotherapies. Findings of greater rates of obesity and unhealthy lipids in PTSD suggest that overeating, overconsumption of high-fat foods, or lack of exercise may contribute to health problems. Further attention to these issues is needed to fully address the needs of individuals recovering from PTSD. From the perspective of managing stress that may contribute to health risks, cognitive–behavioral interventions that have effectively improved daily stress-coping skills and bolstered immune functioning in other populations may serve as effective "lifestyle" interventions in PTSD. However, research is needed to examine the sensitivity of immune parameters to effective treatments currently available for PTSD.

CONCLUSIONS

Chronic stress leads to decreased immune function and a resultant diminished ability to fight disease (Everson et al., 1999). In light of the evidence concerning stress reactions and immune responses in PTSD, it is likely that the long-term negative health effects of PTSD are related to hyperactivity of central stress circuitry along with intermittent excess catecholamine discharge. Excess SNS activity may manifest itself through the peripheral immune system, and changes in immune responsivity and cytokine production may well contribute to deleterious health effects.

The evidence cited here suggests that it would be beneficial to investigate the ways in which treatments for PTSD may impact trauma-related immune, endocrine, and health disruptions. For example, systematic investigations into the relationship of behavioral exposure treatments to immune functioning could provide insight into the sensitivity of immune dysfunction to trauma treatment. Treatment for PTSD often involves medication in conjunction with, or in lieu of, psychotherapy. Antidepressants, specifically the selective serotonin reuptake inhibitor sertraline, have been shown to be effective in treating PTSD (Brady et al., 2000). This type of antidepressant has also been found to be beneficial in treating immune-related diseases, including fibromyalgia (Patkar, Bilal, & Masand, 2003). However, relatively little research has been conducted on the specific effects of antidepressants on immune function (Tucker et al., 2004).

Finally, sleep disruption may be an important mediator between PTSD and immunity and health. Insomnia or even partial sleep deprivation has been shown to decrease NKCC (Irwin et al., 1994). Thus, the high prevalence of considerable sleep deprivation in PTSD may lead to some of the physiological changes associated with the disorder (McEwen, 2003; see also chap. 3, this volume).

KEY POINTS

- Adults who experience chronic posttraumatic stress appear to have poorer health, with up to 2 to 3 times the rate of cardiovascular disease.
- Cardiovascular risk factors with behavioral components appear to be more prevalent in PTSD.
- Immune dysfunction in PTSD, secondary to autonomic nervous system hyperarousal, may also contribute to adverse health outcomes.
- Comprehensive clinical care for PTSD would include health-related prevention and treatment as an adjunct to empirically validated psychotherapies.
- Research is needed to examine the sensitivity of immune parameters to effective treatments currently available for PTSD.

REFERENCES

Ackerman, K. D., Martino, M., Heyman, R., Moyna, N. M., & Rabin, B. S. (1998). Stressor-induced alteration of cytokine production in multiple sclerosis patients and controls. *Psychosomatic Medicine, 60,* 484–491.

Aldwin, C. M., & Yancura, L. A. (2004). Coping and health: A comparison of the stress and trauma literature. In P. P. Schnurr & B. L. Green (Eds.), *Trauma and health: Physical health consequences of exposure to extreme stress* (pp. 99–123). Washington, DC: American Psychological Association.

Altemus, M., Cloitre, M., & Dhabhar, F. S. (2003). Enhanced cellular immune response in women with PTSD related to childhood abuse. *The American Journal of Psychiatry, 160,* 1705–1707.

Amir, N., McNally, R. J., & Wiegartz, P. S. (1996). Implicit memory bias for threat in posttraumatic stress disorder. *Cognitive Therapy and Research, 20,* 625–635.

Antoni, M. H., Baggett, L., Ironson, G., LaPierriere, A., August, S., Klimas, N., et al. (1999). Cognitive–behavioral stress management intervention buffers distress responses and immunologic changes following notification of HIV-1 seropositivity. *Journal of Consulting and Clinical Psychology, 59,* 906–915.

Arata, C. M. (2000). From child victim to adult victims: A model for predicting sexual revictimization. *Child Maltreatment, 5,* 28–39.

Baker, D. G., Ekhator, N. N., Kasckow, J. W., Hill, K. K., Zoumakis, E., Dashevsky, B. A., et al. (2001). Plasma and cerebrospinal fluid interleukin-6 concentrations in posttraumatic stress disorder. *NeuroImmunoModulation, 9,* 209–217.

Baker, D. G., Mendenhall, C. L., Simbarti, L. A., Magan, L. K., & Steinberg, J. L. (1997). Relationship between posttraumatic stress disorder and self-reported physical symptoms in Persian Gulf War veterans. *Archives of Internal Medicine, 157,* 2076–2078.

Baker, G. H., & Brewerton, D. A. (1981, June 20). Rheumatoid arthritis: A psychiatric assessment. *BMJ, 282,* 2014.

Beckham, J. C., Kirby, A. C., Feldman, M. E., Hertzberg, M. A., Moore, S. D., Crawford, A. L., et al. (1997). Prevalence and correlates of heavy smoking in Vietnam veterans with chronic posttraumatic stress disorder. *Addictive Behaviors, 22,* 637–647.

Beckham, J. C., Moore, S. D., Feldman, M. E., Hertzberg, M. A., Kirby, A. C., & Fairbank, J. A. (1998). Health status, somatization, and severity of posttraumatic stress disorder in Vietnam combat veterans with posttraumatic stress disorder. *The American Journal of Psychiatry, 155,* 1565–1569.

Beckham, J. C., Roodman, A. A., Shipley, R. H., Hertzberg, M. A., Cunha, G. H., Kudler, H. S., et al. (1995). Smoking in Vietnam combat veterans with posttraumatic stress disorder. *Journal of Traumatic Stress, 8,* 461–472.

Beckham, J. C., Taft, C., Vrana, S. R., Feldman, M. E., Barefoot, J. C., Moore, S. D., et al. (2003). Ambulatory monitoring and physical health report in Vietnam veterans with and without PTSD. *Journal of Traumatic Stress, 16,* 329–335.

Beckham, J. C., Vrana, S. R., Barefoot, J. C., Feldman, M. E., Fairbank, J. A., & Moore, S. D. (2002). Magnitude and duration of cardiovascular response to anger in combat veterans with and without chronic posttraumatic stress disorder. *Journal of Consulting and Clinical Psychology, 70,* 228–235.

Ben-Eliyahu, S., Shakhar, G., Page, G. G., Stefanski, V., & Shakhar, K. (2000). Suppression of NK cell activity and of resistance to metastasis by stress: A role for adrenal catecholamines and beta-adrenoceptors. *Neuroimmunomodulation, 8,* 154–164.

Bensley, L. S., Eenwyk, J. V., & Simmons, K. W. (2000). Self-reported childhood sexual and physical abuse and adult HIV-risk behaviors and heavy drinking. *American Journal of Preventive Medicine, 18,* 151–157.

Blanchard, E. B. (1990). Elevated basal levels of cardiovascular responses in Vietnam veterans with PTSD: A health problem in the making. *Journal of Anxiety Disorders, 4,* 233–237.

Blascovich, J., & Katkin, E. S. (Eds.). (1993). *Cardiovascular reactivity to psychological stress & disease.* Washington, DC: American Psychological Association.

Boccia, M. L., Scanlan, J. M., Laudenslager, M. L., Berger, C. L., Hijazi, A. S., & Reite, M. L. (1997). Juvenile friends, behavior, and immune responses, to separation in bonnet macaque infants. *Physiology & Behavior, 61,* 191–198.

Boscarino, J. A. (1997). Diseases among men 20 years after exposure to severe stress: Implications for clinical research and medical care. *Psychosomatic Medicine, 59,* 605–613.

Boscarino, J. A., & Chang, J. (1999a). Electrocardiogram abnormalities among men with stress-related psychiatric disorders: Implications for coronary heart disease and clinical research. *Annals of Behavioral Medicine, 21,* 227–234.

Boscarino, J. A., & Chang, J. (1999b). Higher abnormal leukocyte and lymphocyte counts 20 years after exposure to extreme stress: Research and clinical implications. *Psychosomatic Medicine, 61,* 378–386.

Brady, K., Pearlstein, T., Asnis, G. M., Baker, D., Rothbaum, B., Sikes, C. R., et al. (2000). Efficacy and safety of sertraline treatment of posttraumatic stress disorder: A randomized control trial. *JAMA, 283,* 1837–1844.

Brener, N. D., McMahon, P. M., Warren, C. W., & Douglas, K. T. (1999). Forced sexual intercourse and associated health-risk behaviors among female college students in the United States. *Journal of Consulting and Clinical Psychology, 67,* 252–259.

Brosschot, J. F., & Thayer, J. F. (1998). Anger inhibition, cardiovascular recovery, and vagal function: A model of the link between hostility and cardiovascular disease. *Annals of Behavioral Medicine, 20,* 326–332.

Brown, P. J., Read, J. P., & Kahler, C. W. (2003). Comorbid posttraumatic stress disorder and substance use disorders: Treatment outcomes and the role of coping. In P. Ouimette & P. J. Brown (Eds.), *Trauma and substance abuse: Causes, consequences, and treatment of comorbid disorders* (pp. 171–188). Washington, DC: American Psychological Association.

Buckley, T. C., Holohan, D., Greif, J. L., Bedard, M., & Suvak, M. (2004). Twenty-four-hour ambulatory assessment of heart rate and blood pressure in chronic PTSD and non-PTSD Veterans. *Journal of Traumatic Stress, 17,* 163–171.

Buckley, T. C., & Kaloupek, D. G. (2001). A meta-analytic examination of basal cardiovascular activity in posttraumatic stress disorder. *Psychosomatic Medicine, 63,* 585–594.

Burges-Watson, I. P., Muller, H. K., Jones, I. H., & Bradley, A. J. (1993). Cell-mediated immunity in combat veterans with post-traumatic stress disorder. *Medical Journal of Australia, 8,* 55–56.

Burns, V. E., Ring, C., Drayson, M., & Carroll, D. (2002). Cortisol and cardiovascular reactions to mental stress and antibody status following Hepatitis B vaccination: A preliminary study. *Psychophysiology, 39,* 361–368.

Butterfield, M. I., Forneris, C. A., Feldman, M. E., & Beckham, J. C. (2000). Hostility and functional health status in women veterans with and without posttraumatic stress disorder. *Journal of Traumatic Stress, 13,* 735–741.

Carels, R. A., Sherwood, A., & Blumenthal, J. A. (1998). Psychosocial influences on blood pressure during daily life. *International Journal of Psychophysiology, 28,* 117–129.

Carrithers, M. D. (1997). Immune cell traffic in the brain blundering and migration of autoreactive T lymphocytes. *Neuroscientist, 3,* 207–210.

Catania, A., Airaghi, L., Motta, P., Manfredi, M. G., Annoni, G., Pettenati, C., et al. (1997). Cytokine antagonists in aged subjects and their relation with cellular immunity. *The Journals of Gerontology: Series A. Biological Sciences and Medical Sciences, 52,* B93–B97.

Chemtob, C. M., Roitblat, H. L., Hamada, R. S., Carlson, J. G., & Twentyman, C. T. (1988). A cognitive action theory of post-traumatic stress disorder. *Journal of Anxiety Disorders, 2,* 253–275.

Clifford, P. A., Tan, S., & Gorsuch, R. L. (1991). Efficacy of a self-directed behavioral health change program: Weight, body composition, cardiovascular fitness, blood pressure, health risk, and psychosocial mediating variables. *Journal of Behavioral Medicine, 14,* 303–323.

Cohen, H., Kotler, M., Matar, M. A., Kaplan, Z., Loewenthal, U., Miodownik, H., et al. (1998). Analysis of heart rate variability in posttraumatic stress disorder patients in response to a trauma-related reminder. *Biological Psychiatry, 44,* 1054–1059.

Dhabhar, F. S., & McEwen, B. S. (1999). Enhancing versus suppressive effects of stress hormones on skin immune function. *Proceedings of the National Academy of Sciences USA, 96,* 1059–1064.

Dinarello, C. A. (1994). The biological properties of interleukin-1. *European Cytokine Network, 5,* 517–531.

Ditzen, B., Neumann, I. D., Bodenmann, G., Dawans, B. V., Turner, R. A., Ehlert, U., et al. (2007). Effects of different kinds of couple interaction on cortisol and heart rate responses to stress in women. *Psychoneuroendocrinology, 32,* 565–574.

Dunn, A. J. (1988). Systemic interleukin-1 administration stimulates hypothalamic norepinephrine metabolism paralleling the increased plasma corticosterone. *Life Science, 43,* 429–435.

Duram, S. K., & Oppenheim, J. J. (1989). Macrophage-derived mediators: Interleukin-1, tumor necrosis factor, interleukin 6, interferon, and related cytokines. In W. E. Paul (Ed.), *Fundamental immunology* (pp. 639–676). New York: Raven Press.

Edwards, K. M., Burns, V. E., Reynolds, T., Carroll, D., Drayson, M., & Ring, C. (2006). Acute stress exposure prior to influenza vaccination enhances antibody response in women. *Brain, Behavior, and Immunity, 20,* 159–168.

Ehlers, A., & Clark, D. (2000). A cognitive model of posttraumatic stress disorder. *Behaviour Research and Therapy, 38,* 319–345.

Everson, M. P., Kotler, S., & Blackburn, W. D. (1999). Stress and immune dysfunction in Gulf War veterans. *Annals of the New York Academy of Sciences, 876,* 413–418.

Felitti, V. J., Anda, R. F., Nordenberg, D., Williamson, D. F., Spitz, A. M., Edwards, V., et al. (1998). Relationship of childhood abuse and household dysfunction to many of the leading causes of death in adults: The Adverse Childhood Experiences (ACE) Study. *American Journal of Preventive Medicine, 14,* 245–258.

Filakovic, P., Barkic, J., Kadoic, D., Crncevic-Orlic, Z., Grguric-Radanovic, L., Karner, I., et al. (1997). Biological parameters of posttraumatic stress disorder. *Psychiatria Danubina, 9,* 207–211.

Foa, E. B., & Rauch, S. A. M. (2004). Cognitive changes during prolonged exposure versus prolonged exposure plus cognitive restructuring in female assault survivors with posttraumatic stress disorder. *Journal of Consulting and Clinical Psychology, 72,* 879–884.

Folkman, S., Lazarus, R. S., Dunkel-Schetter, C., DeLongis, A., & Gruen, R. J. (1986). Dynamics of a stressful encounter: Cognitive appraisal, coping, and encounter outcomes. *Journal of Personality and Social Psychology, 50,* 992–1003.

Forcier, K., Stroud, L. R., Papandonatos, G. D., Hitsman, B., Reiches, M., Krishnamoorthy, J., et al. (2006). Links between physical fitness and cardiovascular reactivity and recovery to psychological stressors: A meta analysis. *Health Psychology, 25,* 723–739.

Fukata, J., Usui, T., Naitoh, T., Nakai, Y., & Imura, H. (1989). Effects of recombinant human interleukin-1 alpha, -1 beta, 2 and 6 on ACTH synthesis and release in the mouse pituitary tumour cell line AtT-20. *Journal of Endocrinology, 122,* 33–39.

Glaser, R., Kiecolt-Glaser, J. K., Speicher, C. E., & Holliday, J. E. (1985). Stress, loneliness, and change in herpes virus latency. *Journals of Behavioral Medicine, 8,* 249–260.

Glover, D. A., Steele, A. C., Stuber, M. L., & Fahey, J. L. (2005). Preliminary evidence for lymphocyte distribution differences at rest and after acute psychological stress in PTSD-symptomatic women. *Brain, Behavior, and Immunity, 19,* 243–251.

Goldfinger, D. A., Amdur, R. L., & Liberzon, I. (1998). Psychophysiological responses to the Rorschach in PTSD patients, noncombat and combat controls. *Depression and Anxiety, 8,* 112–120.

Goodwin, J. S., Hunt, W. C., Key, C. R., & Samet, J. M. (1987). The effect of marital status on stage, treatment, and survival of cancer patients. *JAMA, 258,* 3125–3130.

Goodwin, R. D., & Stein, M. B. (2004). Association between childhood trauma and physical disorders among adults in the United States. *Psychological Medicine, 34,* 509–520.

Green, B. L., Krupnick, J. L., Stockton, P., Goodman, L., Cocoran, C., & Petty, R. (2005). Effects of adolescent trauma exposure on risky behavior in college women. *Psychiatry, 68,* 363–378.

Gregg, M. E., James, J. E., Matyas, T. A., & Thorsteinsson, E. B. (1999). Hemodynamic profile of stress-induced anticipation and recovery. *International Journal of Psychophysiology, 34,* 147–162.

Harbuz, M. S., Chover-Gonzalez, A. J., & Jessop, D. S. (2003). Hypothalamo–pituitary–adrenal axis and chronic immune activation. *Annals of the New York Academy of Sciences, 992,* 99–106.

Harrell, J. P. (1980). Psychological factors and hypertension: A status report. *Psychological Bulletin, 87,* 482–501.

Herbert, T. B., & Cohen, S. (1993). Stress and immunity in humans: A meta-analytic review. *Psychosomatic Medicine, 55,* 364–379.

Hovens, J. E., Op den Velde, W., Falger, P. R. J., de Groen, J. H. M., Van Duijn, H., & Aarts, P. G. H. (1998). Reported physical health in Resistance veterans from World War II. *Psychological Reports, 82*, 987–996.

Hurwitz, B. E., Brownley, K. A., Motivala, S. J., Milanovich, J. R., Kibler, J. L., Fillion, L., et al. (2005). Sympathoimmune anomalies underlying the response to stressful challenge in human immunodeficiency virus spectrum disease. *Psychosomatic Medicine, 67*, 798–806.

Ironson, G., Wynings, C., Schneiderman, N., Baum, A., Rodriquez, M., Greenwood, D., et al. (1997). Posttraumatic stress symptoms, intrusive thoughts, loss, and immune function after hurricane Andrew. *Psychosomatic Medicine, 59*, 128–141.

Irwin, M., Mascovich, A., Gillin, J., Willoughby, R., Pike, J., & Smith, T. (1994). Partial sleep deprivation reduces natural killer cell activity in humans. *Psychosomatic Medicine, 56*, 493–498.

Jain, S., Mills, P. J., von Kanel, R., Hong, S., & Dimsdale, J. E. (2007). Effects of perceived stress and uplifts on inflammation and coagulability. *Psychophysiology, 44*, 154–160.

Kagan, B. L., Leskin, G., Haas, B., Wilkins, J., & Foy, D. (1999). Elevated lipid levels in Vietnam veterans with chronic posttraumatic stress disorder. *Biological Psychiatry, 45*, 374–377.

Kamarck, T. W., Schwartz, J. E., Shiffman, S., Muldoon, M. F., Sutton-Tyrrell, K., & Janicki, D. L. (2005). Psychosocial stress and cardiovascular risk: What is the role of daily experience? [Special issue]. *Journal of Personality, 73*, 1749–1774.

Kemp, V. H., & Hatmaker, D. D. (1989). Stress and social support in high-risk pregnancy. *Research in Nursing Health, 12*, 331–336.

Kent, S., Bluthe, R. M., Kelley, K. W., & Dantzer, R. (1992). Sickness behavior as a new target for drug development. *Trends in Pharmacological Sciences (TiPS), 13*, 24–28.

Kibler, J. L., Joshi, K., Ma, M., Dollar, K. M., Beckham, J. C., Coleman, M., et al. (2007). A pilot study of posttraumatic stress and cardiovascular risk among young adults [Abstract]. *Annals of Behavioral Medicine, 33*(Suppl.), S175.

Kibler, J. L., & Lyons, J. A. (2004). Perceived coping ability mediates the relationship between PTSD symptoms and heart rate recovery in combat veterans. *Journal of Traumatic Stress, 17*, 23–29.

Kiecolt-Glaser, J. K., Dura, J., Speicher, C., Trask, O., & Glaser, R. (1991). Spousal caregivers of dementia victims: Longitudinal changes in immunity and health. *Psychosomatic Medicine, 53*, 345–362.

Kiecolt-Glaser, J. K., Garner, W., Speicher, C., Penn, G. M., Holliday, J., & Glaser, R. (1984). Psychosocial modifiers of immunocompetence in medical students. *Psychosomatic Medicine, 46*, 7–14.

Kiecolt-Glaser, J. K., Glaser, R., Cacioppo, J. T., MacCallum, R. C., Syndersmith, M., Kim, C., et al. (1997). Marital conflict in older adults: Endocrinological and immunological correlates. *Psychosomatic Medicine, 59*, 339–349.

Kiecolt-Glaser, J. K., Glaser, R., Cacioppo, J. T., & Malarkey, W. B. (1998). Marital stress: Immunologic, neuroendocrine, and autonomic correlates. *Annals of the New York Academy of Sciences, 840,* 656–663.

Kiecolt-Glaser, J. K., Glaser, R., Williger, D., Stout, J., Messick, G., Sheppard, S., et al. (1985). Psychosocial enhancement of immunocompetence in a geriatric population. *Health Psychology, 4,* 25–41.

Kiecolt-Glaser, J. K., McGuire, L., Robles, T., & Glaser, R. (2002). Emotions, morbidity and mortality: New perspectives from psychoneuroimmunology. *Annual Review of Psychology, 53,* 83–107.

Kiecolt-Glaser, J. K., & Newton, T. L. (2001). Marriage and health: His and hers. *Psychological Bulletin, 127,* 472–503.

Kimerling, R., Calhoun, K. S., Forehand, R., Armistead, L., Morse, E., Morse, P., et al. (1999). Traumatic stress in HIV-infected women. *AIDS Education and Prevention, 11,* 321–330.

Klimas, N., Salvato, F., Morgan, R., & Fletcher, M. A. (1990). Immunologic abnormalities in chronic fatigue syndrome. *Journal of Clinical Microbiology, 28,* 1403–1410.

Kosten, T. R., Mason, J. W., Giller, E. L., Ostroff, R. B., & Harkness, L. (1987). Sustained norepinephrine and epinephrine elevation in post-traumatic stress disorder. *Psychoneuroendocrinology, 12,* 13–20.

Krantz, D. S., & Manuck, S. B. (1984). Acute psychophysiological reactivity and risk of cardiovascular disease: A review and methodological critique. *Psychological Bulletin, 96,* 435–464.

Kronfol, Z., & Remick, D. G. (2000). Cytokines and the brain: Implications for clinical psychiatry. *American Journal of Clinical Psychiatry, 157,* 683–694.

Laudenslager, M. L., Aasal, R., Adler, L., Berger, C. L., Montgomery, P. T., Sandberg, E., et al. (1998). Elevated cytotoxicity in combat veterans with long-term posttraumatic stress disorder: Preliminary observations. *Brain, Behavior, and Immunity, 12,* 74–79.

Lazarus, R. S., & Folkman, S. (1984). *Stress, appraisal, and coping.* New York: Free Press.

Lemieux, A. M. (1998). Abuse-related posttraumatic stress disorder: Challenge to the norepinephrine-to-cortisol hypothesis. *Dissertation Abstracts International, 59,* 2B.

Lemieux, A. M., & Coe, C. L. (1995). Abuse-related posttraumatic stress disorder: Evidence for chronic neuroendocrine activation in women. *Psychosomatic Medicine, 57,* 105–115.

Lowe, R., Vedhara, K., Bennett, P., Brookes, E., Lone, G., Munnoch, K., et al. (2003). Emotion-related primary and secondary appraisals, adjustment and coping: Associations in women awaiting breast disease diagnosis. *British Journal of Health Psychology, 8,* 377–391.

Lyons, J. L., McClendon, O., & Dubbert, P. (1994, November). *Exercise motivation and stages of change in veterans with PTSD.* Abstract presented at the annual meeting of the International Society of Traumatic Stress Studies, Chicago, IL.

Maes, M., Lin, A., Delmeire, L., Van Gastel, A., & Kennis, G. (1999). Elevated serum-interleukin 6 (IL-6) and IL-6 receptor concentrations in posttraumatic stress disorder following accidental man-made traumatic events. *Biological Psychiatry, 45,* 833–839.

Malarkey, W., Kiecolt-Glaser, J. K., Pearl, D., & Glaser, R. (1994). Hostile behavior during marital conflict alters pituitary and adrenal hormones. *Psychosomatic Medicine, 56,* 41–51.

Marin, T. J., Martin, T. M., Blackwell, E., Stetler, C., & Miller, G. E. (2007). Differentiating the impact of episodic and chronic stressors on hypothalamic pituitary-adrenocortical axis regulation in young women. *Health Psychology, 26,* 447–455.

McEwen, B. S. (2003). Mood disorders and allostatic load. *Biological Psychiatry, 54,* 200–207.

McFall, M. E., Murburg, M. M., Ko, G. N., & Veith, R. C. (1990). Autonomic responses to stress in Vietnam combat veterans with posttraumatic stress disorder. *Biological Psychiatry, 27,* 1165–1175.

McFarlane, A. C., Achison, M., Rafalowicz, E., & Papay, P. (1994). Physical symptoms in post-traumatic stress disorder. *Journal of Psychosomatic Research, 38,* 715–726.

McNally, R. J., Amir, N., & Lipke, H. J. (1996). Subliminal processing of threat cues in posttraumatic stress disorder? *Journal of Anxiety Disorders, 10,* 115–128.

Meadows, E. A., & Foa, E. B. (1998). Intrusion, arousal, and avoidance: Sexual trauma survivors. In V. M. Follette & J. I. Ruzek (Eds.), *Cognitive–behavioral therapies for trauma* (pp. 100–123). New York: Guilford Press.

Metzger, L. J., Orr, S. P., Berry, N. J., Ahern, C. E., Lasko, N. B., & Pitman, R. K. (1999). Physiologic reactivity to startling tones in women with posttraumatic stress disorder. *Journal of Abnormal Psychology, 108,* 347–352.

Miller, G. E., & Chen, E. (2006). Life stress and diminished expression of genes encoding glucocorticoid reception and $\alpha 2$-adrenergic receptor in children with asthma. *Proceedings of the National Academy of Sciences USA, 103,* 5496–5501.

Miller, R. A. (1996, July 5). The aging immune system: Primer and prospectus. *Science, 273,* 70–74.

Muraoka, M. Y., Carlson, J. G., & Chemtob, C. M. (1998). Twenty-four hour ambulatory blood pressure and heart rate monitoring in combat-related posttraumatic stress disorder. *Journal of Traumatic Stress, 11,* 473–484.

Nieman, D. C. (1994). Exercise, upper respiratory tract infection, and the immune system. *Medicine & Science in Sports & Exercise, 26,* 128–139.

Obrist, P. (1981). *Cardiovascular psychophysiology: A perspective.* New York: Plenum Press.

Ockene, I. S., & Houston-Miller, N. (1997). Cigarette smoking, cardiovascular disease, and stroke. *Circulation, 96,* 3243–3247.

Orr, S. P., Meyerhoff, J. L., Edwards, J. V., & Pitman, R. K. (1998). Heart rate and blood pressure resting levels and responses to generic stressors in Vietnam veterans with posttraumatic stress disorder. *Journal of Traumatic Stress, 11,* 155–164.

Orr, S. P., Pitman, R. K., Lasko, N. B., & Herz, L. R. (1993). Psychophysiological assessment of posttraumatic stress disorder imagery in World War II and Korean combat veterans. *Journal of Abnormal Psychology, 102,* 152–159.

Patkar, A. A., Bilal, L., & Masand, P. S. (2003). Management of fibromyalgia. *Current Psychiatry Report, 15,* 218–224.

Pitman, R. K., Orr, S., Forgue, D., de Jong, J., & Caiborn, J. (1987). Psychophysiologic assessment of posttraumatic stress disorder imagery in Vietnam combat veterans. *Archives of General Psychiatry, 44,* 970–975.

Ramamoorthy, S., Ramamoorthy, J. D., & Prasad, P. D. (1995). Regulation of the human serotonin transporter by interleukin-1 beta. *Biochemical and Biophysical Research Communications, 216,* 560–567.

Resick, P. A., & Schnicke, M. K. (1992). Cognitive processing therapy for sexual assault victims. *Journal of Consulting and Clinical Psychology, 60,* 748–756.

Rivier, C., Vale, W., & Brown, M. (1989). In the rat, interleukin-1alpha and beta stimulate adrenocorticotrophin and catecholamine release. *Endocrinology, 125,* 3096–3102.

Robinson, S. (2000). Body image and body recovery. In A. Y. Shalev & R. Yehuda (Eds.), *International handbook of human response to trauma: The Plenum series on stress and coping* (pp. 163–177). Dordrecht, The Netherlands: Kluwer Academic Publishers.

Rogers, C. S., Norman, S. B., Thorp, S. R., Lang, A. J., & Lebeck, M. M. (2005). Trauma exposure, posttraumatic stress disorder and health behaviors: Impact on special populations. In T. A. Corales (Ed.), *Focus on posttraumatic stress disorder research* (pp. 203–224). Hauppauge, NY: Nova Science.

Sallis, J. F., & Owen, N. (1999). *Physical activity and behavioral medicine.* London: Sage.

Schneiderman, N., Ironson, G., & Siegal, S. D. (2005). Stress and health: Psychological, behavioral, and biological determinants. *Annual Review of Clinical Psychology, 1,* 607–628.

Schnurr, P. P., & Green, B. L. (2004). Understanding relationships among trauma, post-traumatic stress disorder, and health outcomes. *Advances in Mind–Body Medicine, 20,* 18–29.

Schnurr, P. P., & Janikowski, M. K. (1999). Physical health and post-traumatic stress disorder: Review and synthesis. *Seminars in Clinical Neuropsychiatry, 4,* 295–304.

Schnurr, P. P., Spiro, A., & Paris, A. H. (2000). Physician-diagnosed medical disorders in relation to PTSD symptoms in older male military veterans. *Health Psychology, 19,* 91–97.

Selye, H. (1956). *The stress of life.* New York: McGraw-Hill.

Shalev, A. Y., Bleich, A., & Ursano, R. J. (1990). Posttraumatic stress disorder: Somatic comorbidity and effort tolerance. *Psychosomatics, 31,* 197–203.

Shalev, A. Y., Orr, S. P., & Pitman, R. K. (1993). Psychophysiological assessment of traumatic imagery in Israeli civilian patients with posttraumatic stress disorder. *The American Journal of Psychiatry, 150,* 620–624.

Solomon, G. F., Segerstrom, S. C., & Grohr, P. (1997). Shaking up immunity: Psychological and immunologic changes after a natural disaster. *Psychosomatic Medicine, 59,* 114–127.

Southwick, S. M., Yehuda, R., & Morgan, C. A., III. (1995). Clinical studies of neurotransmitter alterations in post-traumatic stress disorder. In M. J. Friedman, D. S. Carney, & A. Y. Deutch (Eds.), *Neurobiological and clinical consequences of stress: From normal adaptation to PTSD* (pp. 335–349). Philadelphia: Lippincott-Raven.

Spivak, B., Shohat, B., Mester, R., Avraham, S., Gil-Ad, I., Bleich, A., et al. (1997). Elevated levels of serum interleukin-1β in combat-related post-traumatic stress disorder. *Biological Psychiatry, 42,* 345–348.

Steptoe, A. (1988). The processes underlying long-term blood pressure reductions in essential hypertensives following behavioural therapy. In T. Elbert, W. Langosch, A. Steptoe, & D. Vaitl (Eds.), *Behavioural medicine in cardiovascular disorders* (pp. 139–148). Oxford, England: Wiley.

Stone, A. A., Mezzacappa, E., Donatone, B. A., & Gonder, M. (1999). Psychosocial stress and social support are associated with prostate-specific antigen levels in men: Results from a community screening program. *Health Psychology, 18,* 482–486.

Surtees, P., Wainwright, N., Day, N., Brayne, C., Luben, R., & Khaw, K. (2003). Adverse experience in childhood as a developmental risk factor for altered immune status in adulthood. *International Journal of Behavioral Medicine, 10,* 251–268.

Tomaka, J., Blascovich, J., Kelsey, R. M., & Leitten, C. L. (1993). Subjective, physiological, and behavioral effects of threat and challenge appraisal. *Journal of Personality and Social Psychology, 65,* 248–260.

Tomaka, J., Blascovich, J., Kibler, J. L., & Ernst, J. M. (1997). Cognitive and physiological antecedents of threat and challenge appraisal. *Journal of Personality and Social Psychology, 73,* 63–72.

Trandel, D. V., & McNally, R. J. (1987). Perception of threat cues in post-traumatic stress disorder: Semantic processing without awareness? *Behaviour Research and Therapy, 25,* 469–476.

Tucker, P., Ruwe, W. D., Masters, B., Parker, D. E., Hossain, A., Trautman, R. P., et al. (2004). Neuroimmune and cortisol changes in selective serotonin reuptake inhibitor and placebo treatment of chronic posttraumatic stress disorder. *Biological Psychiatry, 56,* 121–128.

Tull, M. T., & Roemer, E. (2003). Alternative explanations of emotional numbing of posttraumatic stress disorder: An examination of hyperarousal and experiential avoidance. *Journal of Psychopathology and Behavioral Assessment, 25,* 147–154.

Walker, L. G., Walker, M. B., Heys, S. D., Lolley, J., Wesnes, K., & Eremain, O. (1997). The psychological and psychiatric effects of rIL-2 therapy: A controlled clinical trial. *Psychooncology, 6,* 290–301.

Weiner, E. J., & Stephens, L. (1996). Sexual barrier weight: A new approach. In M. F. Schwartz & L. Cohn (Eds.), *Sexual abuse and eating disorders* (pp. 68–77). Philadelphia: Brunner/Mazel.

Whiteside, T. L., Bryant, J., & Day, R. (1990). Natural killer cytotoxicity in the diagnosis of immune dysfunction: Criteria for a reproductive assay. *Journal of Clinical Laboratory Analysis, 4,* 102–114.

Wilson, A. E., Calhoun, K. S., & Bernat, J. A. (1999). Risk recognition and trauma-related symptoms among sexually revictimized women. *Journal of Consulting and Clinical Psychology, 67,* 705–710.

Wilson, S. N., van der Kolk, B., Burbridge, J., Fisler, R., & Kradin, R. (1999). Phenotype of blood lymphocytes in PTSD suggests chronic immune activation. *Psychosomatics, 40,* 222–225.

Wolfe, J., Chrestman, K. R., Crosby, O. P., Kaloupek, D., Harley, R. M., & Bucsela, M. (2000). Trauma-related psychophysiological reactivity in women exposed to war-zone stress. *Journal of Clinical Psychology, 56,* 1371–1379.

Wrosch, C., Bauer, I., Miller, G. E., & Lupien, S. (2007). Regret intensity, diurnal cortisol secretion, and physical health in older individuals: Evidence for directional effects and protective factors. *Psychology and Aging, 22,* 319–330.

Wu, H., Wang, J., Cacioppo, J. T., Glaser, R., Kiecolt-Glaser, J. K., & Malarkey, W. B. (1999). Chronic stress associated with spousal caregiving of patients with Alzheimer's dementia is associated with downregulation of B-lymphocyte GH mRNA. *The Journals of Gerontology: Series A. Biological Sciences and Medical Sciences, 54,* M212–M215.

Wyatt, G. E., Myers, H. F., Williams, J. K., Ramirez Kitchen, C., Loeb, T., Vargas Carmona, J., et al. (2002). Does a history of trauma contribute to HIV risk for women of color? Implications for prevention and policy. *American Journal of Public Health, 91,* 1–7.

Wyatt, G. E., Vargas-Carmona, J., Burns-Loeb, T., & Williams, J. K. (2005). HIV-positive Black women with histories of childhood sexual abuse: Patterns of substance use and barriers to health care. *Journal of Health Care for the Poor and Underserved, 16,* 9–23.

Yehuda, R. (1998). Psychoneuroendocrinology of post-traumatic stress disorder. *Psychiatric Clinicians of North America, 21,* 359–379.

Yirmiya, R., Avitsur, R., Donchin, O., & Cohen, F. (1995). Interleukin-1 inhibits sexual behavior in female but not male rats. *Brain, Behavior, and Immunity, 9,* 220–233.

Zautra, A. J., Hoffman, J. M., Matt, K. S., Yocum, D., Potter, P. T., Castro, W. L., et al. (1998). An examination of individual differences in the relationship between interpersonal stress and disease activity among women with rheumatoid arthritis. *Arthritis Care and Research, 11,* 271–279.

Zayfert, C., Dums, A. R., Ferguson, R. J., & Hegel, M. T. (2002). Health functioning impairments associated with posttraumatic stress disorder, anxiety disorders, and depression. *The Journal of Nervous and Mental Disease, 190,* 233–240.

Zierler, S., Feingold, L., Laufer, D., Velentgas, P., Kantrowitz-Gordon, I., & Mayer, K. (1991). Adult survivors of childhood sexual abuse and subsequent risk of HIV infection. *American Journal of Public Health, 81,* 572–575.

7

SOCIAL STRESS AND INFLAMMATION IN THE EXACERBATION OF MULTIPLE SCLEROSIS: AN ANIMAL MODEL WITH IMPLICATIONS FOR HUMANS

MARY W. MEAGHER AND C. JANE R. WELSH

Multiple sclerosis (MS) is a chronic inflammatory demyelinating disease of the central nervous system (CNS) that results in significant neural degeneration and disability (Bitsch, Schuchardt, Bunkowski, Kuhlmann, & Bruck, 2000; Brex et al., 2002; Sospedra & Martin, 2005). When Charcot (1868, 1877) first described MS in the 1800s, he suggested that prolonged social stress was related to the onset of MS (Butler & Bennett, 2003). For example, psychological etiological factors frequently cited include

> long continued grief or vexation, such, for instance, as might arise from illicit pregnancy, or the disagreeable annoyances and carking cares which

This research was supported by grants from the National Institutes of Health (R01-NS060822, R01-NS39569, F31-NS50476-2) and the National Multiple Sclerosis Foundation (RG 3128). Additional support was provided by two National Science Foundation graduate fellowships to Robin Johnson and Elisabeth Good Vichaya and by a Texas A&M University postdoctoral fellowship to Erin Young. Tom Welsh, Ralph Storts, Colin Young, Wentao Mi, Andrew Steelman, Mallory Frazier, Jessica Harrison, Patrick Bridegam, Elisabeth Harden, Marilyn Connor, and an army of undergraduate research assistants contributed to the success of this research program.

a more or less false social position entails. This is often the case as regards certain female teachers. Having said so much with respect to women, the question of the male sufferer arises. These are, for the most part, persons who have lost caste, and who, thrown out of the general current, and too impressionable, are ill-provided with the means of maintaining what, in Darwin's theory, is called the "struggle for life." (Charcot, as quoted in Butler & Bennett, 2003, p. 107)

However, it has been only in the past 3 decades that scientific evidence has accumulated to support this hypothesis.

During the 1980s, retrospective studies indicated that patients with MS report significantly more severe life events before disease onset (Grant et al., 1989; Warren, Greenhill, & Warren, 1982). Since then, numerous prospective studies have found that stressful life events predict an increased risk of MS exacerbations (e.g., Ackerman et al., 2002, 2003; Brown et al., 2006; Buljevac et al., 2003; Mohr et al., 2004), as well as the development of new brain lesions found through magnetic resonance imaging (MRI; Mohr, Hart, Julian, Cox, & Pelletier, 2000). Despite clinical evidence of an association between stress and MS, relatively little is known about the mechanisms underlying this phenomenon.

In this chapter, we review human and animal research linking stress with MS and the role of stress-induced exacerbation of inflammation as a mediating pathway. We focus our review on our recent research demonstrating that prolonged social stress exacerbates an animal model of MS. These studies provide evidence that the deleterious effects of social stress are partially mediated by stress-induced changes in proinflammatory cytokine levels. We also show that these adverse effects can be prevented by blocking stress-induced increases in cytokine activity, a finding that may have implications for preventing or reversing the negative effects of social stress on negative health outcomes in humans.

EFFECTS OF STRESS ON PATIENTS WITH MULTIPLE SCLEROSIS

MS affects approximately 2.5 million individuals throughout the world. Infiltration of the CNS by inflammatory cells consisting of plasma cells, macrophages and microglia, and T and B lymphocytes results in damage of the myelin sheath surrounding the axons of neurons. Autoimmune responses to myelin components—myelin basic protein (MBP), proteolipid protein (PLP), and myelin–oligodendrocyte glycoprotein (MOG)—have been detected in MS patients, indicating an autoimmune etiology for MS (Stinissen, Raus, & Zhang, 1997). The clinical symptoms vary depending on the location of inflammatory lesions but can include muscle weakness, numbness, paralysis, loss of bowel or bladder control, vision problems, fatigue, depression, and pain.

Although the etiology of MS remains uncertain, increasing evidence suggests that environmental factors interact with genetic factors to cause disease (Dyment, Ebers, & Sadovnick, 2004; Sospedra & Martin, 2005). Family and twin studies indicate that genetic susceptibility is necessary but not sufficient for disease vulnerability. Though rates of disease are higher among relatives of MS patients, concordance rates for identical twins (approximately 25%) are modest, indicating that environmental factors must be involved.

Potential environmental risk factors include infectious pathogens and stress (Ackerman et al., 2002; Grant et al., 1989; Kurtzke, 1993; Kurtzke & Hyllested, 1987; Mohr et al., 2000, 2004; Soldan & Jacobson, 2001; Sospedra & Martin, 2005; Warren et al., 1982). Both human and animal research suggests that viral infection is a likely environmental trigger of MS (Challoner et al., 1996; Gilden, 2005; Sospedra & Martin, 2005). For example, epidemiological studies indicate that adolescent exposure to certain viruses (e.g., Epstein-Barr, measles, mumps, herpes simplex 6) is associated with later development of MS (Acheson, 1977; Gilden, 2005; Hernan, Zhang, Lipworth, Olek, & Ascherio, 2001; Kurtzke & Hyllested, 1987; Levin et al., 2003; Miguel, Zhang, Lipworth, Olek, & Ascherio, 2001; Moore & Wolfson, 2002; Sospedra & Martin, 2005). In addition, animal models provide experimental evidence demonstrating that viruses can induce demyelination (Dal Canto & Rabinowitz, 1982; Oleszak, Chang, Friedman, Katsetos, & Platsoucas, 2004; Sospedra & Martin, 2005; Theiler, 1934; Welsh, Tonks, Borrow, & Nah, 1990). After establishing a persistent infection of the CNS, these viruses trigger virus- and autoimmune-mediated demyelination.

Other research suggests that stress may be an important cofactor that interacts with viral infection to determine vulnerability to MS (R. R. Johnson et al., 2006; Meagher et al., 2007; Sieve et al., 2004). Support for this hypothesis is provided by both human and animal research. MS patients frequently report elevated levels of stress before initial diagnosis or disease exacerbation (Ackerman et al., 2002, 2003; Brown et al., 2006; Buljevac et al., 2003; Grant et al., 1989; Mei-Tal, Meyerowitz, & Engel, 1970; Mohr et al., 2000, 2004; Mohr & Pelletier, 2006; Rabin, 2002; Warren et al., 1982; Warren, Warren, & Cockerill, 1991). A recent meta-analysis conducted on 14 studies investigating the impact of stressful life events on MS exacerbation found that stress significantly increased the risk of disease exacerbation (Mohr et al., 2004). Of the 14 studies, 13 measured chronic social stressors related to family and work. However, 1 of the 14 studies did not observe a negative effect of stress on MS. This study, which examined the impact of an acute traumatic stressor—missile attacks during the Gulf War—found reduced relapse rates or no change in lesion development (Nisipeanu & Korczyn, 1993). Taken together, these findings suggest that the nature of the stressor determines its impact on initial susceptibility and disease course in MS. Chronic social stressors appear to exacerbate disease, whereas acute stressors may have a beneficial effect.

Though human studies suggest that stress is correlated with the subsequent development of MS disease activity, they do not demonstrate that stress causes disease exacerbation. The problem is that the correlation between subjective reports of stress and disease exacerbation may be due to a third variable. For example, the inflammatory disease process may induce a cytokine-mediated depression that alters patient reports of stress while also exacerbating demyelination. To resolve the issue, animal research is needed to determine whether there is a causal relationship between stress and disease exacerbation. Animal studies are advantageous because exposure to the stressor can be experimentally manipulated and its impact on disease course can be quantified using objective behavioral and physiological markers of disease. Moreover, animal studies can readily identify the biological mechanisms that mediate the relationship between stress and MS-like disease activity.

INVESTIGATING THE EFFECTS OF SOCIAL STRESS ON THEILER'S VIRUS INFECTION

Theiler's Virus Model of Multiple Sclerosis

To investigate the impact of social stress on disease course, our laboratory uses an animal model of MS, Theiler's murine encephalomyelitis virus (TMEV) infection. TMEV is a natural pathogen of mice that induces a biphasic disease process in susceptible strains of mice (Lipton, 1975; Oleszak et al., 2004). The acute phase of infection (1st month) is characterized by CNS inflammation triggered by neuronal and glial infection (Njenga et al., 1997), whereas the chronic phase (3 to 8 months postinfection [pi]) is characterized by immune-mediated demyelination (Oleszak et al., 2004). Mice develop signs of encephalitis and hind limb impairment similar to polio during the acute phase. As the disease progresses, mice develop impairments in gait, motor coordination, and locomotor activity as a result of inflammatory demyelinating lesions and profound dysfunction as a result of axonal severing during late disease (McGavern, Zoecklein, Drescher, & Rodriguez, 1999; McGavern, Zoecklein, Sathornsumetee, & Rodriguez, 2000).

The early immune events occurring during TMEV infection are crucial in the effective clearance of the virus from the CNS (Aubert, Chamorro, & Brahic, 1987). Innate cytokine responses to infection play an important role in shaping downstream innate and adaptive immune responses to infection (Biron, 1998). For example, the cytokine interferon-β plays a pivotal role in the early immune response to TMEV (Fiette et al., 1995). In addition, natural killer cells and CD8+ and CD4+ T cells, which are activated early in infection, play an important role in viral clearance from the CNS (Borrow, Tonks, Welsh, & Nash, 1992; Dethlefs, Brahic, & Larsson-Sciard, 1997;

Kaminsky, Nakamura, & Cudkowicz, 1987; Murray, Pavelko, Leibowitz, Lin, & Rodriguez, 1998; Welsh, Tonks, Nash, & Blakemore, 1987). During chronic disease, CD4+ and CD8+ T cell subsets contribute to demyelination (Clatch, Lipton, & Miller, 1987; Rodriguez & Sriram, 1988).

Vulnerability to the chronic demyelinating phase of the disease is genetically regulated (Brahic, Bureau, & Michiels, 2005). Resistant strains of mice are able to mount an effective immune response and clear that virus from the CNS during the acute phase of disease. In contrast, susceptible strains of mice fail to generate an effective immune response during early infection, resulting in viral persistence and subsequent immune-mediated demyelination during the chronic phase (Lipton & Melvold, 1984; Oleszak et al., 2004). Although susceptibility to late disease is genetically regulated, other factors that influence the initial immune response play a critical role in determining the degree of viral persistence and disease severity (Aubagnac, Brahic, & Bureau, 1999; Brahic et al., 2005; Rodriguez, Pavelko, Njenga, Logan, & Wettstein, 1996). For instance, depletion of CD8 cells or exposure to chronic social stress before infection exacerbates disease (Borrow et al., 1992; R. R. Johnson et al., 2006; R. R. Johnson, Storts, Welsh, Welsh, & Meagher, 2004).

Social Disruption

Our laboratory uses social disruption stress to model the effects of prolonged social stress (see Avitsur, Padgett, & Sheridan, 2006, for a review). In this model, the social hierarchy within a group of three adolescent male mice is disrupted by repeatedly exposing them to a series of older male intruders. The older intruders are preselected to be socially dominant. During a typical session, a dominant intruder is placed into the home cage of the three adolescent mice for a 2-hour session, and the intruder repeatedly chases and pins the resident mice. After these aggressive encounters, the resident mice exhibit submissive responses indicative of social defeat. This procedure is repeated for three consecutive nightly sessions, one night off, followed by an additional three nightly sessions. To minimize habituation to social defeat, a new intruder is used for each social disruption session.

Social disruption induces profound effects on neuroendocrine and immune function, resulting in elevated circulating levels of the stress hormone corticosterone (Avitsur, Stark, & Sheridan, 2001) and increased susceptibility to influenza virus infection and endotoxin challenge in mice (Avitsur et al., 2001; Padgett et al., 1998; Quan et al., 2001). Unlike other commonly used laboratory stressors, social disruption induces a phenomenon known as glucocorticoid (GC) resistance (Avitsur et al., 2001; R. R. Johnson, Storts, et al., 2004; Meagher et al., 2007; Quan et al., 2001). GC *resistance* refers to a decrease in the immune system's capacity to respond to the inhibitory effects of corticosterone in terminating inflammatory responses. With prolonged exposure to high levels of GCs, the immune cells compensate by down-regulating the expression and function of the receptors that bind GCs, thereby making them resistant to the anti-inflammatory effects of GCs. In light of the important role that endogenous GCs play in immune regulation, a reduction in tissue sensitivity to GCs induced by chronic social stress may be one mechanism that increases vulnerability to inflammatory diseases, such as MS.

Stressor exposure has also been shown to intensely activate central noradrenergic neurons (Greenwood et al., 2003), which may provide another potential mechanism though which social stress exacerbates inflammatory disorders such as MS. Indeed, recent evidence suggests that norepinephrine contributes to stress-induced increases in proinflammatory cytokines within the CNS (Blandino, Barnum, & Deak, 2006; J. D. Johnson et al., 2005). Thus, norepinephrine release during social stress may be an important mediator of disease onset and exacerbation in MS by increasing the expression of central proinflammatory cytokines.

Impact of Social Disruption on Acute Theiler's Virus Infection

To elucidate the mechanisms underlying the adverse effects of social stress on MS disease vulnerability, our laboratory has been investigating the impact of social disruption on TMEV infection. We have previously shown that mice exposed to repeated social disruption the week before infection develop more severe behavioral and physiological manifestations of acute and chronic TMEV infection compared with the nonstressed infected control group (R. R. Johnson et al., 2006; R. R. Johnson, Storts, et al., 2004). During acute infection, social stress resulted in greater levels of motor impairment, as indicated by greater hind limb impairment scores, reduced stride length, and reduced grid hang time. Histological analyses of spinal cord and brain revealed that mice exposed to social stress developed higher levels of inflammation, with the most pronounced increases in inflammation occurring in the spinal cord at Day 21 pi. Social stress was also found to alter viral load in the CNS on Days 7 and 21 pi. Although a reduction in CNS viral load was observed in the nonstressed infected mice, viral load remained elevated over time in mice previously exposed to social disruption. This finding is important because disruption of the viral clearance process during the acute phase of TMEV infection appears to increase the risk of developing the chronic demyelinating phase. Taken together, these results suggest that exposure to social stress before infection exacerbates early disease course relative to the nonstressed infected mice.

Glucocorticoid Resistance and Inflammation

Consistent with prior studies (Avitsur et al., 2001; Stark et al., 2001), we found that social disruption increased circulating levels of corticosterone and induced GC resistance before infection (R. R. Johnson, Storts, et al., 2004; Meagher et al., 2007). Under normal conditions, stress-induced increases in corticosterone would be expected to decrease inflammation. However, prolonged exposure to high levels of corticosterone reduced the sensitivity of the immune cells to GC inhibition. Though the development of GC resistance may be adaptive under some circumstances, it appears to dysregulate the magnitude and duration of the CNS inflammatory response, thereby altering both the innate and specific immune response to infection. Supporting this view, exposure to social disruption increased CNS inflammation, viral load, and behavioral signs of infection. The development of GC resistance also helps to explain the paradox of why stress-induced increases in corticosterone, which is normally anti-inflammatory, can result in increased inflammation following chronic stress. Thus, the induction of GC resistance by social stress may be one factor that increases the severity of CNS inflammation and MS disease course. The relevance of GC resistance to human disease is discussed in greater detail in the Implications for Human Disease Vulnerability section.

The finding that prolonged social stress exacerbates acute TMEV infection is relevant in light of epidemiological evidence suggesting that MS may be triggered by viral infection (Acheson, 1977; Kurtzke, 1993). We propose that systemic conditions (e.g., GC resistances, sympathetic activation, and suppressed antiviral immunity) at the time of infection play an important role in modulating immune processes leading to the development of MS. In the next section, we discuss evidence suggesting that social stress may have cascading adverse effects that subsequently alter the later autoimmune phase of MS.

Impact of Social Disruption on Chronic Theiler's Virus Infection

Using a longitudinal design, our laboratory recently examined whether exposure to social disruption the week before infection alters the development of the later autoimmune phase of disease (R. R. Johnson et al., 2006). Consistent with previous studies, mice exposed to social disruption the week prior to infection developed more severe behavioral signs of acute infection, including hind limb impairment, reduced stride length, and reduced spontaneous locomotor activity compared with nonstressed mice. We also observed a stress-induced increase in circulating levels of interleukin-6 (IL-6) on Day 9 pi. After the resolution of the acute phase (4 weeks), mice were monitored monthly until they developed behavioral signs of the chronic disease. Thereafter, weekly behavioral measures were taken to carefully track the development of chronic phase disease. To assess the impact of social stress on the development of autoimmunity, we took blood samples each month to measure levels of circulating antibodies to TMEV and several myelin components (i.e., MBP, MOG, and PLP). We found that the previously stressed mice developed earlier disease onset and more severe behavioral signs of chronic disease, including hind limb impairment, impaired balance and motor coordination on a test where mice are placed onto a rotating rod, reduced stride length, reduced spontaneous locomotor activity, impaired inclined plane performance, and reduced sensitivity to mechanical stimulation, which may reflect a loss of either sensation or motor impairment.

Several acute-phase behavioral and immunological measures predicted disease severity during the chronic phase. For example, behavioral measures collected on Day 7 pi (hind limb impairment and spontaneous locomotor activity) predicted the level of behavioral impairment during the chronic phase (hind limb impairment, foot print stride length, and spontaneous locomotor activity at Day 136 pi; significant r values ranged from 0.33 to 0.72). Moreover, several physiological measures collected early in infection (IL-6 at Day 9 pi; antibody to TMEV, MOG, and MBP at Day 42 pi; and body weights) predicted the level of behavioral impairment during the chronic phase. Correlations were found for both the onset of the chronic phase and the later time points. These results indicate that repeated exposure to social stress subsequently exacerbates both the acute and chronic phase of TMEV infection.

In summary, we have shown that social disruption increases inflammation in the spinal cord and brain of TMEV-infected mice and that this is associated with increased circulating levels of the proinflammatory cytokine IL-6 and the development of GC resistance. These stress-induced increases in inflammation were accompanied by exacerbation of TMEV-induced motor impairment and disruption of viral clearance from the CNS. During late disease, social disruption increases circulating levels of antibodies to myelin and TMEV, suggesting that stress also alters the autoimmune phase of disease. Although the neuroimmune mechanism(s) mediating the adverse effects of social disruption on TMEV infection had not been previously determined, we hypothesized that IL-6 is a likely candidate because it is increased by both TMEV infection (Chang, Zaczynaska, Katsetos, Platsoucas, & Oleszak, 2000; Mi et al., 2006; Palma, Kwon, Clipstone, & Kim, 2003; Sato, Reiner, Jensen, & Roos, 1997; Theil, Tsunoda, Libbey, Derfuss, & Fujinami, 2000) and exposure to social disruption (R. R. Johnson et al., 2006; Merlot, Moze, Dantzer, & Neveu, 2004a; Stark, Avitsur, Hunzeker, Padgett, & Sheridan, 2002).

The Role of Interleukin-6 in Mediating the Adverse Effects of Social Disruption

Recent studies suggest that the adverse effects of social stress on TMEV infection may be mediated by the induction of the proinflammatory cytokine IL-6 (R. R. Johnson et al., 2006; Meagher et al., 2007). Proinflammatory cytokines play a critical role in orchestrating the immune responses involved in viral clearance during early infection and in demyelination during late disease (Oleszak et al., 2004). During acute TMEV infection, IL-6 and other proinflammatory cytokines are elevated in all strains of mice, but higher levels are observed in susceptible mice compared with resistant mice (Chang et al., 2000; Mi et al., 2006; Sato et al., 1997; Theil et al., 2000). Elevated levels of IL-6 have also been found in the lesions and cerebral spinal fluid of MS patients (Padberg et al., 1999; Schonrock, Gawlowski, & Bruck, 2000).

Other research indicates that stressors can increase circulating and central levels of IL-6 and other proinflammatory cytokines (Huang, Takaki, & Arimura, 1997; J. D. Johnson et al., 2005; J. D. Johnson, O'Connor, Watkins, & Maier, 2004; R. R. Johnson et al., 2006; Merlot et al., 2004a; Merlot, Moze, Dantzer, & Neveu, 2004b; Nguyen et al., 1998, 2000; O'Connor et al., 2003; Shintani et al., 1995; Shizuya et al., 1998; Stark et al., 2002). These observations are consistent with reports that circulating levels of IL-6 are elevated in humans with major depression and chronic stress (Kiecolt-Glaser et al., 2003; Maes et al., 1997). As noted previously, prior exposure to a stressor can potentiate or prolong the release of proinflammatory cytokines following immune challenge (J. D. Johnson et al., 2002; R. R. Johnson et al., 2006; Merlot et al., 2004b; Quan et al., 2001). This phenomenon of cross-sensitization may explain how exposure to social disruption stress alters immune cell function and promotes sustained increases in inflammation following TMEV infection. Thus, it seemed plausible that stress-induced increases in central IL-6 production may be one mechanism mediating stress-induced exacerbation of acute and chronic TMEV infection. If stress-induced increases in central IL-6 mediate the adverse effects of social conflict, then blocking the effects of IL-6 during the stress-exposure period should prevent the exacerbation of acute disease.

Before we could test this hypothesis, it was important to determine whether social stress increases IL-6 expression in brain and blood during the stress-exposure period. In addition, we needed to determine whether stress-induced increases in IL-6 could be blocked by central administration of a neutralizing antibody to IL-6. Thus, we conducted a verification study to evaluate these issues. Intracranial cannulae were implanted into the lateral ventricle to allow administration of the neutralizing antibody. Prior to each social disruption session, mice received an injection of either a neutralizing antibody to IL-6 or an equivalent volume of vehicle. Thus, the central effects of stress-induced IL-6 were blocked during the entire week of social disruption. After the last session, mice were sacrificed to measure IL-6 levels in brain and blood using an enzyme-linked immunosorbent assay. As expected, social disruption increased IL-6 levels in both brain and blood, and this effect was reversed by the IL-6 neutralizing antibody treatment.

Next, we conducted a prevention study to determine whether intracranial administration of the neutralizing antibody to IL-6 could reverse the adverse effects of social stress on acute Theiler's virus infection (Meagher et al., 2007). Before each social disruption session, mice in the social stress or no stress groups received either an intracranial injection of a neutralizing antibody to IL-6 or the vehicle. Following their last social disruption session, the mice were infected with TMEV and monitored for the development of sickness behaviors, motor impairment, and physiological indicators of disease course.

During Days 1 and 2 pi we examined several measures of sickness behaviors. The sucrose preference task was used to measure anhedonia, or the loss of pleasure-seeking behavior that occurs during periods of stress or illness. In this test, mice are allowed to drink from two containers: one with tap water and the other with 2% sucrose water. As predicted, social stress caused a decrease in sucrose preference pi, and this effect was blocked by the IL-6 neutralizing antibody administered during the stress-exposure period. In addition, infection caused a significant reduction in body weight that was reversed in the socially stressed mice treated with the IL-6 neutralizing antibody. Exploratory behavior was also reduced by infection, resulting in decreases in horizontal and center time behavior in an open field on Days 1 and 2 pi. These infection-related decreases in exploratory behavior were exacerbated by social stress, and this effect was reversed by administration of the neutralizing antibody to IL-6 during the stress-exposure period. Social stress also caused an increase in infection-related hypersensitivity to mechanical stimulation of the paw with von Frey filaments during the first 24 hours pi. This finding suggests that social stress may be amplifying TMEV-induced allodynia, a phenomenon associated with hyperalgesia that refers to an increase in reactivity to a stimulus that is normally nonpainful. Again, this effect was reversed by IL-6 neutralizing antibody treatment, indicating that the stress-induced enhancement of allodynia is cytokine mediated.

We also assessed whether the IL-6 neutralizing antibody would block the adverse effects of social stress on motor function through Day 21 pi by assessing hind limb impairment, reactivity to mechanical stimulation, stride length, and locomotor activity. As expected, social stress increased TMEV-induced hind limb impairment while decreasing stride length and locomotor activity. Social stress also led to higher paw withdrawal thresholds for mechanical stimulation (von Frey) on Days 14 and 20 pi, which may reflect impairment in either motor or sensory function. On all measures, the deleterious effects of social stress on motor function were prevented by administration of the IL-6 neutralizing antibody during the stress-exposure period.

In addition, the IL-6 neutralizing antibody reversed the adverse effects of social stress on several physiological measures of disease. Social stress was found to increase spleen weights and reduce thymus weights, both signs of altered immunity. This effect was reversed by administration of a neutralizing antibody to IL-6 during the stress-exposure period. Consistent with prior studies, social stress disrupted the normal process of viral clearance in spinal cord and brain. The nonstressed mice cleared the virus by Day 21 pi, whereas the socially stressed mice treated with vehicle failed to clear the virus. Again, this effect of social stress was reversed by IL-6 neutralizing antibody treatment during the stress-exposure period. As expected, social stress increased infection-related inflammation in spinal cord and brain at both Day 7 and Day 21 pi. This stress-induced increase in CNS inflammation was prevented by IL-6 neutralizing antibody treatment.

Taken together, these findings suggest that stress-induced increases in central IL-6 contribute to the adverse effects of social stress during acute TMEV infection. It must be acknowledged, however, that only a partial reversal was observed on some behavioral measures in the stressed mice treated with the IL-6 antibody. Partial reversal suggests that social stress may increase the central expression of other proinflammatory cytokines, such as IL-1β. Therefore, we are currently investigating whether the adverse effects of social stress are partially mediated by IL-1β.

IMPLICATIONS FOR HUMAN DISEASE VULNERABILITY

The present findings may have implications for understanding the biobehavioral mechanisms mediating the adverse effects of social stress on a broad range of diseases affecting humans. Chronic inflammation contributes to the damage induced by a spectrum of central and peripheral degenerative diseases, including MS, Alzheimer's disease, Parkinson's disease, amyotrophic lateral sclerosis, osteoarthritis, rheumatoid arthritis, atherosclerosis, diabetes, cancer, and myocardial infarction (Chen & Miller, 2007; McGeer & McGeer, 2004; Perry, Newman, & Cunningham, 2003; Whitton, 2007). Although acute inflammation is beneficial when it is tightly regulated, chronic inflammation can seriously damage host tissue when sustained at high levels or inappropriately regulated. Chronic inflammation plays a major role in mediating the damage caused by autoimmune diseases (e.g., MS, rheumatoid arthritis) while also greatly influencing the pathogenesis of other diseases in which inflammation plays a modulatory rather than a causal role (e.g., cancer, diabetes, cardiovascular disease). Our research suggests that prolonged social stress is likely to amplify chronic inflammatory diseases by inducing GC resistance and overproduction of the proinflammatory cytokine IL-6. Recent evidence suggests that humans exposed to chronic stress also develop GC resistance and overproduction of IL-6, indicating that similar mechanisms may increase disease risk in humans (Raison & Miller, 2003).

Glucocorticoid Resistance

A growing body of evidence suggests that humans experiencing chronic social stressors develop GC resistance. For example, the parents of children undergoing treatment for cancer exhibit GC resistance (Miller, Cohen, &

Ritchey, 2002; Raison & Miller, 2003). When compared with a matched sample of parents of healthy children, the parents of cancer patients showed reduced sensitivity to the anti-inflammatory action of a synthetic GC, dexamethasone. The capacity of dexamethasone to inhibit the in vitro production of the proinflammatory cytokine IL-6 following immune challenge was suppressed.

Extending this line of work, research has examined the effects of acute and chronic stressors on GC resistance in children with asthma. Previous research had established that acute negative life events nearly doubled the risk of a later asthma attack (Sandberg et al., 2000). Moreover, when the acute stressor occurred within the context of chronic stress, the risk was tripled. Recent evidence suggests that these adverse effects of stress may be mediated by the development of GC resistance (Miller & Chen, 2006). To assess GC resistance, this study measured changes in GC receptor mRNA expression, where a decrease in GC receptor mRNA indicates resistance. The researchers found that chronic family stress was marginally associated with a decrease in GC receptor mRNA expression in white blood cells among children with asthma. Although acute stressors alone did not alter GC receptor mRNA, when these acute events occurred within the context of chronic stress, the result was a 5.5-fold reduction in GC receptor mRNA. This finding suggests that asthmatic children exposed to a combination of acute and chronic stressors experience a profound decrease in GC receptor expression on immune cells, making them less sensitive to the anti-inflammatory effects of endogenous GC. These findings collectively indicate that stress-induced GC resistance may contribute to increased airway inflammatory responses when asthmatic children are exposed to environmental triggers such as allergens and infections.

Mohr and Pelletier (2006) also suggested that the link between stress and MS may be attributable to the development of GC resistance. Supporting this hypothesis, a few studies have suggested that the immune cells of MS patients are less sensitive to the regulatory effects of GC when compared with healthy control participants (DeRijk, Eskandari, & Sternberg, 2004; Stefferl et al., 2001; van Winsen et al., 2005). GC resistance has also been observed in other inflammatory and autoimmune diseases (i.e., lupus, rheumatoid arthritis, asthma, Crohn's disease, ulcerative colitis) and is thought to contribute to disease pathogenesis. In light of the critical role that endogenous GCs play in immune regulation, a reduction in tissue sensitivity to GCs induced by chronic social stress could be one mechanism that increases vulnerability to a broad spectrum of diseases in which inflammation contributes to disease pathogenesis.

Interleukin-6, Chronic Stress, Inflammation, and Disease

Other research indicates that the overproduction of IL-6 is associated with a number of chronic diseases, including osteoporosis, arthritis, cardiovascular disease, Type 2 diabetes, and neurodegenerative diseases, such as Alzheimer's disease, Parkinson's disease, and MS (Elenkov, Iezzoni, Daly, Harris, & Chrousos, 2005; Maggio, Guralnik, Longo, & Ferrucci, 2006; Papanicolaou, Wilder, Manolagas, & Chrousos, 1998; Yudkin et al., 2000). Depression, chronic caregiving, and other stressful life events have also been shown to induce the production of IL-6 and other proinflammatory cytokines in humans (Kiecolt-Glaser et al., 2003; Maes, 2001; Maes et al., 1997). For example, in a longitudinal study of Alzheimer's caregivers, the rate of increase in IL-6 was 4 times larger for caregivers than for noncaregivers. This finding suggests that chronic stress in humans creates a proinflammatory environment that may increase the vulnerability to a host of chronic diseases whose onset and course may be influenced by inflammation. Because animal research has shown that exposure to stress can potentiate and sustain the release of proinflammatory cytokines following immune challenge (J. D. Johnson et al., 2002; R. R. Johnson, 2006; Meagher et al., 2007; Merlot et al., 2004b; Quan et al., 2001), increases in IL-6 may provide a common mechanism explaining the link between chronic stress and inflammatory diseases.

Potential Implications for Multiple Sclerosis and Other Neurodegenerative Diseases

Chronic stress may exacerbate neurodegenerative diseases and CNS infections by creating a proinflammatory environment in the brain that accelerates disease pathogenesis. Specifically, we propose that cross-sensitization of cytokine and microglia responses may provide a common mechanism explaining how stress-induced IL-6 exacerbates inflammatory neurodegeneration in diseases such as MS. This proinflammatory environment may also disrupt antiviral mechanisms, resulting in a disruption of viral clearance from the CNS and increased signs of encephalitis. The cytokine response to viral infection appears to play a key role in the development of subsequent autoimmune responses. Thus, it seems likely that stress-induced increases in central proinflammatory cytokine production during early infection may exacerbate the development of the later autoimmune demyelinating phase of disease.

Treatment Implications

Our work also suggests that the adverse effects of social stress on disease vulnerability in humans may be prevented or reversed by interventions capable of blocking stress-induced increases in proinflammatory cytokine expression. Although additional research will be needed to determine whether this strategy can be safely and effectively implemented in humans exposed to chronic social stress, it is possible that the negative health effects of chronic social stress may be prevented or reversed by a range of anti-inflammatory interventions. For example, research suggests that inhibition of the inflammatory response may reduce the risk of developing neurodegenerative diseases, such as Alzheimer's disease and Parkinson's disease (McGeer & McGeer, 2004; Whitton, 2007). In fact, epidemiological research indicates that regular use of conventional nonsteroidal anti-inflammatory drugs reduces the risk of developing Parkinson's disease by 45% and Alzheimer's disease by 60% to 80% (McGeer & McGeer, 2004). Other anti-inflammatory drugs, such as minocycline, have been shown to inhibit the production of cytokines by microglial cells in the CNS. Minocycline is a derivative of tetracycline that readily penetrates the CNS when administered peripherally, and it is approved by the U.S. Food and Drug Administration for treatment of other medical conditions in humans. Other interventions that have been shown to decrease the expression of proinflammatory cytokines should also be investigated, including exercise, antidepressant medication, omega-3 fatty acids, and mindfulness relaxation training (Carlson, Speca, Patel, & Goodey, 2003; Gielen et al., 2003; Kenis & Maes, 2002; Simopoulos, 2002; see also chaps. 4 and 9, this volume).

CONCLUSIONS

A growing body of evidence suggests that two environmental factors— viral infection and stress—may contribute to the development of MS in genetically susceptible humans and animals. Epidemiological studies indicate that MS is triggered by viral infection. Evidence for a relationship between stressful life events and MS exacerbation is also mounting, including longitudinal studies indicating that naturally occurring stressors predict the occurrence of new lesions. However, these human studies are limited because the association between stress and disease exacerbation may be attributable to a spurious third variable that influences both stress and disease. To determine whether there is a causal relationship between stress and viral infection in MS, animal experiments are essential. Using this approach, we have shown that social stress interacts with TMEV infection to determine the severity of behavioral impairment and CNS inflammation. We have begun to examine the underlying endocrine and immune mechanisms whereby social stress exacerbates CNS inflammation and disease course, including the induction of GC resistance and cross-sensitization of central proinflammatory cytokine activity (IL-6).

Exposure to social stress prior to TMEV infection resulted in more severe manifestations of acute and chronic disease in mice. This finding may have important implications for understanding disease vulnerability in humans. We propose that exposure to social stress prior to infection may result in increased CNS inflammation and dysregulation of the early immune response to infection. The induction of GC resistance and the sensitization of central proinflammatory cytokine expression by social stress may contribute to the dysregulation of central inflammatory responses during early infection. Because early immune responses shape the specific immune response to infection, dysregulation of this response may contribute to the failure to eliminate the pathogen and exacerbation of acute infection. We hypothesize that the establishment of a persistent infection, combined with a heightened inflammatory environment in the CNS, may contribute to the development of autoimmune diseases, such as MS. To test this hypothesis, future research will need to examine whether social-stress-induced GC resistance and central sensitization of IL-6 expression will have cascading effects that increase the severity of the demyelinating phase of disease.

KEY POINTS

- MS is a chronic inflammatory disease of the central nervous system.
- Human and animal research has indicated that prolonged social stress increases the risk of MS in genetically vulnerable individuals, likely through a stress-related increase in inflammation.
- Theiler's virus provides a good animal model for MS and makes it possible to test whether chronic social stress increases the risk of MS.
- IL-6 mediates the negative effects of social stress.
- For humans, chronic inflammation contributes to the damage induced by a number of central and peripheral degenerative diseases, including MS, Parkinson's, Alzheimer's, and amyotrophic lateral sclerosis.
- The adverse effects of social stress on disease vulnerability in humans may be prevented or reversed by interventions capable of blocking stress-induced increases in proinflammatory cytokine expression.

REFERENCES

Acheson, E. D. (1977). Epidemiology of multiple sclerosis. *British Medical Bulletin, 33*, 9–14.

Ackerman, K. D., Heyman, R., Rabin, B. S., Anderson, B. P., Houck, P. R., Frank, E., & Baum, A. (2002). Stressful life events precede exacerbations of multiple sclerosis. *Psychosomatic Medicine, 64*, 916–920.

Ackerman, K. D., Stover, A., Heyman, R., Anderson, B. P., Houck, P. R., Frank, E., & Rabin, B. S. (2003). Relationship of cardiovascular reactivity, stressful life

events, and multiple sclerosis disease activity. *Brain, Behavior, and Immunity,*
17, 141–151.

Aubagnac, S., Brahic, M., & Bureau, J. F. (1999). Viral load and a locus on chromosome 11 affect the late clinical disease caused by Theiler's virus. *Journal of Virology, 73,* 7965–7971.

Aubert, C., Chamorro, M., & Brahic, M. (1987). Identification of Theiler's infected cells in the central nervous system of the mouse during demyelinating disease. *Microbial Pathogenesis, 3,* 319–326.

Avitsur, R., Padgett, D. A., & Sheridan, J. F. (2006). Social interactions, stress, and immunity. *Neurological Clinics, 24,* 483–491.

Avitsur, R., Stark, J. L., & Sheridan, J. F. (2001). Social stress induces glucocorticoid resistance in subordinate animals. *Hormones and Behavior, 39,* 247–257.

Biron, C. A. (1998). Role of early cytokines, including alpha and beta interferons (IFN-a/b), in innate and adaptive immune responses to viral infections. *Seminars in Immunology, 10,* 383–390.

Bitsch, A., Schuchardt, J., Bunkowski, S., Kuhlmann, T., & Bruck, W. (2000). Acute axonal injury in multiple sclerosis: Correlation with demyelination and inflammation. *Brain, 123,* 1174–1183.

Blandino, P., Jr., Barnum, C. J., & Deak, T. (2006). The involvement of norepinephrine and microglia in hypothalamic and splenic IL-1beta responses to stress. *Journal of Neuroimmunology, 173,* 87–95.

Borrow, P., Tonks, P., Welsh, C. J. R., & Nash, A. A. (1992). The role of CD8+ T cells in the acute and chronic phases of Theiler's virus-induced disease in mice. *Journal of General Virology, 73,* 1861–1865.

Brahic, M., Bureau, J. F., & Michiels, T. (2005). The genetics of the persistent infection and demyelinating disease caused by Theiler's virus. *Annual Review of Microbiology, 59,* 279–298.

Brex, P. A., Ciccarelli, O., O'Riordan, J. I., Sailer, M., Thompson, A. J., & Miller, D. H. (2002). A longitudinal study of abnormalities on MRI and disability from multiple sclerosis. *The New England Journal of Medicine, 346,* 158–164.

Brown, R. F., Tennant, C. C., Sharrock, M., Hodgkinson S., Dunn, S. M., & Pollard, J. D. (2006). Relationship between stress and relapse in multiple sclerosis: Part I. Important features. *Multiple Sclerosis, 12,* 453–464.

Buljevac, D., Hop, W. C., Reedeker, W., Janssens, A. C., van der Meché, F. G., van Doorn, P. A., & Hintzen, R. Q. (2003, September, 20). Self reported stressful life events and exacerbations in multiple sclerosis: Prospective study. *BMJ, 327,* 646–651.

Butler, M. A., & Bennett, T. L. (2003). In search of a conceptualization of multiple sclerosis: A historical perspective. *Neuropsychology Review, 13,* 93–112.

Carlson, L. E., Speca, M., Patel, K. D., & Goodey, E. (2003). Mindfulness-based stress reduction in relation to quality of life, mood, symptoms of stress, and immune parameters in breast and prostate cancer outpatients. *Psychosomatic Medicine, 65,* 571–581.

Challoner, P. B., Smith, K. T., Parker, J. D., MacLeod, D. L., Coulter, S. N., Rose, T. M., et al. (1996). Plaque-associated expression of human herpesvirus 6 in multiple sclerosis. *Proceedings of the National Academy of Sciences USA, 92,* 7440–7444.

Chang, J. R., Zaczynaska, E., Katsetos, C. D., Platsoucas, C. D., & Oleszak, E. L. (2000). Differential expression of TGF-b, IL-2, and other cytokines in the CNS of Theiler's murine encephalomyelitis virus-infected susceptible and resistant strains of mice. *Virology, 278,* 346–360.

Charcot, J. M. (1868). Histologie de la sclerose en plaques. *Gazette des Hopitaux, 41,* 554–566.

Charcot, J. M. (1877). *Lectures on the diseases of the nervous system delivered at la Salpetriere* (G. Sigerson, Trans.). London: New Sydenham Society.

Chen, E., & Miller, G. E. (2007). Stress and inflammation in exacerbations of asthma. *Brain, Behavior, and Immunity, 21,* 993–999.

Clatch, R. J., Lipton, H. L., & Miller, S. D. (1987). Class II-restricted T cell responses in Theiler's murine encephalomyelitis virus (TMEV)-induced demyelinating disease: II. Survey of host immune responses and central nervous system virus titers in inbred mouse strains. *Microbial Pathogenesis, 3,* 327–337.

Dal Canto, M. C., & Rabinowitz, S. G. (1982). Experimental models of virus-induced demyelination of the central nervous system. *Annals of Neurology, 11,* 109–127.

DeRijk, R. H., Eskandari, F., & Sternberg, E. M. (2004). Corticosteroid resistance in a subpopulation of multiple sclerosis patients as measured by ex vivo dexamethasone inhibition of LPS induced IL-6 production. *Journal of Neuroimmunology, 151,* 180–188.

Dethlefs, S., Brahic, M., & Larsson-Sciard, E. L. (1997). An early abundant cytotoxic T-lymphocyte response against Theiler's virus is critical for preventing for viral persistence. *Journal of Virology, 71,* 8875–8878.

Dyment, D. A., Ebers, G. C., & Sadovnick, A. D. (2004, February). Genetics of multiple sclerosis. *The Lancet Neurology, 3,* 104–110.

Elenkov, I. J., Iezzoni, D. G., Daly, A., Harris, A. G., & Chrousos, G. P. (2005). Cytokine dysregulation, inflammation, and well-being. *Neuroimmunomodulation, 12,* 255–269.

Fiette, L., Aubert, C., Ulrike, M., Huang, S., Aguet, M., Brahic, M., & Bureau, J. F. (1995). Theiler's virus infection of 129Sv mice that lack the interferon α/β or IFN-γ receptors. *Journal of Experimental Medicine, 181,* 2069–2076.

Gielen, R. S., Adams, V., Möbius-Winkler, S., Link, A., Erbs, S., Yu, J., et al. (2003). Anti-inflammatory effects of exercise training in the skeletal muscle of patients with chronic heart failure. *Journal of American College of Cardiology, 42,* 861–868.

Gilden, D. H. (2005, March). Infectious causes of multiple sclerosis. *The Lancet Neurology, 4,* 195–202.

Grant, I., Brown, G. W., Harris, T., McDonald, W. I., Patterson, T., & Trimble, M. R. (1989). Severely threatening events and marked life difficulties preceding onset or exacerbation of multiple sclerosis. *Journal of Neurology, Neurosurgery, & Psychiatry, 52,* 8–13.

Greenwood, B. N., Kennedy, S., Smith, T. P., Campeau, S., Day, H. E., & Fleshner, M. (2003). Voluntary freewheel running selectively modulates catecholamine content in peripheral tissue and c-Fos expression in the central sympathetic circuit following exposure to uncontrollable stress in rats. *Neuroscience, 120,* 269–281.

Hernan, M. A., Zhang, S. M., Lipworth, L., Olek, M. J., & Ascherio, A. (2001). Multiple sclerosis and age at infection with common viruses. *Epidemiology, 12,* 301–306.

Huang, Q. H., Takaki, A., & Arimura, A. (1997). Central noradrenergic system modulates plasma interleukin-6 production by peripheral interleukin-1. *American Journal of Physiology—Regulatory, Integrative and Comparative Physiology, 273,* R731–R738.

Johnson, J. D., Campisi, J., Sharkey, C. M., Kennedy, S. L., Nickerson, M., Greenwood, B. N., & Fleshner, M. (2005). Catecholamines mediate stress-induced increases in peripheral and central inflammatory cytokines. *Neuroscience, 135,* 1295–1307.

Johnson, J. D., O'Connor, K. A., Deak, T., Stark, M., Watkins, L. R., & Maier, S. F. (2002). Prior stressor exposure sensitizes LPS-induced cytokine production. *Brain, Behavior, and Immunity, 16,* 461–476.

Johnson, J. D., O'Connor, K. A., Watkins, L. R., & Maier, S. F. (2004). The role of IL-1β in stress-induced sensitization of proinflammatory cytokine and corticosterone responses. *Neuroscience, 127,* 569–577.

Johnson, R. R., Prentice, T., Bridegam, P., Young, C. R., Steelman, A. J., Welsh, T. H., et al. (2006). Social stress alters the severity and onset of the chronic phase of Theiler's virus infection. *Journal of Neuroimmunology, 175,* 39–51.

Johnson, R. R., Storts, R., Welsh, T. H., Jr., Welsh, C. J. R., & Meagher, M. W. (2004). Social stress alters the severity of acute Theiler's virus infection. *Journal of Neuroimmunology, 148,* 74–85.

Kaminsky, S. G., Nakamura, I., & Cudkowicz, G. (1987). Defective differentiation of natural killer cells in SJL mice: Role of the thymus. *Journal of Immunology, 138,* 1020–1025.

Kenis, G., & Maes, M. (2002). Effects of antidepressants on the production of cytokines. *International Journal of Neuropsychopharmacology, 5,* 401–412.

Kiecolt-Glaser, J. K., Preacher, K. J., MacCallum, R. C., Atkinson, C., Malarkey, W. B., & Glaser, R. (2003). Chronic stress and age-related increases in the proinflammatory cytokine IL-6. *Proceedings of the National Academy of Sciences USA, 100,* 9090–9095.

Kurtzke, J. F. (1993). Epidemiologic evidence for multiple sclerosis as an infection. *Clinical Microbiology Review, 6,* 382–427.

Kurtzke, J. F., & Hyllested, K. (1987). MS epidemiology in Faroe Islands. *Rivista di neurologia, 57,* 77–87.

Levin, L. I., Munger, K. L., Rubertone, M. V., Peck, C. A., Lennette, E. T., Spiegelman, D., & Ascherio, A. (2003). Multiple sclerosis and Epstein-Barr virus. *JAMA, 289,* 1533–1536.

Lipton, H. L. (1975). Theiler's virus infection in mice: An unusual biphasic disease process leading to demyelination. *Infection and Immunology, 11,* 1147–1155.

Lipton, H. L., & Melvold, R. (1984). Genetic analysis of susceptibility to Theiler's virus induced demyelinating disease in mice. *Journal of Immunology, 132,* 1821–1825.

Maes, M. (2001). Psychological stress and the inflammatory response system. *Clinical Science, 101,* 193–194.

Maes, M., Bosmans, E., De Jongh, R., Kenis, G., Vandoolaeghe, E., & Neels, H. (1997). Increased serum IL-6 and IL-1 receptor antagonist concentrations in major depression and treatment resistant depression. *Cytokine, 9,* 853–858.

Maggio, M., Guralnik, J. M., Longo, D. L., & Ferrucci, L. (2006). Interleukin-6 in aging and chronic disease: A magnificent pathway. *The Journals of Gerontology: Series A. Biological Sciences and Medical Sciences, 61,* M575–M584.

McGavern, D. B., Zoecklein, L., Drescher, K. M., & Rodriguez, M. (1999). Quantitative assessment of neurologic deficits in a chronic progressive murine model of CNS demyelination. *Experimental Neurology, 158,* 171–181.

McGavern, D. B., Zoecklein, L., Sathornsumetee, S., & Rodriguez, M. (2000). Assessment of hind limb gait as a powerful indicator of axonal loss in a murine model of progressive CNS demyelination. *Brain Research, 877,* 396–400.

McGeer, P. L., & McGeer, E. G. (2004). Inflammation and the degenerative diseases of aging. *Annals of the New York Academy of Sciences, 1035,* 104–116.

Meagher, M. W., Johnson, R. R., Young, E. E., Vichaya, E. G., Lunt, S., Harden, E., et al. (2007). Interleukin-6 as a mechanism for the adverse effects of social stress on acute Theiler's virus infection. *Brain, Behavior, and Immunity, 21,* 1083–1095.

Mei-Tal, V., Meyerowitz, S., & Engel, G. L. (1970). The role of psychological process in a somatic disorder: Multiple sclerosis: 1. The emotional setting of illness onset and exacerbation. *Psychosomatic Medicine, 32,* 67–86.

Merlot, E., Moze, E., Dantzer, R., & Neveu, P. J. (2004a). Cytokine production by spleen cells after social defeat in mice: Activation of T cells and reduced inhibition by glucocorticoids. *Stress, 7,* 55–61.

Merlot, E., Moze, E., Dantzer, R., & Neveu, P. J. (2004b). Immune alterations induced by social defeat do not alter the course of an on-going BCG infection in mice. *Neuroimmunomodulation, 11,* 414–418.

Mi, W., Prentice, T. W., Young, C. R., Johnson, R. R., Sieve, A. N., Meagher, M. W., & Welsh, C. J. R. (2006). Restraint stress decreases virus-induced proinflammatory cytokine mRNA expression during acute Theiler's virus infection. *Journal of Neuroimmunology, 178,* 49–61.

Miguel, H., Zhang, S. M., Lipworth, L., Olek, M. J., & Ascherio, A. (2001). Multiple sclerosis and age at infection with common viruses. *Epidemiology, 12,* 301–306.

Miller, G. E., & Chen, E. (2006). Life stress and diminished expression of genes encoding glucocorticoid receptor and beta(2)-adrenergic receptor in children with asthma. *Proceedings of the National Academy of Sciences USA, 103,* 5496–5501.

Miller, G. E., Cohen, S., & Ritchey, A. K. (2002). Chronic psychological stress and the regulation of pro-inflammatory cytokines: A glucocorticoid-resistance model. *Health Psychology, 21,* 531–541.

Mohr, D. C., Goodkin, D. E., Bacchetti, P., Boudewyn, A. C., Huang, L., Marrietta, P., et al. (2000). Psychological stress and the subsequent appearance of new brain MRI lesions in MS. *Neurology, 55,* 55–61.

Mohr, D. C., Hart, S. L., Julian, L., Cox, D., & Pelletier, D. (2004, March 27). Association between stressful life events and exacerbation in multiple sclerosis: A meta-analysis. *BMJ, 328,* 731–735.

Mohr, D. C., & Pelletier, D. (2006). A temporal framework for understanding the effects of stressful life events on inflammation in patients with multiple sclerosis. *Brain, Behavior, and Immunity, 20,* 27–36.

Moore F. G., & Wolfson, C. (2002). Human herpes virus 6 and multiple sclerosis. *Acta Neurologica Scandinavica, 106,* 63–83.

Murray, P. D., Pavelko, K. D., Leibowitz, J., Lin, X., & Rodriguez, M. (1998). CD4 (+) and CD8 (+) T cells make discrete contributions to demyelination and neurologic disease in a viral model of multiple sclerosis. *Journal of Virology, 72,* 7320–7329.

Nguyen, K. T., Deak, T., Owens, S. M., Kohno, T., Fleshner, M., Watkins, L. R., et al. (1998). Exposure to acute stress induces brain interleukin-1beta protein in the rat. *Journal of Neuroscience, 18,* 2239–2246.

Nguyen, K. T., Deak, T., Will, M. J., Hansen, M. K., Hunsaker, B. N., Fleshner, M., et al. (2000). Timecourse and corticosterone sensitivity of the brain, pituitary, and serum interleukin-1beta protein response to acute stress. *Brain Research, 859,* 193–201.

Nisipeanu, P., & Korczyn, A. D. (1993). Psychological stress as risk factor for exacerbations in multiple sclerosis. *Neurology, 43,* 1311–1312.

Njenga, M. K., Asakura, K., Hunter, S. F., Wettstein, P., Pease, L. R., & Rodriguez, M. (1997). The immune system preferentially clears Theiler's virus from the gray matter of the central nervous system. *Journal of Virology, 71,* 8592–8601.

O'Connor, K. A., Johnson, J. D., Hansen, M. K., Wieseler Frank, J. L., Maksimova, E., Watkins, L. R., et al. (2003). Peripheral and central proinflammatory cytokine response to a severe acute stressor. *Brain Research, 991,* 123–132.

Oleszak, E. L., Chang, J. R., Friedman, H., Katsetos, C. D., & Platsoucas, C. D. (2004). Theiler's virus infection: A model for multiple sclerosis. *Clinical Microbiology Reviews, 17,* 174–207.

Padberg, F., Feneberg W., Schmidt, S., Schwarz, M. J., Korschenhausen, D., Greenberg, B. D., et al. (1999). CSF and serum levels of soluble interleukin-6 receptors (sIL-6R and sgp130), but not of interleukin-6 are altered in multiple sclerosis. *Journal of Neuroimmunology, 99,* 218–223.

Padgett, D. A., Sheridan, J. F., Dorne, J., Berntson, G. G., Candelora, J., & Glaser, R. (1998). Social stress and the reactivation of latent herpes simplex virus Type 1. *Proceedings of the National Academy of Sciences USA, 95,* 7231–7235.

Palma, J. P., Kwon, D., Clipstone, N. A., & Kim, B. S. (2003). Infection with Theiler's murine encephalomyelitis virus directly induces proinflammatory cytokines in primary astrocytes via NF-kappaB activation: Potential role for the initiation of demyelinating disease. *Journal of Virology, 77*, 6322–6331.

Papanicolaou, D. A., Wilder, R. L., Manolagas, S. C., & Chrousos, G. P. (1998). The pathophysiological roles of interleukin-6 in human disease. *Annals of Internal Medicine, 128*, 127–137.

Perry, V. H., Newman, T. A., & Cunningham, C. (2003). The impact of systemic infection on the progression of neurodegenerative disease. *Nature Reviews: Neuroscience, 4*, 103–112.

Quan, N., Avitsur, R., Stark, J. L., He, L., Shah, M., Caliguiri, M., et al. (2001). Social stress increases the susceptibility to endotoxic shock. *Journal of Neuroimmunology, 115*, 36–45.

Rabin, B. S. (2002). Can stress participate in the pathogenesis of autoimmune disease. *Journal of Adolescent Health, 30*, 71–75.

Raison, M. C. L., & Miller, A. H. (2003). When not enough is too much: The role of insufficient glucocorticoid signaling in the pathophysiology of stress-related disorders. *American Journal of Psychiatry, 160*, 1554–1565.

Rodriguez, M., Pavelko, K. D., Njenga, M. K., Logan, W. C., & Wettstein, P. J. (1996). The balance between persistent virus infection and immune cells determines demyelination. *Journal of Immunology, 157*, 5699–5709.

Rodriguez, M., & Sriram, S. (1988). Successful therapy of Theiler's virus-induced demyelination (DA strain) with monoclonal anti-Lyt2 antibody. *Journal of Immunology, 140*, 2950–2955.

Sandberg, D., Paton, J. Y., Ahola, S., McCann, D. C., McGuinness, D., & Hillary, C. R. (2000, September 16). The role of acute and chronic stress in asthma attacks in children. *The Lancet, 356*, 982–987.

Sato, S., Reiner, S. L., Jensen, M. A., & Roos, R. P. (1997). Central nervous system cytokine mRNA expression following Theiler's murine encephalomyelitis virus infection. *Journal of Neuroimmunology, 76*, 213–223.

Schonrock, L. M., Gawlowski, G., & Bruck, W. (2000). Interleukin-6 expression in human multiple sclerosis lesions. *Neuroscience Letters, 294*, 45–48.

Shintani, F., Nakaki, T., Kanba, S., Sato, K., Yagi, G., Shiozawa, M., et al. (1995). Involvement of interleukin-1 in immobilization stress-induced increase in plasma adrenocorticotropic hormone and in release of hypothalamic monoamines in the rat. *Journal of Neuroscience, 15*, 1961–1970.

Shizuya, K., Komori, T., Fujiwara, R., Miyahara, S., Ohmori, M., & Nomura, J. (1998). The expressions of mRNAs for interleukin-6 (IL-6) and the IL-6 receptor (IL-6R) in the rat hypothalamus and midbrain during restraint stress. *Life Science, 62*, 2315–2320.

Sieve, A. N., Steelman, A. J., Young, C. R., Storts, R., Welsh, T. H., Welsh, C. J., & Meagher, M. W. (2004). Chronic restraint stress during early Theiler's virus infection exacerbates the subsequent demyelinating disease in SJL mice. *Journal of Neuroimmunology, 155*, 103–118.

Simopoulos, A. P. (2002). Omega-3 fatty acids in inflammation and autoimmune diseases. *Journal of the American College of Nutrition, 21*, 495–505.

Soldan, S. S., & Jacobson, S. (2001). Role of viruses in etiology and pathogenesis of multiple sclerosis. *Advances in Virus Research, 56*, 517–555.

Sospedra, M., & Martin, R. (2005). Immunology of multiple sclerosis. *Annual Review of Immunology, 23*, 683–747.

Stark, J. L., Avitsur, R., Hunzeker, J., Padgett, D. A., & Sheridan, J. F. (2002). Interleukin-6 and the development of social disruption-induced glucocorticoid resistance. *Journal of Neuroimmunology, 124*, 9–15.

Stark, J. L., Avitsur, R., Padgett, D. A., Campbell, K. A., Beck, F. M., & Sheridan, J. F. (2001). Social stress induces glucocorticoid resistance in macrophages. *American Journal of Physiology—Regulatory, Integrative and Comparative Physiology, 280*, R1799–R1805.

Stefferl, A., Storch, M. K., Linington, C., Stadelmann, C., Lassmann, H., Pohl, T., et al. (2001). Disease progression in chronic relapsing experimental allergic encephalomyelitis is associated with reduced inflammation-driven production of corticosterone. *Endocrinology, 142*, 3616–3624.

Stinssen, P., Raus, J., & Zhang, J. (1997). Autoimmune pathogenesis of multiple sclerosis: Role of autoreactive T lymphocytes and new immunotherapeutic strategies. *Critical Reviews in Immunology, 17*, 33–75.

Theil, D. J., Tsunoda, I., Libbey, J. E., Derfuss, T. J., & Fujinami, R. S. (2000). Alterations in cytokine but not chemokine mRNA expression during three distinct Theiler's virus infections. *Journal of Neuroimmunology, 104*, 22–30.

Theiler, M. (1934, August 3). Spontaneous encephalomyelitis of mice: A new virus. *Science, 80*, 122.

van Winsen, L. M., Muris, D. F., Polman, C. H., Dijkstra, C. D., van den Berg, T. K., & Uitdehaag, B. M. (2005). Sensitivity to glucocorticoids is decreased in relapsing remitting multiple sclerosis. *The Journal of Clinical Endocrinology & Metabolism, 90*, 734–740.

Warren, S., Greenhill, S., & Warren, K. G. (1982). Emotional stress and the development of multiple sclerosis: Case-control evidence of a relationship. *Journal of Chronic Disease, 35*, 821–831.

Warren, S., Warren, K. G., & Cockerill, R. (1991). Emotional stress and coping in multiple sclerosis (MS) exacerbations. *Journal of Psychosomatic Research, 35*, 37–47.

Welsh, C. J. R., Tonks, P., Borrow, P., & Nash, A. A. (1990). Theiler's virus: An experimental model of virus-induced demyelination. *Autoimmunity, 6*, 105–112.

Welsh, C. J. R., Tonks, P., Nash, A. A., & Blakemore, W. F. (1987). The effect of L3T4 T cell depletion on the pathogenesis of Theiler's murine encephalomyelitis virus infection in CBA mice. *Journal of General Virology, 68*, 1659–1667.

Whitton, P. S. (2007). Inflammation as a causative factor in the aetiology of Parkinson's disease. *British Journal of Pharmacology, 150*, 963–976.

Yudkin, J. S., Panahloo, A., Stehouwer, C., Emeis, J. J., Bulmer, K., Mohamed-Ali, V., et al. (2000). The influence of improved glycaemic control with insulin and sulphonylureas on acute phase and endothelial markers in Type II diabetic subjects. *Diabetologia, 43*, 1099–1106.

8

ALLOSTASIS: A MODEL FOR WOMEN'S HEALTH

MAUREEN GROËR AND THE WOMEN'S HEALTH RESEARCH GROUP AT THE UNIVERSITY OF SOUTH FLORIDA COLLEGE OF NURSING

The conceptual model of allostasis (McEwen & Seeman, 1999; Schulkin, 2003; Sterling & Eyer, 1988) is a useful paradigm for understanding the deleterious effects of stress in humans. Yet few studies have examined allostasis and allostatic load as an approach for understanding women's health. In this chapter, we present an adaptation of the allostasis model for women's health. We do so by examining the primary mediators, the hypothalamic–pituitary–adrenal (HPA) axis, and the role of inflammation as a response to threat. Next, we present and discuss the term *allostatic load*, a conceptual model that helps explain the relationship between inflammation and disease. The chapter focuses on these processes with an emphasis on the unique stressors experienced by women that are related to gender, social status, role, and development, along with differing responses to stress, gender-specific coping processes, and women's unique vulnerabilities to certain illnesses.

Theresa Beckie, Dorit Breiter, Candace Burns, Janie Canty-Mitchell, Sheila Crowell, Allison Edmonds, Mary Evans, Lois Gonzalez, Cecilia Jevitt, Cecile Lengacher, and Mary Webb coauthored this chapter as part of the Women's Health Research Group.

Allostasis is a model that explains how stress may result in disease. Both predictable high-demand life stages and unpredictable challenges that require biobehavioral adjustment are considered in this approach. The concept was originally introduced by Sterling and Eyer (1988) as a modification of the homeostasis concept that had been the guiding paradigm for understanding physiological adjustments to change. In homeostasis, the concept of maintenance of physiological states within set points is an essential element. As is homeostasis, allostasis is the process of achieving and maintaining stability in the internal environment. The critical difference is the recognition in the allostasis model that stability is achieved through change and that physiological and behavioral states change in response to external environmental and developmental perturbations (Landys, Ramenofsky, & Wingfield, 2006), leading to a state of adaptation outside of the normal physiological ranges.

Allostasis allows organisms to be sufficiently flexible to respond to changing conditions and developmental stages. Primary mediators in allostasis include stress hormones, the immune system, and neurological responses (McEwen & Wingfield, 2003), which are all factors in rapid response to change. Sustained activity of these mediators ultimately produces a particular allostatic state. The primary mediators, though helpful in the short run, may with time cause damage. Such effects are the "costs" of maintaining an allostatic state longer than is optimal for health.

ALLOSTASIS AND ALLOSTATIC LOAD

Key to the allostatic state concept is the idea that over time, allostatic state requirements, when demands continue, may produce an allostatic load on the organism, and that allostatic load over time may cause cumulative effects that contribute to disease and senescence (Stewart, 2006). Four allostatic states may lead to allostatic load: repeated challenges, inability to adapt to repeated challenges, inability to end the allostatic responses after the stressor has been removed, and inability to produce an adequate allostatic response (McEwen, 2003b).

The demands that provoke the allostatic response in humans include external and internal biological and behavioral stressors, both those that are predictable and related to life-cycle events (childbirth and lactation) and those that are unpredictable (such as death of a spouse). Measurement of allostatic load in humans was originally conceptualized as a composite score. Primary mediators were serum dehydroepiandrosterone (DHEA; an antagonist of cortisol), cortisol, and norepinephrine and epinephrine excretion. Secondary effects of the primary mediators included blood pressure, waist–hip ratio, serum high-density lipoproteins and cholesterol, and glycosylated hemoglobin levels (McEwen & Seeman, 1999). Participants in the MacArthur

Study were originally scored on the highest risk quartiles for each of the measures (Singer, Ryff, & Seeman, 2004). The higher scores represent higher allostatic load, and increasing score was associated with higher morbidity and mortality 7 years after the baseline measurements.

In a more recent large study of 18,000 adults, the researchers used 13 measures of allostatic load (Crimmons, Johnston, Haywaerd, & Seeman, 2003). Included in this composite were inflammatory cytokine levels. A significant number of illnesses have been thought of as arising from allostatic load, including hypertension (HTN), obesity, metabolic syndrome, diabetes, cardiovascular disease (CVD), and autoimmune and inflammatory disorders (McEwen & Wingfield, 2003).

It is important to consider gender when calculating allostatic load. Mean values for stress hormones are higher, and DHEA levels are lower for women. Metabolic syndrome biomarkers have higher mean values in men. Thus, allostatic load scores for men and women are not easily comparable. There is an acknowledged need to move to more discrete, time-integrated and molecular tools for measurement of allostatic load. Possibilities for dysregulation in the metabolic, immune, neuroendocrine, and autonomic nervous systems as a result of stress are far more complex than currently measured markers would evaluate (Singer et al., 2004).

Mechanisms by Which Allostatic Load Can Lead to Disease

The mechanisms of diseases that result from allostatic overload are secondary outcomes largely related to the pathophysiological effects of unremitting and chronic exposure of the body systems to the primary mediators. Because the mediators activate defensive functions involving cardiovascular parameters, metabolic functions, immune and inflammatory defenses, and the nervous system, these are the systems that are most likely to suffer from allostatic load. Studies that have supported allostasis have examined the risk of stress-induced illnesses such as CVD (e.g., atherosclerosis, HTN), metabolic disorders (e.g., Type 2 diabetes, metabolic syndrome), neurobehavioral disorders (e.g., depression, anxiety), and immune disorders (e.g., allergy, autoimmunity). Nevertheless, effects of gender have not been thoroughly examined, and implications of allostasis for women's health have not been explicated.

Figure 8.1 depicts an allostasis model, with unique gender influences or variables indicated. The remainder of this chapter explores influences of female gender on aspects of this model.

Perceived Stress and Gender

Central to the model is perceived stress. For an organism to launch a stress response, there must be appraisal of the stressor as innocuous, a danger, or a challenge. This appraisal results in a perception that is often highly individualistic and influenced by gender. Males and females in most animal

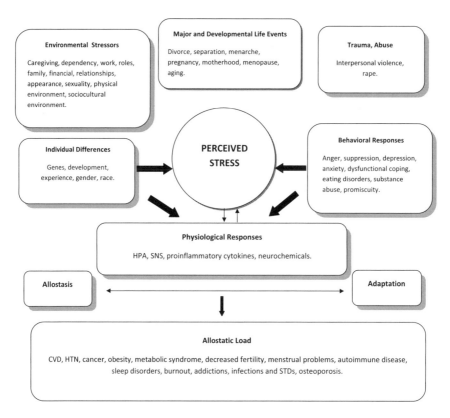

Figure 8.1. An allostatic model of women's health. CVD = cardiovascular disease; HPA = hypothalamic–pituitary–adrenal; HTN = hypertension; SNS = sympathetic nervous system; STD = sexually transmitted disease.

species differ in neuroanatomy, stress axes, neuroendocrinology, and immunology—differences that ultimately would affect allostatic load. Differences may translate into unique gender-specific predilections for diseases, such as depression and autoimmunity for females, and CVD and suicide for males. Many studies have found gender differences in both the HPA axis and the sympathetic adrenomedullary (SAM) system between female and male laboratory animals. Female rodents respond to acute and chronic stressors with greater amplitude responses than do males in both adrenocorticotropic hormone (ACTH) and corticosterone (Armario, Gavalda, & Marti, 1995). Sex differences have also been shown in corticosteroid receptors and neurological responses to stress (Karandrea, Kittas, & Kitraki, 2000).

The human literature is not so clear. A more reactive HPA axis might be etiological in the more frequent occurrence of depression in women. However, many laboratory stress studies have actually demonstrated lower stress reactivity in females. Adult men seem to respond to psychological stress with a greater output of cortisol than do women (Kudielka & Kirschbaum, 2005).

When experimental stressor paradigms, such as the Trier Social Stress Test, are used, there are reproducible HPA activations in both genders. However, women tend to have lower HPA and SAM responses to these types of challenges than do men (Kajantie & Phillips, 2005). Stroud, Salovey, and Epel (2002) critiqued these studies, pointing out that the commonly used laboratory stress paradigms are achievement or instrumentality oriented, and males would find these challenging, whereas social stress might be a more appropriate challenge for females. Their study found that females launched a greater HPA response to social rejection, whereas males responded to achievement-oriented stressors with greater HPA responses.

Another study found that across two cultures (American and Taiwanese), women demonstrated higher relationships between perceived stress and physiological responses than did men (Goldman, Glei, Seplaki, Liu, & Weinstein, 2005). In the MacArthur Study, women with the most negative scores on a social-relationship construct had higher allostatic-load scores than did men with equivalent scores on that construct. This result suggests that social and intimate relationships have greater meaning to women than to men (Singer et al., 2004).

An analysis of animal stress studies (Taylor et al., 2000) pointed out that most stress studies have been done with males, and critiqued the universality of the stereotyped fight-or-flight response. It is not adaptive for females to leave the nest and fight an aggressor, putting both the mother and offspring in jeopardy. Fleeing is not a good option for the offspring's survival. Females, being generally smaller and weaker, are at a greater disadvantage than males when put into predator–prey situations. The more adaptive response to stress for females is to "tend and befriend." Tending is quieting and caring for offspring, and befriending produces social affiliation (usually with other females) so that group members protect offspring. The hormone oxytocin is theorized to be a determinant of the female affiliative behavioral response to stress (Uvnas-Moberg, 1997). Because of its prosocial and physiological effects, we propose oxytocin as a moderator of the stress–allostatic load relationship in women. Indeed, understanding how stress reactivity may be dampened in lactating mothers may provide clues to natural ways that a woman protects herself from allostatic load, particularly during the time when her primary goal is to nurture and care for a newborn infant.

Oxytocin

Although oxytocin is well-known for its role in milk ejection and uterine contractions, the hormone has many additional critical roles in behavior, stress reactivity, cardiovascular and nervous system functioning, endocrine responses, and immune function. Oxytocin appears to be essential for the development of maternal behavior and for bonding between mother and infant (Uvnas-Moberg, 1997). Nipple latch; skin-to-skin contact (Nissen, Lilja, Widstrom, & Uvnas-Moberg, 1995); conscious and unconscious perceptions, such as odors and tastes; and a plethora of emotional responses provoke oxytocin release (Uvnas-Moberg, 1997). Oxytocin is also released by electrical stimulation of afferent nerve fibers originating in the skin (Stock & Uvnas-Moberg, 1988), massage (Agren, Lundeberg, Uvnas-Moberg, & Sato, 1995), sexual activity, touch, warmth, vibration, and electroacupuncture (Uvnas-Moberg, 1997). Psychological influences are also important. A nursing mother merely has to think about her infant or hear its cry to induce a pulse of oxytocin and a subsequent let-down of milk.

Carter and Altemus (1997) proposed that oxytocin and vasopressin are antagonistic and that oxytocin opposes the defense reactions associated with stress, functionally antagonizing vasopressin's effects. If a mother were severely threatened, however, vasopressin release would override oxytocin, allowing for defensive responses.

Oxytocin is an important mediator in the decreased postnatal stress responsiveness of animal mothers. During lactation, oxytocin acts on receptors throughout the hippocampus, hypothalamus, and limbic system, with a general effect of promoting calmness, increasing affiliative and nurturing behavior and social responsivity (Uvnas-Moberg, 1997). Oxytocin's effects may be both energy saving (e.g., sedation, decreased reactivity, increased digestion and anabolic metabolism, decreased blood pressure) and energy transferring (e.g., milk ejection, cutaneous vasodilation, increased levels of glucose). During the last part of pregnancy, ovarian steroids activate the release of oxytocin, which then affects maternal behavior in the early postpartum period. In lab animals with high levels of infanticide, infusion of oxytocin suppressed this behavior markedly (McCarthy, 1990). In addition, an anxiolytic effect of oxytocin has been found: Infusion of oxytocin in 182 healthy men produced increased activation and attenuated arousal and anger (Pietrowsky, Krug, Fehm, & Born, 1992).

Another mechanism of importance in oxytocin's effect on stress reactivity appears to be through vagal regulation. Parasympathetic dominance characterizes the basal autonomic tone of breastfeeding human mothers, possibly through central stimulation of vagal efferent pathways that are affected by oxytocin as well as by other inputs. This activity contributes not only to diminished stress reactivity but also to lower blood pressure, greater lymphocyte responses to mitogens, and decreased cardiac variability in the basal state. The cardiovascular effects of oxytocin include not only the aforementioned vagal effects but also natriuresis and vascular relaxation probably mediated through the atrial natriuretic factor (Gutkowska, Jankowski, Mukaddam-Daher, & McCann, 2000). Breastfeeding women have been reported to have higher vagal tone as estimated from respiratory sinus arrhythmia (Redwine, Altemus, Leong, & Carter, 2001). With respect to the unique aspects of a woman's stress perception and responses, oxytocin may ultimately be a central component that protects and preserves health.

The demands of a woman's multiple roles must be considered in a woman's allostatic model. Much of a woman's life is devoted to caregiving (e.g., husband, children, elderly parents), and conflicts and role stress are inevitable when women work and balance multiple competing demands. The tending instinct is biological and from an evolutionary perspective, absolutely essential. Yet most American women (65%) today work or do not stay at home with their children (Women Employed, n.d.). Economic pressures force some women to work, and occupation and career demands compete with time spent with children. Nearly 40% of American women work in low-paying jobs with unpredictable work schedules, meager benefits, and little opportunity for advancement. This situation is a source of stress for many mothers. The question is whether this stress contributes to allostatic load. For some women it appears that achievement of balance in multiple roles requires resources, such as social support, but allows for a sense of life satisfaction (Rao, Apte, & Subbakrishna, 2003).

There are two opposing frameworks for understanding the effects of multiple roles on women's mental and physical health. The role-strain theory proposes that there is a limit on how a woman can manage multiple roles, and this limit leads to role strain, with negative effects on health. The other approach is the theory of role complementation, in which each additional role brings some benefits (e.g., social resources, self-esteem) that could translate into better health (Baruch & Barnett, 1986). It is likely that circumstances in a woman's life contribute greatly to the impact of multiple roles on allostatic load. Financial, marital, and job status; educational level; and living conditions clearly are important in translating whether multiple roles lead to allostatic load. Another important consideration is that women employed in high-ranking positions are more likely than men to bring their work-related stress home at the end of the day (Lundberg & Frankenhaeuser, 1999). These women have higher work demands than do men, and they have higher norepinephrine levels at work and at home. The health effects of this "spilling over" of stress into other dimensions of a woman's life have not been examined much, but certainly must contribute to allostatic load. Burnout may ultimately be a manifestation of allostatic load in working women's lives.

Although work-related stress is important, marital stress seems to have a much greater influence on women's health. Marital stress in women was associated with higher levels of norepinephrine, epinephrine, and cortisol (Orth-Gomer et al., 2000). Marital stress was also associated with recurrent adverse coronary events in women, whereas work stress seemed to produce greater deleterious coronary events in men (Singer et al., 2004).

Perhaps the effects of being in a "sandwich" generation are significant in middle-age and older women, who potentially have accumulated allostatic load and may face the demands of caregiving for older parents, along with remaining employed and productive. Caregiving for loved ones who are ill or who have dementia has many allostatic costs and has been found to be a major stressor in psychoneuroimmunological studies. For example, the combination of caregiving for a spouse with dementia and life distress was associated with dysfunctional procoagulant responses to acute mental stress in caregivers, a state that potentially could contribute to CVD (von Kanel, Dimsdale, Patterson, & Grant, 2003).

External and health care system environmental factors contribute greatly to allostatic load in women. External environmental conditions include factors such as economic climate, relative wealth, levels of stress and violence, and prevailing norms of a community (Andersen & Davidson, 2001). Health care system environmental factors may influence access, availability, or acceptance of health care services. Findings from reports by organizations such as the Institute of Medicine (Smedley, Stith, & Nelson, 2002) and the Commonwealth Fund (McDonough et al., 2004) indicate that external and health care system environments collectively contribute greatly to disparate health outcomes among women. The burden of cumulative stressors may significantly influence health status and health outcomes (Gee & Payne-Sturges, 2004). Geronimus (1992) termed these stressors the *weathering effect*, a concept not unlike allostatic load. Headley (2004) asserted that chronic morbidity and disparities in African American women's health status may result from women's "extensive and collective experiences with entrenched social, economic, or political barriers" (p. 988).

Major Life Events and Developmental Stages

Women experience many demanding transitions during their life cycles. According to Evans (2003), four important facts about allostasis are relevant to developmental theory: (a) Allostatic load is cumulative over time; (b) the accumulation of multiple small changes in physiological functioning portends morbidity; (c) allostatic load is a joint function of physical and social demands throughout life, genetic predispositions, and lifestyle choices; and (d) elevated allostatic load influences socioemotional and cognitive process as well as physical morbidity. However, only a few investigators have begun to explore allostatic load over the life course. Power, Manor, and Fox (1991) found that accumulated risk factors, beginning in childhood, were related prospectively to health and well-being at age 23. Power and Matthews (1998) found these same cumulative risks influenced health at age 33. Singer and Ryff (1999) found that exposure to accumulated risk factors was associated with higher total allostatic load assessed at age 59. In addition, Felitti et al. (1998) reported that 10 major causes of death in adults were associated with the accumulation of early childhood experiences of abuse and family dysfunction. Research has been limited to retrospective reports of childhood risk factors, and prospective studies are needed.

Evans and colleagues have been engaged in critical research to more fully understand the relationship of development and allostatic load (Evans, 2003; Evans, Kim, Ting, Tesher, & Shannis, 2007). In 2003, he reported a study of cumulative risk and allostatic load among 339 rural children (mean age of 9.2 years). He examined cumulative risk factors, including physical factors, such as crowding and noise in the house and housing quality; psychosocial factors, such as domestic turmoil and violence and child separation from caregivers; and personal characteristics, such as poverty, single parenthood, and maternal high school dropout status. He found that elevated cumulative risk was associated with heightened cardiovascular and neuroendocrine parameters (i.e., cortisol, epinephrine, and norepinephrine), increased deposition of body fat, and a higher summary index of total allostatic load. Also, he found a positive correlation between the number of risk factors and maternal reports of child psychological distress. Of additional concern was his finding that as cumulative risk increased, children were less able to delay gratification and exhibited learned helplessness.

A second study by Evans et al. (2007) reported on cumulative risk, maternal responsiveness, and allostatic load among 207 of the original 339 children in the 2003 study. In 2007, these children had a mean age of 13.37 years. The researchers found that as cumulative risk exposure increased, allostatic load increased, but only for young adolescents with mothers who were low in responsiveness to the child. Youth with more cumulative risk exhibited lower levels of cardiovascular reactivity and slower, less efficient recovery in blood pressure in response to an acute stressor (a mental arithmetic test). These cardiovascular findings were independent of maternal responsiveness. In both studies, Evans et al. examined the potential interactive effects of gender and cumulative risk. Gender was not found to have an interactive relationship with risk or impact on cardiovascular reactivity and recovery. It is important to note that the risk factors identified to this point are gender neutral. For a fuller understanding of allostatic load in women over their lifetimes, additional risk factors specific to women should be included in longitudinal studies.

Trauma and Abuse

One quarter of girls are sexually abused, and more than one third of women report physical or sexual abuse in their lifetimes. In any given year, 3% of women report being subjected to severe physical abuse from their husbands (Rich-Edwards et al., 2001). There has been little investigation of changes in physiological regulatory structures in intimate partner violence (IPV) survivors (Griffin, Resick, & Yehuda, 2005), while exposure to violence is widely accepted as a stressor with both short- and long-term consequences for psychological health (Murali & Chen, 2005). The role of IPV as a precursor to posttraumatic stress disorder (PTSD), an allostatic load outcome, has been clearly documented (Pico-Alfonso, 2005). Women exposed to IPV are subjected to episodes of physical, psychological, or sexual violence that are both repetitive and acute. In addition, their stressors include constant risk associated with life with a violent partner and the sense of constant threat and loss of control (Pico-Alfonso, Garcia-Linares, Celda-Navarro, Herbert, & Martinez, 2004). In a study focused on adolescents (Murali & Chen, 2005), elevated basal levels of cortisol, higher heart rate, and diastolic blood pressure were found in those with greater lifetime exposure to violence. The most pervasive biological effects were exhibited by victims who had the greatest cumulative frequency of experiencing violence.

With regard to allostasis, dysregulation of the HPA axis might account for the increased levels of proinflammatory cytokines that have been reported in victims of trauma and people with PTSD. Interleukin-1β (IL-1β) was reported to be increased in combat veterans with PTSD (Spivak et al., 1997). IL-6 was studied in PTSD survivors of a fire and automobile accident, and found to be elevated. It was even higher in PTSD patients with a history of major depression (Maes et al., 1999). IL-6 release is suppressed by cortisol, which may be lower in PTSD patients. Women who had been raped were examined by Groër, Thomas, Evans, and Helton (2006) and found to have high levels of IL-6, tumor necrosis factor-α (TNF-α), interferon-γ (IFN-γ), and C-reactive protein (CRP) 24 to 72 hours after the rape. These biological responses, if persistent, could help explain the mechanisms by which victims of trauma develop later illness.

Allostasis theory predicts that allostatic load (as measured by stress hormones, inflammatory proteins, and immune changes) leads to physical illness. Physical illnesses of all types appear to be present at higher prevalence in women who have been sexually assaulted. For instance, there is a two- to threefold increase in incidence of arthritis and breast cancer in women with a history of sexual assault (Stein & Barrett-Connor, 2000).

Individual Differences

Risks for secondary and tertiary outcomes are clearly not uniform across all animal species and, we pose, not the same for males and females. Individual differences in how the central nervous system processes stressful stimuli are important, as are an individual's gender, developmental history, behavioral repertoire, and personality. Stress exposure and maternal care interactions during the perinatal period have been shown to program the stress axes of infant mice. The effects appear to be through alteration of gene expression of genes involved in the stress response. Rodent mothers who have high licking and grooming of their pups produce offspring with down-regulated HPA axes, which continues into adult life. The suggestion, then, is that these offspring are more able to tolerate stress and less at risk of stress-related diseases (Caldji, Diorio, & Meaney, 2000). In rats, individual differences in how maternal care is delivered by the mother to the pups are transmitted from mother to daughter, suggesting that individual differences in behavior can be transmitted epigenetically from one generation to the next.

In animals, and now in humans, there is evidence that low birth weight is a sign of adverse fetal programming that is associated with SAM and HPA developmental perturbations (Phillips, Jones, & Goulden, 2006). Girls who were small at birth had greater cardiac sympathetic nervous system activation, both at rest and during stress (Jones, Beda, Jones, Beda, et al., 2005). Salivary cortisol responses were related to fetal growth restriction in boys but not in girls (Jones, Godfrey, et al., 2005). These findings were independent of obesity, education, or social class. Such epigenetic differences in later stress responsivity by fetal growth restriction and by gender are important to consider in the development of allostatic load.

Another consideration is inherent genetic components of behavioral responsiveness to stressors. Rats and mice have been classified as "hawks" or "doves" depending on reactivity to stress (Korte, Koolhaas, Wingfield, & McEwen, 2005). Hawks are proactive, doves reactive in their coping. Neural structures (e.g., hippocampus), neurotransmitters, and stress hormones differ remarkably in accordance with the behaviors of these two types of animals. Girls are genetically endowed and generally socialized to act more in accordance with the dove behavior.

Genetics

Genetic influences on stress responses and stress-related diseases are significant and play a role in allostasis and allostatic load. Regulation of particular inherited variant alleles is nevertheless a function of multiple environmental influences (McEwen, 2000a). Behavioral responses to stress are under some degree of genetic control. The neurochemical substrate from which addiction behaviors emerge is influenced by genes such as those that regulate serotonin, dopamine, and gamma-aminobutyric acid in the brain. Genes also influence the appraisal of stress as well as the production of the physiological stress mediators (McEwen & Seeman, 1999). The morning awakening rise in cortisol shows an inheritability of 40% (Wust, Federenko, Hellhammer, & Kirschbaum, 2000) but appears to be independent of gender (Kudielka & Kirschbaum, 2003).

Behavioral Responses

Immune activators may be involved in the anhedonia of depressive illness and other behavioral effects of anxiety disorders, hostile and aggressive states, PTSD, and abuse of alcohol and other substances, all of which are associated with disorder in diurnal rhythms of serum melatonin, ACTH, and cortisol. The sleep disturbances in depression and other psychiatric illnesses are evidence of this disruption. Allostatic load can cause alterations in brain structures that negatively affect behavioral as well as physiological functioning. Such changes include atrophy of the hippocampus and structural changes in the amygdala and prefrontal cortex (McEwen, 2003b, 2006a). Mild impairment in spatial learning and memory may result. A body of evidence points to an association between dysregulation of the immune system, including cytokines, particularly IL-6 and TNF, and the etiology and pathophysiology of depression. These relationships support depression as a proinflammatory illness (Kim et al., 2007).

Depressive illness and hostility have both been associated with CVD and other systemic illnesses. One major risk factor is the occurrence of childhood experiences of abuse and neglect leading to PTSD and allostatic load in adulthood. Childhood abuse and neglect increases vulnerability to social isolation, a higher incidence of lifetime psychiatric diagnoses (major depressive disorder, dysthymic disorder, generalized anxiety disorder, somatization disorder, and substance abuse), and conditions such as extreme obesity and CVD (Kim et al., 2007; McEwen, 2003a, 2006a). In fact, researchers have shown a link between obesity and depression in women but not in men (Skilton, Moulin, Terra, & Bonnet, 2007). Women, particularly those who have a history of childhood abuse, may be especially vulnerable to the development of a chronic pain syndrome. Research suggests that dysregulation in limbic, paralimbic, and prefrontal brain regions influences stress response modulation and emotional processing, that is, alterations in HPA and autonomic and adrenergic hyperactivity (Meltzer-Brody et al., 2007).

Depression is twice as common in women than men. Maes (1995) found that major depression may be accompanied by systemic immune activation or an inflammatory response with involvement of phagocytic (e.g., monocytic, neutrophilic) cells, T cell activation, B cell proliferation, an acute-phase response, and higher autoantibody (antinuclear, antiphospholipid) titers. Increased production of IL-1β and IL-6 by peripheral blood mononuclear cells in major depressions was also reported.

Those with major depressive illness have allostatic load markers such as impaired immunity, atherosclerosis, obesity, bone demineralization, and atrophy of nerve cells in the brain. These conditions may also be expressed in other chronic anxiety disorders. The brain controls the physiological and behavioral coping responses to daily stressors. The hippocampus expresses high levels of cortisol receptors and is a malleable brain structure important for certain types of learning and memory. It is also vulnerable to effects of stress and trauma (McEwen, 2004).

Women of Color and Allostasis

Chronic morbidity and excess mortality are more pronounced by middle age in Black than in White populations, regardless of socioeconomic status (Geronimus, Hicken, Keene, & Bound, 2006). The weathering hypothesis proposed by Geronimus (1992) posited that Blacks experience early health deterioration as a consequence of the cumulative impact of repeated experiences with social and economic adversity. To test this hypothesis, Geronimus et al. (2006) used data from the National Health and Nutrition Examination Survey (NHANES IV 1999–2002) to examine gender and race differences in age-related allostatic load scores. Blacks had higher allostatic load scores than did Whites, particularly at 35 to 64 years. Black women had the highest allostatic load scores.

Among women residing in the United States, African American women have the highest rates of cardiovascular mortality and morbidity (American Heart Association [AHA], 2006). A key contributor to this excessive disease burden is the high prevalence of HTN in the African American population. Among American women age 20 and older, approximately 45% of African American women have HTN, whereas about 30% of White women have elevated blood pressure (AHA, 2006). A prospective study by Matthews, Kiefe, Lewis, Liu, Sidney, and Yunis (2002) compared the influence of socioeconomic trajectories on incident HTN in a biracial cohort of approximately 3,000 young adults (ages 18–30 at study entry) enrolled in the Coronary Artery Risk Development in Young Adults Study. All participants were normotensive at the time of recruitment. Black women were 5.3 times and Black men were 5.8 times more likely to have become hypertensive by Year 10 of the study compared with White participants.

Chronic exposure to stressors as manifested by cardiovascular reactivity has also been found to influence birth outcomes in Black women. Blacks have consistently demonstrated higher levels of cardiovascular reactivity and recovery than have Whites (Barnes et al., 2000). Hatch et al. (2006) evaluated the influence of cardiovascular reactivity and the risk of preterm delivery in Black military women as compared with Whites. Black women exhibited more cardiac reactivity to computer-controlled laboratory stressors. Despite a relatively low overall risk of preterm delivery (8.2%), the hazard ratio for preterm delivery in Black versus White women was 2.3. The disparity in rates of preterm delivery between Black and White women in the United States is striking. It is possible that the unique stressors that Black women are exposed to may influence the health of their infants as well as their own health. Many women, especially Black women, are employed in occupations classified as being high in job strain. Karasek and Theorell (1990) conceptualized high job strain as employment with high psychosocial demands and low control. Oths, Dunn, and Palmer (2001) tested the influence of high job strain on birth outcomes in southern Black and White women during the first 14 weeks of pregnancy and again at or after the 28th week. At delivery, low birth weight was more than twice as prevalent for Blacks (10.1%) than for Whites (4.7%); women employed in high-strain jobs had babies with lower birth weights than did women who were nonemployed or who worked in low-strain positions. Black women also manifested a larger effect size of job strain on birth weight than did White women (Oths et al., 2001).

PATHOPHYSIOLOGIC OUTCOMES OF ALLOSTATIC LOAD

The factors we have discussed to this point affect the development of allostatic load in women. Next we describe the major pathophysiological outcomes of allostatic load in women as depicted in Figure 8.1.

Cardiovascular Disease

The best studied outcome of allostatic overload is CVD, specifically coronary heart disease (CHD) and HTN. Allostatic elements that contribute to CVD pathophysiology include inflammation, SAM activity, and HPA axis dysregulation. Gabriel, Ahnve, Wretlind, and Martinsson (2000) provided evidence of chronic inflammatory activity in atherosclerosis, corroborating the important role inflammation plays in the pathobiology of CHD. In CHD, chronic elevated proinflammatory cytokines (IL-1, IL-6, TNF-α) associated with atherosclerosis produce allostatic load. Atherosclerosis is hypothesized to be a result of chronic stress and inflammation and, secondarily, oxidative stress. The oxidation-response hypothesis suggests that low-density lipoproteins undergo oxidation in the intima of the vessel wall, inducing expression of several inflammatory mediators by macrophages and vascular endothelium (Blake & Ridker, 2002; Libby, Ridker, & Maseri, 2002; Stocker & Keaney, 2004). Libby et al. (2002) suggested that the inflammatory response in atherosclerosis is an early adhesive process promoting leukocyte adherence to the endothelium. Once these molecules are expressed on the endothelium, migration begins toward the subendothelium, where leukocytes contribute to the inflammatory process and more foam cells are produced. This cascade activates production of TNF-α, which stimulates IL-6, the main hepatic precursor of CRP (Blake & Ridker, 2002). Scientists have tried to quantify clusters of inflammatory markers and their association to CHD risk (Kip et al., 2005). The associations of risk factors with CHD in women are magnified in postmenopause. CHD incidence increases markedly after menopause, as does morbidity from the disease.

Particularly relevant to cardiovascular risk stratification of women is the observation that high levels of inflammatory biomarkers are associated with development of insulin resistance or metabolic syndrome and higher incidence of adverse health events. Highly correlated with CVD, metabolic syndrome is a cluster of correlated abnormalities that include dyslipidemias, central adiposity, glucose intolerance, insulin resistance, HTN, and atherosclerosis.

Elevated blood pressure resulting from allostatic load, along with the long-term deleterious effects of cortisol on blood lipids, glucose, and body fat, is an important influence on the development of atherosclerosis. Strong evidence supports the assumption that the allostatic load associated with repeated experiences of social and economic adversity contributes to the high prevalence of HTN in the United States. Several measures of life stress were found to be predictive of the incidence of HTN during a 20-year period of the Alameda County Study, a longitudinal investigation of behavioral, social, psychological, and economic influences on health (Levenstein, Smith, & Kaplan, 2001). Low education, African American ethnicity, low occupational prestige, worry about job stability, feeling less than very good at one's job, social alienation, and depressive symptoms each had significant age-adjusted associations with incident HTN that were more marked in women than in men.

Though HTN is viewed as a result of excessive tone or reactivity of the SAM system, the role of the parasympathetic system is also important in the maintenance of allostasis (Szanton, Gill, & Allen, 2005). When the parasympathetic system does not counterbalance the SAM system, the continued high-pressure state produces a load on the heart muscle, leading to increased IL-6 (Singh, Kartik, Otsuka, Pella, & Pella, 2002), which further perpetuates inflammation.

Cancer

Allostasis has not been considered in terms of carcinogenesis but has been implicated in the progression of the disease in both men and women. With regard to breast cancer, the relationship between stress and development and progression of cancer is modest. One large study of Finnish women found that life events stress was associated with breast cancer development (Lillberg et al., 2003). When a woman is diagnosed with cancer, she is subject to a bombardment of multiple repeated and chronic stressors associated with the diagnosis and treatment of the disease (Ronson, 2006). In light of the potentially debilitating effects of both the disease and the treatment, plus the emotional stress of cancer, allostatic load is an obvious outcome. With its effects on immune function and the endocrine system, allostatic load would further threaten a woman with cancer and even impair her possibilities for recovery or remission.

Activation of immunocompetent cells enhances the capacity of the immune system to respond to malignant cells, and immune competence is necessary for cancer prevention (Whiteside, 2006). There is considerable documented evidence of a relationship between stress and changes in the immune system (Segerstrom & Miller, 2004). Stress may impair immune competence enough to be one of the most important determinants in the control of certain malignant diseases. Women with cancer face multiple stressors related to both physical and psychological well-being. When the immune system loses its ability to provide effective immunosurveillance, metastasis of cancer cells can result. Antitumor immunity can be suppressed by stress-related increases in HPA or SAM activity (Sephton, Sapolsky, Kraemer, & Spiegel, 2000). An allostasis marker of the cumulative effects of stress is disruption of circadian rhythms, which may then affect cancer progression. Diurnal rhythms are altered in patients with large tumor burdens and liver metastasis (Sephton et al., 2000). As cancer progresses, stress, anxiety, and pain may become severe, interrupting sleep. Poor sleep is also associated with disruptions in the endocrine and immune systems (Vgontzas & Chrousos, 2002), which then can further perpetuate allostatic load.

Several studies have documented that women with breast cancer have dysregulation in several circadian systems and that stress and mood may be indirect contributors to poorer outcomes (Spiegel & Sephton, 2001). In patients with breast cancer, cortisol levels have been reported to be elevated and diurnal profiles flatter compared with control participants (Abercrombie et al., 2004; Porter et al., 2003). Metastatic breast and ovarian cancer patients had abnormal cortisol secretion (Touitou, Bogdan, Levi, Benavides, & Auzeby, 1996). Metastatic breast cancer patients who displayed less variation and a flatter slope in cortisol experienced earlier mortality over a 7-year follow-up (Sephton et al., 2000). In contrast, two studies of cortisol levels in nonmetastatic breast cancer did not support these findings regarding cortisol (Carlson, Campbell, Garland, & Grossman, 2007; Vedhara, Stra, Miles, Sanderman, & Ranchor, 2006). Metastatic progression of breast cancer may be associated with increased or dysregulated cortisol secretion, a phenomenon not present in earlier stages of the disease.

Fatigue is another influence. Flatter cortisol slopes were found in survivors who reported experiencing significant fatigue (Bower, Ganz, & Aziz, 2005). Morning serum cortisol levels were lower in fatigued breast cancer survivors than in nonfatigued survivors (Bower, Ganz, Aziz, & Fahey, 2002). These studies suggest that disturbances in the HPA axis functioning may relate to disease progression or fatigue. In contrast to patients with reproductive system cancer, salivary cortisol was not a predictor of survival in a study of 147 patients with metastatic colorectal cancer (Mormon, Bogdan, Cormont, Touitou, & Levi, 2002).

Inflammatory cytokines, which along with stress hormones are primary mediators in the allostatic model, may also be involved in cancer pathophysiology. Cancers, as well as cancer treatments, produce inflammation. The malignant tumor is itself penetrated by multiple cytokine-secreting cell types, such as macrophages, natural killer cells, neutrophils, dendritic cells, and eosinophils (Ben-Baruch, 2006). Whereas the tumor microenvironment is characterized as inflammatory, the types of cytokines, chemokines, and other molecules secreted act to suppress, rather than enhance, immunity. The inflammatory environment seems to impair the competence of immune cells that would ordinarily recognize and destroy malignant cells (Ben-Baruch, 2006).

Obesity

Elevated cortisol, as seen in Cushing's syndrome and long-term cortisone therapy, has long been associated with central adipose deposition. Central adipose deposition is measured by waist–hip ratios. A waist–hip ratio compares waist measurements at the iliac crest and hip measurements at the largest circumference of the buttocks. Ratios of less than 0.85 indicate that adipose tissue is distributed peripherally, and ratios greater than 0.87 indicate abdominal obesity (Duclos et al., 2001). Women's waist circumferences exceeding 35 inches when measured at the top of the iliac crest indicate central obesity (Brunner, Chandola, & Marmot, 2007). A person can be overweight with a normal waist–hip ratio if fat is stored in the hips and extremities and, conversely, be of normal body mass index with an elevated waist–hip ratio if adipose tissue is stored centrally with lean hips and extremities (Epel et al., 2000). Whether elevated cortisol levels cause central obesity, or whether abdominal adipose tissue can synthesize cortisol from cortisone, is still debated. Cortisol, stress, and obesity research findings are inconsistent and limited by several problems, including that of adjusting cortisol levels for the increased peripheral tissue in obesity (Bjorntorp & Rosmond, 2000).

Hypercortisolemia has been implicated in increased food intake and obesity of melancholic depression (Gold & Chrousos, 1999). Blood leptin and corticosteroid levels increase without decreasing appetite. This apparent leptin resistance may be partially responsible for the formation of central obesity in hypercortisolemia (Newcomber et al., 1998). It has been suggested that the associations between stress, central obesity, and socioeconomic status may be a factor in the social inequality of visceral obesity-related diseases, such as HTN and CVD (Rosmond, Eriksson, & Bjorntorp, 1999). Appetite control and fat deposition are influenced by adrenergic, serotonergic, dopaminergic, and leptinergic systems, which are, in turn, all influenced by stress.

Women naturally carry more weight as fat than do men and require fewer calories per pound of body weight. This extra adiposity is meant to provide fuel for pregnancy and lactation. But excess fat is deleterious to women. Women are more likely than men to become obese. The Centers for Disease Control and Prevention defines *obesity* as a body mass index over 30, and in 2002, 28.7% of men and 34.5% of women in the United States were considered obese (Ezzati, Martin, Skjold, Vander Hoorn, & Murray, 2006). One risk factor unique to women is excessive weight gain during pregnancy, which can lead to later obesity.

Excessive weight is a component of metabolic syndrome and may actually be the leading factor in its development. More than one in five Americans are thought to have metabolic syndrome. Its incidence increases with age, with more than 40% of people in their 60s and 70s having metabolic syndrome (Resnick & Howard, 2002). The excessive deposition of white adipose tissue is central to the development of this disorder. Visceral obesity leads to a chronic state of low-grade inflammation (Bastard et al., 2006). Proinflammatory cytokines produced by white adipose tissue, such as IL-6 and TNF-α, lead to insulin resistance, impaired glucose tolerance, and diabetes. IL-6 may provoke the release of CRP from the liver and contribute to atherosclerosis. Women with all four factors for metabolic syndrome (i.e., HTN, obesity, hypertriglyceridemia, and diabetes) have a much greater mortality rate than do men with the same four factors (Nambi, Hoogwerf, & Sprecher, 2002).

The association of metabolic syndrome with socioeconomic status, as would be predicted by the allostatic model, is well-known and present even in childhood (Huang, Ball, & Franks, 2007). This association was examined in NHANES III and found to be significantly stronger for women of all ethnicities compared with men (Loucks, Rehkopf, Thurston, & Kawachi, 2007).

A number of states (e.g., polycystic ovary disease, Cushing's syndrome, depression, smoking, alcoholism) have patterns of hypercortisolemia, insulin resistance, and hyperinsulinemia with lipid accumulation. Estrogen in premenopausal women causes subcutaneous adipose tissue to turn over faster than gluteal and femoral fat. Mayes and Watson (2004) hypothesized that sex steroids may activate the cyclic adenosine monophosphate cascade, thereby activating hormone-sensitive lipase, yielding lipolysis of adipose tissue. Interventions to reduce cortisol and replace sex hormones should reverse visceral fat accumulation. Estrogen replacement therapy in postmenopausal women appears to reduce central obesity (Mayes & Watson, 2004). However, the serious side effects of estrogen replacement therapy, such as increased risk of venous thrombosis, limit its usefulness.

Reproductive Effects of Allostatic Load

The reproductive effects of stress are well-known. The hypothalamic–pituitary–ovarian axis has not been considered specifically in the allostasis model, but we suggest that it is sensitive to the effects of allostatic load. Fertility and reproductive fitness are clearly influenced by stressors and the stress response in all species. Fear of an unwanted pregnancy can delay onset of the menstrual cycle in a nonpregnant woman. Extreme exercise and weight loss can obliterate the cycle. Both corticotropin-releasing hormone (CRH) and cortisol can directly inhibit the hypothalamic neurons that secrete gonadotropin-releasing hormone, suppressing estrogen and progesterone production. Cortisol can also act on the ovary to make it refractory to sex steroids (Tsigos & Chrousos, 2002).

The menstrual cycle may also influence allostasis. In general, stress reactivity is increased in the luteal phase (Kajantie & Phillips, 2005). Even basic immune responses differ across the cycle. Immunity is directed toward humoral immunity (Th2) in the late luteal phase, perhaps to protect a developing zygote from cellular immune (Th1) attack (Faas et al., 2000). Distress related to the menstrual cycle can profoundly influence a woman's ability to handle stressors in her life. Suicides, commitment of violent crimes, accidents, headaches, asthma, and many infectious and immune diseases are more prevalent during the late luteal and perimenstrual phases. Allostasis recognizes the importance of anticipation in launching stress responses and release of primary mediators, and a women suffering premenstrual syndrome is in a seemingly endless cycle of anticipation of altered functions related to her menstrual cycle.

Pregnancy is a stress-resistant state, but the effects of prenatal stress can be devastating in susceptible women. Prenatal stress is one of the most influential and independent factors causing preterm birth (Wadhwa, Porto, Garite, Chicz-DeMet, & Sandman, 1998). During pregnancy, anxiety and stress may cause increased SAM activity, with concomitant release of catecholamines, as well as HPA axis activation, with release of CRH, ACTH, and glucocorticoids into the maternal and fetal bloodstreams. These neurotransmitters and hormones cross the blood–placenta barrier and circulate in the fetal blood stream in parallel with the mother (Gitau, Cameron, Fisk, & Glover, 1998). Though the HPA system is dampened during pregnancy, the placental CRH responses are stress sensitive. Rising levels of maternal CRH are associated with length of gestation, maternal stress, and infection. In addition, the fetus responds to placental CRH (Sandman et al., 1999) and elaborates increased levels of fetal glucocorticoids. The fetal stress response may play a role in premature rupture of the maternal membranes (Yoon et al., 1998). This could be considered the effect of allostatic load in pregnancy.

Postpartum status and lactational status also appear to influence stress reactivity and thus allostasis. Postpartum women have both higher basal serum cortisol and up-regulated inflammatory response systems (Groër et al., 2005). There is, however, little relationship between life stress, stress perception, dysphoric moods, and endocrine or immune status if women are exclusively lactating compared with formula-feeding (Groër, 2005; Groër & Davis, 2005). It is as if nature protects women, and thus their infants, from stress and infection during this vulnerable time. Nevertheless, some women develop serious mental illness (depression, psychosis) in the postpartum period, and there is also increased vulnerability to certain autoimmune diseases, presumably because of hormonal and endocrine swings that occur at this time of life.

In midlife, women may have accumulated the wear and tear of allostatic adaptation, depending on the many factors we have discussed. In addition, major changes in hormonal milieu may interact with allostasis. Both estrogen and progesterone have significant effects on immunity, with estrogen dependent on dose and progesterone inhibiting immunity. Serum IL-6 rises with age in women and is inversely correlated with estrogen levels (Yasui et al., 2007).

Addictions

Addiction disorders are associated with allostatic load. Women are as likely as men to develop addictions but may have less opportunity. *Addiction* is a term used to describe distinct persistent and recurrent dysregulation in biobehaviors such as gambling, sex, eating, or stealing. Although addictions are of different types, effects on the activities of specific reward areas of the brain may be similar and may be associated with the same neurochemicals (Sadock & Sadock, 2007). An aspect of the way that this hedonic output is produced in the brain is related to metabolism of the addictive substance. There are important gender differences in metabolism of alcohol, with women having lower levels of alcohol dehydrogenase, the enzyme that metabolizes alcohol (Frezza, di Padova, Pozzato, Terpin, Baraona, & Lieber, 1990). They have proportionately less body water for alcohol diffusion, so at an equivalent level of alcohol intake, women have higher blood alcohol concentrations than do men (Frezza et al., 1990).

From an addiction stance, allostasis is the process of maintaining the reward system function stability by changes in brain reward mechanisms. Addiction is an outcome resulting from an allostatic mechanism using natural reward circuits. The allostatic state corresponds to chronic change at the reward set point, the dysregulation of reward circuits, and brain and hormonal stress responses. This allostatic mechanism identifies the neurobiological factors that produce vulnerability to addiction and relapse (Koob & Le Moal, 2001).

McEwen (2000b) pointed out that major risk factors for substance abuse include low socioeconomic status and early childhood experiences of abuse and neglect, which increase allostatic load later in life. Stress and stress reactivity, major contributors to allostatic load, also are major causal factors in alcoholism and exert much of their effects through the HPA axis. Genetic predisposition also accounts for a significant component of risk of substance abuse, although only a few candidate genes that influence addiction behaviors have currently been identified (Zimmermann, Blomeyer, Laucht, & Mann, 2007). A genetically at-risk individual may develop allostatic load from an early age if exposed to significant stress. If the result is alcohol abuse, then the stress response is produced and exaggerated even further, leading to further alcohol abuse. Thus, allostatic load may accumulate through these positive feedback mechanisms.

Women are at greater risk than men of allostatic load related to addictions, particularly alcoholism. Alcoholism in women is more likely to lead to trauma, illnesses, and interpersonal difficulties (Greenfield, Manwani, & Nargiso, 2003). Women tend to have a very different drinking pattern than do men, preferring to drink alone. Separation and divorce also increase women's likelihood of alcohol abuse, as do domestic abuse and violence.

Burnout

Burnout is a subtle process in which an individual gradually becomes mentally fatigued and ultimately completely empty and drained of energy

(Maslach, 1982). Maslach described burnout as a syndrome of emotional exhaustion, depersonalization, and lack of personal accomplishments. Burnout is a result of ineffective coping with enduring work stress. The National Institute of Occupational Safety and Health (NIOSH) defined *job stress* as "the harmful physical and emotional responses that occur when the requirements of the job do not match the capabilities, resources, or needs of the worker" (NIOSH, 1999, p. 6). Sources of occupational stress have been a topic of debate among workers and scientists. Two views predominate. One focuses on worker characteristics, such as personality and ability to cope. The other focuses on work conditions, such as demanding schedules, deadlines, job insecurity, job demands, and shift work (NIOSH, 1999; Sauter & Murphy, 1995; Spence, 1994). For women, low pay, lack of control, and poor working conditions contribute to allostatic load and ultimately lead to burnout.

Many physiological, psychological, and behavioral job-related stress responses have been identified in the literature. Physiologic stress responses to job stress include blood pressure changes (Quick, Quick, Nelson, & Hurrell, 1997), changes in heart rate and rhythm, biochemical (i.e., cortisol, glucose, and thyroxine) changes, and musculoskeletal tension (Baker & Karasek, 2000). Job strain has been found to have a negative effect on workers' neuroendocrine and immunologic status, which results in greater vulnerability to disease (Hurrell & McLaney, 1998; Meijman, van Dormolen, Herber, Rongen, & Kulper, 1995). Burnout is related to job strain and may partly mediate the association between job strain and depression (Ahola et al., 2006). Workers measured as being high in burnout had higher cortisol levels during the workday, a sign of allostasis, which thus potentially increase risk of chronic illness such as CVD (Melamed et al., 1999). Natural killer cell cytotoxicity, a measure of cellular immunity, was reported to be lower in workers who had high scores on the depersonalization subscale of the Maslach Burnout Inventory (Nakamura, Nagase, Yoshida, & Ogino, 1999). In the Finnish Health Study, 3,368 employees ages 30 to 64 were studied for a relationship between burnout and health. Burnout was found to be associated with musculoskeletal diseases among women and with cardiovascular diseases among men. Physical illnesses were associated with all three dimensions of burnout (Hokonen et al., 2006). The relationship to illness is possibly related to the proinflammatory state, as burnout was associated with elevations in both TNF-α (Grossi, Perski, Evengard, Blomkvist, & Orth-Gomer, 2003) and CRP in women (Toker, Shirom, Shapira, Berliner, & Melamed, 2005). In a compelling study of job stress and adiposity, British researchers (Brunner et al., 2007) followed 6,895 men and 3,413 women, ages 35 to 55 years, prospectively for 19 years. A significant dose–response relationship was found between work stress and risk of general and central obesity. Fewer years of education was associated with higher odds of general obesity in women. Both men and women in lower employment grades had higher odds of central obesity. Perceived low social support at work was associated with central obesity in both sexes in a dose-dependent manner. The incidence of obesity increased over 19 years with increasing job stress. Employees experiencing chronic work stress had almost 50% higher odds of obesity than did those without perceived work stress. The researchers suggested that chronic stress stimulates the HPA axis, promoting insulin resistance, increased appetite, and obesity—all of which are indicators of allostatic load.

Sleep Disorders

Sleep deprivation and disturbances can be viewed from several perspectives in the allostasis model. Chronic sleep deprivation in healthy volunteers produces many psychological and physiological effects. Appetite, proinflammatory cytokines, blood pressure, sympathetic activity, evening cortisol, insulin levels, and blood glucose are all reported to increase and parasympathetic activity to decrease following significant sleep deprivation. Adequate sleep promotes resiliency and positive mood (McEwen, 2006b), and thus is a necessary component in preventing accumulated allostatic load. In addition, many mediators of allostasis potentially can disrupt sleep (i.e., proinflammatory cytokines, sympathetic activity). Sleep deficits may produce structural changes in the brain as well as a host of metabolic, oxidative, and behavioral effects that could contribute to allostatic load (McEwen, 2006b). There are multiple interactions between sleep and diseases associated with allostatic load (e.g., diabetes, depression, CVD, and HTN; McEwen, 2006b). Incidence of these diseases increases with aging, and women experience a great number of sleep disorders throughout the perimenopausal period, suggesting a contribution to the risk of allostatic load at this life stage.

Infections

Stress hormones diminish the immune response and enable pathogens to more easily spread. Acute stressors may cause the innate immune system to respond more aggressively to challenge; more chronic stressors may downregulate the immune system's sensitivity to hormonal signals, such as cortisol, that would normally terminate inflammation (Avitsur, Stark, & Sheridan, 2001; Johnson et al., 2002). Research on stressful experiences and acute respiratory infection has yielded evidence that stressors, particularly long-term stressors associated with allostatic load, heighten disease susceptibility through stress-induced disruption of the regulation of proinflammatory cytokines (S. Cohen, 2005).

Both biologically and socially, women are more vulnerable than men to sexually transmitted infections (STIs). The medical consequences of STIs contribute to the morbidity associated with reproductive health, including pelvic inflammatory disease, infertility, ectopic pregnancy, chronic pelvic pain, compromised birth outcomes, and cervical cancer (Watts & Burnhan, 1999). Worldwide, the major route for transmission for women of STIs, including HIV is unprotected heterosexual intercourse. Coexisting genital ulcers, the presence of other STIs, oral contraception use, and menstruation at the time of intercourse increase the risk of contracting HIV for women (Shah & Bradbeer, 2000). Sex hormones influence susceptibility and disease predisposition for many genital tract infections (Brabin, 2002). However, there is immunological vulnerability to infection during the menstrual cycle. During the luteal phase of the menstrual cycle, Th1 is suppressed and Th2 immunity is enhanced. Reductions in Th1 responses are associated with less effective control of fungi, viruses, and intracellular bacteria (Kalo-Klein, Witkin, Kalo-Klein, & Witkin, 1991; Ottenhoff, De Boer, van Dissel, & Verreck, 2003). This finding supports the idea that susceptibility to infections by such pathogens may therefore be exacerbated during the luteal phase.

Studies also support the role of stress in vulnerability to other latent infectious diseases, including herpes simplex virus (HSV). Research involving HSV-1 indicates that long-term distress heightens vulnerability to biologically verified outbreaks of oral herpes, though short-term distress does not yield the same outcomes (F. Cohen et al., 1999; Friedman, Katcher, & Brightman, 1977; Katcher, Brightman, Luborsky, & Ship, 1973; Luborsky, Mintz, Brightman, & Katcher, 1976). HSV-2 research implies that a greater baseline distress increased the likelihood of verified recurrence of HSV-2 symptoms (Goldmeier et al., 1986). Other studies indicate that stressors might trigger genital herpes outbreaks by increasing susceptibility to other infections that compete for the immune system resources needed to keep herpes deactivated (Hoon et al., 1991).

The human papilloma virus is prevalent in women worldwide and is associated with more than 90% of cervical cancer (Lorincz et al., 1992; Schiffman, 1994). Studies have found that immunocompromise impacts development of cervical neoplasms (Penn, 1986; Sillman et al., 1984). These data support the model of allostatic load and its potential effect on immunity and disease.

As a compounding risk, women who are victims of IPV are at increased risk of STI. The allostatic load of stressors of IPV may impact not only risk of contraction of infection but also the course of the disease process (Bauer et al., 2002; Manfrin-Ledet & Porche, 2003).

Autoimmunity

Stress appears to be a factor influencing the expression of autoimmune diseases, which are far more common in women than in men. Systemic inflammatory or autoimmune diseases are associated with loss of function, impairment in the quality of life, and a significantly increased rate of atherosclerosis and CVD, the number one cause of mortality in females. The allostatic model proposes that an inadequate allostatic response to an acute stress will result in lack of containment of damaging mediators, an effect that may contribute to inflammatory autoimmune disease. Another potential allostatic effect would be in chronic stress, during which the Th1–Th2 balance could become shifted toward the Th2 phenotype, thus promoting humoral immunity (autoantibodies) and suppressing cellular immunity. This stress-related shift could then result in first appearance or exacerbation of B-cell-mediated autoimmune diseases, such as Graves' disease (Tsatsoulis, 2006).

Osteoporosis

Osteoporosis occurs at a much higher frequency (4:1) in women compared with men because of women's smaller skeletal frame and decreased bone mass, and the loss of the protective effects of estrogen at menopause. Even more frequent than osteoporosis is low bone mass (osteopenia), which also predominates in women. Loss of bone mineral increases the risk of fractures, causes bone pain, and causes collapse of vertebral bodies leading to a loss in height and stooped posture, tooth loss and periodontal disease, and fatigue. Allostatic load contributes to the development of osteoporosis, which is a little recognized influence. There is a strong association of depression, with its associated hypercortisolism, with osteoporosis. Potentially contributing to bone loss in women with depression are hypogonadism, growth hormone deficiency, and increased concentration of circulating IL-6 (Cizza, Ravn, Chrousos, & Gold, 2001). In a recent study of premenopausal women with depression, the bone mineral density of the women with depression was significantly lower at the lumbar spine and at all sites of the proximal femur (p = .02, .01). Plasma cortisol was significantly higher in the women with depression than in control participants (p = .001; Altindag et al., 2007). Thus, for women particularly, allostatic load contributes significantly to the debilitating problem of osteoporosis in older age.

CONCLUSIONS

Allostasis is a new lens through which to understand women's health and disease. By providing explanatory power to the known health effects of stress, allostasis provides new tools for the prevention of illness or amelioration of symptoms in women. We have provided a broad summary of those links, pointing out how a woman's physiology, development, and psychology might interface with the stressor–stress–illness relationship. Further analyses and much more research are clearly needed to explain these relationships, but if women's health researchers begin to frame their research within the allostasis conceptual model, new discoveries are certain.

KEY POINTS

- Allostasis is a new lens through which to understand women's health and disease. By providing explanatory power to the known health effects of stress, allostasis provides new tools for the prevention of illness or amelioration of symptoms in women.
- Oxytocin, a hormone well-known for its role in milk ejection and uterine contractions, has many additional critical roles in behavior, stress reactivity, cardiovascular and nervous system functioning, endocrine responses, and immune function.
- It is important to consider gender in calculation of allostatic load as allostatic load scores for men and women are not easily comparable.
- Males and females in most animal species differ in neuroanatomy, stress axes, neuroendocrinology, and immunology, differences that ultimately would affect allostatic load.
- Gender differences may translate into unique gender-specific predilections for diseases, such as depression and autoimmunity for females, and CVD and suicide for males.

REFERENCES

Abercrombie, H., Giese-Davis, J., Sephton, S., Epel, E., Turner-Cobb, J., & Spiegel, D. (2004). Flattened cortisol rhythms in metastatic breast cancer patients. *Psychoneuroendocrinology, 29*, 1082–1092.

Agren, G., Lundeberg, T., Uvnas-Moberg, K., & Sato, A. (1995). The oxytocin antagonist deamino-2-D-Tyr-(Oet)-4-Thr-8-Orn-oxytocin reverses the increase in the withdrawal response latency to thermal, but not mechanical nociceptive stimuli following oxytocin administration or massage-like stroking in rats. *Neuroscience Letters, 187*, 49–52.

Ahola, K., Honkonen, T., Kivimaki, M., Virtanen, M., Isometsa, E., Aromaa, A., et al. (2006). Contribution of burnout to the association between job strain and depression: The Health 2000 Study. *Environmental Medicine, 48*, 1023–1030.

Altindag, O., Altindag, A., Asoglu, M., Gunes, M., Soran, N., & Deveci, Z. (2007). Relation of cortisol levels and bone mineral density among premenopausal women with major depression. *International Journal of Clinical Practice, 61*, 416–420.

American Heart Association. (2006). *High blood pressure statistics*. Retrieved April 1, 2007, from http://www.americanheart.org/presenter.jhtml?identifier=2016

Andersen, R., & Davidson, P. (2001). Improving access to health care in America: Individual and contextual indicators. In R. M. Andersen, T. H. Rice, & G. F. Kominski (Eds.), *Changing the U.S. health care system: Key issues in health services policy and management* (2nd ed., pp. 3–30). San Francisco: Wiley.

Armario, A., Gavalda, A., & Marti, J. (1995). Comparison of the behavioural and endocrine response to forced swimming stress in five inbred strains of rats. *Psychoneuroendocrinology, 20,* 879–890.

Avitsur, R., Stark, J., & Sheridan, J. (2001). Social stress induces glucocorticoid resistance in subordinate animals. *Hormones and Behavior, 39,* 247–257.

Baker, D., & Karasek, R. (2000). Occupational stress. In B. S. Levy & D. H. Wegman (Eds.), Occupational health: Recognizing and preventing work-related disease (pp. 419–436). Boston: Little, Brown.

Barnes, V., Treiber, F., Musante, L., Turner, J., Davis, H., & Strong, W. (2000). Ethnicity and socioeconomic status: Impact on cardiovascular activity at rest and during stress in youth with a family history of hypertension. *Ethnicity and Disease, 10,* 4–16.

Baruch, G., & Barnett R. (1986). Role quality, multiple role involvement, and psychological well-being in midlife women. *Journal of Personality and Social Psychology, 62,* 634–644.

Bastard, J., Maachi, M., Lagathu, C., Kim, M., Caron, M., Vidal, H., et al. (2006). Recent advances in the relationship between obesity, inflammation, and insulin resistance. *European Cytokine Network, 17,* 4–12.

Bauer, H., Gibson, P., Hernandez, M., Kent, C., Klausner, J., Bolan, G., et al. (2002). Intimate partner violence and high-risk sexual behaviors among female patients with sexually transmitted diseases. *Sexually Transmitted Diseases, 29,* 411–416.

Ben-Baruch, A. (2006). Inflammation-associated immune suppression in cancer: The roles played by cytokines, chemokines and additional mediators. *Seminars in Cancer Biology, 16,* 38–52.

Bjorntorp, P., & Rosmond, R. (2000). Obesity and cortisol. *Nutrition, 16,* 924–936.

Blake, G., & Ridker, P. (2002). Inflammatory bio-markers and cardiovascular risk prediction. *Journal of Internal Medicine, 252,* 283–294.

Bower, J., Ganz, P., & Aziz, N. (2005). Altered cortisol response to psychologic stress in breast cancer survivors with persistent fatigue. *Psychosomatic Medicine, 67,* 277–280.

Bower, J., Ganz, P., Aziz, N., & Fahey, J. (2002). Fatigue and proinflammatory cytokine activity in breast cancer survivors. *Psychosomatic Medicine, 64,* 604–611.

Brabin, L. (2002). Interactions of the female hormonal environment, susceptibility to viral infections, and disease progression. *AIDS Patient Care and STDs, 16,* 211–221.

Brunner, E., Chandola, T., & Marmot, M. (2007). Prospective effect of job strain on general and central obesity in the Whitehall II Study. *American Journal of Epidemiology, 7,* 828–837.

Caldji, C., Diorio, J., & Meaney, M. (2000). Variations in maternal care in infancy regulate the development of stress reactivity. *Biological Psychiatry, 48,* 1164–1174.

Carlson, L., Campbell, T., Garland, S., & Grossman, P. (2007). Associations among salivary cortisol, melatonin, catecholamines, sleep quality and stress in women with breast cancer and healthy controls. *Journal of Behavioral Medicine, 30,* 45–58.

Carter, C., & Altemus, M. (1997). Integrative functions of lactational hormones in social behavior and stress management. *Annals of the New York Academy of Sciences, 807,* 164–174.

Cizza, G., Ravn, P., Chrousos, G. P., & Gold, P. W. (2001). Depression: A major, unrecognized risk factor for osteoporosis? *Trends in Endocrinology & Metabolism, 12,* 198–203.

Cohen, F., Kemeny, M. E., Kearney, K. A., Zegans, L. S., Neuhaus, J. M., Conant, M. A., et al. (1999). Persistent stress as a predictor of genital herpes recurrence. *Archives of Internal Medicine, 159,* 2430–2436.

Cohen, S. (2005). Keynote presentation at the Eighth International Congress of Behavioral Medicine. *International Journal of Behavioral Medicine, 12,* 123.

Crimmons, E., Johnston, M., Haywaerd, M., & Seeman, T. (2003). Age differences in allostatic load: An index of physiological dysregulation. *Experimental Gerontology, 38,* 731–734.

Duclos, M., Gatta, B., Corcuff, J., Rashedi, M., Pehourcq, S., & Roger, P. (2001). Fat distribution in obese women is associated with subtle alterations of the hypothalamic–pituitary–adrenal axis activity and sensitivity to glucocorticoids. *Clinical Endocrinology, 55,* 447–454.

Epel, E., McEwen, B., Seeman, T., Matthews, K., Castellazzo, G., Brownell, K., et al. (2000). Stress and body shape: Stress-induced cortisol secretion is consistently greater among women with central fat. *Psychosomatic Medicine, 62,* 623–632.

Evans, G. (2003). A multimethodological analysis of cumulative risk and allostatic load among rural children. *Developmental Psychology, 39,* 924–933.

Evans, G., Kim, P., Ting, A., Tesher, H., & Shannis, D. (2007). Cumulative risk, maternal responsiveness, and allostatic load among young adolescents. *Developmental Psychology, 43,* 341–351.

Ezzati, M., Martin, H., Skjold, S., Vander Hoorn, S., & Murray, C. (2006). Trends in national and state-level obesity in the USA after correction for self-report bias: Analysis of health surveys. *Journal of the Royal Society of Medicine, 99,* 250–257.

Faas, M., Bouman, A., Moesa, H., Heineman, M., de Leij, L., & Schuiling, G. (2000). The immune response during the luteal phase of the ovarian cycle: A Th2-type response? *Fertility and Sterility, 74,* 1008–1013.

Felitti, V. J., Anda, R., Nordenberg, D., Williamson, D., Spitz, A., Edwards, V., et al. (1998). Relationship of childhood abuse and household dysfunction to many leading causes of death in adults. *American Journal of Preventive Medicine, 14,* 245–258.

Frezza, M., di Padova, C., Pozzato, G., Terpin, M., Baraona, E., & Lieber, C. (1990). High blood alcohol levels in women: The role of decreased gastric alcohol dehydrogenase activity and first-pass metabolism. *The New England Journal of Medicine, 322,* 95–99.

Friedman, E., Katcher, A., & Brightman, V. (1977). Incidence of recurrent herpes labialis and upper respiratory infection: A prospective study of the influence of biologic, social and psychologic predictors. *Oral Surgery, Oral Medicine, Oral Pathology, 43,* 873–878.

Gabriel, A. S., Ahnve, S., Wretlind, B., & Martinsson, A. (2000). IL-6 and IL-1 receptor antagonist in stable angina pectoris and relation of IL-6 to clinical findings in acute myocardial infarction. *Journal of Internal Medicine, 248,* 61–66.

Gee, G., & Payne-Sturges, D. (2004). Environmental health disparities: A framework integrating psychosocial and environmental concepts. *Environmental Health Perspectives, 112,* 1645–1653.

Geronimus, A. (1992). The weathering hypothesis and the health of African-American women and infants: Evidence and speculations. *Ethnicity and Disease, 2,* 207–221.

Geronimus, A., Hicken, M., Keene, D., & Bound, J. (2006). "Weathering" and age patterns of allostatic load scores among Blacks and Whites in the United States. *American Journal of Public Health, 96,* 826–833.

Gitau, R., Cameron, A., Fisk, N., & Glover, V. (1998, August 29). Fetal exposure to maternal cortisol. *The Lancet, 352,* 707–708.

Gold, P., & Chrousos, G. (1999). The endocrinology of melancholic and atypical depression: Relation to neurocircuitry and somatic consequences. *Proceedings of the Association of American Physicians, 111,* 22–34.

Goldman, N., Glei, D. A., Seplaki, C., Liu, I. W., & Weinstein, M. (2005). Perceived stress and physiological dysregulation in older adults. *Stress, 8,* 95–105.

Goldmeier, D., Johnson, A., Jeffries, D., Walker, G. D., Underhill, G., Robinson, G., et al. (1986). Psychological aspects of recurrences of genital herpes. *Journal of Psychosomatic Research, 30,* 601–608.

Greenfield, S., Manwani, S., & Nargiso, J. (2003). Epidemiology of substance use disorders in women. *Obstetrics and Gynecology Clinics of North America, 30,* 413–446.

Griffin, M., Resick, P., & Yehuda, R. (2005). Enhanced cortisol suppression following dexamethasone administration in domestic violence survivors. *The American Journal of Psychiatry, 162,* 1192–1199.

Groër, M. (2005). Differences between exclusive breastfeeders, formula-feeders, and controls: A study of stress, mood, and endocrine variables. *Biological Research in Nursing, 7,* 106–117.

Groër, M., & Davis, M. (2005). Neuroendocrine and immune relationships in postpartum fatigue: Stress, depression, and infection. *MCN, The American Journal of Maternal/Child Nursing, 30,* 133–138.

Groër, M., Davis, M., Smith, K., Casey, K., Kramer, V., & Bukovsky, E. (2005). Immunity, inflammation and infection in postpartum breast and formula feeders. *American Journal of Reproductive Immunology, 54,* 222–231.

Groër, M., Thomas, S., Evans, G., & Helton, S. (2006). Inflammatory effects and immune system correlates of rape. *Violence and Victims, 21,* 801–814.

Grossi, G., Perski, A., Evengard, B., Blomkvist, V., & Orth-Gomer, K. (2003). Physiological correlates of burnout among women. *Journal of Psychosomatic Research, 55,* 309–316.

Gutkowska, J., Jankowski, M., Mukaddam-Daher, S., & McCann, S. (2000). Oxytocin is a cardiovascular hormone. *Journal of Medical and Biological Research*, *33*, 625–633.

Hatch, M., Berkowitz, G., Janevic, T., Sloan, R., Lapinski, R., James, T., et al. (2006). Race, cardiovascular reactivity, and preterm delivery among active-duty military women. *Epidemiology*, *17*, 178–182.

Headley, A. (2004). Generations of loss: Contemporary perspectives on Black infant mortality. *JAMA*, *96*, 987–994.

Hokonen, T., Ahola, K., Pertovaara, M., Isometsa, E., Kalimo, R., Aromaa, A., et al. (2006). The association between burnout and physical illness in the general population: Results from the Finnish Health 2000 Study. *Journal of Psychosomatic Research*, *61*, 59–66.

Hoon, E., Hoon, P., Rand, K., Johnson, J., Hall, N., & Edwards, N. (1991). A psychobehavioral model of genital herpes recurrence. *Journal of Psychosomatic Research*, *35*, 25–36.

Huang, T., Ball, G., & Franks, P. (2007). Metabolic syndrome in youth: Current issues and challenges. *Applied Physiology, Nutrition, and Metabolism*, *32*, 13–22.

Hurrell, J., & McLaney, M. (1998). Psychological job stress. In W. Rom (Ed.), *Environmental and occupational medicine* (pp. 905–914). Philadelphia: Lippincott-Raven.

Johnson, J., O'Connor, K., Deak, T., Stark, M., Watkins, L., & Maier, S. (2002). Prior stressor exposure sensitizes LPS-induced cytokine production. *Brain, Behavior, and Immunity*, *16*, 461–476.

Jones, A., Beda, A., Osmond, C., Godfrey, K., Simpson, D., & Phillips, D. (2005). Gender specificity of prenatal influences on cardiovascular control during stress in pre-pubertal children: Multiple pathways to the same disease endpoint? *Pediatric Research*, *58*, 1073.

Jones, A., Godfrey, K., Wood, P., Osmond, C., Goulden, P., & Phillips, D. (2005). Fetal growth and the adrenocortical response to psychological stress. *The Journal of Clinical Endocrinology & Metabolism*, *91*, 1868–1871.

Kajantie, E., & Phillips, D. (2005). The effects of sex and hormonal status on the physiological response to acute psychosocial stress. *Psychoneuroendocrinology*, *31*, 151–178.

Kalo-Klein, A., Witkin, S. S., Kalo-Klein, A., & Witkin, S. (1991). Regulation of the immune response to Candida albicans by monocytes and progesterone. *American Journal of Obstetrics & Gynecology*, *164*, 1351–1354.

Karandrea, D., Kittas, C., & Kitraki, E. (2000). Contribution of sex and cellular context in the regulation of brain corticosteroid receptors following restraint stress. *Neuroendocrinology*, *71*, 343–353.

Karasek, R., & Theorell, T. (1990). *Healthy work, stress, productivity and the reconstruction of working life*. New York: Basic Books.

Katcher, A., Brightman, V., Luborsky, L., & Ship, I. (1973). Prediction of the incidence of recurrent herpes labialis and systemic illness from psychological measurements. *Journal of Dental Research*, *52*, 49–58.

Kim, Y., Na, K., Shin, K., Jung, H., Choi, S., & Kim, J. (2007). Cytokine imbalance in the pathophysiology of major depressive disorder. *Progress in Neuropsychopharmacology & Biological Psychiatry, 31,* 1044–1053.

Kip, K., Marroquin, O., Shaw, L., Arant, C., Wessel, T., Olson, M., et al. (2005). Global inflammation predicts cardiovascular risk in women: A report from the Women's Ischemia Syndrome Evaluation (WISE) study. *American Heart Journal, 150,* 900–906.

Koob, G., & Le Moal, M. (2001). Drug addiction, dysregulation of reward, and allostasis. *Neuropsychopharmacology, 24,* 97–129.

Korte, S., Koolhaas, J., Wingfield, J., & McEwen, B. S. (2005). The Darwinian concept of stress: Benefits of allostasis and costs of allostatic load and the trade-offs in health and disease. *Neuroscience and Biobehavioral Reviews, 29,* 3–38.

Kudielka, B., & Kirschbaum, C. (2003). Awakening cortisol responses are influenced by health status and awakening time but not by menstrual cycle phase. *Psychoneuroendocrinology, 28,* 35–47.

Kudielka, B., & Kirschbaum, C. (2005). Sex differences in HPA axis responses to stress: A review. *Biological Psychology, 69,* 113–132.

Landys, M., Ramenofsky, M., & Wingfield, J. C. (2006). Actions of glucocorticoids at a seasonal baseline as compared to stress-related levels in the regulation of periodic life processes. *General and Comparative Endocrinology, 148,* 132–149.

Levenstein, S., Smith, M., & Kaplan, G. (2001). Psychosocial predictors of hypertension in men and women. *Archives of Internal Medicine, 161,* 1341–1346.

Libby, P., Ridker, P., & Maseri, A. (2002). Inflammation and atherosclerosis. *Circulation, 105,* 1135–1143.

Lillberg, K., Verkasalo, P., Kaprio, J., Teppo, L., Helenius, H., & Koskenvuo, M. (2003). Stressful life events and risk of breast cancer in 10,808 women: A cohort study. *American Journal of Epidemiology, 157,* 415–423.

Lorincz, A., Reid, R., Jenson, A. B., Greenberg, M., Lancaster, W., Kurman, R., et al. (1992). Human papillomavirus infection of the cervix: Relative risk associations of 15 common anogenital types. *Obstetrics & Gynecology, 79,* 328–337.

Loucks, E., Rehkopf, D., Thurston, R., & Kawachi, I. (2007). Socioeconomic disparities in metabolic syndrome differ by gender: Evidence from NHANES III. *Annals of Epidemiology, 17,* 19–26.

Luborsky, L., Mintz, J., Brightman, V., & Katcher, A. (1976). Herpes simplex virus and moods: A longitudinal study. *Journal of Psychosomatic Research, 20,* 543–548.

Lundberg, U., & Frankenhaeuser, M. (1999). Stress and workload of men and women in high-ranking positions. *Journal of Occupational and Health Psychology, 4,* 142–151.

Maes, M. (1995). Evidence for an immune response in major depression: A review and hypothesis. *Progress in Neuro-Psychopharmacology & Biological Psychiatry, 19,* 11–38.

Maes, M., Lin, A., Delmeire, L., Van Gastel, A., Kenis, G., De Jongh, R., et al. (1999). Elevated serum interleukin-6 (IL-6) and IL-6 receptor concentrations following accidental man-made traumatic events. *Biological Psychiatry, 45,* 833–839.

Manfrin-Ledet, L., & Porche, D. (2003). The state of science: Violence and HIV infection in women. *Journal of the Association of Nurses in AIDS Care, 14,* 56–68.

Maslach, C. (1982). *Burnout: The cost of caring.* Englewood Cliffs, NJ: Prentice Hall.

Matthews, K., Kiefe, C., Lewis, C., Liu, K., Sidney, S., & Yunis, C. (2002). Socioeconomic trajectories and incident hypertension in a biracial cohort of young adults. *Hypertension, 39,* 772–790.

Mayes, J., & Watson, G. (2004). Direct effects of sex steroid hormones on adipose tissues and obesity. *Obesity Reviews, 5,* 197–216.

McCarthy, M. (1990). Oxytocin inhibits infanticide in female house mice (Mus domesticus). *Hormones and Behavior, 24,* 365–375.

McDonough, J., Gibbs, B., Scott-Harris, J., Kronebusch, K., Navarro, A., & Taylor, K. (2004). *A state policy agenda to eliminate racial and ethnic health disparities.* Retrieved March 6, 2009, from http://www.commonwealthfund.org/Content/Publications/Fund-Reports/2004/Jun/A-State-Policy-Agenda-to-Eliminate-Racial-and-Ethnic-Health-Disparities.aspx

McEwen, B. (2000a). Allostasis and allostatic load: Implications for neuropsychopharmacology. *Neuropsychopharmacology, 22,* 108–124.

McEwen, B. (2000b). Effects of adverse experiences for brain structure and function. *Biological Psychiatry, 48,* 721–731.

McEwen, B. (2003a). Early life influences on life-long patterns of behavior and health. *Mental Retardation and Developmental Disabilities Research Reviews, 9,* 149–154.

McEwen, B. (2003b). Interacting mediators of allostasis and allostatic load: Towards an understanding of resilience in aging. *Metabolism, 52,* 10–16.

McEwen, B. (2004). General introduction to vasopressin and oxytocin: Structure/metabolism, evolutionary aspects, neural pathway/receptor distribution, and functional aspects relevant to memory processing. *Advances in Pharmacology, 50,* 1–50.

McEwen, B. (2006a). Protective and damaging effects of stress mediators: Central role of the brain. *Dialogues in Clinical Neuroscience, 8,* 367–381.

McEwen, B. (2006b). Sleep deprivation as a neurobiologic and physiologic stressor: Allostasis and allostatic load. *Metabolism, 55*(Suppl. 2), S20–S23.

McEwen, B., & Seeman, T. (1999). Protective and damaging effects of mediators of stress: Elaborating and testing the concepts of allostasis and allostatic load. *Annals of the New York Academy of Sciences, 896,* 30–47.

McEwen, B., & Wingfield, J. (2003). The concept of allostasis in biology and biomedicine. *Hormones and Behavior, 43,* 2–15.

Meijman, T., van Dormolen, M., Herber, R., Rongen, H., & Kulper, S. (1995). Job stress, neuroendocrine activation and immune status. In S. Sauter & L. Murphy (Eds.), *Organizational risk factors for job stress* (pp. 113–126). Washington, DC: American Psychological Association.

Melamed, S., Ugarten, U., Shirom, A., Kahana, L., Lerman, Y., & Froom, P. (1999). Chronic burnout, somatic arousal and elevated salivary cortisol levels. *Journal of Psychosomatic Research, 46,* 591–598.

Meltzer-Brody, S., Leserman, J., Zolnoun, D., Steege, J., Green, E., & Teich, A. (2007). Trauma and posttraumatic stress disorder in women with chronic pelvic pain. *Obstetrics & Gynecology, 109,* 902–908.

Mormon, M., Bogdan, A., Cormont, S., Touitou, Y., & Levi, F. (2002). Cortisol diurnal variation in blood and saliva of patients with metastatic colorectal cancer: Relevance for clinical outcome. *Anticancer Research, 22,* 1243–1249.

Murali, R., & Chen, E. (2005). Exposure to violence and cardiovascular and neuroendocrine measures in adolescents. *Annals of Behavioral Medicine, 30,* 155–163.

Nakamura, H., Nagase, H., Yoshida, M., & Ogino, K. (1999). Natural killer (NK) cell activity and the NK cell subsets in workers with a tendency to burnout. *Journal of Psychosomatic Research, 46,* 569–578.

Nambi, V., Hoogwerf, B., & Sprecher, D. (2002). A truly deadly quartet: Obesity, hypertension, hypertriglyceridemia, and hyperinsulinemia. *Cleveland Clinic Journal of Medicine, 69,* 985–989.

National Institute of Occupational Safety and Health. (1999). *Stress at work* (DHHS Publication No. 99-101). Cincinnati, OH: Author.

Newcomber, J., Selke, G., Melson, A., Gross, J., Bogler, G., & Dagogo-Jack, S. (1998). Dose-dependent cortisol-induced increases in plasma leptin concentration in healthy humans. *Archives of General Psychiatry, 55,* 995–1000.

Nissen, E., Lilja, G., Widstrom, A., & Uvnas-Moberg, K. (1995). Elevation of oxytocin levels early postpartum in women. *Acta Obstetrica Gynecologica Scandinavica, 74,* 530–533.

Orth-Gomer, K., Wamala, S., Horsten, M., Schenck-Gustafsson, K., Schneiderman, N., & Mittleman, M. (2000). Marital stress worsens prognosis in women with coronary heart disease: The Stockholm Female Coronary Risk Study. *JAMA, 284,* 3008–3014.

Oths, K., Dunn, L., & Palmer, N. (2001). A prospective study of psychosocial job strain and birth outcomes. *Epidemiology, 12,* 744–748.

Ottenhoff, T., De Boer, T., van Dissel, J., & Verreck, F. (2003). Human deficiencies in Type-1 cytokine receptors reveal the essential role of Type-1 cytokines in immunity to intracellular bacteria. *Advances in Experimental Medicine and Biology, 531,* 279–294.

Penn, I. (1986). Cancer is a complication of severe immunosuppression. *Surgery, Gynecology and Obstetrics. 162,* 603–610.

Phillips, D., Jones, A., & Goulden, P. (2006). Birth weight, stress, and the metabolic syndrome in adult life. *Annals of the New York Academy of Sciences, 1083,* 28–36.

Pico-Alfonso, M. (2005). Psychological intimate partner violence: The major predictor of posttraumatic stress disorder in abused women. *Neuroscience & Biobehavioral Reviews, 29,* 181–193.

Pico-Alfonso, M., Garcia-Linares, M., Celda-Navarro, N., Herbert, J., & Martinez, M. (2004). Changes in cortisol and dehydroepiandrosterone in women victims of physical and psychological intimate partner violence. *Biological Psychiatry*, 56, 233–240.

Pietrowsky, R., Krug, R., Fehm, H., & Born, J. (1992). The effect of "stress hormones" on emotional sensitivity. *Zeitschrift fur Experimentelle und Angewandte Psychologie*, 39, 278–298.

Porter, L., Mishel, M., Neelon, V., Belyea, M., Pisano, E., & Soo, M. (2003). Cortisol levels and responses to mammography screening in breast cancer survivors: A pilot study. *Psychosomatic Medicine*, 65, 842–848.

Power, C., Manor, O., & Fox, J. (1991). *Health and class*. London: Chapman & Hall.

Power, C., & Matthews, S. (1998). Accumulation of health risks across social groups in a national longitudinal study. In S. Strickland & P. Shetty (Eds.), *Human biology and social inequality* (pp. 36–57). New York: Cambridge University Press.

Quick, J. C., Quick, J. D., Nelson, D. L., & Hurrell, J. J., Jr. (1997). *Preventive stress management in organizations*. Washington, DC: American Psychological Association.

Rao, K., Apte, M., & Subbakrishna, D. (2003). Coping and subjective wellbeing in women with multiple roles. *International Journal of Social Psychiatry*, 49, 175–184.

Redwine, L., Altemus, M., Leong, Y., & Carter, C. (2001). Lymphocyte responses to stress in postpartum women: Relationship to vagal tone. *Psychoneuroendocrinology*, 26, 241–251.

Resnick, H., & Howard, B. (2002). Diabetes and cardiovascular disease. *Annual Reviews of Medicine*, 53, 245–267.

Rich-Edwards, J., Krieger, N., Majzoub, J., Zierler, S., Lieberman, E., & Gillman, M. (2001). Maternal experiences of racism and violence as predictors of preterm birth: Rationale and study design. *Paediatric and Perinatal Epidemiology*, 15(Suppl. 2), 124–135.

Ronson, A. (2006). Stress and allostatic load: Perspectives in psycho-oncology. *Bulletin of Cancer*, 93, 289–295.

Rosmond, R., Eriksson, E., & Bjorntorp, P. (1999). Personality disorders in relation to anthropometric, endocrine and metabolic factors. *Journal of Endocrinological Investigation*, 22, 279–288.

Sadock, B., & Sadock, V. (Eds.). (2007). *Kaplan & Sadock's synopsis of psychiatry behavioral sciences/clinical psychiatry* (10th ed.). Philadelphia: Lippincott Williams & Wilkins.

Sandman, C., Wadhwa, P., Glynn, L., Chicz-DeMet, A., Porto, M., & Garite, T. (1999). Corticotrophin-releasing hormone and fetal responses in human pregnancy. *Annals of the New York Academy of Sciences*, 897, 66–75.

Sauter, S. L., & Murphy, L. R. (1995). *Organizational risk factors for job stress*. Washington, DC: American Psychological Association.

Schiffman, M. (1994). Epidemiology of cervical human papillomavirus infections. *Current Topics in Microbiology and Immunology*, 186, 55–81.

Schulkin, J. (2003). *Rethinking homeostasis: Allostatic regulation in physiology and patho-physiology*. Cambridge, MA: MIT Press.

Segerstrom, S., & Miller, G. (2004). Psychological stress and the human immune system: A meta-analytical study of 30 years of inquiry. *Psychological Bulletin, 130*, 601–630.

Sephton, S., Sapolsky, R., Kraemer, H., & Spiegel, D. (2000). Diurnal cortisol rhythm as a predictor of breast cancer survival. *Journal of the National Cancer Institute, 92*, 994–1000.

Shah, R., & Bradbeer, C. (2000). Women and HIV—Revisited ten years on. *International Journal of STD & AIDS, 11*, 277–283.

Sillman, F., Stanek, A., Sedlis, A., Rosenthal, J., Lanks, K., Buchhagen, D., et al. (1984). The relationship between human papillomavirus and lower genital intraepithelial neoplasia in immunosuppressed women. *American Journal of Obstetrics & Gynecology, 150*, 300–308.

Singer, B., & Ryff, C. (1999). Hierarchies of life histories and associated health risks. In N. E. Adler, M. Marmot, B. S. McEwen, & J. Stewart (Eds.), *Socioeconomic status and health in industrial nations* (pp. 96–115). New York: New York Academy of Sciences.

Singer, B., Ryff, C., & Seeman, T. (2004). Operationalizing allostatic load. In J. Schulkin (Ed.), *Allostasis, homeostasis, and the costs of physiological adaptation* (pp. 113–149). Cambridge, England: Cambridge University Press.

Singh, R., Kartik, C., Otsuka, K., Pella, D., & Pella, J. (2002). Brain–heart connection and the risk of heart attack. *Biomedicine and Pharmacotherapy, 56*(Suppl. 2), 257S–265S.

Skilton, M., Moulin, P., Terra, J., & Bonnet, F. (2007). Associations between anxiety, depression, and the metabolic syndrome. *Biological Psychiatry, 62*, 1251–1257.

Smedley, B., Stith, A., & Nelson, A. (Eds.). (2002). *Unequal treatment: Confronting racial and ethnic minorities in healthcare*. Washington, DC: National Academies Press.

Spence, W. (1994). *Stress: A modern epidemic*. Waco, TX: Health EDCO.

Spiegel, D., & Sephton, S. (2001). Psychoneuroimmune and endocrine pathways in cancer: Effects of stress and support. *Seminars in Clinical Neuropsychiatry, 6*, 252–265.

Spivak, B., Shohat, B., Mestre, R., Avraham, S., Gil-Ad, I., Bleich, A., et al. (1997). Elevated levels of serum interleukin-1 in combat-related posttraumatic stress disorder. *Biological Psychiatry, 42*, 343–348.

Stein, M., & Barrett-Connor, E. (2000). Sexual assault and physical health: Findings from a population-based study of older adults. *Psychosomatic Medicine, 62*, 838–843.

Sterling, P., & Eyer, J. (1988). Allostasis: A new paradigm to explain arousal pathology. In S. Fisher & J. Reason (Eds.), *Handbook of life stress, cognition, and health* (pp. 629–649). New York: Wiley.

Stewart, J. (2006). The detrimental effects of allostasis: Allostatic load as a measure of cumulative stress. *Journal of Physiological Anthropology, 25,* 133–145.

Stock, S., & Uvnas-Moberg, K. (1988). Increased plasma levels of oxytocin in response to afferent electrical stimulation of the sciatic and vagal nerves and in response to touch and pinch in anesthetized rats. *Acta Physiologica Scandinavica, 132,* 29–34.

Stocker, R., & Keaney, J. (2004). Role of oxidative modifications in atherosclerosis. *Physiological Reviews, 84,* 1381–1478.

Stroud, L., Salovey, P., & Epel, E. (2002). Sex differences in stress responses: Social rejection versus achievement stress. *Biological Psychiatry, 52,* 318–327.

Szanton, S., Gill, J., & Allen, J. (2005). Allostatic load: A mechanism of health disparities? *Biological Research for Nursing, 7,* 7–15.

Taylor, S., Klein, L., Lewis, B., Gruenewald, T., Gurung, R. A., & Updegraff, J. (2000). Biobehavioral responses to stress in females: Tend-and-befriend, not fight-or-flight. *Psychological Reviews, 107,* 411–429.

Toker, S., Shirom, A., Shapira, I., Berliner, S., & Melamed, S. (2005). The association between burnout, depression, anxiety, and inflammation biomarkers: C-reactive protein and fibrinogen in men and women. *Journal of Occupational Health Psychology, 10,* 344–362.

Touitou, Y., Bogdan, A., Levi, F., Benavides, M., & Auzeby, A. (1996). Disruption of the circadian patterns of serum cortisol in breast and ovarian cancer patients: Relationships with tumour marker antigens. *British Journal of Cancer, 74,* 1248–1252.

Tsatsoulis, A. (2006). The role of stress in the clinical expression of thyroid autoimmunity. *Annals of the New York Academy of Sciences, 1088,* 382–395.

Tsigos, C., & Chrousos, G. P. (2002). Hypothalamic–pituitary–adrenal axis, neuroendocrine factors and stress. *Journal of Psychosomatic Research, 53,* 865–871.

Uvnas-Moberg, K. (1997). Physiological and endocrine effects of social contact. *Annals of the New York Academy of Sciences, 807,* 146–163.

Vedhara, K., Stra, J., Miles, J., Sanderman, R., & Ranchor, A. V. (2006). Psychosocial factors associated with indices of cortisol production in women with breast cancer and controls. *Psychoneuroendocrinology, 31,* 299–311.

Vgontzas, A., & Chrousos, G. (2002). Sleep, the hypothalamic–pituitary–adrenal axis, and cytokines: Multiple interactions and disturbances in sleep disorders. *Endocrinology and Metabolism Clinics of North America, 31,* 15–36.

von Kanel, R., Dimsdale, J. E., Patterson, T. L., & Grant, I. (2003). Acute procoagulant stress response as a dynamic measure of allostatic load in Alzheimer caregivers. *Annals of Behavioral Medicine, 26,* 42–48.

Wadhwa, P., Porto, M., Garite, T., Chicz-DeMet, A., & Sandman, C. (1998). Maternal corticotropin-releasing hormone levels in the early third trimester predict length of gestation in human pregnancy. *American Journal of Obstetrics & Gynecology, 179,* 1079–1085.

Watts, H., & Burnhan, R. (1999). Sexually transmitted diseases, including HIV infection in pregnancy. In K. K. Holmes, P. F. Sparling, P.-A. Mardh, S. M. Lemon,

W. E. Stamm, P. Pilot, & J. N. Wasserheit (Eds.), *Sexually transmitted diseases* (3rd ed., pp. 1089–1132). McGraw Hill: New York.

Whiteside, T. (2006). Immune suppression in cancer: Effects on immune cells, mechanisms and future therapeutic intervention. *Seminars in Cancer Biology, 16,* 3–15.

Women Employed. (n.d.). *About the issues: Overview.* Retrieved March 3, 2009, from http://www.womenemployed.org/index.php?id=7

Wust, S., Federenko, I., Hellhammer, D., & Kirschbaum, C. (2000). Genetic factors, perceived chronic stress, and the free cortisol response to awakening. *Psychoneuroendocrinology, 25,* 707–720.

Yasui, T., Maegawa, M., Tomita, J., Miyatani, Y., Yamada, M., Uemura, H., et al. (2007). Changes in serum cytokine concentrations during the menopausal transition. *Maturitas, 56,* 396–403.

Yoon, B. H., Romero, R., Jun, J. K., Maymon, E., Gomez, R., Mazor, M., et al. (1998). An increase in fetal plasma cortisol but not dehydroepiandrosterone sulfate is followed by the onset of preterm labor in patients with preterm premature rupture of the membranes. *American Journal of Obstetrics & Gynecology, 179,* 1107–1114.

Zimmermann, U., Blomeyer, D., Laucht, M., & Mann, K. (2007). How gene–stress–behavior interactions can promote adolescent alcohol use: The roles of predrinking allostatic load and childhood behavior disorders. *Pharmacology Biochemistry and Behavior, 86,* 246–262.

9

TREATMENTS FOR DEPRESSION THAT LOWER INFLAMMATION: ADDITIONAL SUPPORT FOR AN INFLAMMATORY ETIOLOGY OF DEPRESSION

KATHLEEN KENDALL-TACKETT

As previous chapters have indicated, depression and other negative mental states have an important role in the development of chronic disease. The association likely exists because negative mental states increase inflammation. This chapter examines the link between depression and inflammation from another angle: that of describing the anti-inflammatory effects of treatments for depression. Recent research suggests that all effective treatments for depression appear to lower inflammation and are beginning to be used to treat illnesses other than depression. For example, preliminary studies demonstrate that conventional antidepressants may be useful in treating allergic asthma and septic shock (Roumestan et al., 2007) or in lowering C-reactive protein (CRP) after a heart attack (O'Brien, Scott, & Dinan, 2006).

This research provides another line of evidence that supports an inflammatory etiology of depression. It also suggests an expanded approach to treatment of both depression and chronic illnesses that have depression as a common symptom. The treatment modalities described in this chapter include omega-3 fatty acids, exercise, psychotherapy, St. John's wort, and antidepressants.

OMEGA-3 FATTY ACIDS

In chapter 4, Calder described the potential benefits of omega-3s in treating inflammatory illnesses, such as rheumatoid arthritis. In this chapter, I summarized research on the mental health effects of these fatty acids. A number of recent studies have demonstrated that omega-3 fatty acids are effective for preventing or treating mood disorders. Researchers have documented these effects in a variety of ways, including population studies, randomized controlled trials, and prevention studies. Most demonstrate that omega-3s can benefit mental health. Unfortunately, the diets of many living in Western industrialized countries are deficient in them.

Ratio of Omega-6s to Omega-3s

Over the past century, people living in the United States, Canada, Southern Europe, Australia, and New Zealand have consumed increasingly high levels of omega-6s, while the amount of omega-3s consumed has dropped. For example, in a nationally representative U.S. sample, only 25% of the population reported consuming any omega-3 in the previous 24 hours (Wang et al., 2004). Omega-6s are found in vegetable oils, such as corn and safflower oils, and are a staple of many processed foods. Although omega-6s are necessary for good nutrition, they increase inflammation, particularly when we consume too many of them (Kiecolt-Glaser et al., 2007; Parker et al., 2006). Omega-3 fatty acids are polyunsaturated fats and are found in plant and marine sources.

The result of this dramatic change in the ratio of omega-6s to omega-3s appears to be negatively affecting the health of people in the United States and other industrialized countries. In previous centuries, the ratio of omega-6s to omega-3s has been approximately 2-to-3:1. In contrast, the ratio the average North American consumes ranges from 15-to-17:1 (Kiecolt-Glaser et al., 2007). The parent omega-3 is α-linolenic acid, and it is found in plants and plant oils, such as walnuts, flax seed, and canola oil. With regard to depression and other mental health effects, it is the marine-based, long-chain omega-3 fatty acids that are of interest: eicosapentenoic acid (EPA) and docosahexanoic acid (DHA).

Mental Health Effects of Eicosapentenoic Acid and Docosahexanoic Acid in Population Studies

Researchers conducting population studies were the first to document the mental health effects of EPA and DHA by comparing national rates of fish consumption with rates of depression and other affective disorders across different countries (Kiecolt-Glaser et al., 2007; Maes & Smith, 1998). These studies found that populations who eat more fatty, coldwater fish have higher levels of EPA and DHA and lower rates of affective disorders. Sometimes these results have been surprising. For example, researchers found a surprisingly low incidence of seasonal depression in countries such as Iceland, Finland, and Japan—places where researchers would expect to find it because of their northern latitudes (Parker et al., 2006). Their populations' high rates of fish consumption likely protected them from seasonal depression. Kiecolt-Glaser et al. (2007) also noted that depression is 10 times more common in countries where people eat small amounts of fish.

In a study of 3,204 adults from Finland, researchers assessed both fish consumption and depression via the Beck Depression Inventory (Tanskanen et al., 2001). Multiple logistic regression analysis indicated that depressive symptoms were more likely in participants who ate smaller amounts of fish. Even after controlling for smoking, infrequent exercise, unemployment, and other possible confounds, depression was 31% more likely among individuals who did not consume high amounts of seafood.

Rates of bipolar disorders were also lower in countries where people ate a lot of fish. Noaghiul and Hibbeln (2003) merged mental health data from the 10-nation Cross-National Collaborative Group with national fish consumption data from the World Health Organization. Using logarithmic regression models, they found that greater fish consumption predicted lower rates of Bipolar I disorder, Bipolar II disorder, and bipolar spectrum disorder. The strongest findings were for Bipolar II disorder, which has prominent depressive symptoms. They concluded that their findings were consistent with deficiencies in omega-3s being related to higher risk of mental disorders, even though they could not establish a causal relationship.

Rates of postpartum depression also appear related to fish consumption. Rees et al. (2005) observed that the rates for postpartum depression in North America and Europe are 10 times those in Taiwan, Japan, Hong Kong, and some regions of China. In a population study of 14,000 women from 22 countries, Hibbeln (2002) noted that postpartum depression was up to 50 times more common in countries with low fish consumption. For example, the rate of postpartum depression in Singapore was 0.5%. In South Africa, it was 24.5%. Mothers who ate high amounts of seafood during pregnancy and who had high levels of DHA in their milk postpartum had lower rates of postpartum depression. Rates of postpartum depression were not related to levels of EPA or arachidonic acid.

Omega-3 status has also been related to suicide attempts. In one study, 33 patients who were depressed, but not on medications, were monitored for suicide attempts over a 2-year period (Sublette, Hibbeln, Galfalvy, Oquendo, & Mann, 2006). The researchers assessed plasma polyunsaturated fatty acid levels at the beginning of follow-up. Seven patients attempted suicide. Low

DHA and a high ratio of omega-6s to omega-3s both predicted attempts. Neither arachidonic acid nor EPA levels predicted suicide attempts.

Fish consumption does not always lower rates of depression, however. In a study of 865 pregnant Japanese women, investigators failed to find lower rates of depression in women who ate more fish (Miyake et al., 2006). They found no dose–response effect of fish intake, EPA, DHA, omega-6s, or ratio of omega-6s to omega-3s on postpartum depression. Some methodologic limitations may have influenced these findings, however. First, fatty acid levels were estimated from a dietary questionnaire administered during pregnancy, not assessed directly from participant serum. Second, Japanese men and women have one of the highest fish-consumption rates in the world. It is possible that the researchers encountered a ceiling effect because none of the women were deficient. Finally, depression was assessed any time between 2 and 9 months postpartum. Rates of postpartum depression vary depending on when they are collected. The wide range in assessment times could have influenced the findings.

In summary, men and women who eat more fish appear to have better mental health than do their non-fish-eating counterparts. According to one analysis, people who ate less than 50 lb of seafood a year (1–1.5 lb/person/week) had the highest rates of affective disorders (Noaghiul & Hibbeln, 2003). This finding provides some guidance about how much people need to eat to avoid being deficient. And for those who do not want to eat fish, fish oil supplements may prove an acceptable alternative, as studies examining EPA and DHA as a treatment for depression have found.

Treatment With Eicosapentenoic Acid and Docosahexanoic Acid

The treatment effects of EPA and DHA have also been observed when fish oil supplements are used. In the clinical trials of EPA and DHA, researchers gave either a placebo, EPA alone, or EPA and DHA supplements to people with affective disorders (Parker et al., 2006; Peet & Stokes, 2005). When comparing EPA and DHA, investigators have generally found that EPA is the most effective omega-3 for treating depression. When EPA was added to patients' medication regimen, those who received EPA in addition to their medications were significantly less depressed than were those who received medication and a placebo. EPA has also been used alone to treat depression (Peet & Horrobin, 2002; Peet & Stokes, 2005). The results of these clinical trials are summarized next.

In a study of 20 patients with major depression, patients were randomized to receive either ethyl-EPA (2 g/day) or a placebo in addition to their regular antidepressant medications (B. Nemets, Stahl, & Belmaker, 2002). By the 3rd week of the study, patients who received EPA were significantly less depressed.

EPA and DHA have also been used as a monotherapy for depression. In a study of 28 children ages 6 to 12 with major depressive disorder, children who received 400 mg EPA and 200 mg DHA had significantly improved depression compared with children who received a placebo (H. Nemets, Nemets, Apter, Bracha, & Belmaker, 2006). Investigators assessed the children at baseline and at 2, 4, 8, 12, and 16 weeks. After a month of treatment, the depression of 7 out of 10 children in the EPA and DHA group had dropped by 50%, with no adverse effects noted.

EPA was also useful for patients with bipolar disorder in a 12-week double-blind trial (Frangou, Lewis, & McCrone, 2006). In this study, 75 patients were randomly assigned to one of three adjunct therapies: placebo, 1 g ethyl-EPA, or 2 g ethyl-EPA. Patients receiving either 1 g or 2 g of EPA showed substantial improvement after 12 weeks compared with the placebo. A dose of 1 g was as effective as 2 g, and there was no advantage to 2 g over 1 g. Researchers assessed depression using the Hamilton Rating Scale for Depression and the Clinical Global Impression Scale. Summarizing their findings, the authors noted that EPA was well-tolerated and safe, and that it had an antidepressant effect. They also concluded that patients might find it more acceptable than standard treatment with medications.

EPA and DHA have also been helpful with other emotional states. Hallahan, Hibbeln, Davis, and Garland (2007) tested the efficacy of EPA and DHA supplementation in patients with recurrent self-harm. In this study, 49 patients with repeated acts of self-harm were randomized to receive either a placebo or 1.2 g EPA and 900 mg DHA. After 12 weeks, the patients receiving EPA and DHA had significantly improved depressive symptoms, suicidality, and daily stresses. The authors noted that these were significant markers for suicidality and that supplementation with EPA and DHA had lowered their risk.

These same researchers examined the relationship between EPA and DHA levels and self-harm with another sample (Garland et al., 2007). Their sample included 40 patients who were admitted to the emergency department for self-harm and who met the inclusion criteria (including no current comorbid psychiatric disorder and eating fish no more than once a week). The control group consisted of 27 patients recruited from the medical day ward. Subjects from the control group were also excluded if they ate fish more than once a week. The researchers found that patients with self-harm had significantly lower cholesterol and plasma EPA and DHA levels than did healthy control participants. In addition, patients with self-harm were higher on all measures of pathology, including depression, impulsivity, and alcohol use. Platelet serotonin levels did not account for these differences.

Other researchers found that EPA used alone was an effective treatment for women with borderline personality disorder in a double-blind placebo trial (Zanarini & Frankenburg, 2003). Thirty women with borderline personality disorder were randomly assigned to receive either 1 g of EPA or a placebo for 8 weeks of treatment ($n = 20$ in EPA group, $n = 10$ in the placebo group). After treatment, women who received EPA were significantly less aggressive and depressed than were those in the placebo group.

In summary, an expert panel of the American Psychiatric Association recently concluded that EPA was a promising treatment for mood disorders and that it can be used alone or in combination with DHA or medications, or both (Freeman et al., 2006). Peet and Stokes's (2005) review found that 1 g of EPA/day was the effective dose for treatment. Doses higher than 2 g seemed to have the reverse effect and actually increased depressive symptoms. DHA alone is not an effective treatment for depression (Akabas & Deckelbaum, 2006) but can be used in addition to EPA.

Anti-Inflammatory Effects of Eicosapentenoic Acid and Docosahexanoic Acid

The studies cited in the preceding section indicate that EPA and DHA have a role in the prevention and treatment of depression and other mood disorders. These effects are likely due to EPA and DHA's anti-inflammatory effects (Peet & Stokes, 2005). As described in chapter 4 of this volume, inflammatory eicosanoids are also higher in depressed patients than in their nondepressed counterparts (Parker et al., 2006). Eicosanoids are derived from high levels of arachidonic acid, a long-chain omega-6. Arachidonic acid and EPA compete for enzymes responsible for eicosanoid formation. Higher levels of EPA inhibit both the production of eicosanoids and the proinflammatory cytokines interleukin-1β (IL-1β), IL-6, interferon-γ (IFN-γ), and tumor necrosis factor-α (TNF-α)—the very ones implicated in depression (Jensen, 2006; Parker et al., 2006; Peet & Stokes, 2005).

Kiecolt-Glaser et al. (2007) noted that inflammation levels are lower in patients with either high levels of omega-3s or a lower ratio of omega-6s to omega-3s. In their study of older adults, depression and a high ratio of omega-6s to omega-3s dramatically increased levels of proinflammatory cytokines (IL-6 and TNF-α). (A high ratio of omega-6s to omega-3s can indicate an omega-3 deficiency.) The authors noted that a diet that is low in EPA and DHA increases the risk of both depression and other diseases related to chronic inflammation.

In a large population study ($N = 1,123$), high levels of EPA and DHA were related to lower levels of proinflammatory cytokines (IL-1α, IL-1β, IL-6, and TNF-α) and higher levels of anti-inflammatory cytokines, such as IL-10. For people with low levels of EPA and DHA, the opposite was true: They had high levels of proinflammatory cytokines and low levels of anti-inflammatory cytokines (Ferrucci et al., 2006). This study had several advantages over previous research. It was the first study that specifically examined the relationship between fatty acids and cytokines. The sample in this study was representative of the population, not a specific subgroup. And the fatty acids were directly measured in the plasma rather than estimated from patient dietary reports.

In high doses, however, neither EPA nor DHA appear to have an impact on proinflammatory cytokines. In the first study, 42 healthy adults were randomly assigned to receive EPA (4.7 g), DHA (4.9 g), or a placebo (Kew et al., 2004). EPA or DHA supplements significantly altered the fatty acid composition of the plasma phospholipids and neutrophil lipids, but did not alter the production of TNF-α, IL-10, IL-6, or IL-1β. The authors noted that their findings contradicted earlier findings with smaller dosages. A study by these same investigators, with a sample of 150 healthy men and women, found that (a) EPA or (b) DHA + EPA (1.7 g) or α-linolenic acid (9.5 g) did not alter immune function, including levels of proinflammatory cytokines and the percentage of monocytes engaged in phagocytosis (Kew et al., 2003). The researchers concluded that recommended guidelines could be increased without any harmful effects on the immune system.

What these conflicting findings might reveal is that smaller dosages are more effective in treating mood disorders than are large doses. Indeed, a review of EPA as a treatment for depression revealed that dosages larger than 2 g were related to higher levels of depression (Peet & Stokes, 2005). Kew et al.'s (2003, 2004) findings are consistent with that. Their findings could also mean that EPA and DHA supplements do not harm immune parameters but may indeed modulate immune function so that it is functioning well, but not excessively.

Eicosapentenoic Acid, Docosahexanoic Acid, and the Stress Response

Researchers have examined the impact of EPA and DHA on stress. Physical and psychological stress trigger the stress response, including activation of the inflammatory response system. So the question of interest is whether EPA and DHA have an adaptogenic role in stress by regulating and attenuating the stress response. Several studies have suggested that they may. In a study of college students, researchers found that those students with a high ratio of omega-6s to omega-3s (indicating a deficiency of omega-3s) had more inflammation when exposed to a lab-induced stressor. In contrast, students with higher levels of EPA and DHA had a lower inflammatory response to stress (Maes, Christophe, Bosmans, Lin, & Neels, 2000).

Similarly, Kiecolt-Glaser et al. (2007) found that previous exposure to stress and prior episodes of depression both appear to "prime" the inflammatory response, so that inflammation is hyperresponsive to subsequent stressors. Fortunately, EPA and DHA supplementation seemed to halt that process and its maladaptive impact on mood. In their study of 43 older adults, they noted that "even modest supplementation with n-3 PUFAs [omega-3 polyunsaturated fatty acids] reduces plasma norepinephrine, an important link to the stress response" (p. 221).

A Japanese study investigating the impact of EPA and DHA supplementation on 21 young adults had similar findings (Hamazaki et al., 2005). In a double-blind trial, participants took either a placebo or 762 mg of EPA or DHA for 2 months. Supplementation increased EPA concentrations in the erythrocyte membranes of the supplemented group and also significantly decreased levels of plasma norepinephrine.

In a review article regarding Type 2 diabetes, Delarue, LeFoll, Corporeau, and Lucas (2004) found that fish oil reduced insulin resistance and plasma triglycerides in healthy patients. It also increased resilience to stress by decreasing the activity of the sympathetic nervous system. Unfortunately, fish oil did not have a similar effect on insulin resistance in patients with diabetes. But even in patients with diabetes, fish oil lowered triglycerides. The authors concluded that fish oil showed promise in the prevention of insulin resistance and related health problems.

Not all researchers have found that EPA and DHA attenuate stress, however. In a study of high-stress individuals, researchers randomized participants into no-treatment, placebo, or fish oil groups (Bradbury, Myers, & Oliver, 2005). The placebo group received 6 g/day of olive oil. The treatment group received 6 g of tuna oil, which contained 1.5 g DHA and 360 mg EPA. Compared with the no-treatment group, perceived stress dropped significantly for the EPA and DHA group. But there was no significant difference between the placebo and treatment groups. One possible limitation in this study was that the investigators used a relatively small dosage of EPA. EPA is likely the fatty acid that lowers stress because it lowers levels of proinflammatory cytokines, prostaglandins, and eicosanoids.

Summary

As a large number of studies have demonstrated, EPA and DHA are likely helpful in the treatment of depression. A recent large review (Wang et al., 2004) also found them to be helpful in the treatment of cardiovascular disease. Given the connection between cardiovascular disease and depression, EPA and DHA likely help both because they lower inflammation. As an intervention, EPA and DHA are also appealing because there is little risk associated with their use.[1]

In the next section, exercise, another nonpharmacologic treatment for depression, is described.

EXERCISE

Exercise is another effective treatment for depression. Exercise has traditionally been recommended for people with mild-to-moderate depression.

---

[1]The U.S. Pharmacopeia now tests specific brands of fish oil for contaminants so safe sources are readily available to consumers. These brands are listed on their Web site (http://www.usp.org).

But as two clinical trials have found, exercise can also alleviate major depression as effectively as medications. Many of these studies are of older adults, who are sometimes at higher risk of depression. Medications can be difficult to manage for this population because older adults are frequently taking more than one medication and may metabolize medications more slowly than do younger adults. Exercise is an appealing alternative to medications for this population, and these findings are relevant for younger adults as well. It also appears to lower inflammation and decrease the inflammatory response to stress.

Exercise for People With Depression

A large population study from Finland (N = 3,403) found that exercise lowered depression and helped with feelings of anger, distrust, and stress. Two to three sessions of exercise a week was enough to achieve a mood-altering effect (Hassmen, Koivula, & Uutela, 2000). Exercise helped in other ways as well. Compared with nonexercisers, men and women who exercised perceived their health and fitness as better. Exercise also increased participants' social connections with others.

Thirty-two adults with minor or major depression, ages 60 to 84 years, were randomized to one of two conditions: 10 weeks of lectures or 10 weeks of supervised weight-lifting exercise followed by 10 weeks of unsupervised exercise (Singh, Clements, & Fiatarone Singh, 2001). As predicted, the exercise group was significantly less depressed at 20 weeks than the nonexercise group The researchers did not contact any study participant again until the end of the research period at 26 months. At the 26-month follow-up, exercisers were still less depressed and were significantly more likely to be regularly exercising than were patients in the control condition.

In a similar study, older adults were randomly assigned to either exercise classes or health education for 10 weeks (Mather et al., 2002). All participants were depressed and on medications, but medications were not adequately controlling their depression. At the end of treatment, 55% of the exercise group had significantly less depression compared with 33% of the education group.

Most of the participants in the previously cited studies had mild-to-moderate depression. Babyak et al.'s (2000) study demonstrated that exercise can be helpful for major depression as well. In this clinical trial, older adults with depression were randomly assigned to one of three groups: exercise alone, sertraline (Zoloft) alone, or a combination of exercise and sertraline. After 4 months, all the patients improved, and there were no differences between the groups. People in the exercise-only group did as well as did people in the two medication groups. In addition, people in the exercise-only group were significantly less likely to relapse. Six months after completion of treatment, 28% of the exercise-only group became depressed again versus 51% of the medications-only and medications-exercise groups. The authors concluded that exercise is an effective intervention, even in patients with major depression. Exercise also helps prevent relapse.

This same group of researchers recently replicated their findings (Blumenthal et al., 2007). In the more recent study, 202 adults with major depression were randomized to one of four conditions: sertraline, exercise at home, supervised exercise, or a placebo control. After 4 months of treatment, 41% of the total sample was in remission, meaning that they no longer met the criteria for major depression. Efficacy rates by treatment were as follows: supervised exercise = 45%, home-based exercise = 40%, medication = 47%, and placebo = 31%. Participants in the exercise group walked for 45 minutes on a treadmill at 70% to 85% maximum heart rate capacity, three times a week, for 16 weeks. The home-exercise group received the same instructions, but exercised at home and was therefore not supervised and had minimal contact with the research staff. The authors concluded that the efficacy of exercise was comparable to that of medications. The supervised program was especially effective, but the home program was also comparable to medications. And all treatments were more effective than the placebo.

The mood-altering effects of exercise appear fairly quickly. In a study of 26 women, Lane, Crone-Grant, and Lane (2002) measured anger, confusion, depression, fatigue, tension, and vigor before and after two exercise sessions. The women's moods significantly improved after each exercise session. Depressed mood was especially sensitive to exercise and decreased significantly after each session.

Exercise and Inflammation

As the previously cited studies indicate, exercise is an effective treatment for depression. Several psychosocial explanations have been offered for these effects, including increased social connections, improved perceptions of fitness, and improved self-efficacy (McAuley, Blissmer, Katula, Duncan, & Mihalko, 2000). Researchers also found more recently that exercise lowers inflammation. Exercise initially acts as an acute physical stressor and raises IL-6 and TNF-α. An initial burst of these cytokines does not appear to be harmful. Indeed, and as Goebel, Mills, Irwin, and Ziegler (2000) pointed out, in a normally functioning system, high levels of cytokines trigger the body's anti-inflammatory mechanisms to keep inflammation in check.

Over a longer period of time, however, especially in people with chronically elevated proinflammatory cytokines, exercise lowers inflammation. As was true for exercise studies, in general, the anti-inflammatory effects of exercise have been studied frequently with older adults. Levels of proinflammatory cytokines naturally increase as people age. Indeed, researchers hypothesize that this age-related rise in inflammation creates vulnerability to diseases such as heart disease, cancer, and Alzheimer's (Kiecolt-Glaser et al.,

2007). Because of this increased vulnerability to chronic disease, older adults are frequently the population of choice for studies on exercise, depression, and inflammation.

A study of adults ages 60 to 90 tested the effect of physical activity on perceived stress, mood, and quality of life as well as serum IL-6 and cortisol. The exercise group (n = 10) was instructed to walk for 30 minutes, at a rate that would elevate their heart rate to 60% of its maximum capacity, five times a week for the 10-week study. Adults in the control group (n = 10) did not engage in physical activity. After the 10-week exercise intervention, the exercise group had significantly lower stress on the Perceived Stress Scale and improved mood and quality of life on the SF-36 Health Questionnaire. They reported better physical functioning, more vitality, better mental health, and less bodily pain. They also had a significant decrease in serum IL-6 (Starkweather, 2007). Depression did not mediate these findings; this effect was independent of an association between psychological variables and IL-6.

Another study of older adults compared cardio workouts with flexibility and resistance training to see if either type lowered inflammation (Kohut et al., 2006). In this study, 83 adults, ages 64 to 87, were randomized to one of the two conditions. The cardio workouts were 45 minutes, at 60% to 80% of maximum cardiac effort, three times a week, for 10 months. The flexibility and resistance workouts were 45 minutes of resistance and flexibility training, three times a week, also for 10 months. Both types of exercise led to improved levels of depression, optimism, and sense of coherence. At the end of 10 months, the cardio workout had a stronger effect on inflammation. The cardio workout significantly reduced CRP, IL-6, and IL-18. TNF-α levels improved with both the cardio and flexibility and resistance programs. These effects were independent of psychological variables.

Exercise also had a positive effect on wound healing, an indirect measure of systemic inflammation (Emery, Kiecolt-Glaser, Glaser, Malarkey, & Frid, 2005). In this study, participants were randomized into exercise and control conditions. They were then brought into the laboratory and given a punch biopsy. The researchers then monitored participants' rate of wound healing. The average number of days for the wound to heal in the exercise group was 29 days. In the control group, it was 38 days. Exercise 1 hour a day, 3 days a week lowered perceived stress and improved wound healing. The results of other studies found that wound healing is impaired when stress or hostility levels are high (e.g., Kiecolt-Glaser et al., 2005). Stress and hostility both increase systemic inflammation. When systemic inflammation is high, wound healing is impaired because proinflammatory cytokines are in the bloodstream and not at the wound site, where they belong. The Emery et al. (2005) study indicated that exercise likely improves wound healing by lowering levels of circulating systemic cytokines, thereby increasing them at the wound site.

Overall level of fitness was also related to inflammation in another recent study (Hamer & Steptoe, 2007). The sample was 207 men and women with no history or symptoms of heart disease and who were not being treated for hypertension, inflammatory disease, or allergy. Participants were given one of two mentally stressful tasks in the laboratory (a computerized Stroop test or mirror tracing task). Researchers measured heart rate via a submaximal exercise test. A high-systolic blood pressure indicated a low level of fitness. Participants who responded with higher systolic blood pressure to stress also had a higher IL-6 and TNF-α response. The TNF-α response to stress was 5 times greater in the low-fitness group compared with the high-fitness group. The authors concluded that participants who were physically fit had a lower inflammation response when under stress. They believed that this was another way that exercise protected individuals from heart disease and other conditions.

Summary

Although a relatively new area of study, this research supports the hypothesis that exercise lowers systemic inflammation. And this effect may account for its efficacy in treating depression. Exercise also offers a viable alternative to medications for patients who refuse them.

PSYCHOTHERAPY

Psychotherapy is another treatment modality for depression that has a long track record of success. In particular, cognitive therapy has been shown to be as effective as medications in treating even major depression. Moreover, patients who received cognitive therapy did better on follow-up, were less likely to relapse, and were less likely to drop out of treatment than were those who received medications alone (Antonuccio, Danton, & DeNelsky, 1995; Rupke, Blecke, & Renfrow, 2006).

Cognitive therapy is based on the premise that distortions in thinking cause depression. It teaches patients to recognize and counter these thoughts (Rupke et al., 2006). The goal is to help patients identify distorted beliefs and replace them with more rational ones. Cognitive therapy can also physically change the brain. Two studies compared cognitive therapy with medications on two conditions: obsessive–compulsive disorder (Baxter, Schwartz, Bergman, & Szuba, 1992) and panic disorder (Prasko et al., 2004). In both studies, the outcome variable was change in positron emission tomography (PET) scans of the brain before and after treatment. Before therapy, both groups showed abnormalities in brain metabolism. After treatment, both groups had improved PET scans, but there was no difference between the groups. In other words, cognitive therapy caused the same changes in the brain that medications had in both studies.

Interpersonal therapy is a newer modality, but it too is proving effective even for more serious depressions. In a recent National Institute of Mental Health collaborative research study, interpersonal psychotherapy was as effective as tricyclic antidepressants and cognitive therapy, and was effective for almost 70% of the participants (Tolman, 2001). Interpersonal psychotherapy is based on attachment theory and the interpersonal theories of Sullivan. It is time limited and focuses on the client's interpersonal relationships. Disturbances in the key relationships are hypothesized as being responsible for depression. Clients review information about key relationships, the nature of current communications, and how key relationships may have recently changed (Grigoriadis & Ravitz, 2007).

Interpersonal psychotherapy has shown effectiveness with high-risk populations, and was used to treat low-income, depressed adolescents in five school-based mental health clinics in New York City (Mufson et al., 2004). In this study, 63 teens with depression or dysthymia were randomly assigned to receive 16 weeks of interpersonal psychotherapy or 16 weeks of treatment as usual. The sample was 84% girls and 71% Hispanic. By the end of the intervention, teens receiving interpersonal therapy had significantly fewer depressive symptom, better social functioning, greater clinical improvement, and a greater decrease in clinical severity on the Clinical Global Impressions Scale. The authors noted that the largest treatment effects occurred for the older and more severely depressed adolescents.

Interpersonal psychotherapy has also proven helpful in preventing postpartum depression in high-risk women (Zlotnick, Miller, Pearlstein, Howard, & Sweeney, 2006). In this study, 99 low-income pregnant women were randomly assigned to receive standard antenatal care or standard care plus an intervention based on interpersonal therapy. The goal of the intervention was to improve women's close personal relationships, change their expectations about these relationships, build their social networks, and help them master their transition to motherhood. The intervention was delivered in a group setting. At 3 months postpartum, 4% of the intervention group became depressed compared with 20% of the control group.

Anti-Inflammatory Effects of Psychotherapy

Although evidence is preliminary, both cognitive therapy and interpersonal psychotherapy likely have an anti-inflammatory effect. Interpersonal psychotherapy's effect is due to increasing amount and quality of support. The inflammation effect of social isolation and lack of support is described in chapter 5 of this volume. When support increases, inflammation will likely decrease.

The same might prove to be true with cognitive therapy. As described in chapter 5, a number of past studies have examined the physiological effect of one's beliefs and cognitions. Hostility is of interest to the present discussion because it is a particular way of looking at the world. People high in hostility tend to attribute negative motives to others and have difficulty trusting others and establishing close relationships. Hostility also specifically raises inflammation. As described earlier, in one study, hostility was associated with higher levels of IL-1α, IL-1β, and IL-8 in 44 women, and the combination of depression and hostility led to the highest levels of IL-1β, IL-8, and TNF-α (Suarez, Lewis, Krishnan, & Young, 2004).

Kiecolt-Glaser et al. (2005) found that couples who were high in hostility had higher levels of circulating proinflammatory cytokines. As a result, the rate of wound healing for the high-hostility couples was 60% slower than for low-hostility couples. High-hostility couples had fewer cytokines at the wound site, where they were supposed to be, and high levels circulating systemically, where they were more likely to impair health and increase the risk of age-related diseases.

Cognitive therapy specifically addresses beliefs such as hostility. Because negative cognitions increase inflammation, we could predict that reducing their occurrence would lower inflammation. That is indeed what Doering, Cross, Vredevoe, Martinez-Maza, and Cowan (2007) found in their study of women after coronary bypass surgery. They found that clinically depressed women had a higher incidence of in-hospital fevers and infections in the 6 months after surgery, resulting in part from decreases in natural killer cell cytotoxicity. An 8-week program of cognitive–behavioral therapy reduced depression, improved natural killer cell cytotoxicity, and decreased IL-6 and CRP. Because the immune system was functioning more effectively, this intervention decreased postoperative infectious diseases.

Summary

The two types of psychotherapy reviewed in this section likely decrease inflammation, but through different mechanisms. Interpersonal psychotherapy focuses on improving social support, which buffers stress and downregulates the inflammatory response. Cognitive therapy lowers inflammation by changing the negative beliefs that upregulate the stress and inflammatory response. Both are effective treatments for depression and appear to be anti-inflammatory.

ST. JOHN'S WORT

Another treatment modality for depression is St. John's wort (*Hypericum perforatum*), the most widely used herbal antidepressant in the world (Dugoua, Mills, Perri, & Koren, 2006). Herbalists have used St. John's wort since the Middle Ages. It derives its name from St. John's Day (June 24) because it blooms near this day on the medieval church calendar. *Wort* is the Old English word for a medicinal plant. It is a common wildflower in Great Britain, northern Europe, and the northeastern and north central United States (Balch, 2002).

Efficacy of St. John's Wort

A large body of evidence indicates that St. John's wort effectively treats depression (Sarris, 2007; Werneke, Turner, & Priebe, 2006). Evidence for St. John's wort's effectiveness can be found in both review articles and results of randomized clinical trials, where it is proven as effective as tricyclic anti-depressants and selective serotonin reuptake inhibitors (SSRIs). These findings are briefly summarized next.

One trial compared St. John's wort (*Hypericum* extract STEI 300) to a placebo and imipramine. The subjects were 263 primary-care patients with moderate depression. The authors found that St. John's wort was as effective as imipramine for moderately depressed patients after 4, 6, and 8 weeks of treatment (Philipp, Kohnen, & Hiller, 1999). Patients in this trial also tolerated St. John's wort better.

In one study, 87 patients with major depression, recruited from Canadian family practice physicians, were randomly assigned to receive either St. John's wort or sertraline (van Gurp, Meterissian, Haiek, McCusker, & Bellavance, 2002). At the end of the 12-week trial, both groups improved, and there was no difference between the two groups. But there were significantly more side effects in the sertraline group at 2 and 4 weeks. The authors concluded that St. John's wort, because of its effectiveness and benign side effects, was a good first choice for a primary-care population.

Anghelescu, Kohnen, Szegedi, Klement, and Kieser (2006) compared the efficacy and safety of *Hypericum* extract WS 5570 with paroxetine for patients with moderate to severe depression. The acute phase of treatment lasted for 6 weeks, with another 4 months of follow-up to prevent relapse. The patients improved on both treatments, with no significant difference in efficacy between paroxetine and St. John's wort. The authors noted that St. John's wort was an important alternative to standard antidepressants for depressed patients.

Mechanism for Efficacy

Researchers still do not understand the exact mechanism for St. John's wort's antidepressant effect. St. John's wort is standardized by percentage of hypericin, one of 10 active constituents that have been identified so far. Hypericin was once considered the primary antidepressant component, but this is no longer true. Hyperforin is now thought to be the antidepressant constituent (Lawvere & Mahoney, 2005; Muller, 2003; Wurglies & Schubert-

Zsilavecz, 2006). Hyperforin appears to inhibit the reuptake of the serotonin, the same mechanism found in the SSRIs (e.g., fluoxetine, sertraline; Kuhn & Winston, 2000; Werneke et al., 2006).

Of interest to the present discussion is that hyperforin is also anti-inflammatory (Dell'Aica, Caniato, Biggin, & Garbisa, 2007; Kuhn & Winston, 2000; Werneke et al., 2006; Wurglies & Schubert-Zsilavecz, 2006). Hyperforin inhibits the expression of intercellular adhesion molecule (Zhou et al., 2004), and it specifically lowers levels of the proinflammatory cytokines involved in depression (Hu et al., 2006). Hu et al. (2006) used an animal model to test whether St. John's wort could counter the toxic side effects of chemotherapy. The researchers specifically investigated whether St. John's wort had an impact on the levels of proinflammatory cytokines, including IL-1β, IL-2, IL-6, IFN-γ, and TNF-α. They found that St. John's wort did protect rats receiving chemotherapy by inhibiting proinflammatory cytokines and intestinal epithelium apoptosis. Although not a study of depression, it was the first to demonstrate that St. John's wort inhibits the cytokines that are high in depression.

Summary

Hyperforin is showing promise as an anti-inflammatory agent in animal models, and it lowers the proinflammatory cytokines that tend to be high in depression. Furthermore, by inhibiting inflammation, it may also increase serotonin by decreasing degradation of its precursor—tryptophan (Maes & Smith, 1998).

ANTIDEPRESSANT MEDICATIONS

The final treatment modality for depression described in this chapter is antidepressants. Until recently, researchers believed that antidepressants' efficacy was due to their effects on the monoamine neurotransmitters, such as serotonin and norepinephrine. That conceptualization is accurate but likely incomplete. Recent studies have noted that antidepressants have some specific anti-inflammatory actions. Moreover, anti-inflammatory drugs appear to have an antidepressant effect and likely modulate the inflammatory response (Szelenyi & Vizi, 2007). These findings suggest that antidepressants have usefulness in treating inflammatory physical diseases and that other anti-inflammatory medications may be useful in treating depression.

A recent study compared CRP levels in patients with major depression before and after treatment with SSRIs. These were cardiac patients who were taking one of three antidepressant medications following a heart attack: sertraline, fluoxetine, or paroxetine. In these patients, CRP dropped significantly after treatment, independent of whether depression resolved (O'Brien et al., 2006).

An animal model demonstrated the anti-inflammatory and anti-nociceptive (antipain) effects of antidepressants in rats. The researchers found that the antidepressants imipramine, amitriptyline, trazodone, and clomipramine were anti-inflammatory as measured by paw edema. Fluoxetine reduced paw edema in a dose–response way. Only sertraline did not reduce edema; it increased it. The most effective of these medications for pain management were amitriptyline and trazodone (Abdel-Salam, Nofal, & El-Shenawy, 2003).

An in vitro study of inflammation was designed to test whether the antidepressant venlafaxine would modulate the inflammatory response. Vollmar, Haghikia, Dermietzel, and Faustmann (2008) hypothesized that the norepinephrine–serotonin system modulated inflammatory diseases, such as depression, given the growing body of evidence that antidepressants have immunoregulatory effects. Venlafaxine is a norepinephrine–serotonin reuptake inhibitor. In an astroglia–microglia coculture, they demonstrated that venlafaxine reduced signs of inflammation by decreasing IL-6 and IL-8, and they concluded that venlafaxine was anti-inflammatory. They hypothesized the antidepressant effect of this medication might be due to monoamine-mediated immunomodulation.

Another study tested the anti-inflammatory effects of two antidepressants—fluoxetine and desipramine—in two animal models of human disease: septic shock and allergic asthma (Roumestan et al., 2007). The authors noted that antidepressants affected anti-inflammatory signals and might be useful adjuncts to treatments for these conditions. They also noted that part of antidepressants' efficacy could be due to attenuating brain expression or action of the proinflammatory cytokines. Antidepressants also decrease peripheral inflammation. In their model of septic shock, both antidepressants decreased TNF-α levels. In a model of allergic asthma, they found that fluoxetine and the steroid prednisolone reduced several types of leukocytes, including macrophages, lymphocytes, neutrophils, and eosinophils. Desipramine reduced only macrophages. The authors concluded that antidepressants had a direct peripheral anti-inflammatory effect. They noted that antidepressants can be useful in treating inflammatory conditions, especially with comorbid depression, pointing out that antidepressants may allow patients to cut down on steroid use.

Antidepressants also increase glucocorticoid receptor function and decrease IL-1β and TNF-α. Some antidepressants that have shown these effects include desipramine, clomipramine, fluoxetine, paroxetine, and citalopram (Pace, Hu, & Miller, 2007). Inflammatory cytokines, such as IL-1 and TNF-α, induce the secretion of the prostaglandin cyclooxygenase-2 (COX-2). In contrast, when COX-2 is inhibited, it helps regulate glucocorticoid receptor function as it relates to inflammation and stress-induced neuroendocrine pathways. Anti-inflammatory COX-2 inhibitors (such as Celebrex) attenuate glucocorticoid resistance and could explain why COX-

2 inhibitors boost the effectiveness of the antidepressant reboxetine in patients with major depression. COX-2 is a signaling molecule that can contribute to glucocorticoid resistance. Pace et al. (2007) recommended that future therapies target these immunologic processes that are relevant to the pathophysiology of psychiatric disorders, such as depression.

CONCLUSIONS

The findings presented in this chapter indicate that there are a number of effective treatments for depression. Until recently, researchers tended to study these modalities individually, rather than considering common elements among them. That limited view is beginning to change as researchers examine the anti-inflammatory effects of these treatments. Another interesting aspect of this research is that it often is conducted by researchers who are not necessarily studying depression but may be studying illnesses that have depression as a symptom.

These findings suggest that combining treatments in novel ways can increase the effectiveness of these treatments. Examples include using COX-2 inhibitors or EPA to boost the actions of antidepressants. Conversely, antidepressants may be steroid sparing for patients with immune-related and autoimmune disorders. Combining treatments in these novel ways may be some of the more practical results that come from PNI research. These novel treatment approaches will also lead to an increased understanding of the pathophysiology of various diseases, which will pave the way for prevention.

KEY POINTS

- The omega-3 fatty acids EPA and DHA are effective in treating both cardiovascular disease and depression, often in combination with medications.
- Higher levels of EPA and DHA are associated with increased stress resilience.
- Exercise is as effective as antidepressants for treating even major depression. It also increases wound healing and stress resilience by lowering systemic inflammation.
- Cognitive therapy can improve functioning of the immune system and decrease inflammation in patients with depression.
- The antidepressant constituent of St. John's wort, hyperforin, is specifically anti-inflammatory and lowers proinflammatory cytokines in animal studies.
- Preliminary evidence suggests that all effective treatments for depression lower inflammation, and several specifically lower proinflammatory cytokines and CRP in depression.

- These findings also suggest some novel uses for antidepressants and a combination of nonpharmacologic and medication treatments for depression.

REFERENCES

Abdel-Salam, O. M., Nofal, S. M., & El-Shenawy, S. M. (2003). Evaluation of the anti-inflammatory and anti-nociceptive effects of different antidepressants in the rat. *Pharmacology Research, 48*, 157–165.

Akabas, S. R., & Deckelbaum, R. J. (2006). Summary of a workshop on n-3 fatty acids: Current status of recommendations and future directions. *American Journal of Clinical Nutrition, 83*, 1536–1538.

Anghelescu, I. G., Kohnen, R., Szegedi, A., Klement, S., & Kieser, M. (2006). Comparison of Hypericum extract WS 5570 and paroxetine in ongoing treatment after recovery from an episode of moderate to severe depression: Results from a randomized multicenter study. *Pharmacopsychiatry, 39*, 213–219.

Antonuccio, D., Danton, W. G., & DeNelsky, G. Y. (1995). Psychotherapy versus medication for depression: Challenging the conventional wisdom with data. *Professional Psychology: Research and Practice, 26*, 574–585.

Babyak, M., Blumenthal, J. A., Herman, S., Khatri, P., Doraiswamy, M., Moore, K., et al. (2000). Exercise treatment for major depression: Maintenance of therapeutic benefit at 10 months. *Psychosomatic Medicine, 62*, 633–638.

Balch, P. (2002). *Prescription for herbal healing.* New York: Avery.

Baxter, L. R., Schwartz, J. M., Bergman, K. S., & Szuba, M. P. (1992). Caudate glucose metabolic rate changes with both drug and behavioral therapy for obsessive-compulsive disorders. *Archives of General Psychiatry, 49*, 681–689.

Blumenthal, J. A., Babyak, M. A., Doraiswamy, P. M., Watkins, L., Hoffman, B. M., Barbour, K. A., et al. (2007). Exercise and pharmacotherapy in the treatment of major depressive disorder. *Psychosomatic Medicine, 69*, 587–596.

Bradbury, J., Myers, S. P., & Oliver, C. (2005). An adaptogenic role for omega-3 fatty acids in stress: A randomized placebo controlled double blind intervention study [Electronic version]. *Nutrition Journal, 3*, 20.

Delarue, J., LeFoll, C., Corporeau, C., & Lucas, D. (2004). N-3 long-chain polyunsaturated fatty acids: A nutritional tool to prevent insulin resistance associated to Type 2 diabetes and obesity? *Reproduction, Nutrition, Development, 44*, 289–299.

Dell'Aica, I., Caniato, R., Biggin, S., & Garbisa, S. (2007). Matrix proteases, green tea, and St. John's wort: Biomedical research catches up with folk medicine. *Clinical Chimica Acta, 381*, 69–77.

Doering, L. V., Cross, R., Vredevoe, D., Martinez-Maza, O. L., & Cowan, M. J. (2007). Infection, depression and immunity in women after coronary artery bypass: A pilot study of cognitive behavioral therapy. *Alternative Therapies in Health and Medicine, 13*(3), 18–21.

Dugoua, J.-J., Mills, E., Perri, D., & Koren, G. (2006). Safety and efficacy of St. John's wort (Hypericum) during pregnancy and lactation. *Canadian Journal of Clinical Pharmacology, 13*, e268–e276. Retrieved from http://www.cjcp.ca/pdf/CJCP05-036_e268-e276F.pdf

Emery, C. F., Kiecolt-Glaser, J. K., Glaser, R., Malarkey, W. B., & Frid, D. J. (2005). Exercise accelerates wound healing among healthy older adults: A preliminary investigation. *The Journals of Gerontology: Series A. Biological Sciences and Medical Sciences, 60*, M1432–M1436.

Ferrucci, L., Cherubini, A., Bandinelli, S., Bartali, B., Corsi, A., Lauretani, F., et al. (2006). Relationship of plasma polyunsaturated fatty acids to circulating inflammatory markers. *The Journal of Clinical Endocrinology & Metabolism, 91*, 439–446.

Frangou, S., Lewis, M., & McCrone, P. (2006). Efficacy of ethyl-eicosapentaenoic acid in bipolar depression: Randomized double-blind placebo-controlled study. *The British Journal of Psychiatry, 188*, 46–50.

Freeman, M. P., Hibbeln, J. R., Wisner, K. L., Davis, J. M., Mischoulon, D., Peet, M., et al. (2006). Omega-3 fatty acids: Evidence basis for treatment and future research in psychiatry. *Journal of Clinical Psychiatry, 67*, 1954–1967.

Garland, M. R., Hallahan, B., McNamara, M., Carney, P. A., Grimes, H., Hibbeln, J. R., et al. (2007). Lipids and essential fatty acids in patients presenting with self-harm. *The British Journal of Psychiatry, 190*, 112–117.

Goebel, M. U., Mills, P. J., Irwin, M. R., & Ziegler, M. G. (2000). Interleukin-6 and tumor necrosis factor-alpha production after acute psychological stress, exercise, and infused isoproterenol: Differential effects and pathways. *Psychosomatic Research, 62*, 591–598.

Grigoriadis, S., & Ravitz, P. (2007). An approach to interpersonal psychotherapy for postpartum depression: Focusing on interpersonal changes. *Canadian Family Physician, 53*, 1469–1475.

Hallahan, B., Hibbeln, J. R., Davis, J. M., & Garland, M. R. (2007). Omega-3 fatty acid supplementation in patients with recurrent self-harm. Single-centre double-blind randomized controlled trial. *The British Journal of Psychiatry, 190*, 118–122.

Hamazaki, K., Itomura, M., Huan, M., Nishizawa, H., Sawazaki, S., Tanouchi, M., et al. (2005). Effect of omega-3 fatty acid-containing phospholipids on blood catecholamine concentrations in healthy volunteers: A randomized, placebo-controlled, double-blind trial. *Nutrition, 21*, 705–710.

Hamer, M., & Steptoe, A. (2007). Association between physical fitness, parasympathetic control, and proinflammatory responses to mental stress. *Psychosomatic Medicine, 69*, 660–666.

Hassmen, P., Koivula, N., & Uutela, A. (2000). Physical exercise and psychological well-being: A population study in Finland. *Preventive Medicine, 30*, 17–25.

Hibbeln, J. R. (2002). Seafood consumption, the DHA content of mothers' milk and prevalence rates of postpartum depression: A cross-national, ecological analysis. *Journal of Affective Disorders, 69*, 15–29.

Hu, Z. P., Yang, X. X., Chan, S. Y., Xu, A. L., Duan, W., Zhu, Y. Z., et al. (2006). St. John's wort attenuates irinotecan-induced diarrhea via down-regulation of intestinal pro-inflammatory cytokines and inhibition of intestinal epithelial apoptosis. *Toxicology and Applied Pharmacology, 216*, 225–237.

Jensen, C. L. (2006). Effects of n-3 fatty acids during pregnancy and lactation. *American Journal of Clinical Nutrition, 83*, 1452S–1457S.

Kew, S., Banerjee, T., Minihane, A. M., Finnegan, Y. E., Muggli, R., Albers, R., et al. (2003). Lack of effect of foods enriched with plant- or marine-derived n-3 fatty acids on human immune function. *American Journal of Clinical Nutrition, 77*, 1287–1295.

Kew, S., Mesa, M. D., Tricon, S., Buckley, R., Minihane, A. M., & Yaqoob, P. (2004). Effects of oils rich in eicosapentaenoic and docosahexaenoic acids on immune cell composition and function in healthy humans. *American Journal of Clinical Nutrition, 79*, 674–681.

Kiecolt-Glaser, J. K., Belury, M. A., Porter, K., Beversdoft, D., Lemeshow, S., & Glaser, R. (2007). Depressive symptoms, omega-6: omega-3 fatty acids, and inflammation in older adults. *Psychosomatic Medicine, 69*, 217–224.

Kiecolt-Glaser, J. K., Loving, T. J., Stowell, J. R., Malarkey, W. B., Lemeshow, S., Dickinson, S. L., & Glaser, R. (2005). Hostile marital interactions, proinflammatory cytokine production, and wound healing. *Archives of General Psychiatry, 62*, 1377–1384.

Kohut, M. L., McCann, D. A., Konopka, D. W. R., Cunnick, J. E., Franke, W. D., Castillo, M. C., & Vanderah, R. E. (2006). Aerobic exercise, but not flexibility/resistance exercise, reduces serum IL-18, CRP, and IL-6 independent of β-blockers, BMI, and psychosocial factors in older adults. *Brain, Behavior, and Immunity, 20*, 201–209.

Kuhn, M. A., & Winston, D. (2000). *Herbal therapy and supplements: A scientific and traditional approach.* Philadelphia: Lippincott Williams & Wilkins.

Lane, A. M., Crone-Grant, D., & Lane, H. (2002). Mood changes following exercise. *Perceptual and Motor Skills, 94*, 732–734.

Lawvere, S., & Mahoney, M. C. (2005). St. John's wort. *American Family Physician, 72*, 2249–2254.

Maes, M., Christophe, A., Bosmans, E., Lin, A., & Neels, H. (2000). In humans, serum polyunsaturated fatty acid levels predict the response of proinflammatory cytokines to psychologic stress. *Biological Psychiatry, 47*, 910–920.

Maes, M., & Smith, R. S. (1998). Fatty acids, cytokines, and major depression. *Biological Psychiatry, 43*, 313–314.

Mather, A. S., Rodriguez, C., Guthrie, M. F., McHarg, A. M., Reid, I. C., & McMurdo, M. E. T. (2002). Effects of exercise on depressive symptoms in older adults with poorly responsive depressive disorder: Randomized controlled trial. *The British Journal of Psychiatry, 180*, 411–415.

McAuley, E., Blissmer, B., Katula, J., Duncan, T. E., & Mihalko, S. L. (2000). Physical activity, self-esteem, and self-efficacy relationships in older adults: A randomized controlled trial. *Annals of Behavioral Medicine, 22*, 131–139.

Miyake, Y., Sasaki, S., Yokoyama, T., Tanaka, K., Ohya, Y., Fukushima, W., et al. (2006). Risk of postpartum depression in relation to dietary fish and fat intake in Japan: The Osaka Maternal and Child Health Study. *Psychological Medicine, 36,* 1727–1735.

Mufson, L., Dorta, K. P., Wickramaratne, P., Nomura, Y., Olfson, M., & Weissman, M. M. (2004). A randomized effectiveness trial of interpersonal psychotherapy for depressed adolescents. *Archives of General Psychiatry, 61,* 577–584.

Muller, W. E. (2003). Current St. John's wort research from mode of action to clinical efficacy. *Pharmacology Research, 47,* 101–109.

Nemets, B., Stahl, Z., & Belmaker, R. H. (2002). Addition of omega-3 fatty acid to maintenance medication treatment for recurrent unipolar depressive disorder. *The American Journal of Psychiatry, 159,* 477–479.

Nemets, H., Nemets, B., Apter, A., Bracha, Z., & Belmaker, R. H. (2006). Omega-3 treatment of childhood depression: A controlled, double-blind pilot study. *The American Journal of Psychiatry, 163,* 1098–1100.

Noaghiul, S., & Hibbeln, J. R. (2003). Cross-national comparisons of seafood consumption and rates of bipolar disorders. *The American Journal of Psychiatry, 160,* 2222–2227.

O'Brien, S. M., Scott, L. V., & Dinan, T. G. (2006). Antidepressant therapy and C-reactive protein levels. *The British Journal of Psychiatry, 188,* 449–452.

Pace, T. W., Hu, F., & Miller, A. H. (2007). Cytokine-effects on glucocorticoid receptor function: Relevance to glucocorticoid resistance and the pathophysiology and treatment of major depression. *Brain, Behavior, and Immunity, 21,* 9–19.

Parker, G., Gibson, N. A., Brotchie, H., Heruc, G., Rees, A.-M., & Hadzi-Pavlovic, D. (2006). Omega-3 fatty acids and mood disorders. *The American Journal of Psychiatry, 163,* 969–978.

Peet, M., & Horrobin, D. F. (2002). A dose-ranging study of the effects of ethyl-eicosapentaenoate in patients with ongoing depression despite apparently adequate treatment with standard drugs. *Archives of General Psychiatry, 59,* 913–919.

Peet, M., & Stokes, C. (2005). Omega-3 fatty acids in the treatment of psychiatric disorders. *Drugs, 65,* 1051–1059.

Philipp, M., Kohnen, R., & Hiller, K.-O. (1999, December 11). Hypericum extract versus imipramine or placebo in patients with moderate depression: Randomized multicenter study of treatment for eight weeks. *BMJ, 319,* 1534–1539.

Prasko, J., Horocek, J., Zalesky, R., Kopecek, M., Novak, T., Paskova, B., et al. (2004). The change of regional brain metabolism (18FDG PET) in panic disorder during the treatment with cognitive behavioral therapy or antidepressants. *Neuroendocrinology Letters, 25,* 340–348.

Rees, A.-M., Austin, M.-P., & Parker, G. (2005). Role of omega-3 fatty acids as a treatment for depression in the perinatal period. *Australia & New Zealand Journal of Psychiatry, 39,* 274–280.

Roumestan, C., Michel, A., Bichon, F., Portet, K., Detoc, M., Henriquet, C., et al. (2007). Anti-inflammatory properties of desipramine and fluoxetine. *Respiratory Research, 8,* 35.

Rupke, S. J., Blecke, D., & Renfrow, M. (2006). Cognitive therapy for depression. *American Family Physician, 73*, 83–86.

Sarris, J. (2007). Herbal medicines in the treatment of psychiatric disorders: A systematic review. *Phytotherapy Research, 21*, 703–716.

Singh, N. A., Clements, K. M., & Fiatarone Singh, M. A. (2001). The efficacy of exercise as a long-term antidepressant in elderly subjects: A randomized, controlled trial. *The Journals of Gerontology: Series A. Biological Sciences and Medical Sciences, 56*, M497–M504.

Starkweather, A. R. (2007). The effects of exercise on perceived stress and IL-6 levels among older adults. *Biological Research for Nursing, 8*, 1–9.

Suarez, E. C., Lewis, J. G., Krishnan, R. R., & Young, K. H. (2004). Enhanced expression of cytokines and chemokines by blood monocytes to in vitro lipopolysaccharide stimulation are associated with hostility and severity of depressive symptoms in healthy women. *Psychoneuroendocrinology, 29*, 1119–1128.

Sublette, M. E., Hibbeln, J. R., Galfalvy, H., Oquendo, M. A., & Mann, J. J. (2006). Omega-3 polyunsaturated essential fatty acid status as a predictor of future suicide risk. *The American Journal of Psychiatry, 163*, 1100–1102.

Szelenyi, J., & Vizi, E. S. (2007). The catecholamine cytokine balance: Interaction between the brain and the immune system. *Annals of the New York Academy of Sciences USA, 1113*, 311–324.

Tanskanen, A., Hibbeln, J. R., Tuomilehto, J., Uutela, A., Haukkala, A., Viinamaki, H., et al. (2001). Fish consumption and depressive symptoms in the general population of Finland. *Psychiatric Service, 52*, 529–531.

Tolman, A. O. (2001). *Depression in adults: The latest assessment and treatment strategies.* Kansas City, MO: Compact Clinicals.

van Gurp, G., Meterissian, G. B., Haiek, L. N., McCusker, J., & Bellavance, F. (2002). St. John's wort or sertraline? Randomized controlled trial in primary care. *Canadian Family Physician, 48*, 905–912.

Vollmar, P., Haghikia, A., Dermietzel, R., & Faustmann, P. M. (2008). Venlafaxine exhibits an anti-inflammatory effect in an inflammatory co-culture model. *International Journal of Neuropsychopharmacology, 11*, 111–117.

Wang, C., Chung, M., Lichtenstein, A., Balk, E., Kupelnick, B., DeVine, D., et al. (2004). *Effects of omega-3 fatty acids on cardiovascular disease* (AHRQ Publication No. 04-E009-1). Rockville, MD: Agency for Healthcare Research and Quality.

Werneke, U., Turner, T., & Priebe, S. (2006). Complementary medicines in psychiatry: Review of effectiveness and safety. *The British Journal of Psychiatry, 188*, 109–121.

Wurglies, M., & Schubert-Zsilavecz, M. (2006). Hypericum perforatum: A "modern" herbal antidepressant: Pharmacokinetics of active ingredients. *Clinical Pharmacokinetics, 45*, 449–468.

Zanarini, M. C., & Frankenburg, F. R. (2003). Omega-3 fatty acid treatment of women with borderline personality disorder: A double-blind, placebo-controlled pilot study. *The American Journal of Psychiatry, 160*, 167–169.

Zhou, C., Tabb, M. M., Sadatrafiei, A., Grun, F., Sun, A., & Blumberg, B. (2004). Hyperforin, the active component of St. John's wort, induces IL-8 expression in human intestinal epithelial cells via a MAPK-dependent, NF-kappaB-independent pathway. *Journal of Clinical Immunology, 24*, 623–636.

Zlotnick, C., Miller, I. W., Pearlstein, T., Howard, M., & Sweeney, P. (2006). A preventive intervention for pregnant women on public assistance at risk for postpartum depression. *The American Journal of Psychiatry, 163*, 1443–1445.

EPILOGUE:
INFLAMMATION AND CHRONIC DISEASE: CLINICAL IMPLICATIONS AND FUTURE DIRECTIONS

KATHLEEN KENDALL-TACKETT

I frequently speak to audiences of health care providers about the role of inflammation in mental and health disease. Every once in a while, someone in the audience will ask whether this line of research is the latest health fad. It is a fair question. We have all seen today's hot topic in health become tomorrow's unhelpful advice. I answer by saying that I believe that this line of research is here to stay. When researchers from all over the world who start with completely different research questions all end up in the same place, it is clear we are on to something. Researchers examining a wide range of "unrelated" health issues (e.g., heart disease, diabetes, sleep problems, trauma, postpartum depression) have discovered the same inflammatory link.

THE MIND–BODY CONNECTION IN HEALTH

Mind–body connections in health have an enormous amount of scientific support. The next step should be to integrate these findings into health care settings, to prevent and treat illness. In this epilogue, I describe some possible future directions and clinical implications of the findings to date.

Health care providers routinely screen for so-called hard symptoms of disease—cholesterol levels, blood pressure, and triglycerides. They also discuss behavioral aspects of health, such as smoking, abusing substances, high-risk sexual behavior, and overweight and obesity. But these same health care providers generally do not discuss—and indeed, may not even be aware—that negative emotions, such as depression and hostility, can have the same deleterious health effects as high cholesterol or smoking. Furthermore, patients with chronic negative emotions are more likely to die prematurely.

It is important not only to address and treat negative mental states but also to monitor treatments for effectiveness. Some studies have recognized the importance of treating depression, for example, but their interventions were only partially effective. I found an interesting example of this recently while writing an article summarizing research on the long-term effects for babies of in utero antidepressant exposure. As most of the authors pointed out, the risks of leaving depression untreated were at least as harmful for the baby as medication exposure because depression increases the risk of preterm birth. No decision in these cases, including the decision to not treat, was risk free. So medication decisions during pregnancy need to be based on risk-benefit analyses. When does the risk of antenatal depression outweigh the use of antidepressants during pregnancy? Often, medications are the safer choice. However, I read one particular study that examined whether in utero exposure to antidepressants increased behavioral teratogenicity (i.e., the development of internalizing and externalizing symptoms; Misri et al., 2006). The mothers in the study had been on antidepressants for a long time, but at the initial follow-up, 73% were still depressed. Four years later, 50% were still depressed. So the babies were doubly affected: They were exposed to both maternal depression and antidepressants. One wonders why the women's health care providers did not notice that their patients were still depressed and try another treatment to alleviate their depression.

This research highlights the need for follow-up in treatment for depression. It cannot simply be assumed that because someone is taking a prescription medication for depression that he or she is no longer depressed. Along these same lines, we might think about targeting both the negative mental states and inflammation. Some studies found that depression was alleviated, even though inflammatory markers did not change (Moorman et al., 2007). Others found that inflammation improved independent of whether depression lessened (O'Brien, Scott, & Dinan, 2006). Recognizing the mind–body connection, we might want to measure and treat both.

If the treatment for depression is not working, practitioners need to try something else. That may include targeting inflammation more specifically. As some of the studies in chapter 9 described, novel combinations of treatments may be helpful in these cases. Some examples include combining antidepressants with omega-3s and anti-inflammatory medications (such as nonsteroidal anti-inflammatory drugs [NSAIDs] or cyclooxygenase-2 inhibitors). Given the wide range of effective treatments for depression, practitioners have many other tools capable of alleviating depression and may not need to use antidepressants at all. Even cognitive–behavioral therapy lowered proinflammatory cytokines in at least one study (Doering, Cross, Vredevoe, Martinez-Maza, & Cowan, 2007).

Another factor to consider in future studies is individual and group differences in vulnerability to the effects of stress. As chapters 5, 6, 7, and 8 detailed, those who experienced traumatic events—especially if those events occurred in childhood—are more vulnerable to subsequent stressors. Once trauma has changed the way their bodies react, what can trauma survivors do? Can cognitive–behavioral therapy or exercise help them downregulate their stress response and resulting inflammation? Research to date suggests that these techniques would likely be helpful, but they have never been specifically tried with trauma survivors.

We also know that there are gender differences in some of these effects, although the pattern is not entirely clear. For example, regarding these effects in women, are women more or less vulnerable in certain stages of life? The research to date suggests that premenopausal women may be more stress-resilient than women later in life, as reflected in older women's vulnerability to heart disease (see chap. 1). Is that because the change in hormones for women in that stage of life makes them more vulnerable to the inflammatory effects of stress? Is it due to the protective effect of oxytocin, which downregulates the stress response and is high during pregnancy and lactation? It is a topic that demands further investigation.

Ethnic-group differences in health are another possible topic to consider from a psychoneuroimmunology (PNI) perspective. We already know that a number of ethnic minority groups have significantly higher rates of a whole range of inflammatory illnesses, particularly heart disease and diabetes. What accounts for this increased vulnerability? Are there genetic vulnerabilities? And do these disappear once we account for the health effects of poverty and racism? What can be done to help minority patients not succumb to these diseases? More to the point, how can these diseases be prevented in the first place?

In the discussion of prevention, it is also important to consider protective factors. One factor that is appropriate to consider in a PNI framework is social capital (Melton, Holaday, & Kimbrough-Melton, 2008). Why might people in one neighborhood, where there are high levels of social engagement and social capital, have better health than do people in neighborhoods where social capital is low? Research described in chapter 5 of this volume demonstrates the importance of social support and social integration. People with low social integration, or who perceive that they are lower on the social hierarchy, experience measurable negative effects on their health. Can this knowledge be used to encourage situations that are health protective? Can it be applied to minority health? That too would be worth investigating.

WHAT CAN PATIENTS DO?

Finally, we need to consider the question of what patients can do. Quite often, patients tend to assume that the physiological changes that occur in the wake of traumatic events are immutable. They are not. Rather, they should be understood as vulnerabilities that will likely always be present. After trauma, the body does become more vulnerable to stress, but there is much that trauma survivors can do to counter these effects. I believe that this information is relevant to everyone who lives in our high-stress culture.

The first thing patients can do to increase their stress resiliency is to exercise. The body initially experiences exercise as a stressor. However, as exercise becomes more regular and level of fitness improves, exercise reduces stress. Exercise not only lowers stress but specifically lowers the inflammatory response to stress. This makes the patient less vulnerable to subsequent stressful events (Starkweather, 2007).

The second step, as several chapters described, is to specifically lower inflammation. One way to do that is through chronic use of NSAIDs, as these can decrease the risk of neurodegenerative diseases, including Alzheimer's disease and multiple sclerosis (see chaps. 2 and 7). Because these are potentially risky to use long-term (particularly concerning is the risk of gastrointestinal bleeds), patients should do so only when under the care of a health care provider. Another way to lower inflammation is to supplement with eicosapentaenoic acid (EPA) and docosahexaenoic acid (DHA). Omega-3s are showing a lot of promise in treating both physical and mental health problems, and they do not appear to have the negative side effects that NSAIDs do, except at the very highest dosages (see chap. 4). The potential benefits of EPA and DHA supplementation appear to far outweigh any risks associated with their use.

CONCLUSION

We can surely expect that vital discoveries in this field will continue to be made over the next decade. These findings will have application to both preventing and treating disease. To date, researchers have done an excellent job of documenting the phenomenon of an inflammatory role in disease and the impact of stress on that inflammatory process. Our next step is to complete treatment studies that fully integrate what we have learned. We also want patients to use this research information to enhance their well-being—and their lives. I believe that these goals are within our grasp. The future of this field looks bright indeed.

REFERENCES

Doering, L. V., Cross, R., Vredevoe, D., Martinez-Maza, O. L., & Cowan, M. J. (2007). Infection, depression and immunity in women after coronary artery bypass: A pilot study of cognitive behavioral therapy. *Alternative Therapies in Health and Medicine, 13*(3), 18–21.

Melton, G. B., Holaday, B. J., & Kimbrough-Melton, R. J. (2008). Community life, public health, and children's safety. *Family & Community Health, 31*, 84–99.

Misri, S., Reebye, P., Kendrick, K., Carter, D., Ryan, D., Grunau, R. E., et al. (2006). Internalizing behaviors in 4-year-old children exposed in utero to psychotropic medications. *The American Journal of Psychiatry, 163*, 1026–1032.

Moorman, A. J., Mozaffarian, D., Wilkinson, C. W., Lawler, R. L., McDonald, G. B., Crane, B. A., et al. (2007). In patients with heart failure elevated soluble TNF-receptor 1 is associated with higher risk of depression. *Journal of Cardiac Failure, 13*, 738–743.

O'Brien, S. M., Scott, L. V., & Dinan, T. G. (2006). Antidepressant therapy and C-reactive protein levels. *The British Journal of Psychiatry, 188*, 449–452.

Starkweather, A. R. (2007). The effects of exercise on perceived stress and IL-6 levels among older adults. *Biological Research for Nursing, 8*, 1–9.

INDEX

and PTSD, 135–136
Borderline personality disorder, 224
BOSS (Biomarkers of Oxidative Stress
	Study), 36–37
Brain
	allostatic load and structural changes in,
		193–194
	communication between immune sys-
		tem and, 14–15
	inflammation in, 23, 27–29
	lipid peroxidation in, 24
Breast cancer, 197, 198
Breastfeeding, 188, 201
Burnout, 202–204
Butler, M. A., 159–160

Cancer, 197–198
Cardiovascular disease (CVD). See also Heart
		disease
	and adverse childhood experiences,
		133–134
	and allostatic load, 185, 186, 194, 196–
		197
	and depression, 114–116
	and hostility, 117
	and marital strife, 119
	and physical inactivity, 136
	and PTSD, 134–139
	racial differences in, 195
	and smoking, 136
	and social status, 121
	and stress reactivity, 137–138
	and Type 2 diabetes, 118
Cardiovascular recovery, 138
Caregivers
	allostatic load of, 189–190
	glucocorticoid resistance of, 169–170
	immune function of, 142
	interleukin-6 levels of, 171
Carmichael, C. L., 120
Catecholamines, 10, 11, 140–141
CBSM. See Cognitive–behavioral stress man-
		agement
CD4 (CD4+) T cells
	PTSD and levels of, 145, 146
	in TMEV infection, 162, 163
CD8 (CD8+) T cells
	PTSD and levels of, 145, 146
	in TMEV infection, 162, 163
CD14 gene, 28
Cell function, sleep and, 63–64
Cell-mediated immunity, PTSD and, 146–147

Central adipose deposition, 198–200
Central sleep apnea (CSA), 59
Cerebrospinal fluid, lipid peroxidation in,
		32–33, 36, 38
Challenge appraisals, 139–140
Charcot, J. M., 159–160
CHD. See Coronary heart disease
Chemoattractants, 86
Chemotaxis, leukocyte, 77, 86, 87, 96
Chemotherapy, St. John's wort and, 234
Chen, E., 170
Childhood abuse
	and allostatic load, 194
	and immune function, 145
Childhood experiences, cardiovascular risk
		and, 133–134
Child maltreatment, inflammation and, 123
Chronic disease
	and inflammation, 58
	and mind–body connection, 243–245
	parenchymal damage in, 23
	recommendations for patients with, 246
	and sleep, 57–61
Chronic disease model, for Alzheimer's dis-
		ease, 34
Chronic heart failure, 115
Chronic inflammation, 169
Chronic pain syndrome, 194
Chronic stressors, 9
	acute stressors with, 142, 170
	cardiac reactivity from, 195
	and immunity, 142, 204
	and multiple sclerosis, 161
Clomipramine, 235
Coagulability
	of caregivers, 190
	of patients with depression, 115–116
	of patients with PTSD, 124
Cognitions, of PTSD, 139–140
Cognitive action theory, 139
Cognitive appraisal theory of stress and cop-
		ing, 140
Cognitive–behavioral stress management
		(CBSM), 144, 147
Cognitive therapy, 230–232
Communication, between brain and immune
		system, 14–15
Congestive heart failure, 116
Continuous positive airway pressure (CPAP),
		59–60
Coping mechanisms and strategies
	maladaptive, 10

Thoughts, negative, 143, 144
TMEV. *See* Theiler's murine encephalomyelitis virus
TNF-α. *See* Tumor necrosis factor-α
Total sleep time (TST), 55
Trait hostility, 116–118
Trauma, allostatic load and, 191–192
Trauma-relevant stressors, 137–138
Trazodone, 235
Troxel, W. M., 120
TST (total sleep time), 55
Tuberculosis, 23
Tumor necrosis factor-α (TNF-α), 4, 13
    antidepressant effect on, 235
    in atherosclerosis, 196
    and burnout, 203
    in cross-sensitization studies, 15
    in depression, 114, 194
    and exercise, 228–230
    in HIV, 65, 66
    in insomnia, 60
    in obstructive sleep apnea, 59–60
    and omega-3 fatty acids, 88–89, 224
    of rape victims, 192
Type 2 diabetes
    and allostatic load, 185
    and cardiovascular disease, 118
    C-reactive protein levels in, 13
    fish oil in prevention of, 226
    and sleep duration, 61
    and sleep quality, 57, 58

Ulcerative colitis, 93, 94
Unsaturated fatty acids, 78, 79. *See also* Polyunsaturated fatty acids (PUFAs)
Upper respiratory infection, 143

Vaccination, 141
Vagal nerve activity, 10, 11, 188
Vascular inflammation, 121
Vasopressin, 188
Venlafaxine, 235
Viral infections, multiple sclerosis and, 161, 165
Viral load, social stress and, 164

Waist–hip ratio, 199
Weathering effect, 190, 194
Weight
    birth, 193, 195
    body, 135–136, 168
White blood cells, 146. *See also* T cells
Women
    alcohol metabolism and alcoholism in, 202
    daytime sleepiness of, 62
    health care services use by, 123
    hostility and metabolic syndrome in, 118
    marriage health effects for, 118–119
    model of health for. *See* Allostatic load
    obesity and PTSD in, 135–136
    sleep and inflammation in, 66–67
    vulnerability to stress, 245
    work-related stress of, 189–190
Women of color, allostasis for, 194–195
Working mothers, 189–190
Work-related stress, 189
Wort, 233
Wound healing
    and exercise, 229
    and hostility, 232

ABOUT THE EDITOR

Kathleen Kendall-Tackett, PhD, a health psychologist and an International Board Certified Lactation Consultant, is a clinical associate professor of pediatrics at Texas Tech University School of Medicines, Amarillo, and a fellow of the American Psychological Association (APA) in Divisions 38 (Health Psychology) and 56 (Trauma Psychology). She is editor of *Family & Intimate Partner Violence Quarterly* and associate editor of *Psychological Trauma: Theory, Research, Practice, and Policy*, and she serves on the editorial boards of four other journals in family violence and perinatal health. In addition to serving as acquisitions editor for Hale Publishing, Dr. Kendall-Tackett has authored more than 200 journal articles, book chapters, and other publications and has authored or edited 17 books in the fields of trauma, women's health, depression, and breastfeeding. A founding member of APA's Division 56, she currently serves as division secretary.